Elements of
Banking and Insurance

Elements of
Banking and Insurance

THIRD EDITION

JYOTSNA SETHI
Former Associate Professor
Department of Commerce
Jesus and Mary College
University of Delhi

NISHWAN BHATIA
Associate Professor
Department of Commerce
Jesus and Mary College
University of Delhi

PHI Learning Private Limited
Delhi-110092
2024

₹ 925.00

ELEMENTS OF BANKING AND INSURANCE, Third Edition
Jyotsna Sethi and Nishwan Bhatia

ISBN-978-93-91818-40-1 (Print Book)
ISBN-978-93-91818-41-8 (e-Book)

Published by PHI Learning Private Limited, Rimjhim House, 111, Patparganj Industrial Estate, Delhi-110092 and Printed by Glorious Printer, Delhi-110092.

By the Grace of Guru

We dedicate our work
to
The Academic Fraternity
and
Our Inquisitive Students

Contents

Preface

The need for third edition has emerged out of the global headwinds and uncertainties surrounding us. While the world was still reeling under the Covid-19 pandemic, it has been hit by the Russia–Ukraine conflict. The RBI, in its report 'Scars of the Pandemic' (April 2022), projects output losses at 52 lakh crores for last three years and contemplates that it shall take 12 years to overcome these losses. The Geo-political situation on international trade has resulted in unprecedented slow down in cargo movement, unavailability of essential components especially chips used in electronic and automobile sectors, soaring input prices, stretched working capital cycles, exchange rate volatility and disruption in payment mechanism.

Numerous changes by the regulatory authorities have been made in the Financial and Insurance Sectors to minimize the adverse impact of the above. We have attempted to incorporate the same in the present edition.

We are indeed thankful to our dear students and esteemed colleagues for the overwhelming response to our book *Elements of Banking and Insurance.*

We are sure that the readers will find the third edition even more useful. Your valuable comments and suggestions are welcome.

Jyotsna Sethi
Nishwan Bhatia

Preface to the First Edition

The financial sector constitutes one of the major components of the services sector and within the financial sector *Banking* and *Insurance* have a significant role to play. There has been a manifold increase in the demand for banking services along with a commensurate increase in insurance services to cover various commercial and personal risks arising out of increasing complexities of modern life.

The past few years have witnessed myriad institutional and structural changes paving the way for the entry of a number of private and foreign players in these fields. These, in turn, have thrown up numerous opportunities as well as challenges for banking and insurance companies.

The present book is an attempt to describe the role of banking and insurance sectors in the current era of globalization, privatization and liberalization. Besides, the strides made in the field of information technology in recent years, have significantly impacted the operating environment resulting in increased competitive pressures and changing customer demands. A corollary of this is the increased employment opportunities in these sectors, directly or indirectly.

Many universities have exhibited great foresight by introducing the subjects of Banking and Insurance at the undergraduate level. Delhi University in particular, has offered an Application Course in Banking and Insurance for the third year students of B.A. (restructured) programme. The subject of Insurance has also been offered as a discipline course for the B.A. (restructured) programme.

We hope that the lucid style of the text presentation which has been supported with suitable tables, figures and illustrations will prove useful to our students in the understanding of these subjects as well as help them to keep abreast of the current developments taking place in these areas. It is also expected that this text will aid fellow teachers in clarifying certain theoretical and conceptual issues as well as provide useful insight to professionals in the fields of banking and insurance.

Despite our best efforts, we acknowledge our human limitations and possible errors. We, therefore, invite constructive suggestions as they would be instrumental in further improving our work.

We are deeply indebted to our families whose support and understanding helped bring this effort to fruition.

Jyotsna Sethi
Nishwan Bhatia

Abbreviations

ATM	Automated Teller Machine
CAR	Capital Adequacy Ratio
CBS	Core Banking Solution
CRR	Cash Reserve Ratio
DD	Demand Draft
DP	Depository Participant
DRI	Differential Rate of Interest
ECS	Electronic Clearing Service
EFT	Electronic Fund Transfer
EMT	Electronic Mail Transfer
EPZ	Export Promotion Zone
FD	Fixed Deposit
FDI	Foreign Direct Investment
FDR	Fixed Deposit Receipt
HUDCO	Housing and Urban Development Corporation
IDBI	Industrial Development Bank of India
L/C	Letter of Credit
LAB	Local Area Bank
M&A	Mergers and Acquisitions
MF	Mutual Fund
MICR	Magnetic Ink Character Recognition
MT	Mail Transfer
NABARD	National Bank for Agriculture and Rural Development

NAV	Net Asset Value
NBFC	Non Banking Finance Companies
NBFI	Non Banking Finance Intermediaries
NGO	Non-governmental Organisation
NHB	National Housing Bank
NPA	Non-performing Advance/Assets
NSDL	National Security Depository Ltd.
NSE	National Stock Exchange
PAN	Permanent Account Number
PC	Personal Computer
PER	Price Earning Ratio
PIN	Personal Identification Number
PLR	Prime Lending Rate
PMRY	Prime Minister's Rozgar Yojana
RBI	Reserve Bank of India
RRB	Regional Rural Bank
RTGS	Real Time Gross Settlement
SCB	Scheduled Commercial Bank
SDR	Special Drawing Rights
SEBI	Securities and Exchange Board of India
SENSEX	Sensitive Index
SFC	State Financial Corporation
SGSY	Swarnjayanti Gram Swarojgar Yojana
SHG	Self-help Group
SIDBI	Small Industries Development Bank of India
SJSRY	Swarna Jayanti Shahari Rozgar Yojana
SLR	Statutory Liquidity Ratio
SSI	Small-scale Industries
SWIFT	The Society for Worldwide Inter-bank Financial Telecommunication
TT	Telegraphic Transfer
VAT	Value Added Tax

1

Introduction to Banking Business

Learning Objectives

After going through this chapter we will be able to:

- Understand the role of banking sector.
- Identify the features of banking business that distinguish it from other businesses.
- Describe the functions performed by commercial banks.
- Identify the business prohibited for banking companies.
- Enumerate the types of deposits accepted by banks.

Money makes the mare go is an old saying which is relevant even today. Money and credit provide the pivot around which all the economic activities cluster. Banks are institutions that accept various types of deposits and use these funds for granting loans. By pooling the saving of widely scattered economically surplus units, banks form a vast pool of social capital. This helps in capital formation and capital accumulation. However, banks are not merely the storehouses of the country's wealth but they are reservoirs of resources necessary for economic development—be it building of infrastructure, setting up of basic and key industries, modernization of agricultural sector, boosting domestic and international trade, and so on. By discharging this function efficiently and effectively, a commercial bank increases the productive capacity of the nation and thereby plays a pivotal role in accelerating the pace of economic development.

Banks today are an important part of the payment mechanism of the economy, and it is through them that the monetary and fiscal policies of the government are concretized. By creating credit, banks are in a position to affect prices, nominal national income and other macro-economic variables. Banks are at the heart of the financial system. They are a class of financial institutions which the public views as safe and convenient outlets for its savings. The importance of a viable, sound and safe banking system cannot be overemphasized.

1.1 BRIEF HISTORY

Banking in its simplest form is as old as authenticated history. In India, references about banking habits and regulation exist in our scriptures and ancient texts. During the vedic times (2000–1400 B.C.), moneylending and 'Rna' or debt are repeatedly mentioned in the vedic literature[1]. During the smriti period, which followed the vedic period and epic age, Manu the great law giver of that time spoke of vaishs earning money through interest. He observed that "a sensible man should deposit his money with person of good family, good conduct, well acquainted with the law, veracious, having money, many relatives, wealthy and honourable". He also talks about regulations governing credit—interest on loan to bankers, usurers, renewal of commercial papers, etc[2].

Chanakya's Arthshastra (about 300 B.C.) is full of facts to show that there were powerful guilds of merchant bankers in existence who received deposits, advanced loans and carried on the other banking functions[3]. B.K. Bhargava adds that bankers in the smriti period accepted deposits from the public, granted loans against pledges and personal security, granted simple loans, acted as bailee for his customers, subscribed to public loans by granting loans to king, acted as a treasurer and banker to the State and managed the currency of the country[4].

A system of banks had also been devised as early as 2000 B.C. by the Babylonians. In ancient Greece and Rome, the practice of granting credit was widely prevalent. The Bank of Venice, which was established in 1157, is considered to be the most ancient bank. In Florence, 'Monte' was established in 1336, and a public bank was set up in 1401 in Barcelona[5]. For fulfilling the needs of merchants, the Bank of Amsterdam was set

---

[1] Kripa, S.S., *Development of Commercial Banks in India,* Sunrise Publications, New Delhi, 2007, p. 1.

[2] Kripa, S.S., op.cit., p. 2

[3] Nigam, B.M. Lal, *Banking Law & Practice,* Konark Publishers, New Delhi, 1988, p. 13.

[4] Kripa, S.S., op.cit., p. 2.

[5] Shekhar, K.C. and Shekhar Lekshmy, *Banking Theory and Practice,* Vikas Publishing House, New Delhi, 2005, p. 1.

up in 1609 (and most European Banks at that time were formed on this model).

Early history apart modern banking began with the goldsmiths of London in the 17th century. At that time money was held in the form of gold and silver coins. As the goldsmiths had excellent strong rooms, people started keeping their money with them for safe keeping in return for a fee. The goldsmiths used to issue receipts for the same which began to be transferred from one trader to another for settlement of debts. In this manner, the trader avoided the hassle of withdrawing their coins from the goldsmith to make the payment to their creditors. The creditors, in turn, were saved from the necessity of having to deposit the same with the goldsmith for safe keeping. To make such transactions simpler, the goldsmith started issuing receipts in convenient denominations and made them payable to bearer. The goldsmith soon observed that at a time only a small proportion of coin were needed for making payment, so they started lending the surplus money and charging certain interest for doing so. The goldsmith began entrusting reserves to the 'exchequer' under the sanction and care of the King. Unfortunately, King Charles II shut up the exchequer one day and that caused the ruin of the goldsmiths. However, this proved to be a turning point in the history of English banking with the growth of private banking and the Bank of England in 1694. At this point, it is pertinent to mention that apart from the goldsmiths, the moneylenders and merchants also had a strong role to play. Each of these was closely concerned in dealing of money which in those days was in the form of coins made of precious metals. Merchants were trustworthy people to whom people gave their monies for safe keeping. They also issued receipts acknowledging their liabilities and honoured them when the receipts were presented. Moneylenders in villages too lent money to people on interest. This money was usually their own, but sometimes, it also belonged to people with surplus money who gave it to them. Moneylenders, thus, became embryonic banks by serving as money borrowers as well as moneylenders. As these money changers transacted their business sitting on benches (equivalent of English 'Bench', German 'Banck', Italian 'Banco' and French 'Banqui'), they came to be known as '**banks**'.

In India our historical, cultural, social and economic factors have resulted in the Indian money market being characterized by the existence of both the unorganized and the organized sectors.

Unorganized sector: The unorganized sector comprises moneylenders and indigenous bankers which cater to the needs of a large number of people especially in the rural areas. They have been meeting the financial requirements of the rural populace since times immemorial. Indigenous bankers are private firms or individuals whose functions are similar to banks—they receive deposits, lend money and deal in *Hundies,* whereas the primary business of moneylenders is money lending and not banking. Moneylenders can be professional—those whose sole business is to lend money like *Sahukars* and *Mahajans*. Non-professional moneylenders lend their surplus money and are also engaged in some other business, like *Zamindars*. At the time of Independence, the most important source of rural credit was moneylenders who accounted for 71.6 per cent of the total rural credit.

The indigenous bankers are different from the proper banks in a number of ways. For instance, they combine banking activities with trade whereas trading is strictly prohibited for banks in the organized sector. They do not believe in formalities or paper work for making deposits or withdrawing money. In fact, since a substantial percentage of their clientele is illiterate, they frequently take a thumb impression of their customers on a blank paper. Even if they use a 'Hundi' as a negotiable instrument yet it will not be indicated on its face whether the transaction is supported by valuable consideration or it is merely as a result of mutual accommodation. The rate of interest charged by them fluctuates directly with the need of the borrower and may sometimes be as high as 300 per cent! They are insulated from all type of monetary and credit controls as they fall outside the purview of the RBI. Though they are still the major source of funds for small borrowers, but now their market has started shrinking because of the fast expansion of branches of banks in the unorganized sectors.

Organized sector: The organized sector of the money market comprises specialized banking institutions like Industrial Development Bank of India (IDBI), Small Industries Development Bank of India (SIDBI), National Bank for Agriculture and Rural Development (NABARD), Export-Import (EXIM) Bank and National Housing Bank (NHB) which are the apex institutions in their respective fields. The commercial banks are the oldest institutions in the organized money market. They have a huge geographical network and enjoy tremendous public confidence. This sector also includes the public sector banks, private sector banks and foreign banks as well as cooperative banks.

The evolution of Indian banking system can be categorized into three distinct phases: (1) The pre-Independence phase, i.e., before 1947, (2) second phase from 1947 to 1991, and (3) third phase 1991–92 and beyond, i.e., after the financial sector reforms.

Phase 1 The pre-Independence phase was charaterized by the presence of a large number of banks (more than 600); most of them being small in size and suffering from high rate of failures. As a result, public confidence in banks was low and deposit mobilization was also very slow.

Phase 2 With the introduction of economic planning an attempt was made for aligning monetary and banking activity with the requirements of planning. This phase was characterized by nationalization. The State Bank of India Act, 1955, was passed and the Imperial Bank was renamed the State Bank of India (SBI). The seven subsidiary banks of SBI were nationalized in 1960 and then in 1969, 14 major banks were nationalized followed by 8 more banks in 1980. The flow of agricultural and industrial credit was widened and deepened after nationalization. The Deposit Insurance Corporation was formed to insure deposits of small depositors. The weak banks were compulsorily merged with bigger financially viable banks.

Phase 3 The post-1991 saw a remarkable transition in the banking sector as capital base of banks was strengthened; prudential norms were introduced in line with international standards, interest rates were de-regularized, new private sector banks were opened and other initiatives were taken to enhance productivity and competitiveness of this sector.

Some of the main differences between the moneylenders (unorganized) and the banks (organized) sectors have been summarized below in Table 1.1.

Table 1.1 Differences between Unorganized and Organized Sectors

Moneylenders (Unorganized sector)	*Banks (Organized sector)*
Lend from own savings.	Lend from deposits received from general public.
Frequently combine banking with trading activity.	Are prohibited from carrying on any trading activity.
Usually charge very high rate of interest, rates fluctuates with the needs of borrowers.	Rate of interest are comparatively lower.
Formalities/procedures for borrowing are bare minimal if at all.	Paper work, formalities, procedures are much more stringent.
Usually money has to be returned after a fixed period.	Money has to be returned on demand
No restrictions as to mode of demand (cheque, etc.) or time and place.	Demand can be made only through cheques, drafts, order, etc. during working hours in bank premises.
Does not provide other agency/general utility services.	They provide a number of agencies and general utility services.
Hardly use any procedure or any technology.	Usually all operations are computerized and use high technology for most purposes.

1.2 BUSINESS OF BANKING

Banks are institutions that accept various types of deposits and use those funds for granting loans. The business of banking is that of an intermediary between the saving and investment units of the economy. It collects the surplus funds of millions of individual savers who are widely scattered and channelizes them to the investors. (See Figure 1.1).

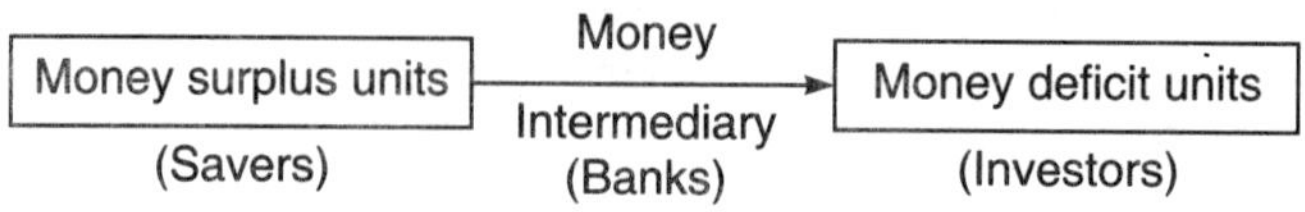

Figure 1.1 Business of banking.

In simple terms, banks serve as a middle man from the money surplus unit to be money deficit unit. They are intermediaries, who transfer funds from savers to investors through grants for business, commerce, education, housing and other purposes. They perform the basic purpose of intermediation through the following four transformation mechanisms:

Liability-asset transformation. The deposits of money that banks accept from the public are liabilities for the bank. These are converted by them into assets such as loans and investments.

Size transformation. Banks create a reservoir of funds from the numerous small deposits collected from customers, and then provide large loans to investors.

Maturity transformation. The liquidity preferences of borrowers and lenders differ. Banks offer savers deposits according to their time or demand liability preferences, and at the same time banks provide short, medium or long-term loans to the borrowers according to their preferences.

Risk transformation. The risks to which savers are exposed, are distributed by the bankers through diversification.

In this manner commercial banks mobilise savings from the general public, through their extensive network of branches, and channelize them into productive purposes. They finance industry as well as domestic and foreign trade and agriculture. They are instrumental in raising the standard of living of people by advancing loans for housing, consumer durables, education, etc. the success of the monetary policies of the central bank also depends upon the efficient, functioning of the commercial banks.

1.2.1 Meaning of Banking

According to section 5(b) of the Banking Regulation Act, 1949, "banking" means the accepting, for the purpose of lending or investment, of deposits of money from the public, repayable on demand or otherwise, and withdrawable by cheque, draft, order or otherwise. *Banking company* means any company which transacts the business of banking in India. No company can carry on the business of banking in India unless it uses as part of its name at least one of the words *bank, banker* or *banking.*

Any company which is engaged in the manufacture of goods or carries on any trade and which accepts deposits of money from the public, merely for the purpose of financing its business, such manufacturer or trader shall not be deemed to transact the business of banking. The essence of banking business is receiving money as deposits from the public, which are always repayable on demand. Banks also create credit; other commerical enterprises do not perform these functions.

1.2.2 Functions of Bank

According to section 6 of the Banking Regulation Act, 1949, the primary functions of a bank are:

The borrowing, raising or taking up of money; the lending or advancing of money either upon or without security; and drawing, making, accepting, discounting, buying, selling, collecting and dealing in bills of exchange, hundies, promissory notes, coupons, drafts, bill of lading, railway receipts, warrants, debentures, certificates, scrips and other instruments, and securities whether transferable or negotiable or not. Besides the two main functions of lending and investment, a commercial bank performs a variety of other functions.

Other functions: Banks provide the following services:

- Carry out the standing instructions of customers for making payments; including subscriptions, insurance premium, rent, electricity and telephone bills, etc.
- Undertake government business like payment of pension, collection of direct tax (e.g., income tax) and indirect taxes (like excise duty).
- Collect dividends, cheques, bills of exchange, promissory notes.
- Underwrite and deal in stock, funds, shares, debentures, etc.
- Act as agents for any government or local authority or any other person or persons; also carry on agency business of any description including the clearing and forwarding of goods, giving of receipts and discharges, and otherwise acting as an attorney on behalf of customers, but excluding the business of a Managing Agent or Secretary and Treasurer of a company.
- Contract for public and private loans and negotiating and issuing the same.
- The effecting, insuring, guaranteeing, underwriting, participating in managing and carrying out of any issue, public or private, of State, municipal or other loans or of shares, stock, debentures or debenture stock of any company, corporation or association and the lending of money for the purpose of any such issue.

- Many banks also act as trustees, executors and administrators to undertake the supervision of investments and distribution of income on behalf of their customers.
- The issue of letters of credit, international money orders, travellers' cheques (both in Indian Rupee and foreign currency), foreign currency, circular notes and bank drafts.
- Safe custody services through provision of lockers and safe deposit vaults for safe keeping of documents, cash, jewellery, etc.
- Remittance of funds through electronic funds transfer (EFT) service, bank draft, etc.
- Deals in debit and credit cards and ATM cards.

It is pertinent to mention that services provided by banks have undergone a sea change in recent years. The use of internet technology has become a very powerful force changing the very core of traditional banking. Changing lifestyles and intense competition have further enlarged the range of services provided by banks. Banks are increasingly focusing on fee-based activities like cards, electronic transfers and clearances, mobile banking, loan syndication, hedging and a host of other activities. A brief summary of functions performed by most commercial banks today are given in Table 1.2. For convenience, they have been grouped into **primary**, **agency** and **general utility services**.

Table 1.2 Functions of Commercial Banks

Primary		*Agency*	*General utility*
Acceptance of deposits • Saving • Fixed • Demand	Advancing of loans • Loans • Overdraft • Discounting of bills	Collection of interest, dividend, salary, pension Buying/selling of foreign exchange Payment of rent, insurance premium, electricity and telephone bills Collection of cheques, promissory notes, bills	Issue of letter of credit, travellers' cheques, credit cards, debit cards, ATM cards Safe custody of valuables and documents, lockers Specialized advisory service to customers, electronic transfer of funds Internet banking, mobile banking, bancassurance

1.2.3 Business Prohibited for Banking Company

According to section 8 of the said Act, no banking company shall directly or indirectly deal in the buying or selling or bartering of goods, except in connection with the realization of security given to or held by it, or engage in any trade, or buy, sell or barter goods for others otherwise than in connection with bills of exchange received for collection or negotiation. The banking system is integral to a country's financial stability and economic growth. Also banks deal largely in other people's money and therefore they are subject to numerous statutory regulations, e.g., the liquidity norms. Banks are also subject to priority sector lending norms and have to open rural branches for more balanced regional development.

1.2.4 Difference between Banking and Other Businesses

Though other businesses can also raise deposits from the public to finance their business or give loans, yet they cannot be called banks as they are very different. Some of the main differences between banking and other businesses have been summarized in Table 1.3.

Table 1.3 Difference between Banks and Other Businesses

Banking business	*Other businesses (Manufacturing, Trading/services)*
Deal in money and financial products like deposits, loans, etc.	Deal in goods and services.
Banks create credit and cannot deal in goods and services.	Do not have the power to create credit, engage in manufacturing trading and providing other services.
Banking business is directly controlled/ regulated by RBI and other regulatory authorities to ensure trust and confidence of investors.	Business is not directly controlled by any statutory authority.
A substantial portion gets locked up to meet liquidity requirements like CRR/ SLR.	There are no statutory restrictions regarding liquidity, almost the entire resources can be used.
Have to balance profitability with social justice and welfare.	Have comparatively far greater freedom to organize business.
Tallying of accounts is done on daily basis.	Usually accounts are prepared once a year.
Banking operations need to be automated much more due to need for control and the routine/repetitive nature of business.	Business operations do not have a dire need for automation.
Deposits with banks are liabilities of banks.	Deposits with bank are assets.

1.3 BANKER CUSTOMER RELATIONSHIP

The moment an individual opens an account with the banker, he becomes a customer of the bank. There exists a special relationship between the banker and its customer. To understand this relationship, it is important to know who is a banker and who is a customer.

1.3.1 Banker

A banker is one, who performs the business of banking. The term *banking* has already been defined earlier. Some of the salient features of this definition are as follows:

- A banking company must perform both of the essential functions, viz. (a) accepting of deposits, (b) lending or investing the same. If the purpose of accepting of deposits is not to lend or invest, the business will not be called **banking business**. The explanation to section 5(c) makes it clear that any company which is engaged in the manufacture of goods or carries on any trade and which accepts deposits of money from the public, merely for the purpose of financing its business as such is not deemed to transact the business of banking.
- For the purpose of opening an account the banker accepts deposits of money and not of anything else. The word *public* implies that banker accepts deposits from anyone who is capable of contracting and who offers his/her money for such purpose.
- The definition also specifies the time and mode of withdrawal of deposits. The depositor must make a demand for withdrawing his/her money. The demand should be made in a proper manner and through an instrument in writing and not merely by verbal order or a telephonic message.

  The banker is, thus, an intermediary and deals with money belonging to the public. A number of other institutions which also deal with money are not designated as banking institutions because they do not fulfil all the above-mentioned prerequisites.

1.3.2 Customer

There is no statutory definition of the term customer. However, the legal decisions on the matter throw some light on the meaning of the term. As such a *customer* is defined as a person who opens a deposit or current account or negotiates an advance on current or loan account. Accordingly, a person who goes to encash a bearer cheque in the bank, or visits a bank to deposit application money for allotment of shares of a company shall not be termed as a *customer*. Dr. Hart defines a customer as "one who has an account with a banker or for whom a banker habitually undertakes to act as such". In law a person can be an individual or, a firm, company, society or any legal entity including a government department and a corporation incorporated by, or under any law.

Account Opening Procedure: To open a bank account the customer has to fill the requisite form, savings, fixed, current etc. He has to give details of name, date of birth, occupation, residential address. All KYC norms have to be fulfilled. Copies of Pan Card/Aadhaar have to be submitted. He also has to submit photographs and give specimen signatures. A proper introduction from an existing customer needs to be provided.

1.3.3 Relationship between Banker and Customer

The general relationship between banker and customer is that of debtor and creditor. Sometimes, the banker acts as an agent or trustee of the customer as explained below. To constitute a customer, a person must

- Open a bank account—saving, current or fixed deposit, in his name by making necessary deposit of money only and not anything other valuables like gold or shares etc.
- The dealing between the banker and the customer must be in the nature of banking business. The business of banking, is the accepting of deposits and lending of money. So, if a person goes to the bank for any other purpose like payment of income tax, utility bills, etc., he will not be considered to be a customer of the bank.

Relationship as debtor and creditor: The moment the customer opens an account with the banker, he becomes debtor of the customer and the customer becomes his creditor. The banker is then bound to return an equivalent amount of money, by paying a similar sum to the depositor when he is asked for it. However, this relationship is reversed when the customer takes an overdraft—then the customer becomes the debtor and the banker becomes a creditor. The debtor-creditor relationship between banker and customer is also different from similar relationship in other commercial transactions in the following respects:

The creditor must demand payment. In case of ordinary commercial debt, the debtor repays the money on the specified date, or as per the terms of the contract. But in case of a deposit in the bank, the debtor/banker is not required to repay the amount on his own accord. The depositor/creditor must make a demand for the payment.

Demand must be made in the proper manner. The withdrawal should be effected through an order, cheque and draft or otherwise. These days bankers also make payments when requested through electronic cheques, ATMs, credit cards and debit cards.

Proper place and time of demand. If the payment is not being demanded through electronic mode, then the customer/creditor has to make the demand at the proper place and proper time. In other words, he can demand payment only from that branch of the bank, where he has an account and that too during working hours on a working day. In ordinary commercial transaction, money can be demanded anytime and anywhere.

1.3.4 Banker as Trustee

Under certain circumstances, bankers enter into fiduciary relationship of a trustee with their customers. A trustee holds money or assets and performs certain functions for the benefit of some other person called the **beneficiary**. For instance, when a banker receives valuables for safe custody, he acts as a trustee. This property does not pass on to the banker and it is not available for distribution amongst his general creditors in case of liquidation.

1.3.5 Banker as Agent

A banker acts as an agent of his customer in many ways, e.g., when he buys or sells securities or makes payment of various dues of his customers, or collects cheques on his behalf. In all these cases, the banker acts as an agent of his customer.

1.4 BANK DEPOSITS

It is the taking of deposits and granting of loans that single out a bank. These are the core activities of a bank. Initially, all accounts are opened with a deposit of money by the customer and hence these accounts are called **deposit accounts**. Public deposits comprise the major proportion of a bank working funds which are used primarily to make loans and advances and to purchase securities. The size of deposits is a fair reflection of the confidence, reposed by the public in that bank. The growth and prosperity of a bank depends on how they are managed to maximize profits. The banker solicits deposits from the members of the public belonging to different walks of life, engaged in numerous economic activities. The nature of banking facility sought by them, therefore, varies widely, e.g., some want to earn interest, some want their money to be safe, others use banking facilities for conducting business. As a result, different types of accounts with various facilities and privileges are offered by banks to their customers. Banks accept various types of deposits, which are generally categorized as demand or time deposits.

Time deposit: Any deposit which is not repayable on demand is a time deposit, e.g., a fixed deposit.

Fixed deposits. A fixed deposit is an account with the banker, which is repayable on the expiry of a specified period, that's why such deposits are also called **term deposits**. They are a genuine saving medium. The banker can utilize such amounts more profitably since he knows before hand when this money will be demanded. As a result, a much higher rate of interest is offered to the customer on such deposits. These deposits have different maturity periods and the rate of interest is proportionate to the maturity period. When a person deposits money with the banker on a fixed deposit, a fixed deposit receipt (FDR) is given to him by way of acknowledgement for the amount deposited. A fixed deposit can be opened singly or jointly. It mentions the date of opening and maturity, the amount deposited, the rate of interest and instructions for payment of interest whether monthly, quarterly, yearly or on maturity. Senior citizens usually get another 0.5% additional interest on their fixed deposits. In case payment is desired before maturity then rate payable will be less. This deposit receipt is not a negotiable instrument. However, it can be assigned provided due notice of assignment to the banker.

Recurring deposit. This scheme was started by banks to provide more incentives for saving and also to encourage people to save on a regular basis. If a person opts to invest in a recurring deposit then as the name suggests they deposit a sum of their choosing say ₹100 or any multiple thereof every month for a period of their choice. This period usually ranges between one to three or five years. Interest paid under this system is more than that paid on a saving account and slightly less than that of a fixed deposit.

Demand deposits. Demand deposits are those where customers expect to be able to withdraw money at anytime. These include savings deposits and deposits in current accounts.

Saving bank accounts. Such accounts are usually maintained by people who wish to save a part of the current income to meet the future needs and also to earn some interest. For banks the need of keeping cash reserves against such deposits is comparatively more as compared to fixed deposits but smaller as against current deposits. The banker pays interest against these accounts to the customers though at a lower rate than in case of fixed deposits, it is three percent at present, though it varies across banks. For operating a savings bank account, the customer has to abide by some rules—The customer has to maintain a minimum balance in his account. A chequebook is issued to customer to withdraw money however there is a restriction as to the number of withdrawals he can make. Records of the transactions are maintained in a passbook or through a monthly bank statement.

Current account. Such accounts are opened by businessmen/corporates who do not want any restriction on the operation of their account. It is running and active account and the banker is under an obligation to repay these deposits only when the customer demands payment through a cheque, card or otherwise, and that's why these are termed as **demand liabilities**.

Generally, a much higher level of minimum balance has to be maintained by the customer in this account. He is issued with a chequebook and a passbook, but no interest is paid to him on these deposits. In fact, he has to pay bank charges to the banker for maintaining this account for him. Clean or secured overdraft facilities are also granted against such accounts. Banks also extend free outstation cheque collection facility and issue of demand drafts to such account holders.

Note: The various loans and advances granted by banks have been discussed in Chapter 5.

KEY TERMS

Bancassurance Distribution of financial products particularly life and non-life insurance by banks as corporate agents through their various branches.

Hundi A negotiable instrument not by statute but by custom or usage written in an oriental language.

Intermediary Go between people and organizations.

Macro-economic variable National income, output and employment.

Negotiable Negotiable Instrument is an instrument that is transferable by delivery so that the transferee becomes the holder thereof. For example, a cheque and a promissory note.

KYC (Know your Customer) It is mandatory for all prospective customers to fill a KYC form at the time of opening an account and all customers have to fill this form periodically. All information regarding the name, date of birth, occupation, address proof, copy of pan-card or Aadhar along with photographs have to be submitted.

REVIEW QUESTIONS

1.1 'Banks are not just institutions for accepting of deposits and lending of money'. Comment on the statement and explain the role of the banking sector in the national economy.

1.2 Distinguish between the organized and unorganized sectors of the money market.

1.3 Define the term 'banking' and explain how the functions of a bank have changed over the years.

1.4 Will a person who goes to deposit income tax in a bank be deemed to be a customer of that bank? Give reasons for your answer and also explain the procedure for opening an account in a bank.

1.5 Explain about the various types of deposits offered by a bank to its customers.

2

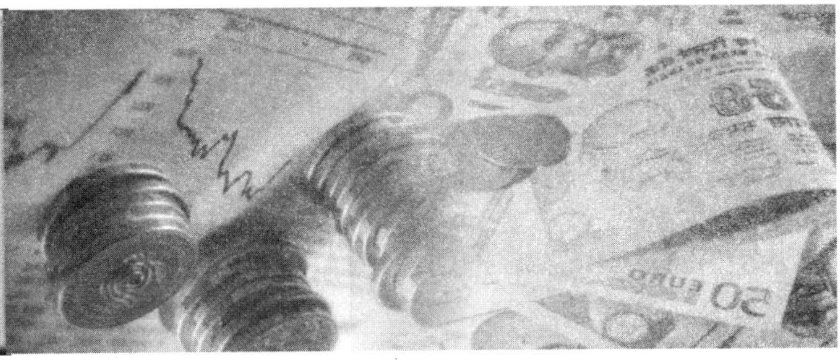

Structure of Commercial Banks in India and Apex Banking Institution

Learning Objectives

After going through this chapter we will be able to:

- Understand the structure of the banking system in India.
- Describe the role and functions of the Reserve Bank of India.
- Differentiate between Public sector and Private sector banks.
- Learn about the structure of Regional Rural banks.
- Understand the operations of Indian and foreign banks. Explain the features of Co-operative banks.
- Differentiate between commercial banks and cooperative banks. Learn about Apex level Banking Institutions—NABARD, NHB, SIDBI, IDBI, EXIM.

The structure of banking varies widely from country to country. Often a country's banking structure is a consequence of the regulatory regime to which it is subjected. The banking system in India works under the constraints that go with social control and public ownership. Nationalization, for instance, was a structural change in the functioning of commercial banks which was considered essential to better serve the needs of development of the economy in conformity with national policy and objectives. Similarly to meet the major objectives of banking sector reforms, government stake was reduced up to 51 per cent in public sector banks. New private sector banks were allowed and foreign banks were permitted additional branches.

2.1 STRUCTURE OF INDIAN BANKING SYSTEM

The Indian financial system comprises a large number of commercial and cooperative banks, specialized developmental banks for industry, agriculture, external trade and housing, social security institutions, collective investment institutions, etc. The banking system is at the heart of the financial system.

The Indian banking system has the RBI at the apex. It is the regulatory body for all banks in India. It is the central bank of the country under which there are the commercial banks including public sector and private sector banks, foreign banks and local area banks. It also includes regional rural banks as well as cooperative banks. The structure of the Indian banking system is given in Figure 2.1.

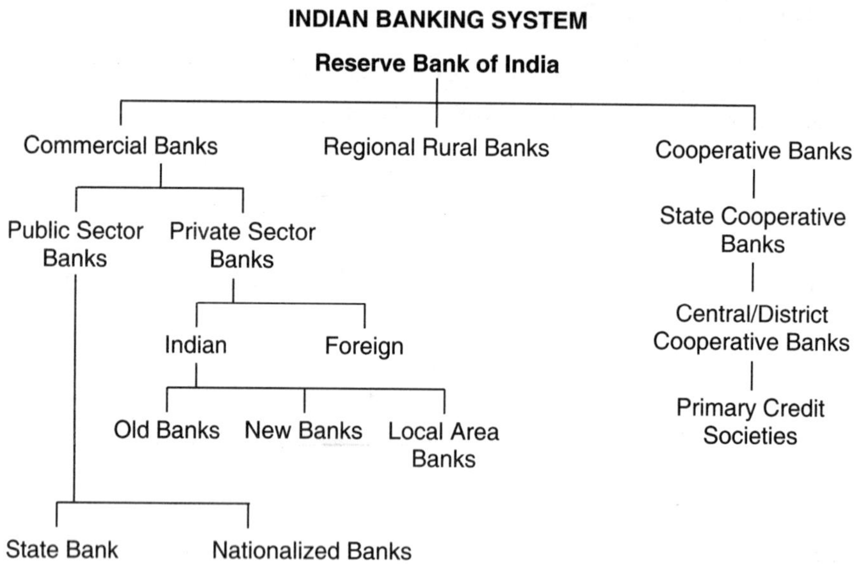

Figure 2.1 Structure of Indian Banking System.
(N.B. All subsidiaries of SBI have been merged in the SBI)

2.2 RESERVE BANK OF INDIA

The importance of central banking institution has gained recognition as a leader bank and symbol of economic activity in most civilized countries of the world. It has no direct interaction with the public but it is a banker to other banks and the government. Most central banks are normally responsible for monetary control, and in addition are involved in prudential regulation and placing government debt on the most favourable terms. The Reserve Bank of India, the central bank of our country, was established in 1935 under the aegis of Reserve Bank of India Act, 1934. It was a private shareholders institution till January 1949, after which it became a state-owned institution under the Reserve Bank (transfer of public ownership) of India Act, 1948. It is the oldest central bank among the developing countries. As the apex bank, it has been guiding, monitoring, regulating and promoting the destiny of the Indian financial system.

2.2.1 Objectives of RBI

RBI is a state-owned organization, that functions as a corporate body with special powers and obligations for serving the national interest. Objectives are to ensure stability of interest and exchange rates, to provide liquidity, an adequate supply of currency, and flow of credit to productive sectors It issues bank notes and keep reserves with a view to secure monetary stability in the country. It operates the currency and credit system. It plays a lead role in the development of a sound financial system, which reflects national and economic priorities, and ensures that financial transactions can be safely and efficiently executed. Due to the peculiar nature of the developing economy, the bank has also acquired additional responsibility to render regulatory, supervisory, developmental and promotional functions.

2.2.2 Functions of RBI

The primary function of a central bank is to formulate, execute and monitor the country's monetary policy, maintain stability and accelerate growth. The Preamble of the RBI Act, 1934, describes its basic functions as 'to regulate the issue of Bank Notes and keeping of reserves with a view to securing monetary stability in India and generally to operate the currency and credit system of the country to its advantage'. The RBI thus not only performs its traditional monetary functions, but also a number of regulatory, promotional and developmental functions.

Traditional Functions: RBI has played an important role in the development of money and capital markets in India, through its various traditional functions discussed hereinafter.

- *Note issuing authority.* RBI has the sole right to issue currency notes (excluding one rupee note and coins which are issued by the Finance Secretary to the Government of India) in the following denominations: ₹2, 5, 10, 20, 50, 100, 500 and 1,000. However ₹2 and 5 have since been discontinued. These notes including one rupee notes and coins are unlimited legal tender throughout India. The department for issue of notes is called the **issue department**, and is separate from the banking department which performs the general banking business. The issue department issues bank notes against the security of gold coins and bullion, foreign securities, rupee coins, Government of India rupees securities and such bills of exchange and promissory notes as are eligible for purchase by the bank. The aggregate value of gold coin and bullion was not supposed to be less than 40 per cent of these assets but after 1956, this system was abandoned, and a minimum value of total approved assets came to be adopted as a cover for note issue.

- *Banker's bank and lender of the last resort.* Just as individuals and corporates have accounts with banks all banks operating within the nation have accounts with the Reserve Bank of India. The RBI enables efficient and swift transfer of funds and settlement of inter-bank transactions. Banks hold non-interest earning current account with the RBI through which they can electronically transfer payments to other banks using Real Time Gross Settlement (RTGS). Banks can also electronically manage their funds position through the Deposit Account Department. The RBI also provides short-term loans and advances to banker/financial institutions to facilitate lending for specified purposes. In times of need the banks borrow funds from RBI and hence it is called the **banker of last resort/ lender of last resort**. It grants accommodation to scheduled banks by (i) Rediscounting or purchase of eligible bills (including commercial bills, bills for financing agricultural operations, cottage and small-scale industries, bills for holding or trading in government securities and foreign bills), and (ii) Loans and advances against certain securities (including stocks, funds and securities other than immovable property), gold or silver or documents of title to the same, such bills of exchange and promissory notes that are eligible for purchase or rediscount by the RBI as stated earlier or guaranteed by the state government as to the repayment.
- *Banker to the government.* In accordance with the Reserve Bank of India Act, 1934, the Central Government has to entrust the Reserve Bank with all its money, remittances, exchange and banking transactions in India as well as with the management of its public debt. As a banker to the government, the RBI works out the overall fund position and sends daily advice and monthly statements showing balances in its books. It receives and pays money on behalf of various government departments, acts as a banker to all state governments barring those of Jammu & Kashmir and Sikkim.

  The RBI also provides ways and means advances – a short-term interest bearing advance to the governments to tide over the temporary mismatches in their receipts and payment. Since 1976, every ministry and department has been allotted a specific public sector bank for handling its day-to-day transactions so that the RBI is absolved from these responsibilities.

- *Custodian of foreign exchange reserves.* The RBI plays the role of a custodian for safeguarding foreign currency, gold and other securities. Under section 40 of the RBI Act, the RBI is required to maintain the stability of the external value of the rupee. For this all foreign exchange reserves including gold, foreign assets and government balances held abroad, are centralized with the RBI. All foreign exchange receipts and payments are required to be transacted through RBI, or its authorized dealers (mainly major commercial banks).

  Besides, maintaining the official rate of exchange in which all foreign transactions are conducted, the Reserve Bank administers the exchange controls of the country by acting as the custodian of India's reserve of international currencies.

- *Controller of credit.* The Reserve Bank of India functions as the controller of credit by regulating the quality of credit, and the rate at which it is made available. It exercises control over the credit granted by the commercial banks through **Quantitative methods** like cash reserve ratio, bank rate, statutory liquidity ratio and open market operations or **Selective methods** pertaining to the amount, purpose of loan, etc. explained later.

  (i) ***Quantitative Methods***

  - *Cash Reserve Ratio (CRR)* The banks are required to keep a certain percentage of their total demand and time liabilities in the form of cash with the RBI. At present this ratio is 4.5% (June 22).
  - *Statutory Liquidity Ratio (SLR)* It is the reserve requirement banks are expected to keep before offering credit to the customers. Every banking company in India is required to maintain in cash, gold, unencumbered approved securities, an amount which shall not at the close of business on any day be less than the minimum specified percentage of SLR. At present it is 18% (June 22).
  - *Bank Rate* Bank rate is the rate of interest at which the RBI makes advances to the commercial banks.

CRR, SLR and bank rate are all used as tools for credit control. When there is excessive credit supply in the market it will lead to inflation and speculative activities. The RBI will increase the limit of CRR, SLR and the bank rate. This will result in a decrease in money supply and help to keep inflation in check.

- *Open market operations* Open market operations means buying and selling of securities by the Reserve bank. If the RBI wants to increase the money supply in the system then it will start purchasing securities and if it wants to decrease the money supply then it will start selling the securities.

  (ii) *Selective Credit Control* Apart from the above methods the RBI uses certain methods of selective credit control. By issuing directives under section 21 of the Banking Regulation Act pertaining to the following:

  The purpose of advances for which they may or may not be made available, the maximum amount to be advanced to any borrower, the maximum amount upto which guarantee may be given and the margins to be maintained in case of secured assets and the rate of interest to be charged.

Regulatory and Supervisory Functions The RBI has the authority to regulate and administer the entire banking and financial system under the provisions of the Banking Regulation Act 1949 and the RBI Act of 1934 with the objectives to check malpractices and protect the interest of depositors and maintain safety and soundness of the banking and financial system of the country.

Regulatory Functions In view of the growing complexities and inter-connectedness in the system and the potential systemic risks that could arise, the RBI performs a number of regulatory functions.

Disclosure Norms As per RBI's directives banks are required to make disclosures in their Annual Reports and other documents about their capital adequacy, asset quality, liquidity, earning aspect and penalties imposed on them by the Regulator. If the RBI feels the need at any time, it can put a bank under PCA (Prompt Corrective Action) meaning that a bank could collect deposits but do very little commercial lending if their lending records are bad and NAPs very high.

Prudential Norms These norms refer to the ideal/responsible norms maintained by banks with a view to strengthen their balance sheets—asset recognition, capital adequacy, investment portfolios and capital market exposures. The RBI has also issued guidelines under Bassel II for risk management. The RBI can also merge weak banks with strong ones to strengthen balance sheets of banks which are struggling under a mountain of debt and to enable the merged entity to make increased credit offering.

Know Your Customer (KYC) It has become an integral part of the banking process through which the bank verifies information about the identity and address of the customer at the time of opening of their account. The bank also periodically updates identification data of their customers including photos, proof of identity and proof of address. This is done with a view to prevent money laundering and other criminal activities and to minimize financial frauds.

Prompt Corrective Action (PCA) The RBI can put a bank under PCA if the bank's performance does not meet the minimum criteria laid down by the central bank. PCA was introduced in 2002 for commercial banks but now it is applicable to Urban Co-operative Banks (March 2022) and it shall become applicable to NBFCs from 1st October 2022. NABARD too has developed a PCA for all RRBs also. Foreign Banks branches operating in India are also covered under this.

If a bank is put under PCA it means that they can collect deposits but do very little commercial lending. This is done generally when a bank has poor lending record, high NPAs and high leverage. In the last financial year out of the ₹2,000 crores infused in five state owned lenders, ₹11,500 crores had gone to three banks under PCA namely UCO Bank, Indian Overseas Bank and Central Bank of India (ET 25.12.21). The RBI triggers the first threshold of PCA when a bank reports two years of consecutive negative ROA and if it extends to three years then the second threshold is triggered. The last criterion is the total debt or leverage, which measures the financial risk of the bank.

Deposit Insurance and Credit Guarantee Corporation (DICGC) to protect the interest of small depositors in case of bank failure. The DICGC provides insurance cover to all eligible depositors up to a maximum of ₹1 lakh. In this regard India's limit is very low as compared to some other countries. In dollar terms its 1,404 in India, 72,436 in China, 111,327 in the UK and 250,000 in the US. (This limit has since been increased to ₹5 lakh on 4.2.20).

2.2.3 Supervisory Functions

Licensing of banks The RBI grants licenses without which no bank can operate. A company desirous of starting a banking business has to satisfy the central bank regarding minimum capital requirements, reserves, liquid assets and other parameters laid down by the RBI only then a license will be granted. RBI is also empowered to cancel the license of a bank if it feels that the business of the bank is not being carried out satisfactorily.

Branch expansion The RBI exercises control over expansion of branches by banks through the bank's branch licensing policy.

Inspection of banks The RBI has powers to carry out periodical inspection and auditing of banks. It examines banks against various parameters like organizational structure, mobilization of deposits, investments, credit portfolio management, branch expansion, deployment of credit to priority sector among others. It can also conduct investigation if a complaint is made regarding major irregularities or frauds against any bank.

Control over Amalgamation and Liquidation It's a pre-requisite for banks to obtain RBI's permission for voluntary amalgamation. In consultation with the central government, RBI also has the power for compulsory amalgamation of weak banks to improve their financial efficiency, e.g. the New Bank of India was merged with the Punjab National Bank in 1993, Dena and Vijaya Banks were merged with the Bank of Baroda in 2019.

RBI also supervises banks under liquidation to ensure that proper procedures are being followed.

2.2.4 Promotional and Development Functions

The RBI has been aiding development and promoting saving and banking habits. It has fostered a number of specialized financial institutions to meet the growing needs of trade, commerce, industry and agriculture. By opening more and more branches in rural and semi-urban areas the RBI has succeeded in developing a banking habit among people in such areas which led to greater monetization, given a boost to provision of rural credit, and reduced the dependance on money lenders and indigenous bankers.

2.2.5 Agriculture Credit

Development of institutional agriculture credit and other rural activities has been an area of focus for the central bank. The predominant influence of agriculture on the Indian economy has necessitated the urgent need to expand and co-ordinate the credit facilities available to the rural sector. The RBI does not provide finance directly to the agriculturists but through co-operative banks, Land development banks, commercial banks. After establishment of National Bank for Agriculture and Rural Development (NABARD) in July 1982, all functions relating to rural credit have been transferred to this new agency.

2.2.6 Industrial Finance

There was a complete absence of financial institutions for providing medium- and long-term credit. The RBI has set up a number of Financial Institutions at all India and regional levels to function as specialized institutions for long-term lending. The important ones include:

(i) Industrial Finance Corporation of India (IFCI), 1948
(ii) Sate Financial Corporations (SFCs), 1953
(iii) Industrial Development Bank of India (IDBI), 1964
(iv) National Bank for Agricultural and Rural Development (NABARD), 1982
(v) Unit Trust of India (UTI)

2.2.7 Development of Bills Market

There was a complete absence of an organized bill market in India even after the establishment of the RBI. The RBI made concerted efforts for the development of bills market and in 1954, all scheduled banks were directed to develop and encourage financing through trade bills. By the end of 1958, the bill market was extended to cover export bills also.

2.2.8 Other Activities of RBI

Training RBI imparts training to its own staff through its staff training college. It conducts different courses for senior and Intermediate officers as well as special short-term courses in Co-operative marketing and Land mortgage Banking at Regional Co-operative Training centres.

Research The RBI conducts research studies related to banks and other financial sectors including money supply, agricultural credit, international trade, foreign exchange, etc. It also conducts technical studies.

- *Collection and publication of data.* The Reserve Bank of India has a separate Department of Statistics for collecting, compiling and disseminating statistical information on money and banking. It publishes Reserve Bank Bulletin and Annual Report apart from other publications.

Management: The bank is managed by a Central Board of Directors, which exercises overall control. The central board comprises the governor, four deputy governors and fifteen directors nominated by the Central Government. The directors of four local boards at Delhi, Kolkata, Chennai and Mumbai advise the Central Board. There is also a committee of the Central Board of Directors. Apart from the banking and issue departments, there are at present twenty other departments and three training establishments at the central office of the bank. The head office of the Reserve Bank is at Mumbai.

2.3 COMMERCIAL BANKS

In the organized sector of the money market, commercial banks and cooperative banks have been in existence for the past several decades. A commercial bank is run on commercial line that is to earn profits unlike a cooperative bank which is run for the benefit of a group of members of the cooperative body, e.g., a housing cooperative society. The commercial banks are spread across the length and breadth of the country, and cater to the short-term needs of industry, trade and commerce and agriculture unlike the developmental banks which focus on long-term needs. These days the commercial banks also look after other needs of their customers including long-term credit requirements.

The banking sector has been undergoing drastic metamorphosis. The rapid progress witnessed in the realm of banking services has been engineered by the trends in globalization, liberalization and privatization. The technological revolution and demographic changes have also helped to change the face of banking in India. More banks are switching over to virtual banking from the brick and mortar banks, and are providing a vast array of products through very innovative channels and at highly competitive prices. Banks are now free to quote their own interest rates on loans/advances and term deposits. They now have to manage their investments and loans portfolios based on the international norms and practices of risk management including asset liability management.

Commercial banks operating in India may be categorized into public sector, private sector, and Indian or foreign banks depending upon the ownership, management and control. They may also be differentiated as scheduled or non-scheduled, licensed or unlicensed.

2.3.1 Scheduled Banks

A scheduled bank means a bank included in the second schedule of the Reserve Bank of India Act, 1934. A bank is included in this schedule if, i.e.,

1. It is carrying on the business of banking in India.
2. Its paid-up capital and reserves are not less than ₹5 lakh.
3. It is:
   - (i) A state cooperative bank.
   - (ii) A company as defined in the Companies Act of 1956.
   - (iii) An institution notified by the central government in this behalf.
   - (iv) A corporation or company incorporated by, or under any law in force in any place outside India.

All nationalized banks, e.g., Canara Bank, Syndicate Bank and almost all private sector banks, such as Axis, ICICI and HDFC are commercial scheduled banks in India. Foreign banks like ABN Amro and HSBC are also scheduled banks in India. Since 1965, the state cooperative banks have also been made eligible to be included in the second schedule. At present, scheduled commercial banks (SCBs) consist of 28 public sector banks, 9 new private sector banks, 20 old private sector banks and 31 foreign banks.

A scheduled bank enjoys certain privileges like becoming eligible for availing the facilities of accommodation from the Reserve Bank, dealing in foreign exchange, etc. It also has certain obligations like maintaining statutory reserves with the Reserve Bank.

2.3.2 Non-scheduled Banks

Those banks which are not included in the second schedule of the Reserve Bank of India Act are termed as **non-scheduled banks**. Usually they are small sized institutions which restrict their activities to local areas. Their paid-up capital and reserves do not aggregate up to more than ₹5 lakh. Their banking activities are also limited, e.g., they cannot deal in foreign exchange. The classification of Indian commercial banks into scheduled and non-scheduled banks had significance prior to nationalization but now almost all commercial unscheduled banks have been weeded out. Their role has become infinitesimally small in terms of deposits as well as number of branches. It carries little practical meaning except that of academic interest.

2.3.3 Licensed Banks

No bank can carry on the business of banking unless it holds a license granted by the Reserve Bank of India. Provisions regarding licensing are contained in section 22 of the Banking Regulation Act, 1949. A license is usually granted if the RBI is satisfied that the bank has the capacity to pay its depositors as and when their claims accrue, and that its operations are not detrimental to the interests of the depositors. Licensing is done to ensure that the working of individual banks improves, and that the weaker and unsound ones can be weeded out. Licenses can be cancelled at any time if the RBI feels that the affairs of a bank are not being carried on in a satisfactory manner.

2.4 PUBLIC SECTOR BANKS

Public sector banks have acquired a place of prominence since nationalization. These continue to be the major lenders in the economy due to their sheer size and penetration of network. The public sector banks comprise 19 nationalized banks, the State Bank of India (Annexure 2). Till 1955 they were used to be only private commercial bank—whether scheduled or non-scheduled, licensed or unlicensed, foreign or Indian, they were all owned and controlled by private entrepreneurs and shareholders. There were three phases of bank nationalization. First was in July 1955, when Government of India nationalized the Imperial Bank of India to create the State Bank of India. It was a pioneering attempt in introducing public sector banking in the country. In 1959, eight state banks of erstwhile princely states were also nationalized to form the subsidiaries of the State Bank of India. But now only seven of them are in existence, since the state banks of Bikaner and Jaipur were merged. The second phase of public sector banking came into existence when 14 major commercial banks were nationalized on July 19, 1969. This was done with the view to serve the needs of development of the economy in conformity with national priorities and objectives. On April 15, 1980, six more private sector banks were nationalized. This led to the dominance of public sector banks as nearly 90 per cent of the banking activity in the country was brought into the public sector. Most people generally rely on nationalized banks backed by the government. The public sector banks were socially controlled and publicly owned. It was done with the objective of giving a professional bent to bank management and provision of adequate credit for agricultural and rural sector, small industries, exports and a new class of entrepreneurs. It also aimed to professionalize bank management through adequate training of bank staff.

In retrospect, it appears that political motives dominated the decision about the two nationalizations. Large-scale branch expansion, mass recruitment of staff to take banking to grass roots level, direct investments and credit programmes, administered interest rate regime, credit dispensation towards poverty alleviation programmes through loan melas, etc., ruled the roost in the Indian banking scene for over two decades. However, when faced with stiff competition from private sector and foreign banks, the public sector banks have reinvented themselves, and have markedly improved their services and operational results.

After the massive merger of Public Sector Banks the total number of PSBs in India has come down from 27 in 2017 to 12 in 2021. The SBI is the largest PSB in India with 25% share of total loan and deposit market. PSBs have performed better than the private sector banks with year-on-year profit growth of 140% as compared to 28% in private sector banks. (Business Standard 22.8.2021)

2.5 PRIVATE SECTOR BANKS

Private sector banks have existed for over a century in India. Prior to the first major nationalization in 1969, private capital called the shots in commercial banking. The Tatas owned the Central Bank of India, the Birlas—the United Commercial Bank (UCO Bank now), and so on. Following the recommendations of the Narasimham committee on financial sector (1991), the Reserve Bank of India issued guidelines for the setting up of new private sector banks in India in January 1993. It was hoped that these financially viable, technologically sound and professionally managed banks will infuse greater competition and propel the entire banking sector to much higher levels of productivity and efficiency. At present, there are 21 private sector banks (MINT 1.1.2020). The new private sector banks are aggressive, professionalized and fastest growing. The old private sector banks are typically smaller with the specific regional buyers and less than satisfactory performance. The guidelines of the RBI for the entry of private sector banks are as follows:

Formation: Such a bank shall be listed as a public limited company under the Companies Act, 1956. It will be governed by the provisions of Reserve Bank of India Act and Banking Regulation Act. The decision regarding licensing and inclusion under second schedule of the RBI shall be final. At the time of granting of licences preference may be given to those banks which propose to have their headquarters located in a centre, which does not have headquarters of any other bank. The voting rights of an individual shareholder shall be governed by the ceiling of one per cent (which was raised to 10 per cent in 1994).

Capital: The minimum paid-up capital shall be ₹100 crore with promoter's contribution being 25 per cent. In case the capital is more than ₹100 crore, then the promoter's contribution shall be 20 per cent. NRI participation can be to the extent of 40 per cent. The shares of the bank should be listed on stock exchanges. The bank shall be subject to prudential norms in respect of banking operations norms for income recognition, asset classification and provisioning as well as capital adequacy of 8 per cent of the risk weighted average.

Operations: The bank shall have to observe priority sector lending targets as applicable to other banks, though some modifications in their composition may be allowed by the RBI in the initial three years. RBI instructions with respect to export credit will also have to be complied with. For at least three years after its establishment they will not be allowed to set up a subsidiary or mutual fund.

Opening of branches: Branch licensing shall be governed by the existing policy whereby banks are free to open any branches without prior approval of the RBI, if they satisfy capital adequacy and prudential accounting norms. If the RBI so directs, they might be required to open branches in rural and semi-urban areas.

Revised guidelines issued by the RBI in January 2001 brought in some changes. The major changes are:

- Minimum paid-up capital for a new bank should be ₹200 crore which shall be increased to ₹300 crore in subsequent three years after commencement of business.
- A non-banking financial company (NBFC) may convert into a commercial bank, if it satisfies the prescribed criteria.
- A large industrial house should not promote any new bank.
- Preference would be given to promoters with expertise of financing priority areas, and in setting up banks specializing in the financing of rural and agro-based industries.

2.6 PUBLIC SECTOR BANKS VS. PRIVATE SECTOR BANKS

Both public and private sector banks are integral to Indian banking system and operate under the RBI's regulations nevertheless their ownership and functioning differ vastly.

Table 2.1 enumerates the main differences between public sector and private sector banks.

Table 2.1 Differences between Public Sector and Private Sector Banks

Public sector banks	*Private sector banks*
At least 51 per cent ownership vests with the government PSBs include SBI, its subsidiaries and nationalized banks.	Majority shareholding lies with the general public, include both old private sector banks like Bank of Rajasthan, South Indian Bank, Jammu & Kashmir Bank Ltd., as well as new private sector banks like HDFC, AXIS, ICICI, Kotak Mahindra.
They have old set-up, therefore, capital assets are more.	Have lower balance sheet size and are set up with lower capital base.
Branches are more including those in rural areas, therefore, penetration and geographical reach is far more.	Branches are comparatively less including those in rural areas.
Number of employees is much more, and they are organized in Trade Unions.	Less number of personnel and unions do not pose a problem.
Fund income is more as concentration is more on loans and advances. Some have forayed into credit cards, mutual funds, etc.	Fee income is more as they earn commission from loan syndication, equipment leasing, credit cards, mutual funds, insurance, etc.
Are less technology savvy.	Use state-of-the-art technology which helps them to grow faster, with less investment.
Though a number of changes have been made yet government control is more.	In the last 4–5 years, there has been further deregulation, and these banks have comparatively more freedom to operate.
NPAs are much higher.	NPAs are much lower.

The PSBs are not entirely guided by the profit maximization goal alone and financial inclusion goals have been integrated in their objective function unlike the private sector banks. The contention that their performance is not as good as the private sector banks is not entirely correct as they weathered the Covid-19 pandemic shock quite well. They also have the highest share of branches in rural and semi-urban areas. The private sector banks meet their PSL targets but not through organic lending but through investment in priority sector lending certificates especially in agriculture and small and marginal farmers category. The recent mega merger of 10 state owned banks has resulted in consolidation of the sector, creating stronger and more robust banks (MINT 19.8.22).

2.7 LOCAL AREA BANKS

To meet the long standing need of developing a decentralized banking system, the union budget 1996–97 announced a very important policy measure regarding the development of commercial banking in India, namely, the setting up of local area banks (LABNKs) as commercial banks in the private sector. It was hoped that the large number of problems faced by RRBs and other commercial and cooperative banks would be addressed by the local area banks especially in the rural areas. These banks were thus set up with the twin objectives of (i) providing an institutional mechanism for promoting rural and semi-urban savings, and (ii) for providing credit for viable economic activities in the local areas. These banks were established as public limited companies in the private sector, and were promoted by either individual, corporates, trusts or societies. The minimum paid-up of such banks was ₹5 crore with promoter's contribution at least ₹2 crore. Unlike the RRBs which can operate in many districts with large number of banks, the local area banks can operate and open branches in maximum of three geographically contiguous districts. The local area banks are governed by the provisions of the RBI Act, 1934, the Banking Regulation Act, 1949 and other relevant statutes. They are to be registered as a public limited company under the Companies Act, 1956. The concept of the local area banks has remained a non-starter. There were only five such banks in 2003, and their assets amounted to only ₹119 crore and ₹146 crore in 2001–02 and 2002–03, respectively. Most of them had moderate to high credit-deposit ratios, and they were generally profitable.

2.8 INDIAN BANKS

As observed earlier, banks in India may be commercial banks incorporated as joint stock companies, public sector banks or cooperative banks or regional rural banks or foreign banks. Indian banks operate nationally through a colossal network of branches. Since, they have a large and varied clientele with a diverse spectrum of needs, the Indian banks specialize in different geographical regions—urban and rural, different sectors—industry both large and small, agriculture, trade, housing, exports, etc. However, all of them in the organized sector come under the purview of the RBI Act and the Banking Regulation Act.

The main strength of the Indian banks is their vast number of employees who are well conversant with the social and cultural fabric of their customers. The Indian banks by and large focus on core banking operations. They also strictly comply with the RBI guidelines as to liquidity requirements, interest rates and priority sector lending amongst other provisions.

2.9 FOREIGN BANKS

Till the 1950s they were called **Exchange Banks** because they alone transacted most of the import and export financing business of India. The foreign banks are branches of joint stock companies incorporated abroad, but operating in India. They are foreign in origin, and have their head office located in their parent country. Many foreign banks opened their offices, and expanded branches after the opening up of the Indian economy in the 1990s. These banks created an entirely new playing field in the banking sector through their range of products and services including ATMs, electronic services, credit cards and portfolio management. They provide foreign currencies for bona fide purposes like trade, travel or for study abroad. Most foreign banks have a very strong parent bank commitment, superior technology and provide a very high level of customer service. This has resulted in very strong performances of these banks both in the retail sector (home loans, credit cards, distribution of third party products including mutual funds and insurance services) as well as the corporate sector (derivatives, structured products, other risk management products and the debt capital markets).

Licensing of foreign banks: In order to operate in India, the foreign banks have to obtain a licence from the Reserve Bank of India. For granting this licence, the following factors are considered:

- Financial soundness of the bank.
- International and home country rating.
- Economic and political relations between home country and India.
- The bank should be under consolidated supervision of the home country regulator.
- The minimum capital requirement is US$ 25 million spread over three branches—$ 10 million each for the first and second branch and $ 5 million for the third branch.
- Both branches and ATMs require licences and these are given by the RBI in conformity with WTO's commitments.

Functions of foreign banks: The main business of foreign banks is the financing of India's foreign trade which they can handle most efficiently with their vast resources. Recently, they have made substantial inroads in internal trade including deposits, advances, discounting of bills, mutual funds, ATMs and credit cards. A large part of their credit is extended to large enterprises and MNCs located mostly in the tier one cities—mainly the metros, though some banks are now foraying in the rural sector as well. Technology used by these banks has been a major driver of change in the Indian banking industry. A highly trained and efficient workforce and the huge pool of capital resources at the disposal of these banks have created tremendous goodwill and prestige of foreign banks in India.

Apart from their main businesses, foreign banks are also instrumental in shaping the attitudes, perceptions and policies of foreign governments, corporates and other clients towards India, especially in the following areas:

(i) Bringing together foreign institutional investors and Indian companies.
(ii) Organizing joint ventures.
(iii) Structuring and syndicating project finance for telecommunication, power and mining sectors.
(iv) Providing a thrust to trade finance through securitization of export loan.
(v) Introducing new technology in data management and information systems.

Performance: Foreign banks are not subject to the stringent norms regarding opening of rural branches, priority sector lending or bound by the social philosophy of Indian banks. These factors combined with the financial, technical and human resources of the foreign banks have ensured a healthy growth of these banks in India.

2.10 INDIAN BANKS VS. FOREIGN BANKS

The structure, scope, nature of banking activities as well as the RBI norms for the Indian and foreign banks differ in a number of respects. Table 2.2 highlights the main differences between Indian and foreign banks.

The entry of private sector banks and foreign banks has enhanced efficiency and productivity of the public sector banks. The competition in the banking sector has intensified as a result of which there has been a rapid increase in product innovations and changes in business strategy. The share of private sector banks and foreign banks in total assets, which was less than 10 per cent at the inception of reforms, has steadily increased to about 25 per cent at the end of March, 2005. These banks have also compelled other banks to usher in new technology to try and improve their market share.

Table 2.2 Differences between Indian Banks and Foreign Banks

Indian banks	*Foreign banks*
It is a joint stock company incorporated in India.	It is the branch of a joint stock company incorporated outside India.
Area of operations extends to whole of India.	Operations are concentrated in metros and tier 1 cities.
Operations are mostly local.	Operations are international.
Cater more to middle and lower income groups.	Focus more on high income groups, large corporates and MNCs.
Income is more from core banking operations.	Income is more fee based and from new products like credit cards, ATMs, mutual funds, etc.
Main strength lies in their huge number of branches and the number of employees.	Main strength lies in their technology and vast capital resources as well as their networking.
Obtaining a licence from RBI is comparatively easier.	It is more difficult to obtain a licence from RBI.
RBI norms regarding NPAs, rural sector branches and social responsibility, etc. are more stringent.	These norms are comparatively more lenient.

2.11 REGIONAL RURAL BANKS

RRBs are Indian scheduled commercial banks operating at regional level in different states for development of agriculture, trade, commerce and industry to boost rural economy. 19 regional rural banks (RRBs) were set up by the Government of India under the Regional Rural Banks Act of 1976 with the specific purpose of providing credit and other facilities to the small and marginal farmers, agricultural labourers, artisans and small entrepreneurs in rural areas. The then existing credit agencies, namely, the cooperative and commercial banks, were unable to meet the requirements of the rural people in general and the rural poor in particular. The cooperative banks had a weak structure, and were heavily dependent upon the RBI. They were unable to mobilize resources or provide post-credit supervision or recover loans. Though the commercial banks did not share these shortcomings, but because of their urban orientation, they were not familiar with the local customs, thinking patterns or problems, and so could not understand their needs. At the same time because of high overheads, they could not provide cheap credits. By 1993, 172 out of 196 RRBs were recorded unprofitable. In March 2011 number of RRBs stood at 82, in 2013 it was 64 and 57 in 2014. The road map was to bring them down to 38 or below (ET 24.2.19). This move is aimed to consolidate them for the better operational efficiencies and economies of scale and optimum use of technology, in line with government's big rural focus. At present there are 43 RRBs, the highest number-36 in UP and least-2, in Kerala (MINT 1.4.2020).

Top five RRBs according to business size are

Name	*Business size in ₹ Crores*
Baroda UP Bank	72,015
Karnataka GB	54,856
Aryavart Bank	48,649
Andhara Pradesh GVB	43,999
Kerala GB	38,607

(TOI 11.4.22)

Incidentally the largest RRB-Baroda UP Bank is bigger than the largest Small Finance Bank whose business size is ₹70,588 crores as in March 2021.

Structure: RRBs have been jointly set up by the government of India, the state government and the sponsor commercial bank. Each RRB operates within specified local limits. If necessary, a RRB can establish branches or agencies at places notified by the government, which are usually adjoining districts. Initially they were set up with a capital of ₹1 crore which was raised to ₹5 crore by RRB Amendment Act of 1987. Of the issued capital 50 per cent is subscribed by the central government, 15 per cent by the state government and 35 per cent by the sponsor bank. Apart from subscribing to the share capital, sponsor banks also provide managerial assistance, help in recruitment and training of personnel during the initial period of its functioning.

Functions: Every rural regional bank is authorized to carry on the business of banking as defined in the Banking Regulation Act, 1949. It may also carry on any other businesses, specified in section 6(1) of the Act. It is engaged in

- Granting loans and advances to small and marginal farmers and agricultural labourers both at the individual level as well as in groups, to cooperative societies including agricultural marketing societies or farmers service societies for agricultural and related operations.
- Granting loans and advances to artisans, small entrepreneurs and persons of small means engaged in trade, commerce, industry or other production activities within its area of operations, so that they can start their own farming activities including purchase of land, seeds and manure.
- RRBs charge a lower rate of interest and thus provide credit at lower cost in rural areas.

Management: Management of each RRB is vested in a nine-member board of directors, headed by a Chairman, appointed by the Government of India. While discharging their functions they have to cover the commercial angle, and at the same time follow the directive principle issued by the government. For example, they can appoint officers and employees, but their salary structure is prescribed by the government according to the one existing in the state where the bank is located.

After the RRB Amendment Act of 1987, the following changes have come into force:

- Authorized capital was raised from ₹1 to ₹5 crore.
- The chairman is to be appointed by the concerned sponsor bank in consultation with NABARD.
- Sponsor banks have to subscribe to the share capital as well as impart training to personnel, and provide managerial and financial assistance for the first five years of its functioning.
- Amalgamation of two or more RRBs can be done in consultation with NABARD, concerned state government and the sponsor bank.
- Sponsor banks have been empowered to monitor the progress of their RRBs from time to time, to conduct inspections, internal audits and to suggest measures to RRBs wherever necessary.
- As from July 5, 2007, RBI has allowed RRBs to accept foreign currency deposits from NRIs and persons of Indian origin[1].

Problems faced by RRBs

- Lack of coordination in Branch expansion
- Difficulties in Deposit mobilization
- Slow progress in lending activity
- Urban-orientation of staff
- Procedural rigidities

2.12 COOPERATIVE BANKS

Co-operative banks are those co-operative societies whose principal business is banking. They play a crucial role in providing credit to people of small means. Cooperative banks are a part of the set of institutions, which are engaged in financing rural and agriculture development. The other institutions in this set include the RBI, NABARD, commercial banks and regional rural banks. Cooperative banking is small-scale banking carried on a *no profit, no loss* basis for mutual cooperation and help. They were conceived to supplant moneylenders and indigenous bankers

[1] *The Economic Times,* July 6, 2007, p. 20.

by providing adequate short-term and long-term institutional credit at reasonable rates of interest. There are 1,540 cooperative banks with 86 million depositors having a total savings of about 5 lakh crores. (ET 6.2.20)

Features of cooperative banks

- These banks are government sponsored, government supported and government subsidized financial agencies in India.
- They help in developing saving habits among the general public and thus encourage savings and investments in the economy.
- Commercial banks are owned by shareholders and/or government but a co-operative bank is a financial entity that belongs to it's owners and customers, as it's depositors are it's shareholders and vice-versa. This can lead to disastrous consequences at times.
- Unlike commercial banks which focus on profits, cooperative banks are organized and managed on principles of cooperation, self help and mutual help. They function on a "no profit, no loss" basis.
- They perform all the main banking functions but their range of services is narrower than that of commercial banks. However, their geographic coverage is the widest.
- Some of them are scheduled banks but most are unscheduled banks.
- They are governed under state laws as well as RBI norms.
- Co-operative banks belonging to one state are regulated by the registrar of co-operative societies of the concerned state while multi-state cooperatives are regulated by the central government. With the Banking Regulation Amendment Act 2020 the RBI's regulatory control has increased significantly in terms of management, capital, audit and liquidation.
- They have a federal structure of three-tier linkages and vertical integration.
- Cooperative banks are financial intermediaries only, particularly because a significant amount of their borrowings is from the RBI, NABARD, the central and state governments and cooperative apex institutions.
- There has been a shift of cooperative banks from the rural to the urban areas as the urban and non-agricultural business of these banks has grown over the years.

Organization structure: Cooperative banks have a three-tier set-up with the state cooperative bank at the apex, the district cooperative bank at the district level and the primary credit societies at the village level.

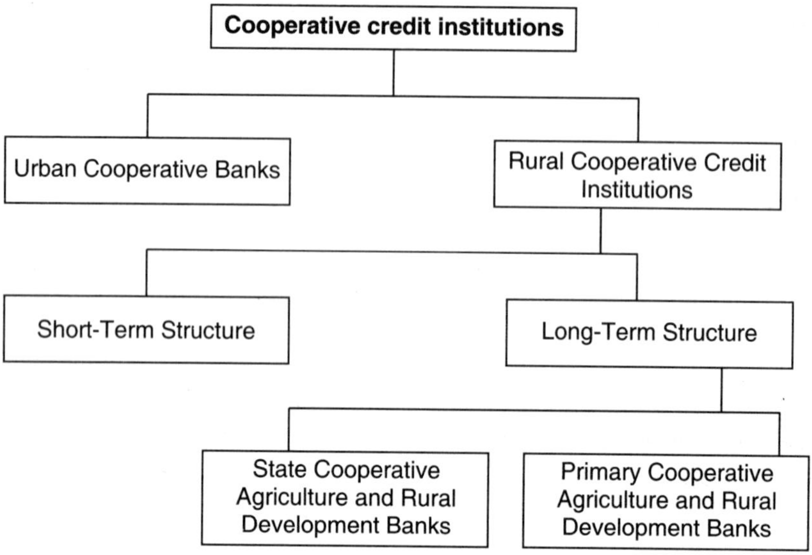

Figure 2.2 Structure of cooperative credit institutions.

The cooperative banking structure is federal in character, with three-tier linkages between state, district and village level institution. At the state level, we have state cooperative banks (SCBs), at the district level the central cooperative banks (CCBs) or the district central cooperative banks (DCCBs) and then at the village level the primary agricultural credit societies (PACSs).

Weaknesses: The rate of mortality of cooperative banks is very high. On an average 16 such banks default and die annually. Cooperative banks suffer from too much dependence on RBI, NABARD and the government.

They have a low capital base as they lack sources to raise capital which till recently was restricted to members only. Other problems faced by them include poor credit management, lack of professional management and absence of certain regulatory and supervisory powers of RBI. These issues have since been addressed. (Banking Regulation Amendment 2020, Chapter 10).

They are subject to too much officialization and politicization. Both the quality of loans assets and their recovery are poor. The primary agricultural cooperative societies—a vital link in the cooperative credit system—are small in size, very weak and many of them are dormant.

The cooperative banks suffer from existence of multiple regulation and control authorities.

Many urban cooperative banks have failed or are in the process of liquidation.

Cooperative banks have increasingly been facing competition from commercial banks, LIC, UTI and small savings organizations.

2.13 COMMERCIAL VS. COOPERATIVE BANKS

The nature scope and functioning of the commercial and cooperative banks vary in numerous ways. The main differences between commercial banks and cooperative banks have been summarized in Table 2.3.

Table 2.3 Differences between Commercial Banks and Cooperative Banks

Commercial bank	*Cooperative bank*
Function on business lines, for profit.	Work on principles of self-help and mutual cooperation for benefit of members.
Are organized as joint stock companies or registered as public corporations under separate acts of Parliament.	Are established under the cooperative society acts of different states.
Are organized on unitary basis.	Have a three-tier set-up—the state cooperative bank at the apex, the district cooperative bank at the district level and the primary credit societies at the village level.
Branch network is spread far and wide within the country and some banks have set up branches abroad.	Area of operation is restricted to a particular local boundary or district or state.
Traditionally have been urban oriented, though now they also finance the rural sector.	Are basically rural oriented and have been financing agriculture and allied activities.
Most commercial banks are scheduled banks, e.g., SBI, PNB, HDFC.	Most are non-scheduled, e.g., Maharashtra state cooperative bank, Junnar cooperative society, though some are scheduled, e.g., Saraswat cooperative bank ltd.
Are governed by all sections of the Banking Regulation Act, 1949.	Only some sections of the Act are applicable to them.

2.14 APEX-LEVEL BANKING INSTITUTIONS

In spite of the phenomenal geographical expansion of commercial banks, the existence of cooperative banks, regional rural banks, etc., it was mostly the short-term credit needs of industry, trade, commerce and agriculture that were being met. A need was felt for the creation of some apex-level banking institutions to cater to the specific requirements of agriculture (NABARD), housing (NHB), industry (IDBI and SIDBI) and foreign trade (EXIM). These institutions facilitate the flow of credit and perform many promotional and development functions and coordinate the activities of various agencies engaged in similar activities. A brief description of their roles and functions is given below.

2.15 NATIONAL BANK FOR AGRICULTURE AND RURAL DEVELOPMENT (NABARD), 1982

Vast areas in the rural hinterland remain outside the purview of the organized money market in spite of the presence of a number of commercial and co-operative banks, land development banks, cooperative societies and regional rural banks. Access to bank finance and credit remains a distant dream for a vast majority of people living in these areas. In order to promote integrated and sustainable rural development and secure prosperity of rural areas the National Bank for Agriculture and Rural Development (NABARD) was set up as an apex development bank under the National Bank for Agriculture and Rural Development Act, 1981. It came into existence on July 12, 1982. It not only facilitated the flow of credit for promotion and development of agricultural, small scale, cottage and village industries, handicrafts and other rural crafts, but it also took over the entire undertaking of Agricultural Refinance and Development Corporation (ARDC). The refinancing function of the Reserve Bank in relation to the state cooperative banks and regional rural banks—the two institutions, which together account for disbursement of more than 50 per cent of the rural credit was also taken over by NABARD. NABARD also collaborates with National Commodities and Derivatives Exchange Ltd. (NCDEX) and Multi Commodity Exchange (MCX) in order to actively participate in the spot as well as futures agriculture markets in India.

A brief summary of NABARD's role as facilitator of rural prosperity is given below.

2.15.1 Credit Functions

- NABARD provides refinance to lending institutions in rural areas like commercial banks, state cooperative banks rural development banks, RRBs and other eligible financial institutions. It reported an all time high refinance disbursement of ₹2.68 lakh crore during 2021–2022. A concessional refinance of ₹15,000 crores was disbursed to regional rural banks and cooperative banks for boosting capital formation in agriculture (ET 12.7.22).
- Through the rural infrastructure development fund it sanctions finance for irrigation, building rural roads and bridges as well as for soil conservation, forest management, flood protection and drinking water schemes.
- It issues Kisan Credit Cards through a vast rural banking network.
- It grants financial assistance to tribal families under the tribal development fund.
- It also provides financial support under the farm innovation and promotion fund.

2.15.2 Development Functions

- It extends assistance to the Government, the Reserve Bank of India and other organizations in matters relating to rural development. It also offers training and research facilities for banks, cooperatives and other organizations working in the area of rural development. NABARD has so far granted assistance of ₹947 crores to 6,395 farmer producer organizations and created a corpus of ₹1,000 crore for a credit guarantee fund. Around 1.18 crore SHGs have been covered cumulatively under the SHG-Bank Linkage Programme. It has undertaken initiatives like piloting net zero-ground water use in watersheds, development of simple tools for climate change analysis among others. Cumulatively close to 10 lakh youth have been trained to take up wage and employment activities (ET 12.7.22).

2.15.3 Regulatory Functions

- NABARD evaluates, monitors and inspects client banks to assess their financial and operational soundness, managerial efficiency and compliance to statutory provisions so that the interest of depositors and stakeholders is protected.
- It acts as a regulator for cooperative banks and RRBs.

2.16 NATIONAL HOUSING BANK (NHB)

Even though the housing and real estate sector contribute significantly to the GDP of the nation, yet for a long time the planners neglected these sectors. It was only in the Seventh Five- Year Plan that a recommendation was made to the RBI to set up a National Housing Bank as an apex level autonomous institution for providing housing finance. As a result, the NHB was set up on July 9, 1988 under the National Housing Bank Act, 1987. It is wholly owned by the RBI which contributed its entire paid-up capital of ₹100 crore. The NHB is expected to operate as a principal agency to promote housing finance at local as well as regional levels and to provide financial and other support to other such institutions. Its mission is to serve the housing needs of all segments of the population with the focus on low and moderate income housing. Its head office is in New Delhi.

Objectives: NHB hopes to promote a sound, healthy, viable and cost effective housing finance system through a network of dedicated housing finance institutions. Not only does it hope to make housing credit more affordable but it also encourages supply of buildable land and building materials to upgrade housing stock in the country.

2.16.1 Regulatory Functions

- NHB determines the policies and issues directions to housing finance institutions so that they are not detrimental to the interest of the depositors.
- It regulates the entry of housing finance market through a system of registration for all housing finance companies and also conducts their onsite and offsite surveillance.

2.16.2 Financing Functions

- NHB extends refinance facilities to different primary lenders including scheduled banks, RRBs, housing finance companies, state level apex cooperative housing societies, etc. These primary lenders provide finance to individual borrowers, builders, corporate houses for purchase or construction of new houses and for repair or upgradation of existing houses.
- It provides guarantee and underwriting facilities to housing finance institutions.
- NHB has also launched RESIDEX for tracking the movement of prices of residential housing segment in India. For doing this it collects data from real estate agents, private consultants and research organizations of national repute, banks and housing finance companies. This data is updated quarterly.

2.16.3 Promotional Functions

To improve and strengthen the credit delivery network for housing NHB performs a number of promotional functions.

- It has issued the Model Memorandum and Articles of Association, guidelines for equity participation of housing finance companies and schemes for their refinance support.
- It also guarantees the bonds issued by these companies.
- NHB provides technical and administrative assistance to housing finance companies.
- It has designed and conducted various training programmes for their personnel also.

2.17 SMALL INDUSTRIES DEVELOPMENT BANK OF INDIA (SIDBI)

To cater to the needs of the small scale sector, the Small Industries Development Bank of India was set up in 1990 under an Act of Parliament as the principal financial institution for promotion, financing and development of the Micro Small and Medium Enterprises (MSME) and for coordinating the functions of other institutions engaged in similar activities. It is among the top 30 development banks of the world. It was established as a wholly owned subsidiary of the Industrial Development Bank of India and took over its financial activities relating to the small scale sector. Its head office is in Lucknow, Uttar Pradesh.

Initially most of the bank's income was earned from indirect lending that is through refinancing but by the late 1990s this scenario changed drastically and direct assistance was stepped up increasingly. Its sources of funds come through deposits from commercial banks including foreign banks which have to deposit money to the extent of short fall in their priority sector lending. Its domestic sources include those which are recycled to it from the National Industrial Credit (long-term operations) Fund. Its off-shore sourcing of funds come from Japan and Germany.

Objectives: The definition of MSMEs has changed many times to make it more relevant to the changing economic conditions. The current Classification (w.e.f 13.05.2020) is as follows:

Manufacturing and services

Micro	Investment < ₹ 1 crore and turnover < ₹ 5 crore
Small	Investment < ₹10 crore and turnover < ₹50 crore
Medium	Investment < ₹20 crore and turnover < ₹100 crore

SIDBI aims to make the MSME sector strong, vibrant and globally competitive. It facilitates and strengthen credit flows and addresses financial and development gaps in the MSME ecosystem. It provides direct finance and refinance of term loans granted by banks, State Finance Corporation (SFC), State Industrial Development Corporation (SIDC) for setting up of industrial projects as well as for their expansion, modernization or diversification.

2.17.1 Financing Functions

- SIDBI provides direct assistance in the form of term loans and working capital term loans and bills discounting to small industries and service sector units with project cost of up to ₹25 crore.
- It provides equity type assistance under the National Equity Fund to entrepreneurs and also by way of seed capital.
- It grants refinance against loans granted to small units by banks, state level finance corporations, state industrial development corporations, etc., for setting up, expansion and modernization of industrial projects.

- Direct discounting and rediscounting of bills arising out of sale of machinery or capital equipment by manufacturers in the small scale sector on deferred credit.
- Rediscounting of short term trade bills arising out of sales of products of the small scale sector.
- SIDBI's Bill Finance Scheme provides medium and short term finance to manufactures of indigenous machinery, capital equipment, components, sub-assemblies, etc.
- It also provides international finance facilities in domestic and foreign currencies.
- It provides pre- and post-shipment credit, foreign currency term loans, opening of LCs for international finance schemes.

2.17.2 Promotional and Developmental Functions

- SIDBI partners with NGOs, financial institutions, corporate bodies, research and development laboratories, marketing agencies, etc. for national level promotion and development programmes.
- It sets up industrial estates and develops industrial areas to provide support to National Small Industries Corporation of India and other institutions concerned with the small industries.
- It provides increased amenities for smooth operation of SSIs as well as for setting up of warehousing facilities for their products.
- India SME Asset Reconstruction Company (ISARC) was established by SIDBI along with other PSBs/Financial Institutions to unlock the idle NPA assets of MSMEs for productive purposes, to recycle and enhance flow of credit from banking sector to MSMEs.
- SIDBI and ISRAC have developed a DIY (Do-it-Yourself) web module which can prepare restructuring proposals by keying in data of past financials, future plans/projections and restructuring requirements. This can be submitted on-line or through hard copy along with prescribed documents.

2.17.3 Coordination Functions

SIDBI coordinates with the Government subsidy schemes for promotion and development of the small scale industries by making use of the network of banks and state level financial institutions which have retail outlets.

2.18 INDUSTRIAL DEVELOPMENT BANK OF INDIA LIMITED

Industrial Development Bank of India is the apex banking institution in the field of long-term bank finance. It was constituted under Industrial

Development Bank of India Act, 1964 as a development financial institution and came into existence on July 1, 1964. Originally, it was established as a fully owned subsidiary of the Reserve Bank of India but it was delinked from it in February 1976 and was made into an autonomous corporation owned by the Government of India. It continued to serve as a DFI for 40 years till the year 2004 when it was transformed into a bank. For this purpose, the Industrial Development Bank (Transfer of Undertaking and Repeal) Act, 2003 was passed and a new company under the name of Industrial Development Bank of India Ltd. (IDBI Ltd.) was incorporated as a Government company on September 27, 2004 and came into effect on October 1, 2004. Since then it has been functioning as a bank in addition to its earlier role of a financial institution.

With the aim of achieving faster inorganic growth of the bank, IDBI Bank Ltd., a wholly owned subsidiary of IDBI Ltd. was amalgamated with IDBI Ltd. The merger became effective from April 2, 2005. Thereafter, the United Western Bank Ltd. (UWB) a Satara-based private sector bank was also merged with IDBI Ltd. The merger came into effect on October 3, 2006. In order that the name of the bank truly reflects the functions carried on by it the name of bank was changed to IDBI Bank Ltd. The new name became effective from May 7, 2008. Since then, it has been functioning in its present name of IDBI Bank Ltd.

The IDBI Bank Ltd. finances all types of industrial enterprises including manufacturing, mining, processing and service industries covering shipping, transport and hotel industries both in the private and public sectors. The government had placed IDBI Bank Ltd. under PCA in May 2017 after it exceeded the limits set by the central bank for bad loans and it's subsequent weakening of capital position. This negatively impacted it's legacy business of project and corporate loans (TOI 11.3.21). It was reclassified as a private sector bank by the RBI on January 21, 2019 but was still open to scrutiny by CAG and CVC due to government ownership. (The LIC currently owns 49.24% stake and GOI 45.48%). IDBI bank received a capital infusion of 9,300 crore in the financial year 2019–2020 from the LIC and the government (ET 25.7.22). RBI's financial supervision board reviewed IDBI's performance on Feb. 18, 2021. The bank had earned a net profit of ₹378 crore in quarter ended Dec. 2020 and qualified to exit RBI's PCA frame work. Though it will be under continuous monitoring.

Objectives: The main objectives of IDBI are to coordinate the workings of institutions engaged in financing, promotion and development of industry in conformity with the national priorities. It also assists in the development of such institutions for providing credit and other facilities for the development of industry.

2.18.1 Financing Functions

- IDBI provides direct assistance in the form of term loans.
- It refinances term loans given by eligible institutions to medium and large-scale units.
- It accepts discounts or rediscount bona fide commercial bills or promissory notes of industrial concerns.
- It provides venture capital for development and use of indigenous technology as well as for adaptation of imported technology.

2.18.2 Promotional Activities

- IDBI undertakes promotional activities market and investment research, surveys and techno-economic studies.
- It also provides technical and administrative assistance to industrial enterprises for promotion, management or expansion.

2.19 EXPORT IMPORT BANK OF INDIA (EXIM BANK)

The Export Import Bank of India was set up in 1982 under the Export-Import Bank of India Act, 1981. Since then it has been a catalyst as well as a key player in the promotion of cross-border trade and investment. It has particularly helped the small and medium enterprises in their globalization efforts, through import of technology, export product development, export production, export marketing, pre-shipment, post shipment and overseas investment etc. A more detailed account of EXIM Bank and its functioning is given in Chapter 7.

KEY TERMS

Cash Reserve Ratio (CRR) It is the reserve requirement that a commercial bank has to keep in liquid cash with the RBI before offering credit to the customer. The bank does not earn interest on it nor can it use this amount for lending or investment purposes. Currently it is 4.9%.

Financial Inclusion Refers to the availability and equality of opportunities in accessing financial services including banking, loan, equity and insurance products at affordable rates and in a timely manner.

Jan Dhan Yojna Launched in 2014 by GOI, this scheme aims to expand affordable financial services such as bank accounts, remittances, credit, insurance and pensions to Indian citizens.

Prompt Corrective Action (PCA) RBI can put a bank under PCA when it fails to meet financial parameters as articulated by RBI.

Repo Rate It is the interest rate at which the central bank lends to the commercial banks in their hour of need and that is why it is called as Lender of the Last Resort.

Reverse Repo Rate is the rate at which the RBI borrows money from banks for short-term.

Statutory Liquidity Ratio (SLR) It is the minimum percentage of deposits that a commercial bank has to maintain in the form of liquid cash, gold or other securities. The RBI is empowered to change this to check liquidity position. SLR is 18% since February 2021.

The government uses CRR and SLR to regulate inflation and fuel growth, to ensure solvency of banks and also compels banks to invest in government securities like bonds.

REVIEW QUESTIONS

2.1 Over the years the RBI's promotional and developmental roles have taken precedence over its regulatory role. Comment upon the statement and discuss the functions of the Reserve Bank of India.

2.2 Explain the rationale of public sector banks. How does their functioning differ from that of commercial banks?

2.3 Distinguish between
- (i) Public sector banks and private sector banks
- (ii) Indian banks and foreign banks

2.4 'The rate of mortality of cooperative banks is very high'. In view of the above enumerate the various measures taken by the RBI for strengthening the functioning of cooperative banks.

2.5 Write short notes on
- (i) Challenges faced by Regional Rural Banks
- (ii) Role in promoting rural development
- (iii) NABARD
- (iv) Role of Small Industries Development Bank of India (SIDBI) in promoting MSMEs

3

Banking Sectors

Learning Objectives

After going through this chapter we will be able to:

- Differentiate between Corporate and Retail banking.
- Study the characteristics of International banking.
- Understand the multidisciplinary approach to Rural banking.
- Learn about non-banking financial intermediaries, insurance companies and mutual funds.

Modern banking in India has traversed a long way since independence. If one traces the evolutionary path that the banks have taken, one turning point was the nationalization of 14 leading banks in 1969 to bring them under social control. This forced banks to operate under a highly regulated environment wherein they had to comply with quantitative restrictions on credit flows, follow administrated interest rate structures, divert funds to the priority sector and curtail liquidity by setting aside their assets under statutory reserve ratios. All these translated into banks being plagued with low productivity, inefficiency and mounting bad debts. The second turning point came with the reform measures initiated by the Reserve Bank of India following the Narasimham Committee recommendations in 1991.

3.1 RECENT DEVELOPMENTS IN BANKING INDUSTRY

The financial sector reforms introduced strict prudential norms for higher operational efficiency and improved productivity and profitability. They also ushered in healthy competition by allowing new banks in the private sector. These banks brought about a paradigm shift in service standards in terms of choices of services offered, the speed of delivery, the superior technology employed by them and their market orientation. The public sector banks had no option, but to get out of their lethargic and inefficient state and gear themselves to face the onslaught of their competitors.

Liberalization and deregulation of the financial sector, the use of technology and the changing nature of customers who are time, quality and price conscious as well as demanding in a number of other ways has ushered in a new era in the banking sector. Banks can no longer afford to be insulated from these changes. The traditional face of banking which concentrated on deposits and loans now has to cater to a whole range of services—personal loans for education, housing or automobiles, equipment financing, remittances from abroad, international letters of credit, loan syndication and insurance, to name a few.

3.2 BANKING SECTORS

The spectrum of needs and requirements of individuals, organizations and sectors of the economy is very vast and diverse. Banks have come up with a whole range of banking products and services to suit the requirements of their clients. Banking sectors include corporate banking, retail banking, international banking and rural banking.

3.3 CORPORATE BANKING

Corporate banking typically serves the financial needs of large corporate houses—both domestic and multinational—public sectors and governments. Sometimes, it is also referred to as wholesale banking compared to retail banking. The corporate clients are a few in number but they keep high balances and make high value transactions. Traditionally, banks had primarily been focusing on production based activities and financed working capital requirements as well as term loans to corporates due to following reasons:

- From the beginning till the pre-reform era, business houses were heavily dependent on banks for their financial needs. The capital markets were not well developed, joint venture norms had not been liberalized, mergers and acquisitions were not the preferred route and numerous restrictions were placed on raising finance from overseas markets.
- The banking institutions too showed a preference for providing credit to the corporates. The banking institutions have primarily been focusing on demands of economic development and production-based activities and showed a preference for providing credit to the corporates. The risk for banks was considerably less as

corporate borrowings were made against collaterals after verifying their capacity for repayment.

- Since the client base was small the paper work involved was also minimal. The government had also earmarked priority sectors, and as such banks had to comply with the targets allotted to them.
- After liberalization, many corporates could not face the competition and went into the red. Though from the year 2007 till mid 2014 banks gave more loans to industry. (In fact these loans peaked in February 2013 when they stood at 46.1% of total loans), but then these loans began to slow down. Economic downturn and recessionary environment resulted in poor performance of many borrowers especially in the textile, steel and real estate sectors. Further the rise in investment in intangible assets like R&D, branding, organizational development and software made it more difficult for banks to give loans to corporates unlike earlier when they could sell the physical assets given as collateral, for recovery in case of default.

3.3.1 Features

Corporate banking serves the need of corporates, those having a legal entity. They offer business current accounts, make commercial loans, participate in syndicated lending and are active in inter-bank markets to borrow/lend from/to other banks. Many banks offer structured products, capital market services and corporate solutions. Corporate banking involves comparatively fewer borrowers, and the account size is usually large and sometimes it can run into billions of dollars.

3.3.2 Services

Corporate banking services include

(i) Working capital and term loans, overdrafts, bill discounting, project financing.

(ii) Cash management including both short-term holdings of cash and funds held for longer periods.

(iii) Financing of exports and imports including export credit arrangements.

(iv) Project finance.

(v) Transmission and receipt of money.

(vi) Handling foreign currency and hedging against changes in value.

(vii) Bank guarantees, letters of credit, discounting of bills.

In recent times, there has been a marked shift from corporate to retail banking. There has been a reduction in demand for credit by large corporates for working capital requirements because of enhancement in activities like productivity and sales realization corporates now also have access to tapping public deposits apart from issuance of shares and debentures. The major reason for avoiding corporate accounts is the mounting non-performing corporate accounts. Difficulty in pricing the services and high risks involved are some of the other reasons for overlooking corporate accounts.

However, this is a very lucrative segment provided care is taken in identifying and focusing on selected business segments and catering to their requirements, e.g., for the SME segment, credit is paramount whereas for big corporates, customized solutions are needed. Furthermore, banks are expected to have greater financing opportunities in the area of project finance, especially in the infrastructure sector, given the conversion of two major financial institutions (FIs) into banks. Banks have been focusing mainly on syndication of debt to ensure wider participation in project finance and wholesale lending segment. Systematic account planning process can help to identify the profitable customers, and pricing of services can help the bank to get rid of asset quality problem[1]. Most developed nations banks have separate corporate bank divisions which help them to avoid the pit falls of *one-size-fits-all* policies.

3.4 RETAIL BANKING

Retail banking means delivery of banking products to the ultimate consumer. Unlike corporate banking which caters to the needs of big corporate houses, retail banking serves the needs of individuals. The importance of retail loans has increased for both PSBs and private sector banks. Because of subdued profitability and deleveraging by corporates, banks shifted their focus away from large infrastructure and industrial loans to retail loans. Credit continues to be driven by retail credit. Private sector banks account for 50.4% of credit growth and PSBs 44.7%. Retail credit stands at 30.5% with housing loans having the largest share. Industrial loans share is 28.9% (TOI 11.4.22).

Retail banking encompasses deposit and asset linked products as well as other financial services offered to numerous personal banking customers and small businessmen. It tends to be domestic rather than international. Retail banking is largely intra bank: The bank itself accepts deposits and makes many small loans[2]. Products offered by retail banking include credit cards, educational loans, housing loans, consumption loans for consumer durables like refrigerators, washing machines, music systems, convenience/flexi deposit accounts, and so on.

---

[1] Sharma, Vinod, *India Needs Better Corporate Banking: Professional Banker*, The ICFAI University Press, September 2004, p. 50.

[2] Heffernan, Shelagh, *Modern Banking*, John Wiley & Sons, West Sussex, England, p. 47.

3.4.1 Characteristics of Retail Banking

Large number of small customers: Retail banking is characterized by the existence of a large number of small customers, who consume personal banking and small business services. The relationship size of each account is small but the number of relationship is huge. The essential prerequisite of retail banking is its orientation towards the consumer whether it is in size, price, delivery channels or product profile.

Multiple products: A basket of products including flexi deposits, cards, insurance, medical expenses, auto loans are offered to the consumers. Besides these, there are a number of value added services like de-mat accounts, issue of free ATM cards, portfolio management, payment of water, electricity and telephone bills.

Multiple delivery channels: To increase penetration and access banks are not limiting themselves to branches but are making extensive use of internet, call centres, kiosks, etc.

For repayment of retail loans EMI is fixed after taking into account the principal amount, rate of interest and the time period of loan. The EMI has to be paid every month.

Private sector banks accounted for 50.4% of credit growth and PSBs contributed 44.7%. Retail credit stands at 30.5%—the largest share of all scheduled commercial banks, industrial loans have 28.9% share. Within retail loans housing loans have the largest share (TOI 11.4.22).

3.4.2 Origin of Retail Banking

Origin of retail banking in India can be traced to a number of developments.

Financial sector reforms and liberalization: Before opening up of the economy during the decade of the nineties, corporate banking had been the preferred goal for bankers. Banks relied on blue chip companies for deployment of funds. As observed earlier, after the reforms it no longer remained so. Corporates could now go in for external commercial borrowing (ECB) from any internationally recognized bank, export credit agency, international capital market or supplier of equipment. They could also opt for mergers and acquisitions. So banks had to look for other avenues than the corporate sector for growth and expansion.

Spreading of risk: Another consequence of liberalization was industrial recession, economic downturn, industrial sickness which resulted in failure of many big corporates. Mounting non-performing assets made banks more cautious about lending to business houses, and diverting their funds into the retail segment, as retail banking has the advantage of minimizing the risk and maximizing the returns. The returns from retail segment are 3 to 4 per cent as compared to 1 to 2 per cent from the corporate segment.

Growth in banking technology and automation of banking processes: Technology has opened up new vistas for the banking industry and redefined its nature, scope and extent. State-of-the-art electronic technology has helped to increase penetration through ATMs without opening more branches. Internet has made possible banking to be done from home. Telebanking and phone banking are some other new technologies which have revolutionized banking.

Changing profile of customers: An ever-increasing middle class, with more disposable income, higher education and a desire for higher standard of living have fuelled the demand for retail banking services. More and more people seemed to have embraced the credit culture, and are demanding consumer goods, holidays, education and a host of other value added banking services.

Retail banking has the potential to provide decent return for banks with an extended clientele base in an era of thinning margin and non-performing advances. Banks need to invest in expensive technology and use it a driver for growth, know their customer, go in for product innovation and have transparency in pricing of their products in order to get an edge over their rivals.

3.5 INTERNATIONAL BANKING

International banking is a logical extension of domestic banking. It dates back to the 13th century. More recently there has been a rapid increase in the scale of international banking from about mid 1975, when the main banks of western countries established an extensive network of global operations.

Reasons for growth of International banking

- Increase in cross border trade for exports and imports of goods and services
- Investment of capital globally
- Migration of labour who send remittances back home
- Existing customers expanding their businesses abroad and banks providing better services through setting up their branches in those countries
- Intense competition at home prompting banks to expand operations in other countries
- Growth of technology

International banking services are delivered for the benefit of non-resident Indians, exporters, importers, tourists, foreign entities and banks. These services include corporate lending, loan syndication, merchant banking, handling international letters of credit, collection of clean and documentary credits and remittances.

3.5.1 Characteristics of International Banking

Banking activities are carried across different geographical borders: When branches and subsidiaries are carrying out operations in different countries, then question is to which supervisory authority will have jurisdiction over these arise. Effective coordination can be achieved only if there is good communication between countries, and global compliance standards are in place. Generally foreign banks have to comply with local laws as well as laws of their country of origin.

Currency of transaction is different from the home currency of the bank. They also have to deal with different time zones and languages.

Risks in international banking are both pecuniary as well as political: Apart from the financial risks inherent in all businesses, fluctuating rates of currencies of different countries can also pose problems giving rise to the need for hedging and other measures. Political instability like coups or fall of governments, changing economic and fiscal policies can all become a major cause of concern. The current Ukraine-Russian conflict and resultant geo-political tensions have fueled inflation and recessionary trends across the globe. RBI has predicted that the negative impact of the Covid-19 pandemic will last for 12 years.

Non-interest income is substantially more than interest income: Income from fund based activities like commission on bills, guarantees, letters of credit, syndication fees, loan processing and counselling fees, etc. are more than the interest earned from lending operations.

3.5.2 International Banking Services

Some services offered under International banking including remittances, export credit and international letter of credit and bank guarantee are explained as follows:

Remittance: Remittance is a facility by which the bank makes funds available from a customer at one place to him, or anyone authorized by him, at another place within India and abroad. International remittances can be inward or outward.

International inward remittance. There is a huge pool of Indians working abroad who regularly send money back home. There are numerous inter-bank transactions between corporates and countries. International inward remittances ensure quick and safe delivery of funds from exchange houses and banks to beneficiaries in India. Remittances can be transferred easily and swiftly in any of the following ways:

(i) **Transfer through SWIFT**—Most branches of all leading banks like SBI, ICICI, HDFC, Axis, etc., are directly connected to the globe via

SWIFT. The SWIFT message is a highly secure, fast and efficient method of fund transfer electronically, for example, when an Indian bank has to send money to someone in New York they will send it through NOSTRO.

(ii) **Transfer through telex**—If SWIFT facilities are not available from any place, then one can remit funds through texted telex messages.

(iii) **Demand drafts**—These can also be used to send money into India from abroad.

International outward remittances. When any person, firm, organization or resident in India desires to transfer funds to any place outside India, it gives rise to foreign outward remittances. Banks that have been named as authorized dealers are delegated powers to affect outward remittances on behalf of their constituents, subject to certain conditions and completion of formalities as enumerated in the exchange control manual as amended up to date.

3.5.3 Pre-Shipment and Post-Shipment Credit for Exports

Before the goods are exported, exporters need finance for purchasing, manufacturing, processing, transporting, etc. of goods, i.e., **pre-shipment finance**. After exports of goods and before payment is realized, exporters again need finance to tide them over that period. This is termed as **post-shipment finance**. All this is arranged by commercial banks as part of their international banking operations. These have been explained in detail in Chapter 7.

3.5.4 International Letter of Credit

A letter of credit facilitates trade transactions betweens two parties who are not familiar with each other. It is a commercial instrument of assured payment through which the buyer's bank undertakes to make payment to the seller on production of documents stipulated in the credit. Under this facility the buyer's bank gives commitment of payment to the seller through his bank. International letter of credit facilitates global commerce through the banking channel. These letters are by and large irrevocable. The letter of credit specifies conditions regarding proof of dispatch of goods or services by sellers, submission of all relevant documents, and stipulation as to payment being made on presentment of documents or at some future date, and so on.

Main parties and a typical LC transaction

- Applicant/importer who requests his bank to open an LC in favour of the exporter.
- *Issuing bank:* Importer's bank who issues LC.

- *Advising bank:* The banker in exporter's country to whom issuing bank sends LCs.
- *Negotiating bank:* The exporter's bank. If the exporter is satisfied as to the terms, etc., of LC, he will make arrangement for shipping the goods and present the LC to his bank, i.e., the negotiating bank to verify all documents along with LC.
- The exporter's bank will then negotiate the bill.
- The LC issuing bank will receive the bill and documents from the exporter's bank and give them to the importer.
- After receiving the bill and checking documents the importer accepts/pays the bill and gets the shipping documents covering the goods purchased by him.
- The LC issuing bank reimburses the amount to negotiating banks if all documents are in order.
- The exporter receives the payment on realization.

3.5.5 Bank Guarantee

Bank guarantee includes both a finance guarantee as well as performance guarantee. Under finance guarantee, the bank guarantees the beneficiary (the person named in the guarantee to receive the guaranteed sum), certain amount on behalf of its customer who has commercial relationship with the beneficiary. Under performance guarantee, the bank guarantees performance of a contract of goods/services supplied under a contract by its customer.

3.6 RURAL BANKING

Even though nearly 68 per cent of India's population lives in villages yet India's banking penetration remains low. The geographic reach of banking is uneven. Till 1955 when the State Bank of India came into being only ₹5 crore of rural credit, accounting for hardly 0.9 per cent of total credit requirement was provided by banks. As a result, neither there was effective machinery for mobilization of rural savings, nor could the poor farmers and agricultural labourers get out of the clutches of rich landlords and moneylenders.

The SBI tried to address this problem by setting a target of opening 400 branches in five years in the district and sub-district level. Another turning point came when fourteen banks were nationalized in 1969. The liberalized branch licensing policy of the RBI provided further impetus to opening of more branches in rural areas. In spite of all these measures, the problem of rural finance remained. The strong nexus between banks and big industrial houses did not allow credit to percolate down to the common man or small industries and agriculture, i.e., to the grass-roots level. In fact, the populist government policies which allowed cheaper credit to the needy without proper controls led to defaults in repayment, which were later written off for political as well as administrative reasons. Consequently, the trends over the years have clearly shown that the banking system in India finds a more profitable business in the urban regions as compared to the rural ones.

The failure of the formal delivery channels in bridging the credit gap has helped to spawn the well-organized informal delivery channels like moneylenders and chit funds. This dependence has been said to be as high as 78 per cent according to a Pricewaterhouse Coopers study[3]. The reasons cited for this include better delivery mechanisms offered by them, ease in purchase and greater flexibility in repayment. The commercial banks in their attempt to serve these two desparate areas suffered from liquidity constraints, asymmetric information, and high transaction costs which decreased their efficiency and profitability[4].

3.6.1 Multi-agency Approach to Rural Credit

Before nationalization cooperative system was the only agency for dispensing rural credit. In order to address the need of the rural sector, numerous attempts were made including setting up of regional rural banks, schemes for micro-finance, setting up of self-help groups, primary credit societies and other cooperative banks and local area banks. As already explained in Chapter 2, RRBs were set up as specialized rural financial institutions for developing the rural credit delivery and ensure financial inclusion. It was hoped that the RRBs by combining the feel and familiarity of rural problems, characteristic of cooperatives with the professionalizm and large resource base of commercial banks, shall go a long way in providing credit to this hither to neglected area. It was envisaged that the RRBs would mobilize local savings and meet the entire credit needs of all medium and small cultivators. They would implement programmes of supervised credit, set up and maintain godowns, supply inputs and agricultural equipment, provide assistance in marketing and generally help in the overall development of the villages in their area. By providing access to finance they shall help in empowerment of the vulnerable sections of society.

Since, in most states cooperative banking structure is behest by weaknesses so a multi-agency approach to rural credit has been in operation for quite sometime. Along with rural banks other methods of extending credit facilities in the countryside include setting up of more

---

[3] Bandhopthyay, Tamal, *Revolutionizing Rural Banking*, http//in.rediff.com/money/feb/26guest1.htm, February 26, 2004.

[4] Bhattacharya, Sugata, *Rural Banking: An Opportunity for Growth, Professional Banker*, The ICFAI University Press, Hyderabad, Special Issue, March 2006, p. 59.

branches of commercial banks, financing of credit societies, providing micro-credit through SHGs and NGOs which at times raise fears of overlapping. But fears about overlapping and duplication of banking facilities are not entirely true. The large credit gap both quantitative and qualitative that exists in rural areas necessitates the coexistence of all the credit agencies albeit with proper coordination. RRBs are preferred over commercial banks for purveying direct finance to farmers owing to their low cost structure and rural ethos. In any case, in view of the formidable problems of personnel and management, it is not possible for commercial banks to cover the rural area adequately. However, they are important for extending refinancing facility to rural banks. Commercial banks also play a supporting role in relation to cooperatives. The expansion of commercial banks branches in rural areas should be regulated and monitored, so that the commercial banks as well as rural banks support the role of cooperatives which are the primary credit institutions in rural area. Where cooperatives have failed to make development loans, but are in a position to look after short-term needs, commercial banks should lend only for the developmental purposes by entering into special arrangements with the cooperators.

As of March 19 India had over two lakh ATMs out of which only 35,649 were in rural areas. So government has asked PSBs and Private sector banks to open 15,000 branches in FY21 in rural areas (ET 6.1.20). The mandate from the finance ministry is to open a branch within 15 km radius of a village where there is no banking facility available.

It was hoped that through these formal and semi-formal channels, the rural households will have access to credit. Cooperative banks, regional rural banks and local area banks have already been discussed in the Chapter 2. The role of micro-credit and self-help groups in delivering credit to the rural sectors is being examined hereinafter.

RBI recommendations for supply of rural credit: The recommendations of the RBI to examine issues relating to rural credit include the business facilitator model and the business correspondent model. It is hoped that these models would provide a whole range of financial services encompassing savings, credit and remittance, insurance and pension products in rural areas.

Business facilitator model: This model proposed that banks could use a wide array of civil society organizations and others for supporting them by undertaking non-financial services. These would include NGOs, farmers' clubs, functional cooperatives, IT enabled rural outlets of corporates, postal agents, insurance agents, well functioning panchayats, and so on.

Business correspondent model: This model proposed using institutional agents/other external entities for supporting the banks for extending financial services. They would function as "pass through" agencies to provide credit related services such as disbursal of small value credit, recovery of principal/collection of interest and sale of micro-insurance/ mutual fund products/pension products, etc. NGOs micro-finance institutions registered NBFCs with significant rural presence, IT enabled rural outlets or corporates and post offices may function as the business correspondents.

Micro-finance: Micro-finance and micro-credit are frequently used interchangeably. Micro-credit is the provision of very small loans to poor borrowers who typically lack collateral, steady income or a verifiable credit history. Micro-finance is a wider term which encompasses a broad offering of financial services for low-income communities including loans, insurance, savings, pension, etc. Over the past decade the micro-finance industry in India has grown at a compounded annual growth rate of 26% to reach ₹2.36 trillion (Mint 23.4.21). This has helped 55 million economically vulnerable people in India, out of which the vast majority—99% are women, to become financially independent and live a life of dignity. At the grass root level micro-finance has transformed the lives of millions by fostering financial inclusion. Their vital role has been acknowledged by the RBI also as is evident from the fact that out of the 10 Small Finance bank licenses granted 8 were given to micro-finance institutions.

Micro-credit: In spite of the phenomenal outreach of formal credit institutions, the rural poor still depend upon the informal sources of credit. Two major causes for this are the large number of small borrowers with small and frequent needs. Also the ability of these borrowers to provide collateral is very limited. Besides, the long and cumbersome bank procedures and their risk perception have also been limiting factors. Micro-credit has emerged as the most suitable and practical alternative to conventional banking in reaching the hitherto untapped poor population.

The terms Micro-credit or micro-finance are frequently used interchangeably. Micro-credit means providing very poor families who typically lack collateral, steady income or a verifiable credit history with very small loans to help them engage in productive activities or grow their tiny businesses. Micro-finance is a wider term which encompasses a broad offering of loans, insurance, savings, pension, etc. Over time, the concept of micro-credit been broadened to include a whole range of financial and non-financial services like credit, equity and institution. Micro-finance institution is an organization that provides financial services to people with limited income who have difficulty in accessing the formal banking sector. The objectives of micro-finance is to provide appropriate financial services to significant numbers of low-income, economically active people in order to finance micro-enterprises and non-farm income generating activities including agro-allied activities and ultimately improve their condition as well as that of local economies.

As per RBI micro-finance is the provision of thrift, credit and other financial services and products of very small amount to the poor in rural, semi-urban and urban areas for enabling them to raise their income levels, and improve their living standard. Micro-credit institutions are those that provide these facilities. The micro-finance approach has emerged as an important development in banking for channelizing credit for poverty alleviation directly and effectively. The micro-credit extended by banks to individual borrowers directly or through any agency is regarded as a part of banks priority sector loans.

The RBI has made the following recommendations:

- Institutions such as NABARD and SIDBI may provide bulk lending support to start-up MFIs and funds of state/central development/ finance corporations.
- Micro-credit portfolio of the regulated MFIs may be made eligible for direct finance from NABARD.
- The MFIs may be rated to help banks/financial institutions to decide about engaging them as their agents and funding them.
- Accounting standards for SHGs and NGOs may be developed, codified and standardized by NABARD.

While micro-finance institutions have made remarkable progress but a lot more needs to be done. To compliment their micro-credit initiatives these MFIs need to promote financial literacy, as well as provide a thrust to social-development projects and community connect initiatives. Loans should be given for productive purposes after proper assessment of borrower's ability to repay. Focus should be maintained on capacity building at the bottom of the pyramid.

Self-help groups (SHGs): SHG is an Indian micro-finance model introduced in 1992 under the guidelines of RBI and NABARD. SHGs help to improve the lives of the poor and marginalized segments of the society and foster financial inclusion. They have been launched to combat the problem of growing poverty at the grass roots level. Small, cohesive and participative groups of the poor are formed who regularly pool their savings to make small interest bearing loans to its members. In the process, they lean the nuances of financial discipline. Initially bank credit is not a primary objective. It is only after the group stabilizes and gains ability to undertake productive activity and bear risk that micro-credit comes into play.

The SHG bank linkage programme (launched in 1992) has proved to be the major supplementary credit delivery system with a wide acceptance by banks, NGOs and various government departments. It encourages the rural poor to build their capacity to manage their own finances, and then negotiate bank credit on commercial terms. There are about one crore

SHGs with active bank linkages involving 10 crore Indians, aggregate bank balance of 7000 crores. 90% of SHGs in India consist exclusively of women. In India there are three models of SHG bank linkages, namely:

Model 1	SHGs formed and financed by bank
Model 2	SHGs formed by NGOs and formal organizations, but directly financed by the banks
Model 3	SHGs financed by banks using NGOs and other agencies as financial intermediaries

Norms to be observed by SHGs. Certain norms have to be observed in the formation of SHGs. To become a member, a person has to be below the poverty line. Only one member of a family can become a member and that person cannot become a member of more than one SHG. There is no limit of maximum number of members for irrigation projects, but for other groups the numbers of members can be between 10 and 20. Members of SHGs are supposed to meet regularly, that is, once a week or once a fortnight. However, registration is optional and left to the discretion of the members.

While individuals find it difficult to break the chain of poverty, as SHGs they have better prospects for bank credit (often without collateral) and higher chances of income generation. SHGs frequently act as pressure groups in Gram Panchayats and help in fight against dowry and alcoholism. In this manner they help in social upliftment of women and the marginalized.

3.7 NON-BANKING FINANCIAL INTERMEDIARIES

As already observed financial intermediaries are institutions that serve as "middleman" in the transfer of funds from savers (millions of households) to those who invest in real assets such as houses, equipment, factories, etc. These funds can be channelled from surplus units either directly, e.g., through stocks, bonds or other debt instruments, or indirectly through financial intermediaries who hold these primary claims as investments, obtain funds from them by issuing secondary claims on themselves like safe deposits, insurance policies, mutual funds, etc., and sell them to the surplus units (savers). While banks primarily provide payment and other liquidity related services, the NFBIs offer equity and risk-based products. However, this distinction is getting blurred these days as some NFBIs are converting themselves into banks and financial integration is proceeding at a rapid pace.

Banks are the biggest financial intermediaries. Many non-banking institutions like UTI, LIC, GIC also act as intermediaries, and when they do so they are known as **non-banking financial intermediaries (NBFI)**. Some non-intermediaries, e.g., IDBI, IFC, NABARD have been set up by the government to fulfil the credit needs of the certain sectors. Since, they have been set up by the government, they are called **non-banking statutory financial organizations (NBSFO)**. The Indian financial system also comprises a large number of privately owned, decentralized and relatively small-sized financial intermediaries which are either primarily engaged in fund based activities, while the others primarily provide financial services. For convenience the former are called **non-bank financial companies (NBFCs)** and the latter **non-bank financial services companies (NBFSCs)**[5]. Non-banking financial companies represent a heterogeneous group of institutions engaged in hire purchase, housing finance, lease finance, investors, etc. The number of such companies runs into thousands but only a small proportion of them report to/file return with the RBI. Four types of institutions categorized in terms of their primary business activity and under the regulatory purview of the Reserve Bank are: equipment leasing companies, hire purchase companies, loan companies and investment companies. The residuary non-banking companies (RNBCs) have been classified as a separate category as their business does not confirm to any of the other defined classes of NBFC business. Besides, there are other NBFCs, viz., miscellaneous non-banking companies (chit funds), mutual benefit finance companies (nidhis and potential nidhis) and housing finance companies which are either partially regulated by the Reserve Bank or are outside the purview of the Reserve Bank.

There is a considerable overlap in the functioning of these institutions—both mobilize savings and facilitate financing of different activities. However, the difference lies in fact that banks accept deposits which are repayable on demand (i.e., they have cheque facility), their deposits liabilities constitute a major part of money supply and banks also create credit.

NBFIs play an important dual role in the financial system. They complement the role of commercial banks by filling gaps in their range of services. At the same time, they also compete with banks and force them to be more efficient and responsive to the needs of customers. They have helped to bridge the credit gaps in several sectors wherein the banks were unable to do so. Their role in delivering credit to the unorganized sector including farms and small borrowers at the local level on a sustained basis is widely recognized. They provide a diversified range of functions to individuals, corporate and institutions clients. The NBFIs are very effective as they have the ability to take quicker decisions, assume greater risks and customize their services. This is because FIs have access to private information such as loan application deposit history, incomes, assets, liabilities and credit history. They are also able to monitor the borrower's activities better and so are better equipped to make more rational loan

---

[5] Bhole, L.M., *Financial Institutions and Markets, Structure Growth and Innovations*, Tata McGraw-Hill, New Delhi, 2004.

decisions. They provide the lender information, diversification and financial expertise. They benefit the borrower by reducing transaction costs through broadening the rate of instrument, denomination and maturities that deficit spenders can issue.

3.7.1 Insurance Companies

Insurance companies are one of the major types of financial intermediaries, and they collect large amounts of premiums from the investors and channelize funds to the government's other sectors. Previously the insurance companies were very active in the fields of life, health and general insurance both property liability and property casualty. Now, they have begun to operate the pension schemes and mutual funds also.

The institutions providing insurance services have gone through three distinctive phases. Before independence, there were a large number of insurance companies (total 352 comprising 245 life insurance companies and 107 general insurance companies), and all of them were in the private sector and truly competitive. Life insurance was nationalized in 1952 by passing of the LIC Act, 1956 and General Insurance was nationalized in 1972 after passing of General Insurance Services (Nationalization) Act, 1972. Nationalization transformed the competitive private insurance industry into monopolistic and oligopolistic state or public sector insurance industry in India.

The insurance regulatory and development body (IRDA) which became a statutory body in April 2000 opened up the insurance sector to let some Indian and foreign private companies to enter the insurance business. At present, there are a total of 24 companies—7 general insurance companies, 11 life insurance companies in the private sector, LIC, GIC and its 4 subsidiaries carrying on life and general insurance business in India. In addition, there is post office life insurance business also. The major distinction between the life and general insurance is that in the life insurance companies liability is fixed and certain as well as fairly long-term—sometimes even 30, 40 or even 50 years. As a result liquidity is not a problem for them. In case of general insurance companies, their liabilities are mostly short-term and unpredictable because their claims are uncertain, their amount is variable and ascertainable only sometimes after the happening of the event (accident, fire, etc.). As a result, liquidity is a major consideration in their investment policy.

The assets of these companies are also different. For LIC government securities, mortgage and housing loans, loans to electricity boards and power companies, loans for water supply and sewerage, other infrastructural loans, industrial securities and term loans to companies are important assets. The GIC invests in corporate securities, government securities, and mortgage and housing loans. Dues from subsidiaries, special deposits with the government; loans to banks are its other major investments.

Both life insurance companies and general insurance companies are powerful players in the market and their decisions have a significant impact on the financial markets in India. LIC and GIC have now diversified their activities significantly in areas like mutual funds, pension schemes, housing finance, venture capital, and so on. In fact, the financial resources of the postal life insurance business have accumulated to a substantial size.

3.7.2 Mutual Funds

Investors in India have traditionally been investing in real estate, FDs and gold. From 2008 though, real estate took a back seat and mutual funds began to gain a lot of popularity as an investment option. The latest figures highlight that Equity MFs get 15,900 crore in April, up 5 times despite volatility (TOI 11.5.22) and total mutual funds assets hit a record high of 38.9 lakh crores. Small investors invariably do not posses adequate time, knowledge, expertise and resources for directly accessing highly profitable avenues in capital and money markets, so they are unable to decide in which shares or securities to invest.

Mutual fund companies raise funds from the potential investors for investing in shares and securities. The company that raises and manages the funds is known as an Asset Management Company (AMC). The AMC divides the funds so raised into a specific number of units usually with a value of ₹10 each. The investors in the mutual fund are given a share in the total funds which is proportionate to their investments and which is evidenced by the Unit Certificates. However, unlike the shareholders of a company the shareholders in mutual funds have no voting rights. The mutual fund companies invest in a broad range of shares and securities wherein small investments can be easily made. The professional managers of the fund also split the corpus of the fund into debt and equity so that the risk arising out of market volatility can be minimalized. In the secondary market units can be purchased and sold at their Net Asset Value (NAV). The NAV is required to be declared at least once a week. This provides liquidity to the investors.

Mutual fund schemes can be open-ended or close-ended. Open-ended schemes do not have any maturity period. The investor can exit from the fund on any business day by surrendering units for redemption at a price related to its NAV. In close-ended schemes there is a fixed maturity period. Investors can buy the units during the initial issue but can redeem them only at the end of the maturity period unless the unit scheme is listed on the stock exchange, then units can be bought or sold at any time.

While investing in MFs, investors should be aware that though they can expect good returns on their investments, especially if they hold them for a long period, yet there are risks involved viz; market risk, inflation risk, interest rate risk especially MFs are subject to the volatility in the market.

Mutual funds are pure intermediaries, and perform the basic function of buying and selling securities on behalf of its unit holders. The savings of their members are collected and invested in a diversified portfolio of financial assets. The investors in the mutual fund are given a share in its total funds, which is proportionate to their investments and which is evidenced by the unit certificates. However, unlike the shareholders of the company, the shareholders in mutual funds do not have any voting rights. Mutual funds or units may be either growth oriented or income oriented or both income and growth oriented. In addition, they may offer many other financial services such as insurance, share exchange, housing and bank loans to their customers. Mutual funds distribute the income to its members on a pro-rata basis. Small investors invariably do not possess adequate time, knowledge, expertise, experience and resources for directly accessing highly profitable avenues in capital and money markets. The portfolio investment and management by specialists in the trust help the small investors to obtain 'high return-low risk' combination. These experienced professionals not only judicially take investment decisions but continuously monitor, supervize and analyze investments, so that the investors keep enjoying a high and secure return on their savings. Since, mutual funds portfolios are diversified, some people maintain that though there is reduction of risk, returns from them are average. Mutual funds may not be a channel for getting rich quickly but they provide long-term growth avenues.

KEY TERMS

Acquisition It refers to one company taking over controlling interest in another company.

Loan syndication When groups of banks and financial institutions come together and contribute the necessary finance for a transaction.

Merchant banking That branch of banking which advises corporates on financial alternatives, corporate mergers, underwriting new issues, and so on.

Mergers A merger is a friendly coming together of two or more companies to form one unit for overall increase in efficiency and profits.

Net Asset Value or (NAV) is the market value of the assets of the fund less its liabilities.

NOSTRO means 'our account with you', e.g. an Indian bank in New Delhi maintaining a US$ account with its branch or correspondent bank in Paris is said to have a NOSTRO account with the Paris branch/bank.

Systematic Investment Plan (SIP) Through SIP one can invest a fixed amount in a Mutual Fund scheme at regular intervals, say every month instead of a lumpsum investment.

SWIFT Society for Worldwide Inter-bank Financial Transactions. It is a vast messaging network of banks and other financial institutions to quickly, accurately, and securely send and receive information, such as money transfer instructions. It is a crucial part of global financial infrastructure—in 2021, 11,000 global SWIFT members institutions sent an average of 42 million messages per day through this network.

REVIEW QUESTIONS

3.1 Differentiate between corporate and retail banking. Which sector is growing faster and why?

3.2 Describe the characteristics of international banking.

3.3 Do you think micro-finance is a more suitable alternative to provide finance to the rural poor? Give reasons for your answer.

3.4 Write short notes on:

- (i) International letter of credit
- (ii) Non-banking financial intermediaries
- (iii) Mutual Funds
- (iv) Corporate banking
- (v) Micro-finance
- (vi) SHGs

4

Electronic Banking

Learning Objectives

After going through this chapter we will be able to:

- Understand the concept and reasons for growth of e-banking.
- Know about the different modes of electronic fund transfer—NEFT, RTGS, IMPS, UPI.
- Learn the difference between debit, credit and smart cards.
- Appreciate the risks involved in e-banking.

The enhanced role of the banking sector in the Indian economy, the increasing levels of deregulation and globalization in the Indian banking industry have placed numerous demands on the banks. It is no longer adequate for banks to provide only traditional banking services. To meet varied financial needs, banks have to offer a wider and flexible range of financial products tailored for all types of customers and do this in a most efficient manner in terms of cost, time and convenience.

Technological innovations witnessed by the corporate sector during the nineties have introduced new business paradigms, wherein information technology is increasingly playing a significant role in improving the banking services. Technology has made banking seem-less, swift and low cost. Sweeping changes have taken place both in the financial services being offered as well as in the manner in which customers are accessing them. For example, more and more banking services are now being accessed remotely rather than through branch banking. In fact, technology has not only assumed the role of a facilitator, but it is also a source of competitive advantage for banks.

Demographic changes which have resulted in higher levels of education, breaking up of joint families, more women opting for paid employment, and the resultant changes in lifestyles, have all helped to fuel demand for different types of banking products and services.

4.1 MEANING OF E-BANKING

Going by its exponential growth, e-banking has become one of the most preferred method of banking in recent years. The following data for the month of March 22 highlights the volume of e-banking in the sphere of cards—7.3 crore credit card users spent 68,327 crores online and 33,773 crores in stores using card swipe machines. During the same month 91.7 crore debit card users used their cards for 20.8 crore transactions (worth 40,831 crores) in stores and 11.9 crores transactions (worth 22,687 crores) online (TOI 24.5.22). E-banking refers to the use of technology which allows customers to perform banking transactions electronically without visiting a brick and mortar institution. On-line means direct linking of an operation or equipment to a computer system, so that any stimulus provided by that operation or equipment is immediately accepted by the computer system.

Banking business has now shifted to an online environment. For the customer, Internet banking has translated into convenience and numerous choices. For banks it has become a cost-effective means for global expansion through innovative product delivery.

Electronic services allow a bank's customers and other stake-holders to interact and transact with the bank seamlessly through a variety of channels such as the internet, wireless devices, ATMs, on-line banking, phone banking and telebanking. Other services offered under e-banking include electronic funds transfer, electronic clearing service and electronic payment media including the credit card, debit card and smart card. On-line banking helps consumers to overcome the limitations of place and time as they can bank anywhere, anytime as these services are available 24 hours, 365 days a year without any physical limitations of space like a specific bank branch, city or region. They also bypass the paper based aspect of traditional banking.

India has emerged as one of the fastest growing markets for e-banking in the world.

4.2 AUTOMATED TELLER MACHINE

An automated teller machine or automatic teller machine (ATM) is a computerized telecommunications device that provides a bank's customers a secure method of performing financial transactions in a public space without human intervention. An ATM provides these services round the clock, throughout the year.

An earlier version of an ATM was developed in 1939 in New York, by the then City Bank of New York, but removed only after 6 months of installation due to the lack of customer acceptance! This status quo was maintained for nearly 25 years till Barclays Bank of UK installed an ATM in 1967 in London. ATMs first came into wide use during the early eighties to mid-eighties in the West and picked up later in the 1990s in India.

On-site ATMs can be interior (i.e., located in the branch premises) Off-site or exterior ATMs (located anywhere outside the branch premises, e.g., at railway stations, airports, shopping malls, etc.). Banks do not need to obtain permission of the RBI for installation of ATMs at branches and extension counters for which they hold licences issued by the Reserve Bank. They can also install offsite ATMs without RBI approval. However, they should obtain a licence from the regional office of DBOD (Department of Banking Operations and Development) of RBI, before operationalizing the ATM, so as to be in conformity with section 23 of the Banking Regulation Act. The minimum space needed for ATM installation is 40 square feet to 100 square feet.

4.2.1 Operation

For using an ATM, a customer requires an ATM card. Initially an ATM card worked on various principles including radiation and low-coercivity magnetism that was wiped by the cards reader to make fraud more difficult. However, most modern ATM card are made up of plastic with a magnetic stripe or a plastic smart card with a chip. Customer has a special card number that is referred to as a PIN (personal identification number) usually of four or more digits. The customer has to insert the card in the machine and quote his or her PIN number. Upon successful entry of the PIN, the customer may perform a transaction. After the completion of the transaction, a transaction record is printed, usually stating the action taken, date and time, location, any applicable fees and available balance. On completion of the transaction, the customer's card is ejected. However, if the PIN number is entered incorrectly and that too several times, then usually after the third attempt most ATMs retain the card as a security precaution to prevent an unauthorized user from discovering the PIN by guesswork.

Initially ATMs were only used for withdrawing cash. However, they provide many other services. A consumer can use an ATM for:

- Deposits/withdrawals of cash, usually in India the amount that can be withdrawn through an ATM is limited between 10 to 15 thousand ruppees in 24 hours.

- Making balance enquiry
- Obtaining an account statement for previous limited transactions
- Inter account transfer of funds (restricted to accounts of the same customer at same or different centres)
- Making utility payment of bills, e.g., electricity, telephone, etc.
- Requisition of chequebooks
- All withdrawals using an ATM are immediately deducted from the customer's account. Beyond a few transactions fee is charged on additional withdrawals during a month. For instance SBI allows 8 free transactions per month including 5 in SBI and 3 in other banks in metros and 10 in non-metro areas 5 each in SBI and other bank ATMs. These charges vary from ₹8–20, depending on the nature of the transaction. If a customer loses their ATM card the bank levies fee (₹50–500), for replacement.

4.3 INTERNET BANKING

Internet banking is the ability to use one's personal computer to communicate with one's bank. Internet banking and on-line banking is an outgrowth of PC banking. PC banking enables customers to execute bank transactions from their personal computer via a modem through a financial software of the bank. Internet banking has become a strategic necessity for most commercial banks. It is being used as a distribution channel to build up customer contracts in a systematic way in order to inform, counsel and sell products and services.

As observed earlier, customer behaviour has changed drastically due to technological advancement and changes in lifestyles. The use of financial services is today characterized by individuality, mobility, independence of time and place and flexibility. Internet is being viewed as a new distribution channel to provide complex products at lower cost to more and more potential customers who can consume them at any time from anywhere in the world. The internet has helped banks to enlarge their market area without building new offices, and to increase their market share and profits.

All banks, which propose to offer internet services, should obtain prior approval from RBI. Only those banks which are licensed and supervised in India and have a physical presence in India will be permitted to offer internet banking products to residents of India. Thus, both banks and virtual banks incorporated outside the country and having no physical presence in India will not, for the present, be permitted to offer internet banking services to Indian residents.

A number of routine issues which are simple in nature but time-consuming can be handled through the internet, e.g., customer's request for opening an account, balance enquiries, FD renewals, request for chequebooks, foreign exchange rates, on-line bill payments, stop payment request, request for debit cards, transfer of funds on-line and monthly statement by e-mail. No staff intervention is required in all these cases and the bank can provide all these services to their customers at a fraction of the cost. Internet banking not only ensures saving in the salary of staff, but also enhances the bank's ability to increase their customer base without having to invest in exorbitantly priced real estate for opening more physical branches. According to some estimates, the cost per transaction over the internet is one-eighth of the cost to the bank if performed through branch banking.

4.3.1 Advantages

Internet banking provides

- Anywhere and anytime banking as services are provided round the clock
- Worldwide connectivity as it transcends geographical boundaries
- Easy access to recent and historical data
- Direct customer control of international movement of funds
- Greater processing speed and accuracy

However, there are certain limitations of internet banking also—it presupposes computer literate customers who can develop trust in this technology which is not always the case especially in a country like India. The fear of hacking is very real in people's minds so the risk management of the system of the banks poses new challenges.

4.4 ELECTRONIC CLEARING SERVICE (ECS)

The scheme for electronic clearing service was introduced by RBI in 1994 in four metro centres and extended to sixteen other centres later. The scheme facilitates credit of dividend into customer's accounts. Apart from increasing the speed of payment, it also ensure that frauds are avoided. There are two types of ECS—ECS credit and ECS debit. ECS credit facilitates bulk payment. It is a medium of payment used by an organization to pay interest, dividend, salary, pension, etc. to a large number of beneficiaries. The payment can be made electronically resulting in saving of time and cost. ECS debit is the opposite of ECS credit. It is a medium that helps organizations to collect the proceeds of bills, premium, instalments on due date based on mandates received from the users of their services. Maximum ceiling of ₹2 crore per transaction had been fixed earlier by the RBI but this ceiling was removed on October 26, 2004.

4.5 ELECTRONIC FUNDS TRANSFER (EFT)

For making inter-city payments customer usually make payments through demand drafts, mail transfers and telegraphic transfers. In 1996, RBI devised an electronic funds transfer (EFT) system to facilitate fast transfer of funds electronically. The funds can be transferred between any two bank accounts even if the sender and the receiver are located in different cities or deal with different banks. EFT has accelerated the movement of funds across the globe. E-cash or cyber-cash plays a predominant role in world commerce. Such electronic funds movements amounting to a few trillion dollars are settled on a daily basis in major international financial centres. Society for worldwide inter-bank financial telecommunication (SWIFT) is a classic example of EFT among banks with its own standards for messages, which ensures speed, reliability, security and accuracy. The objective of establishing an EFT system is to facilitate an efficient, secure, economical, reliable and expeditious system of funds transfer and clearing in the banking sector throughout India, and to relieve the stress on the existing paper based funds transfer and clearing system.

4.5.1 Advantages

- Funds can get transferred easily and conveniently without delays and paper work.
- Built-in security measures ensure safety of funds during transfer.
- Losses and frauds are minimized due to easy tracking of transactions/customers.

It is not only in India but online transfer of funds is vital and essential service in the global banking industry. These systems have revolutionized the banking sector and provided momentum to the growth of a digital and cashless economy. At present 40% of all transactions in India are digital and in 2021 payments worth $3 trillion were processed by digital instruments. By the year 2026 this market is expected to more than triple to $10 trillion (ET 3.6.22). The three systems that are most frequently used for electronic transfer of money include NEFT, RTGS and UPI. All three are safe and secure methods for making payments and are monitored by the RBI.

4.5.2 National Electronic Fund Transfer (NEFT)

All customers having a saving or current account are eligible to transfer money online through NEFT. In case the person wants to make payment through some bank he will have to deposit cash in the nearest NEFT enabled branch of any bank and transfer the money to the beneficiary having an account with an NEFT enabled bank and some charges will have to be paid. Maximum limit for such transfer is ₹50,000. For transfers made online there are no charges. Though there is no limit on minimum amount but a maximum amount of ₹10,00,000 is fixed for online payments. Before 2019 the RBI had fixed timings for NEFT transfers—between 8 am to 6.30 pm from Monday to Friday, and 8 am to 12 pm on Saturdays but after 2020 these transactions can be done 24×7. NEFT is one-to-one payment facility, however according to RBI guidelines NEFT payments are processed on a deferred settlement basis and settled in half-hour batches. It is done during banking hours and if the transfer cannot be completed over weekends or bank holidays it shall be completed on the next working day. For transferring payment through this system, the following details have to be given to the bank—the name of the beneficiary, his account number, account type, name of his bank along with the IFSC (Indian Financial System Code). Cost of transaction is very reasonable and is usually in the range of ₹2.50 – ₹25.

4.5.3 Real Time Gross Settlement (RTGS)

RTGS is a fund transfer system based on gross settlements and funds are moved from one bank to another in real time on a one to one basis and not in batches. It is primarily designed for high value transactions and when payment needs to be processed immediately. The minimum amount that can be transferred through RTGS is ₹2,00,000, there is no maximum limit though banks might place a maximum limit according to their risk perception. All customers having a saving or current account are eligible for transferring payment online. Money is remitted within thirty minutes. Sender and receiver bank should be RTGS enabled. This list is available on the RBI website. Cost of transaction is slightly more than NEFT, usually ₹30 for a payment of ₹5 lakh. For transfer of money the following information has to be provided—account number of remitter, name, account number of beneficiary, along with the bank and branch name and IFSC code of receiving bank.

4.5.4 Immediate Payment Service (IMPS)

IMPS was launched in 2010 and is used for transferring money instantly. Remittances can be made 24×7, 365 days of the year irrespective of weekends and bank holidays. Money can be transferred using phones, ATMs, Internet banking and mobile money identifiers (MMID).

- Requirements
- MMID of the recipient
- 7 digit MMID No.
- MMID of receiver
- Beneficiaries' name, mobile number, account number, IFSC code.

4.5.5 Unified Payments Interface (UPI)

This is an instant real-time payment system developed by the National Payments Corporation of India. It facilitates peer to peer and person to merchant transactions. It was introduced on 11th of April, 2016. Its market includes India, Bhutan, Nepal, Malaysia, Singapore, United Arab Emirates through international cross border agreements. UPI is a payment system that allows one to transfer money to someone else using the IMPS payment framework, without having to know their bank account number or their IFSC code. UPI is a system that powers multiple bank accounts into a single mobile application (of any participating bank). UPI is continuing to growth at a very fast pace-clocking 5.95 billion transactions worth ₹10.41 lakh crore last month, especially in person-to-person (P2P) fund transfers and low value merchant (P2M) payments (ET 3.6.22). It is expected to account for all digital payment volumes by FY26. They crossed 6.28 billion transactions in July (MINT 9.8.22). UPI enabled apps allow transactions up to ₹1 lakh with any smartphone using a VPA (Virtual Payment Address). Steps involved for transfer are fewer, money is transferred faster, it does not need personal details like credit card/debit card or bank account numbers. There are no charges and money can be transferred round the clock.

4.6 TELEBANKING

Any branch of a commercial bank which has computerized operations can offer telebanking facility to its customers with the help of suitable software for this purpose. Telebanking or bank-on-phone allows customers to interface with the bank via telephone. Digitalization of voice has enabled the introduction of this technological marvel. The customer can dial a designated number and perform a number of transactions from the convenience of their premises. Facilities offered through telephone banking include request for balance enquiries, enquiries about collections or specific credits/debits, transfer of funds, request for statement of account, etc. Banks are also offering services such as account opening, ordering for demand drafts, stop payment requests as well as report of the loss of a debit, credit or ATM card. A password for security and protection is given by the banker to the customer.

4.7 ELECTRONIC CHEQUES

In the year 2002, an amendment was made under section 6 of Negotiable Instrument Act, to include an electronic cheque as a negotiable instrument. It is valid like a paper cheque. When a cheque is issued in electronic form instead of its normal physical form by the use of digital signature, it is called an **electronic cheque**. It contains an exact mirror image of the paper cheque and is generated, written and signed in a secured system by ensuring the minimum safety standards with the use of digital signature, with or without biometrics signatures (identification on basis of face, retina, fingerprints, etc.) and asymmetric crypto system.

4.8 CREDIT CARDS

There are various ways of making payment through the banking system. These include cheques, direct debits, bank drafts, electronic transfer, international money orders, letters of credit, etc. Since, the beginning of 1980s, the banks introduced a new facility for making payments, i.e., the credit card. The use of credit card is essentially a method of postponing payment. When the customer makes a purchase, the actual payment is made later when he issues a cheque for the payment on his bank. These cards are made of plastic, hence they are referred to as *plastic money*. Plastic money refers to substitution of currency at the time when a payment is taking place by using a card. It has become the best alternative to cash and made life simpler, easier and faster than before. Plastic money has increasingly become an alternative payment system in most developed and developing countries. There are myriad factors responsible for this. First and foremost the technical revolution in the banking sector has eliminated physical and geographical banking and replaced it with anytime anywhere banking. This has played a crucial role in the payment card industries. Secondly, there has been a sea change in consumer behaviour. They want the convenience and safety in making payments. With the use of credit card there is no need to stand in queues in the bank branch, where they have an account, during banking hours on a working day. The use of credit card also enables its holder to minimize the use of hard cash and, thus, provides safety to the cardholder. Data on credit and debit cards realized by RBI in the month of March 2022 shows that banks increased their card base from 6.2 crores to 7.3 crores in the previous 12 months. The highest growth was reported by ICICI (22.5%) followed by Axis Bank (26%) and SBI (16%). Foreign banks lost most American Bank had a decline of 1.5 lakh users, Standard Chartered Bank 1.3 lakh users.

4.8.1 Features

1. A credit card is synonymous with a short term revolving credit to the card holder. It is an instrument which provides instantaneous credit facilities to its holder—usually between 30 and 45 days.
2. A credit card is made of plastic. Each card carries embossed characters giving the name of the holder, his account number and its period of validity. On the reverse side, it gives the holder's signature.
3. Plastic money lasts anywhere from 2 to 5 times as longer than paper money. It cannot get torn, mutilated or discoloured like paper currency. It is harder to counterfeit and unlike paper currency, plastic currency does not shed tiny bits of ink and dust that can disable ATM by confusing their optical reader.
4. They reduce the need to carry cash and can prove to be of immense help in case of emergencies like sudden illnesses.

5. It is a payment device that can be used in local, national and sometimes even in international markets, during travel, at ATMs, etc. for purchase of all kinds of goods such as households, consumer durables and services like hotels, airways, railways, and so on.
6. The credit card reduces the need for the customer to hold money balances at any given time by helping to synchronize the receipt of income with the expenditure of goods.
7. The use of credit card also eases the pressure on RBI to issue currency and on use of cheques.
8. Having a bank account is not a prerequisite for issuing a credit card, some banks insist on the credit card holder having an account in their bank, others don't.
9. Each credit card holder is given a credit limit on his credit card. This is the maximum amount one can spend at one point if time. This limit is fixed by the bank for the customer (depending upon his financial standing and past financial history), which is entirely separate from his normal bank account and is maintained by the banks' credit cards' department.
10. The Banks offer reward programmes on credit card usage. Credit card holders earn points, discounts and other benefits which can be redeemed in purchase of FMCGs, air travel, hotels, restaurants, etc.
11. Credit cards are time saving as goods and services can be paid for without wasting time on money dealings and even over the Internet.
12. Universal acceptability — while travelling paper currency in different countries but many credit cards are accepted in a number of countries.
13. Some banks like SBI give a choice of three different types of insurance cover like health, accidents or card loss or theft.

4.8.2 Operation

There are three parties to a credit card, namely:

(i) The issuing bank

(ii) The cardholder

(iii) The member merchant establishment/retail outlet

The issuing bank enrolls member establishments who are willing to accept payment through credit cards. At the time of making a payment the magnetic strip on the card which contains coded information about the customer and his account is read by special card reader in the ATM (automated teller machine) and point of sale (PoS) terminals. When a card holder makes a purchase, he signs a charge slip. The retail outlet gives one copy each of this charge slip to the customer and the bank. The bank makes the payment to the retailer after deducting its commission and charges. Bills are sent to cardholders periodically, generally monthly.

4.8.3 Advantages

The use of credit card offers numerous advantages to the merchant, customer as well as the bank.

Benefits to merchants:

- Because of the ease and convenience of using credit cards, the sales of the retail outlets increase manifold.
- Credit cards provide instantaneous validation/verification of details of the customer so the merchant is not subject to risk.
- The bad debts of the merchant are reduced as he gets payment from the bank.

Benefits to customers:

- The customer can purchase goods or services anywhere, anytime whenever he desires.
- The card holder is neither required to pay interest to the bank nor pay a higher price to the retailer for making paperless payment.
- Since, it is a document of credit worthiness, it enables the customer to obtain credit at designated places. He usually enjoys the credit facility for anything between 30 and 45 days.
- Use of credit card saves the customer from the necessity of carrying hard cash.
- All transactions of the customers are recorded in the statements sent by his bank. So, there is no confusion.
- The customer has to issue a single cheque to cover payment of numerous transactions made during his billing cycle.
- Payment of utility bills becomes fast and easy as the need to stand in long queues is dispensed with.

Benefits to bank:

- The credit card business is very lucrative for the banker as they get upto 40 per cent return on the capital employed in spite of their funds being blocked for a period of 30 to 45 days.
- Banks can increase their outreach without having to open more branches or ATMs by encouraging customers to use credit cards.
- Banks can sell other products like insurance along with credit cards and generate additional income.
- If a customer fails to make the payment due on their card the bank can charge interest fees to their account.

4.8.4 Drawbacks

Use of credit card encourages impulsive purchases. The customers can end up spending more money than they have. This can lead to financial problems as consumers can easily be lured into the debt trap if not careful. There are chances of the card being misused if it falls into the hands of an unscrupulous person as evidenced from the number of credit card frauds which are reported across the globe every year.

4.9 DEBIT CARDS

Like the credit card a debit card too is a payment mechanism which allows the holder to make purchases electronically without making any immediate cash payment. It appears that plastic money appears to be the preferred mode of payment for more and more people. While the use of credit cards and debit cards has increased manifold both in terms of value and volume of transactions yet the growth in use of debit cards has been at a much faster rate than in the case of credit cards.

4.9.1 Features

A debit card is a variant of an ATM card. It has the following features:

- Whereas an ATM card can be used only where the ATMs are provided by the banks, and that too only for cash withdrawals, the debit card can be used in any merchant outlet that is linked with the customer's bank for making payment.
- Credit card is issued to clients after a proper assessment of their credit standing. But for a debit card holder there is no need to make such an assessment.
- At the time of making payment through a debit card, the amount is instantly debited to the customer's account unlike payment made through the credit card where the account of the customer is debited after a certain period.
- Debit card frees the card holder from carrying cash for his/her purchases.
- Debit card is like a blank cheque, so it must be used carefully otherwise an unscrupulous person can wipe the entire balance in the bank account of the holder.
- There are no chances of the debit card user to fall into the debt trap, since payment is immediately debited to his account, as he can only use the money which is available in his account.
- There are no transaction costs and no question of late fee payment in the use of debit card.
- Bankers also avoid the risk of bad debts.

4.10 SMART CARD

As the name suggests this plastic card is smarter than the credit card and debit card. A smart card is a magnetic strip card that is embedded with a computer microchip and designed with a far greater capacity. The microchip provides the smart card intelligence and memory. It is small enough to be conveniently carried around, and has manifold application. In fact, it is almost like carrying a portable computer in one's pocket.

4.10.1 Features

1. Smart card can be used for storing personal informations like name/address, driving licence details, medical records, e.g., blood group, any history of heart disease, blood pressure, diabetes or allergy problems which can prove very useful in emergencies; equipment maintenance records and any other information which is required to be stored.
2. These cards can be used as a personal identification device anywhere, e.g., for making hotel bookings or purchase airlines ticket.
3. Smart card can be used for carrying out financial transactions like the payments of telephone and electricity bills, road toll taxes, ATM cash vending for withdrawing cash, etc.
4. One of the best features of smart cards is the security provided by such cards. In present days of heightened terrorist activities, smart card can be conveniently used for airport security, defence services, controlling access to data in the computer industry and so forth.
5. Apart from the above security features, smart card can help to prevent card related crimes.

   With all the above features it would not be very surprising if in the future smart card replaces the use of debit cards and credit cards.

4.11 RISKS IN E-BANKING

Risks in banking business can be in the nature of any of the following:

1. *Strategic risk* This can arise because of faulty business decisions and improper implementation. It can be current or prospective. If the senior management takes decisions to meet competitive pressures without cross-checking the cost benefit analysis.
2. *Transaction risk* This can arise because of fraud, negligence, error, etc. if adequate service levels are not maintained.

3. *Compliance risk* If the bank does not comply with legal provisions and ethical standards, it can result in monetary loss as well as reduced business.
4. *Reputation risk* The reputation of the bank can be tarnished because any of the above or because of inferior service.

In case of e-banking nothing in the internet is secure. Use of high technology has brought the operational risk in the form of security risk not only in the world but in India also cyber fraud has increased manifold. Customers fear that their money may be targeted by cyberspace robbers. In an environment of large scale use of technology, there is a need for surveillance monitoring and auditing to detect unusual usage patterns and deficiencies. This calls for putting in place appropriate and adequate safeguards to ensure security covering physical and other aspects.

To minimize transaction risks banks should have a security policy duly approved by the Board of Directors. They should also introduce logical access controls to data, systems, application softwares, utilities, telecommunication lines, etc. At the minimum, they should use firewall system so that there is no direct connection between internet and bank's system. **Bankway** and **Flexcube** are the most popular e-banking solutions used for securing electronic transactions in India. Biometrics which is the science of identifying an individual by means of personal characteristics like face, finger prints, retina or voice, is another security paradigm, which can empower banks to verify the actual identity of a person rather than merely depending upon a PIN number.

Banks should also ensure that the products that they offer should be restricted to account holders only and services should include only local currency products. They should immediately report any breach or failure of security systems and procedure to the RBI. Banks should also make mandatory disclosures of risks, responsibilities and liabilities of the customers in doing business through internet.

It will be naïve to assume that in case of e-banking there are only transaction risks. This is because transaction risks will give rise to legal issues and ultimately all these will have a monetary implication as well as affect the reputation of the bank and trust in the entire financial system.

KEY TERMS

Decryption Process of converting the coded text to its original form.

Electronic Operations performed by the action of electrons, characterized by the prevalence of electronic equipment.

Encryption Process of converting normal text to a coded message by means of an electronic method.

FMCGs Fast moving consumer goods.

Low coercitivity magnetism Use of low level magnetic force.

Paradigm A model, an overall concept accepted by most people in explaining a complex idea.

Phishing Internet fraudsters 'fish' for passwords and security details and use them for committing fraud on the internet.

Tele-communication Communication by electronic or electric means as through radio, telephone, telegraph, television or computers.

REVIEW QUESTIONS

4.1 Discuss the different modes of electronic money transfer. In your opinion which option might be used by a small entrepreneur of New Delhi to make a payment of 1,00,000 to his supplier of raw materials in Ahmedabad? Give reasons.

4.2 'Plastic money has replaced paper money'. Comment on the above statement and differenciate between debit and credit cards.

4.3 Write short notes on

(i) Operation of ATM cards

(ii) Benefits of credit cards to banker

(iii) Smart card

(iv) Risks in e-banking

5

Loans and Advances

Learning Objectives

After going through this chapter we will be able to:

- Understand principles of sound lending.
- Know about the main methods of granting loans and advances.
- Learn about the various types of securities accepted by banks for granting loans.
- Learn how Lien, Pledge, Assignment and Mortgage are used to create a charge on assets.

The primary function of a commercial bank is that of a broker and dealer in society's money. Banks mobilize a large fraction of the liquid savings of the nation, and allocate them successfully and productively to those who need it, such as, industry, agriculture and households. The major portion of banks' funds is employed by way of loans and advances from wherein banks earn interest, discounts and conversion fees.

5.1 PRINCIPLES OF SOUND LENDING

The business of lending carries certain inherent risks, and banks can afford to take only calculated risks as they deal in other people's money. Another important facet of bank operations is the need to have ready cash as a bank is under an obligation to return the customer's money whenever it is demanded. Hence, the nature of bank functions is such that it requires a very prudent and diligent handling of bank funds. It is advisable that the following general principles of sound lending should be followed by a banker at the time of granting advances.

5.1.1 Principle of Liquidity

As already observed banks accept customer's money, a substantial part of which is repayable on demand. Liquidity implies the ability to produce cash on demand, and the banker must be able to meet these liabilities whenever they are demanded. While it is true that all businesses have to devote considerable attention to liquidity management, but for a banker it can affect its credit, and for a banker, credit is the very foundation of his business. So a banker must ensure that there is no mismatch of resources and that the money he invests or lends should be repaid in the stipulated period, so that his obligation to pay his depositors is not affected. Liquidity also implies shiftability without loss. If the security accepted is readily shiftable, e.g., discounting of first class bills which can be rediscounted with the RBI in case of need, then the banker can obtain funds easily. On the other hand, if security is in the form of land, then such security can be converted into cash only after an interval.

5.1.2 Principle of Safety and Security

As observed earlier, bankers loan funds which are entrusted to him. Safety of funds means that the borrowers repay the loan along with interest as per the agreement. To ensure safety and security, the banker must take into account (i) the capacity of the borrower to pay, and (ii) the willingness of the borrower to repay. Capacity depends upon the financial strength of the borrower, his tangible assets and success of his business. Willingness depends upon the honesty, integrity and reputation of the borrower. In other words, both the tangible worth of the security offered as well as the creditworthiness of the borrower should be carefully analyzed before granting an advance. The banker must take some tangible security as collateral for the loan and this should have sufficient margin. In case of unsecured loans the prospects of bad loans increase significantly.

5.1.3 Principle of Profitability

Banks are essentially commercial ventures, and as such they have to ensure that their lending operations are sufficiently profitable to cover their cost of funds, cost of interest and risk cost, and leave sufficient income to allow for full prudential provisioning, allocation to capital and reserves for expansion, growth and for maintaining its competitive viability. Though banks are subjected to numerous regulations like priority sector lending yet they cannot afford to sacrifice profitability for social objectives. Banks need to maintain a judicial balance between the two so that both profitability and social objectives can be maintained.

5.1.4 Principle of Purpose

At the time of granting an advance the banker must enquire about the purpose of the loan. If it is for speculative or unproductive purposes, it may prove to be a burden on cash generation and repayment capacity of the borrower. On the other hand, it can be reasonably anticipated that loans meant for productive purposes like business, trade, industry, agriculture, profession or vocation. This will help generate incremental income that will facilitate prompt repayment of the loan.

5.1.5 Principle of Diversification of Risks

The old maxim *do not keep all the eggs in one basket* is very apt as far as the bankers' portfolio of loans and advances is concerned. A prudent banker should always try and spread risk by granting loans to different borrowers from different trades, industries, sectors and regions, so that risks arising from change in government policies, natural calamities or technological breakthroughs and so forth do not put his position in jeopardy.

5.1.6 Principle of Social Responsibility

At the time of evaluation of a loan project, bankers should not put an overdue emphasis on the size of the borrower, and the security that he is offering. The technical competency of the borrower and the economic viability of his project should also be considered. The priority sector guidelines have also to be followed by the bankers, if they want to contribute in the process of economic development by helping more and more entrepreneurs to run successful ventures. For a long time banks in India were used as an instrument of socio-economic development. Social obligations took precedence over profitability for the banks. The principle of social responsibility does not, however, mean that adequate attention should not be paid to other principles.

In conclusion, it is pertinent to mention that none of the principles should be considered in isolation. While evaluating a loan proposal, a judicious balance of all the cardinal principles of sound lending are called for. This has become more imperative after 1991. Before liberalization, banking business did not face much competition. As it was concentrated in a few hands, the policy environment was characterized by close regulation and control, and profitability was not the dominant criterion on which the banks were supposed to function. But now the commercial principles of viability, efficiency, prudence and profitability are receiving as much attention as social banking.

5.2 METHODS OF GRANTING ADVANCES

Lending may be fund based, non-fund based or asset based. Fund-based lending is the most direct form of lending with an actual outflow of cash. In non-fund based lending, there was no actual outflow of cash but there is a contingent liability, e.g., LCs, bank guarantee, etc. In the case of asset-based lending, e.g., project securitization/project finance, the bank depends upon the earning capacity of the asset being financed. In this case, bank has no or only limited recourse to the borrowers.

For granting advances, banks can use any of the following methods.

5.2.1 Cash Credit

Cash credit accounts for around two-thirds of total bank credit as it is the most favoured method for availing credit in India. It is a form of revolving credit. This offers flexibility to borrowers because it permits withdrawals from the line of credit at any time. Also, payment can be made of whole or part of outstanding loan as and when the borrower has cashflows. Under this system the banker fixes a cash credit limit on an annual basis, and the customer is at liberty to withdraw any amount as and when he needs. Thus, the cash credit account is an active and running account to which deposits and withdrawals may be affected frequently.

Features:

- The bank fixes the cash credit limit of the borrower after studying the financial capacity, projected sales and past utilization of such limits.
- The borrower has to provide security of tangible assets (in the form of pledge or hypothecation) or guarantees.
- The borrower can withdraw from this account whenever he requires and whatever amount he needs, provided the amount does not exceed the cash credit limit.
- Interest is charged only on the actual amount withdrawn, and for the actual period for which it is utilized.
- Even though the advances sanctioned under this system are made for the period of one year but in reality they 'roll over' a period of time. Initially a commitment charge of 1 per cent was levied on the unutilized amount, but it was withdrawn. RBI has now left this upon the discretion of individual banks.

  From the bankers' point of view, there are certain limitations of the system. He stands to lose interest on the unutilized amount, he also has to keep adequate funds to meet the demands of the customer as and when they arise. He is not in a position to verify the end use of the advance by the borrower. However, he does enjoy some operative convenience as only one account has to be maintained which avoids repetitive documentation.

5.2.2 Overdraft

An overdraft is a short-term credit facility. It is given to a current account holder, by which he is allowed to withdraw more money from his account then what actually stands to his credit.

Features:

- For granting an overdraft limit, the banker may insist on either a collateral security or grant it on the personal security of the borrower.
- The customer can withdraw as much money as is needed subject to a maximum of the overdraft limit which has been sanctioned.
- Interest is charged on the actual amount utilized and for the period that it is utilized.
- Sometimes in the absence of an express agreement for an overdraft facility, such an agreement can be inferred from the course of business between the banker and customer.
- If the lending bank so desires, the overdraft facility can be discontinued or recast.
- The main differences between cash credit and overdraft are that the former is granted for a longer period whereas overdraft is of a temporary nature. A new account has to be opened for cash credit where as there is no such need in case of overdraft. Usually cash credit is granted against security of goods through pledge or hypothecation but overdraft may be given against personal security of the customer or financial security like shares or bonds.

5.2.3 Bills Discounting

Another short-term facility for providing working capital is through discounting and purchasing of bills. When the customer provides a bill of exchange as security, the banker deducts a certain amount, called **discount**, from the face value of the bill, and advances the rest of the amount to the customer. The bill is presented on the due date on maturity to the drawee for payment. Bills are considered highly liquid security and, therefore, they are highly favoured especially by the conservative banks.

In addition to advancing money by discounting bills, a banker purchases them outright at face value and less bank charges. Purchase of bills is normally confined to bills payable on demand.

5.2.4 Loan System

The term *loan* is popularly used to denote the granting of an advance in lump sum, usually on the basis of some acceptable securities. Under the loan system, credit is given for a definite purpose and for a predetermined period. Traditionally loans were provided for working capital funds for business operations, but banks have extended their lending activities to investment in long-term bonds and open-end securities, both government and private. Furthermore, loans are advanced not just for financing trade and industry, but also to government units as well as to consumers for a range of personal products like housing, automobiles, education, etc.

Features:

- The purpose of the loan is clearly defined. This ensures a greater degree of self discipline on the borrower and makes it easier for the banker to monitor and control the use of bank credit as compared to advances made by way of cash credit or overdraft.
- Funds are provided at one go for a single transaction. If additional funds are required, the customer has to apply afresh and renegotiate terms for a new loan or even for renewal of the existing loan. To avoid this sometimes borrowers tend to borrow in excess of their requirements.
- Though loans are given for a fixed period, in practice they tend to roll over as frequently they are renewed.
- Repayment is usually made in instalments, though sometimes it can be repaid on demand.
- Interest is to be paid on the entire amount whether it is utilized fully or not.
- Operating costs of a loan for a banker are lower than in case of other methods of advances.

Types of loans: Loans can broadly be categorized on the basis of the security, the period sanctioned or on the basis of the purpose of the loan. On the basis of security loans can either be secured or unsecured. On the basis of period, they can be short-term, medium-term or long-term loan or a bridge loan. They can be composite or consumption loans depending on their purpose. A brief description follows:

Short-term loans. Short-term loans are loans which are granted for a period not exceeding one year. These are advanced to meet the working capital requirements, against security of movable assets like goods, commodities, shares, debentures, etc. They are usually taken to meet the working capital requirements of business.

Term loans. Medium and long-term loans are usually called **term loans**. These loans are extended for periods ranging from one year to about eight or ten years on the security of existing industrial assets or the assets purchased with the loan. Term loans are used for purchase of capital assets for establishment of new industrial units, for expansion, modernization or diversification. They involve an element of risk as they are intended to be repaid out of the future profits over a period of years. Consequently, apart from the financial appraisal of such loans, the technical feasibility and managerial competency of the borrower should also be studied. Banks can charge fixed rates of interest for the entire period or different prime lending rates for different maturities, provided transparency and uniformity of treatment is maintained.

Bridge loans. It is a type of gap financing arrangement. Bridge loans are essentially short-term loans that are granted pending disbursement of sanctioned term loans. These help borrowers to get immediate cash flow to meet their urgent and critical needs during the period when formalities for availing of the term loans sanctioned are being fulfilled. They are repaid out of the amount of such loans or from the funds raised in the capital market if these loans are granted by financial institutions. Through such loans businesses can get liquidity to tap business opportunities and individuals can manage finances especially in sale/purchase of property.

Composite loans. If a loan is taken for buying capital assets as well as for meeting working capital requirements, it is called a **composite loan.** Usually such loans are availed by small entrepreneurs, artisans and farmers.

Consumption loans. Traditionally, banks used to focus on loans for productive purposes, but during the recent past banks have increasingly started giving loans for consumption purposes like education, automobiles, housing loans, consumer durables, etc.

5.3 SECURED ADVANCES

In accordance with the principles of safety and security of sound lending, commercial banks prefer to make advances against securities. According to section 5 (a) of the Banking Regulation Act 1949, a secured advance or loan means a loan or advance made on the security of assets the market value of which is not at any time less than the amount of loan or advance, or against personal security (Book debts, bills receivables) or other guarantees. An advance which is not secured is called an **unsecured advance**.

The basic objective of obtaining securities is to recover the unpaid amount of loan if any, through the sale of these securities. Hence, the securities should be clearly identifiable (in physical form as well as in value terms), be easily marketable, have stability (price should not be subjected to high fluctuations), and their title should be clear and easily transferable.

5.3.1 Classification of Securities

Based on their nature, securities can be divided into various categories.

Personal securities: These are also called **intangible securities**. In case of these, the banker has a personal right of action against the borrower, e.g., promissory notes, bills or exchange, a security bond, personal liability of guarantor, etc.

Tangible securities: These are forms of impersonal security, such as, land, buildings and machinery. In the event of recovery of loans, banks have to get such securities enforced or sold through the intervention of court.

Primary securities: These are those securities or assets which are created with the help of finance made available by the bank, like machinery or equipment purchased with the help of bank finance.

Collateral security: This security is not what is financed out of the bank advance. It is additional security given by the borrower where the primary security is not enough to recover the loan amount at the time of realization, e.g., the land of the factory is given as security along with the machinery purchased out of the bank loan.

Securities can also be classified as liquid security (those which are easily convertible to cash), government security or gilt edged securities (bonds, promissory notes, treasury bills issued by government), stock exchange securities (shares, debentures), and blue chip securities (shares of pool A companies).

5.4 MODES OF CREATING CHARGES

In case of secured loan, a charge is created on the asset in favour of the bank. In other words, the banker obtains a legal right to get payment of the loan amount out of the security charged. According to the nature of security, charges can be of the following types as mentioned in Table 5.1.

Table 5.1 Types of Charge and Nature of Security

Type of charge	*Nature of security*
Lien	Goods and securities
Pledge or hypothecation	Movable properties
Assignment	Book debts
Mortgage	Immovable property

Charges can also be categorized according to their nature such as fixed charge or floating charge. A fixed charge is created on assets whose identity does not change, e.g., land and buildings. In the case of floating charge, the identity of the asset keeps fluctuating, e.g., stocks.

The legal provisions regarding modes of creating charge over tangible assets and the rights and obligations of various parties are explained hereinafter.

5.4.1 Lien

Lien means the right of the creditor to retain the goods and securities owned by the debtor until the debt due from him is repaid. The creditor gets only the right to retain the goods and not the right to sell. Lien can be either particular or general. The right of particular lien can be exercised by a person who has spent his time, money or labour on the goods, e.g., a car mechanic, a tailor, etc. It can be exercised against only those goods for which charges have to be paid. A banker, however, enjoys the right of general lien.

Features:

- The right of **general lien** confers a blanket right, on the banker and is applicable in respect of all amounts which are due from the debtor such as security handed over to the banker for a machinery loan after its repayment can also be used by the banker in respect of any other advance outstanding in his name, e.g., against an overdraft taken by the borrower.
- Even though this right is conferred upon the banker by the Indian Contract Act, yet it is advisable to take a letter from the customer mentioning that the goods have been entrusted to the banker as security, and he may exercise his right of lien against it.
- The bankers' right of lien is tantamount to an implied pledge. Unlike as in the case of particular lien the creditor can only retain the goods till the amount due is paid, but the banker has the right to sell the goods kept as security in case of the customer does not repay the loan.
- Sometimes even a negative lien can be entered into. Under this arrangement, the borrower has to (i) give a declaration that the assets given as security are free from any charge or encumbrance, (ii) that no charge will be created on them nor will the borrower dispose of those assets without the consent of the banker. The banker's interests are only partially safe by securitizing a negative lien as he cannot realize his dues from these assets.

5.4.2 Pledge

Pledge is the bailment of goods as security for payment of a debt or performance of a promise. When a borrower secures a loan through a pledge, he is called a **pawner** or **pledger**, and the bank is called the **pawnee** or **pledgee**.

Features:

- The goods can be pledged by the owner, a joint owner with consent of other joint owners, a mercantile agent or in some cases by an unpaid seller.

- The banker can retain the goods for the payment of the debt, for any interest that has accrued on it as well as any expenses incurred by him for keeping the goods safe and secure.
- Goods can be retained for any subsequent advances also, but not for any existing debt which is not covered by the pledge.
- In case of non-payment, the banker has the right to sell the goods and recover the amount of loan along with the interest and expenses, if any.
- In case of default by the pledger, the banker has the right either to
  - (a) File a civil suit against the pledger and retain the goods as additional security; or
  - (b) Sell the goods. In case of sale, banker must give due notice of sale to the borrower before making a sale.
- This right is not limited by the law of limitation.
- Banker's right of pledge prevails over any other dues including government dues except worker's wages.
- Banker must take good care of goods and return them after the payment is made along with accretion, if any.

5.4.3 Hypothecation

Hypothecation is an extended idea of pledge, whereby the creditor permits the debtor to retain possession of goods, either on behalf of or in trust for himself.

Hypothecation is a charge made on movable property in favour of a secured creditor without delivery or possession. Charge is created only on movable goods like stocks, machinery and vehicles. The borrower binds himself to give the possession of the goods to the banker, whenever the latter desires. It is a convenient device in the circumstances in which the transfer of possession is either inconvenient or impracticable such as buses and taxies, which are given as security by taxi operators, but are used by them. The agreement is entered into through a deed of hypothecation.

The bank cannot take possession of goods without the consent of the borrower, but after taking possession, the banker is free to exercise the right of a pledgee, and sell the assets without intervention of the court.

5.4.4 Assignment

Assignment of a contract means transfer of contractual rights and liabilities to a third party. The transferor or borrower is called the **assignor**, and the transferee or banker is called the **assignee**. The borrower can assign any of his rights, properties or debts to the banker as security for a loan. These might be existing or future. Generally the 'actionable claims' are assigned by the borrower. An actionable claim is a claim to any debt, other than a debt secured by mortgage of immovable property, or by hypothecation or pledge of movable property, or to any interest in movable property not in the possession, either actual or constructive, of the claimant which the civil court recognizes as affording ground of relief, whether such debt or beneficial interest be existent, accruing, conditional and contingent. Usually the borrower may assign books debts, money due from government or semi-government organizations or life insurance policies.

Although notice of assignment of the debtor is not required under law (section 130 of Transfer of Property Act, 1881), nevertheless it is in the interest of the assignee to give notice to the debtor because in the absence of the notice, the assignee is bound by any payments which the debtor might make to the assignor in ignorance of the assignment. For example, if the borrower assigns his life insurance policy in favour of his banker as security for a loan, the bank should give a notice to the Life Insurance Corporation (LIC), otherwise if any payment is made by the LIC to the borrower, the banker will not be able to claim it.

Assignment may be legal or equitable. A legal assignment is effected through an instrument in writing signed by the assignor. The assignor too informs the debtor in writing about the assignment, the assignee's name and address. The assignee also serves a notice on the debtor of the assignor, and seeks confirmation of assigned balance. If the above conditions are not fulfilled, i.e., assignment is not done in writing, or notice of assignment is not given to debtor, then such assignment is called **equitable assignment**.

5.4.5 Mortgage

When a customer secures an advance on the security of specific immovable property the charge created thereon is called a **mortgage**. Section 58 of the Transfer of Property Act, 1882, defines a mortgage as, *The transfer of an interest in a specific immovable property for the purpose of securing the payment of money advanced or to be advanced by way of loan, an existing or future debt, or the performance of an engagement which may give rise to pecuniary liability.* The instrument through which it is affected is called a **mortgage deed**, the customer (transferor) is called the **mortgagor** and the bank (transferee) is called the **mortgagee**. The payment so secured which includes both the principal money and the interest thereon is called the **mortgage money**.

Section 58 of the Transfer of Property Act, recognizes six types of mortgagers which are discussed hereinafter.

Simple mortgage: In case of simple mortgage, the mortgagor does not give possession of property, but binds himself personally to pay the mortgage money. He agrees expressly or impliedly that in case he fails to make the payment according to the contract, then the mortgagee shall have right to cause the mortgage property to be sold and proceeds of sale to be applied, as far as may be necessary, in payment of the mortgage money. The mortgagee himself cannot sell the property, but has to seek intervention of the court.

Mortgage by conditional sale: Under this form of mortgage the mortgager ostensibly (on the face of it) sells the mortgaged property with any one of the following conditions:

(i) on default of payment of mortgage money, the sale shall become absolute.

(ii) on payment being made on a certain date, the sale shall become void.

(iii) when the payment is made, the buyer shall transfer the property to the seller.

Usufructuary mortgage: Unlike the simple mortgage which is non-possessory, in case of usufructuary mortgage, the mortgagor delivers possession of the mortgaged property. The mortgagee is also entitled to receive rents and profits accruing from the property and appropriate the same in lieu of interest or in payment of mortgaged money or both. When the debt is so discharged or repaid, the mortgagor is entitled to recover possession of his property. There is no personal liability on the mortgagor.

English mortgage: In case of English mortgage, there is transfer of ownership on the condition that the mortgagee will re-transfer the same on the payment of mortgage money. Further, the mortgagor personally undertakes to repay the mortgaged money. In case of default, the mortgagee has the right to sell the property without seeking permission of the court in the special circumstances mentioned in section 69 of the Transfer of Property Act.

Mortgage by deposit of title deeds (equitable mortgage): This mortgage is affected by deposits of title deeds of the property by the debtor in favour of the creditor to create a security thereon. This type of mortgage is called **equitable mortgage** in English law. In India, it is restricted to the cities of Delhi, Mumbai, Kolkata and Chennai or any other town which the concerned state government may notify in the official gazette in this behalf. No registration is necessary and delivery can be either actual or constructive. There is personal liability of the mortgagor to pay, and the mortgagee can sell the property with the sanction of the court if the mortgaged money is not repaid.

Anomalous mortgage: A mortgage which is not simple mortgage, mortgage by conditional sale, usufructuary mortgage, English mortgage and mortgage by deposit of title deeds (equitable mortgage) is called an **anomalous mortgage**. If the terms of the mortgage do not strictly adhere to any of the above five types, e.g., in case of simple mortgage if the mortgagee is allowed to use the mortgage property, then it will not be called simple or usufructuary but an anomalous mortgage. Under this the rights and liabilities of the parties are determined by the terms agreed upon in the mortgage deed, and in the absence of such a deed by the local usage.

5.4.6 Legal Mortgage vs. Equitable Mortgage

From the point of view of transfer of title to the mortgaged property, a mortgage may either be a legal mortgage or an equitable mortgage.

Legal mortgage: Legal mortgage can be enforced only if the mortgage money is ₹100 or more. It is affected by transfer of legal title to the mortgage property by the mortgagor in favour of the mortgagee. All this involves expenses in the form of stamp duty and registration charges. At the time of repayment of mortgaged money, the property is retransferred to the mortgagor.

Equitable mortgage: In case of equitable mortgage, only documents of title are transferred in favour of the mortgagee and not the legal title. No registration is necessary and no stamp duty or registration charges have to be paid. Through the memorandum of deposit, the mortgagor undertakes to execute a legal mortgage in case of default in payment within the stipulated time. The reputation of the mortgagor is not affected, since in absence of registration no one comes to know about the mortgage. However, this can prove risky also if through negligence or fraud, another party is induced to advance money on the security of the mortgaged property as the subsequent mortgagee will have priority over the first.

KEY TERMS

Bailment Delivery of goods from one party (bailor) to another (bailee) to be returned or otherwise disposed of after the accomplishment of the purpose.

Cardinal principles The most important principles on which decisions depend.

Floating charge Charge created on assets which undergo change in quantity and value (e.g. stock of goods).

Judicious Applying sound judgment and being wise and careful while taking decisions.

REVIEW QUESTIONS

5.1 Explain the cardinal principles a banker should follow while granting loans and advances to a customer.

5.2 Describe the various ways in which a commercial bank renders financial assistance to borrowers.

5.3 Discuss the importance of secured advances advances and describe the various types of securities used for granting loans by a bank.

5.4 What are the various types of charges that can be created on:

(i) goods and securities

(ii) movable properties

5.5 Compare the relative advantages and drawbacks of equitable and legal mortgage.

6

Priority Sector Lending

Learning Objectives

After going through this chapter we will be able to:

- Understand the rationale of priority sector lending.
- Identify bank targets for priority sector lending.
- Describe various segments of priority sector.

Bank finance plays a pivotal role in the economic development of a region. Priority Sector Lending (PSL) is used as a development tool for economic upliftment of the poorer and weaker sections of the society as opposed to focus on the financial sector only. PSL is an important policy through which the RBI stipulates banks to provide a specified portion of bank lending to few specified sectors. PSL norms are applicable to every commercial bank including Regional Rural Banks (RRBs), Small Finance Banks (SFBs), Local Area Banks (LABs), Primary Urban Co-operative Bank (UCB) and foreign banks.

Directed credit policy has been an important part of the Indian banking sector. It started in 1966, but was defined as such in the RBI report in 1972. Under this policy stipulated amounts have to be provided by commercial banks as loans to the priority sector which include those areas of economic activity which are socially desirable, but had not been adequately financed or had been wholly neglected by the commercial banks earlier. The objective of priority sector programme is to ensure that there is adequate flow of credit to strengthen the vulnerable sector of the economy which had hitherto been neglected because of low profitability.

The categories of priority sector are as follows

(i) Agriculture
(ii) Micro, Small and Medium Enterprises
(iii) Export Credit (not applicable to RRBs and LABs)
(iv) Education
(v) Housing
(vi) Social Infrastructure
(vii) Renewable Energy
(viii) Others (including SHG/JLGs, construction of toilets, setting up of schools, drinking water and sanitation facilities, startups, health infrastructure and renewable energy) (ET September 4, 2020).

6.1 RATIONALE OF PRIORITY SECTOR

Priority sector lending is an important role given by the RBI to the banks for providing a specified portion of the bank lending to few specified sectors. These sectors are considered as important for development of the basic needs of the country by the government of India and the RBI and they have to be given priority over other sectors for provision of timely and adequate credit. Though India has one of the oldest banking sectors in the world yet the growth of the sector has been very lopsided. Prior to the formation of the State Bank of India in 1955, bank capital was in the hands of a few private entrepreneurs. As a result, vast sections of the Indian population were unable to consume banking services. At that time, more than 70 per cent people lived in the rural areas. For all their needs whether for land, housing, seeds, fertilizers, cattle, tubewells, and so on, they were heavily dependent on moneylenders and powerful Zamindars. Needless to say they were badly exploited and could not get out of their clutches. So much so that many a times, their children continued to repay their parents' debts. It was in this background that the State Bank of India was formed, which set up more than 400 branches in rural areas. This was followed by nationalization of 14 banks in 1969 and social control over banks was introduced. It was hoped that the hitherto neglected sectors like agriculture, small-scale industries, small entrepreneurs, artisans, etc. would be able to access bank finance. Apart from the quantum of bank credit, its deployment, composition and direction are equally important in the realization of the country's various macro-economic goals. The banking system in India works under the constraints that go with social control and public ownership. Not only the public sector banks, but also the private sector and foreign banks are required to meet targets in respect of sectoral deployment of credit, regional distribution of branches and regional credit deposit ratios. All banks, in general, have to pay attention to balance profitability with liquidity, but the public sector banks which incidentally perform nearly 90 per cent of total banking in India, have to be especially cautious in balancing the principle of profit maximization with those of social welfare, social justice and promotion of regional balance in development.

At the meeting of the National Credit Council held in July 1968, it was emphasized that the commercial banks should increase their involvement in the financing of priority sectors. No direction of the sector was formalized till 1972, when certain guidelines were provided by RBI indicating the scope of the items to be included in this sector. Priority sector lending means the priority in disbursement of loans over other lending sectors, as decided by the Central Government. Banks have been adhering to the RBI guidelines without insisting on adequate security and providing credit at concessional rates of interest. The bank's staff also help the borrower in completing the application form wherever necessary and see to its fast disposal. Prior to nationalization of commercial banks, these banks were mostly urban based and profit oriented, and generally not responsive to the needs of development and growth. With the PSL guidelines it was hoped that there will be increased penetration of credit to credit deficient areas, increased lending to small and marginal farmers and weaker sections, to poor people for housing, poor students for education and a boost to renewable energy, health and infrastructure.

6.1.1 Targets

Initially, no specific targets were fixed in respect of priority sector lending, but in November 1974, banks were advised to raise the shares of these sectors in their aggregate advances to the level of 33.3 per cent by March 1979. This was later raised to 40 per cent in March 1983. Since then, there have been several changes in the scope of priority sector lending and targets and sub-targets applicable to various bank groups. PSL directions last revised in September 2020, require domestic and foreign banks to achieve a credit disbursement target of 40% of lending book while regional rural banks and small finance banks need to attain 75%. Reserve Bank has prescribed the targets for lending to the priority sectors by commercial banks as follows.

Public and private sector banks:

Overall priority sector target of net bank credit (NBC) 40 per cent, of which,

Agricultural advances	18 per cent
Advances to weaker sections	10 per cent

Foreign banks operating in India:

Overall priority sector target of net bank credit (NBC) 32 per cent, of which,

Advances to small scale sector (SSI)	10 per cent
Export credit	12 per cent

Domestic scheduled commercial bank having a short fall in priority sector lending are required to make contribution to the Rural Infrastructure Development Fund (RIDF) established in NABARD. However, banks are urged to take appropriate steps to increase the flow of credit to priority sector agricultural and weaker section so as to achieve stipulated targets. Reserve Bank has also stipulated that in the case of foreign banks, if there is a shortfall in priority sector lending from the above targets and sub-targets, the concerned bank should deposit an amount equivalent to the shortfall with the Small Industries Development Bank of India at an interest rate of 8 per cent per annum.

In addition to the above overall limits, the RBI sets sub-limits for certain sub-sectors within the priority sector, i.e., it has been further stipulated that within the agriculture sector, 10 per cent of NBC has to be given to weaker sections. Weaker sections include small and marginal farmers (land-holdings up to 5 acres), landless labourers, tenant farmers, share croppers, artisans, village and cottage industries, scheduled castes, scheduled tribes, beneficiaries of SGSY and SJSRY as well as to SHGs. There was no SSI overall target for Indian banks, but within the SSI group, 40 per cent credit should be given to those SSIs with investment in plant and machinery upto ₹5 lakh, 20 per cent to those with investment between ₹5 lakh to ₹25 lakh and 40 per cent to those with investment more than ₹25 lakh.

6.2 DIFFERENT SEGMENTS OF PRIORITY SECTOR ADVANCES

6.2.1 Agriculture

Agriculture finance includes: Farm Credit, Agriculture Infrastructure and Ancillary Activities. It can be short-term, medium-term or long-term. Agriculture finance can be Direct or Indirect. **Direct Finance** is any finance which is given directly to the farmers for their agricultural and allied activities is called direct finance, e.g. crops, purchase of agricultural implements, etc. **Indirect Finance** is that which is given to borrowers who are not directly engaged in agriculture but assist those who are, e.g. dealers of fertilizers, pesticides agricultural tools, etc.

Direct finance: It is given in the form of

Crop loans. Upto ₹5,000, short-term crop loans are given to farmers against pledge/hypothecation of the agricultural produce for a period not exceeding 3 months.

Development loans. Medium and long-term loans are provided for financing production and development needs. Development loans are given for

- Purchase of agricultural implements and machinery including transport equipments, sugar cane crushers, thresher machines, tractors, trailers, jeeps, bullock-carts, etc.

- Development of irrigation potential for construction of tube wells, tanks, boring and electrification of wells, construction of lift irrigation, purchase of generator sets, and so on
- Reclamation and land development schemes for levelling of land terracing and wasteland development
- Construction of farm buildings and structures including bullock-sheds, tractor and truck-sheds and farm stores
- Construction and running of storage facilities like warehouses, godowns, silos, cold storages, etc.
- Production and processing of hybrid seeds of crops
- Payment of irrigation charges for hired water from wells, tube wells and canals
- Other types of direct finance to farmers, e.g., short-term loans to non-traditional plantations, horticulture and allied activities such as dairying, fishery, piggery, poultry and bee-keeping

Medium and long-term loans are given for the development of plantations, horticulture, forestry, fisheries, poultry and wasteland.

Indirect finance: It is given in the form of

- Credit for financing the distribution of fertilizers, pesticides, seeds, etc.
- Loans to electricity boards for reimbursing the expenditure incurred for low tension connections
- Finance for hire purchase schemes for distribution of agricultural machinery and implements
- Loans for construction and running of storage facilities
- Advances for maintaining tractors, bulldozers, and well-boring equipment
- Loans to cooperative marketing societies and cooperative banks
- Loans to agro-industries corporations

6.2.2 Micro, Small and Medium Enterprises (MSMEs)

The Micro, Small and Medium sector is considered the backbone of the Indian economy. At present there are more than 6.33 crores MSMEs in India that account for around 27% of GDP, contribute around 40% to exports and provide employment to more than 11 million people. The definition of this sector has undergone numerous changes since 2006 when the Micro, Small and Medium Enterprise (MSME) Act was introduced. Major changes introduced in their definition on 13.5.2020 to be realistic in time and to establish an objective system of classification and to provide ease of doing business. MSMEs are now classified on the basis of the composite criteria of investment in plant and machinery and turnover. The difference between manufacturing and service units has been done away with. Exports will not be counted in terms of turnover for any enterprise whether Micro, Small or Medium. The definition of Medium enterprise was again changed on 1.7.20. The current criteria for MSMEs is as under

Industry	Investment in Plant & Machinery	Turnover
Micro	less than ₹1 crore	less than ₹5 crore
Small	less than ₹10 crore	less than ₹50 crore
Medium	less than ₹50 crore	less than ₹250 crore

The target for PSL for the MSME sector is 7.5% of ANBC or credit equivalent amount of off-balance sheet exposure which ever is higher. The classification of retail and wholesale trade under MSME targets can be of help to banks for meeting their PSL targets.

6.2.3 Small Road and Water Transport Operators (SRWTO)

Advances to such operators are given, provided they do not own more than 10 vehicles including the one proposed to be financed. Advances are also given to NBFCs for lending to truck operators and SRWTOs other than truck operators satisfying the eligibility criteria.

6.2.4 Retail Traders

Retail traders dealing in essential commodities like fair price shops and consumer cooperative stores as well as private retail traders with credit limits not exceeding ₹5 lakh are eligible for priority sector lending.

6.2.5 Professionals and Self-employed Persons

Loans to professionals and self-employed persons include loans for the purpose of purchasing equipment, repairing or renovating existing equipment, acquiring and repairing business premises, purchasing tools and/or for working capital requirements to medical practitioners including dentists, chartered accountants, cost accountants, practising company secretaries, lawyers or solicitors, engineers, architects, surveyors, construction contractors or management consultants accredited journalists and cameramen.

6.2.6 State Sponsored Organizations for Scheduled Castes/ Scheduled Tribes

These include advances sanctioned to state sponsored organizations for scheduled castes/scheduled tribes for the specific purpose of purchase and supply of inputs to the marketing of outputs of the beneficiaries of these organizations.

6.2.7 Education

Educational loans should include only those loans and advances which are granted to individuals for the educational purposes including vocational courses, and not those granted to institutions. It will include all advances granted by banks under special schemes, if any, introduced for the purpose. The amount of loans that can be granted are up to ₹20 lakh. The earlier limit was ₹10 lakh. Loans currently classified as PSL will continue till maturity.

6.2.8 Housing

Housing finance includes both direct as well as indirect finance.

Direct finance includes advances made to all categories of borrowers for housing in rural and urban areas. The limit for such advance was raised from ₹3 lakh to ₹5 lakh in 1997.

Indirect finance includes assistance given to any governmental agency for the purpose of constructing houses exclusively for the benefit of scheduled castes/tribes and low income groups, where the loan component does not exceed ₹2 lakh per unit. It also includes assistance to any governmental agency for slum clearance and rehabilitation of slum dwellers. As on June 2021 housing loans eligible for PSL are (i) Loans to individuals up to ₹35 lakh in metropolitan centres (with population of ten lakh and above) and up to ₹25 lakh in other centres, for purchase/ construction of a dwelling unit per family, provided the overall cost does not exceed ₹45 lakh and 30 lakh respectively. Loans for repairs to damaged houses will not exceed 10 lakh and 6 lakh respectively for metropolitan and other centres. However housing loans to banks own employees will not be eligible for classification under the priority sector.

6.2.9 Consumption Loans

Pure consumption loans are provided for the welfare of the weaker sections. The total amount of such loans should not exceed ₹1,000 per family per year.

6.2.10 Funds Provided to RRBs

The entire amount of the refinance provided by sponsor banks to their sponsored RRBs for the purpose of on-lending, will be treated as priority sector lending of the sponsor banks—50 per cent of funds may be treated as indirect agricultural lending and 40 per cent of the funds shall be treated as advances to weaker sections.

6.2.11 Loans to Self-help Groups (SHGs)/NGOs/Micro-credit

Loans not exceeding ₹1 lakh, provided directly by banks to individuals or individual members of SHGs/JLG provided that the borrowers income does not exceed ₹1 lakh in rural areas and 1.6 lakh in others. Loans not exceeding ₹2 lakhs provided directly to SHGs/JLG for activities other than agriculture or MSMEs, e.g. for building toilets. They will be reckoned as priority sector lending. Such loans shall be included as part of bank's lending to weaker sections.

6.2.12 Food and Agro-based Processing Sector

As per RBI's Master Directions dated 4.9.2020, all credit to food and agro-based processing sector should be included under the priority sector. A special fund of ₹2000 crore has been set up in NABARD to provide credit at affordable rates to boost this sector covering individual entrepreneurs, cooperatives, Farmer Producer Organizations, corporates, joint ventures, etc.

New norms for priority sector lending: RBI has revamped norms for priority sector loans as under (ET 5.9.20):

6.2.13 Health and Infrastructure Sectors

The RBI has doubled it's limit for health and infrastructure sector to ₹10 crore.

6.2.14 Renewable Energy

Clean energy is the need of the hour so it is not at all surprising that this area is receiving a lot of attention. Loans up to ₹30 crores granted for renewable energy projects will now be eligible under priority sector. Individual households can get loans up to ₹10 lakh for renewable energy.

6.2.15 Startups

According to the new norms Startups (as defined by the industry ministry) can qualify as PSL for loans up to ₹50 crores. This will reduce their cost of capital by allowing them better access to bank credit.

Banks can also give loans up to ₹5 crores for setting up schools, drinking water and sanitation facilities as post-covid these have emerged as focus areas.

It is pertinent to mention that under the mixed economy system of our country, banks have been subjected to a lot of social control. As a result, they sometimes had to sacrifice principles of profit maximization for those of social responsibilities. Before liberalization, this did not pose major problems. As for decades, banks were isolated from the competition, and the profitability was not the primary criterion on which they functioned. All this translated into low efficiency and productivity, overstaffing and union pressure. Banking regulations on liquidity, rate of interest to be charged and norms for priority sector lending began to put a heavy strain on the banking system, which began to reel under bad debts, defaults and mounting NPAs.

While it is desirable that sectors wherein the roots of economic development lie should get precedence over other sectors, in other words, the priority sectors should not be neglected, yet lending to these sectors should not be allowed to degenerate into irresponsible lending. At the time of evaluation of a loan proposal relating to the priority sector, the principles of underlying social responsibility should receive prominence, but it is imperative that equal attention should also be paid to commercial principles of viability, efficiency and profitability.

KEY TERMS

Deployment Spread of funds to reach a broader spectrum of people.

Micro-credit Provision of credit of very small amounts to poor people in rural, semi-urban and urban areas.

Self-help groups (SHGs) Small groups of rural poor who come together for mutual benefits.

Venture capital Capital for financing proposals which involve new products and technology which are risky, but have a potential of high returns.

REVIEW QUESTIONS

6.1 Write a short note on the rationale of priority sector lending.

6.2 Explain the targets set for public sector banks for priority sector lending. How are these different from similar targets of foreign banks?

6.3 "There is a dire need of balancing principles of social lending with those of sound lending". Comment on the above statement in view of the targets prescribed by RBI for priority sector lending by the commercial banks.

6.4 Enumerate the different sectors under priority sector. Which new sectors have been added recently?

7

Export Credit

Learning Objectives

After going through this chapter we will be able to:

- Understand the meaning of export credit.
- Know the difference between export and import finance.
- Explain various types of export credit.
- Differentiate between pre-shipment/packaging credit and post-shipment finance.
- Delineate the role of ECGC.
- Describe the functions of EXIM bank.

Exports have a most crucial role to play in the growth and development of any economy. To put India's exports on a higher growth trajectory, there can be little doubt that exports will remain a priority sector for a long time. Banks should, therefore, treat exports as a preferred sector in dispensation of credit both from the point of view of availability as well as cost.

7.1 EXPORT AND IMPORT FINANCE

Exports involve movement of goods and services across national boundaries and matching settlements in various currencies. Export finance is different from the domestic financing of trade in a number of ways as it is subjected to the existence of both commercial risks as well as country risks.

7.1.1 Commercial Risks

Though commercial risks like insolvency of buyer, failure of buyer to accept goods or to make payment in specified time, etc. exist for both, yet risks get compounded in case of foreign trade because of various reasons. The operating cycle also becomes longer due to the long time taken for transit of goods to reach the buyer, hence the need for bill discounting becomes more important. The geographic distances involved make it difficult to scrutinize the integrity of buyer or supplier closely. Problems are also posed because of difficulties in communication due to different languages and cultural norms. Differen[t] currencies pose risks of exchange rate fluctuations. A cursory understanding of the different legal systems, time zones, and so on is also advisable.

7.1.2 Country Risks

Apart from the above risks, there are certain other country risks which exist in foreign trade. Problems can arise because of outbreak of war, a revolution, civil war or coup. A change in government policy regarding import or export or the use of trade routes can also pose problems. For example, closure of the Suez Canal to international traffic from 1967 to 1975 during the Arab–Israeli war, then ships between Europe and India had to take a very lengthy route via the Cape of Good Hope in Africa. Poltical disturbances have been witnessed by many countries in the middle east, including Syria, Libya, Egypt, and Yemen. The Covid-19 Pandemic and the current Ukraine–Russia conflict and subsequent NATO sanctions have introduced a new element of uncertainty in the global outlook. The world is under severe inflationary pressure and global recession seems imminent.

In view of the critical importance of exports for a developing country and the nature of foreign trade, export trade is regulated by the Directorate General of Foreign Trade (DGFT) under the Ministry of Commerce and Industry, which announces the policies and procedures required to be followed for exports from India. These procedures are articulated in the Foreign Trade Development and Regulation Act, Exim Policy Handbook. The movement of currency is regulated by Reserve Bank (through Foreign Exchange Issue Regulations, Exchange Control Manual). There is also a negative list of exported goods and services under the category of prohibited items, canalized items and restricted items.

7.2 RBI MEASURES TO PROMOTE EXPORT CREDIT

RBI has undertaken several measures to ensure timely and hassle free flow of credit to the export sector. RBI has directed commercial banks to ensure free flow of credit to exporters at concessional rates. It has also directed that no worthwhile export proposal should suffer from want of credit. In fact, an application for export credit cannot be rejected by a competent authority of the bank without the approval of the next higher authority. They also have to be disposed off within the prescribed time. Banks are free to fix lower interest rates for exporters on the basis of their actual cost of funds, operating expenses and creditworthiness of the borrower as the RBI sets the ceiling under which the banks have the flexibility to fix any interest rate. The RBI has also drawn up a Gold Card Scheme with a view to further simplifying access to bank credit by exporters, especially small and medium exporters and making it borrower friendly in terms of procedure and credit terms. This scheme would not be applicable to those exporters who are blacklisted by the Export Credit Guarantee Corporation or included in the Reserve Bank defaulter's list.

Export finance can be needed even before the execution of the order for purchases, manufacturing, etc. and again after sending the goods, but before realization of payments to avoid a liquidity crunch. Depending on the stage of need, export finance is broadly classified as pre-shipment or packing credit and post-shipment finance.

7.3 PRE-SHIPMENT OR PACKING CREDIT

As the name suggests, pre-shipment or packing credit implies the financial assistance provided to exporters prior to shipment of goods. Export credit scheme to finance exporters was introduced in 1967 with the object of providing working capital finance to exporters at internationally competitive interest rates to facilitate exports. Banks are permitted to decide appropriate interest rates based on the risk perception, the borrower's credit worthiness and market practices.

Packing credit (PC) is a short-term working capital finance provided to an exporter to enable him to process/manufacture goods and arrange for transportation, warehousing and shipment of finished goods. It is usually extended as PC either in rupees or in foreign currency. It is essentially working capital made available for financing/purchasing/processing/manufacturing/transporting/warehousing of goods meant for export. All costs prior to shipment are eligible for being financed under packing credit. This is given on the basis of confirmed and irrevocable order or any other evidence including letter of credit, for the export of goods from India. It is also given as advance against duty drawback as well as cheques/drafts received as an advanced payment or against incentives receivable from the governments.

7.3.1 Guidelines for the Grant of Pre-shipment or Packing Credit

The following factors are considered by banks for disbursal of export credit:

1. The viability of proposal, the integrity of the borrower and the capacity of the exporter to execute the order must be carefully examined.
2. The export contract/purchase order/letter of credit should be valid, operative and contain all essential details. It should also be devoid of ambiguities.
3. The quantum of finance has to be need-based and worked out against specified order/orders. Generally, the value of the advance so granted does not exceed FOB value of the goods.
4. The exporters should have complied with the exchange control regulations, for example, the exporter should have a valid importer-exporter code number allocated by Director General of Foreign Trade, Ministry of Commerce.
5. The commodity to be exported should be allowed for export and where necessary the applicant should have licence, quota, export endorsement, etc.
6. Exporter should not be in the caution list of RBI or the selected approval list of ECGC.
7. Separate accounts should be opened for each packing credit except when running account facility is allowed.
8. Packing credit advances are generally granted on secured basis only, in some exceptional cases a clear packing credit may be advanced at the initial stage, but once the goods are acquired by the exporter, the banks usually convert the clean advance into hypothecation/ pledge.

The export finance is normally available at a lower rate of interest as compared to the finance for domestic activity. The Reserve Bank of India has instructed banks to finance exporters in foreign currency or provide finance in rupees. Interest in export finance is charged in the following manner:

Rate of interest: In case of rupee finance, at a rate of interest not exceeding 2.5 per cent less than PLR, and in case of foreign currency finance, at a rate of interest not exceeding 50 basis points (0.5 per cent) over LIBOR (rates of interest prevailing in international markets).

Period of finance: Pre-shipment finance is granted to an exporter normally for 180 days. In case the bank approves, it can be extended for another 90 days with the prior approval of RBI.

Running account facility: Running account facility means that the first debit in the account can be set-off by the first credit with the condition that no debit entry is outstanding for more than the stipulated period.

With effect from 14-3-1992, the banks may give packing credit without insisting on the prior submission of an export order of the letter of credit under the running account facility subject to the following conditions:

- This facility may be granted by the bank if it is satisfied that the need for such facility by the exporter is genuine.
- It may be extended only to those exporters whose track record has been good.
- Where such facility has been given, letter of credit of conformed orders should be produced within a reasonable period of time.

7.4 POST-SHIPMENT FINANCE

Post-shipment finance facility is granted to bridge the gap between the shipment of goods and the realization of proceeds. This is because once the goods are exported; there is some time gap in getting the proceeds of the bill. The time gap depends on many factors like transit period, any credit extended by the exporter (bills on usance basis), etc. As a result the exporter's funds are blocked, and this may result in a liquidity crunch. Banks grant financial support by extending credit generally in the form of purchase/discount, negotiation of bills under L/C, advance against export bills sent on collection, etc. The documents required for this facility include export bills payable and demand/usance export bills, claims for duty drawback, freight differential claims, etc.

7.4.1 Period Within which Export Value of Goods is to be Realized

The export value should be repatriated to India within six months from the date of export in normal circumstances, and within 15 months in case of goods exported to a warehouse established outside India. In certain cases, e.g., when goods are exported from a special economic zone, the amount can be realized within 12 months.

7.4.2 Precautions to be Taken by the Bank in Case of Post-shipment Finance

1. The export documents should be submitted within the period of 21 days, from the date of export unless a prior approval of Reserve Bank has been obtained.
2. These documents, e.g., invoice, packing list, weight list, insurance certificate/policy certificate or original bills of lading/AWB should not be inconsistent with each other.
3. The insurance policy/certificate should be adequate and properly signed, dated and stamped.

4. Bill of lading/AWB should also be properly signed, dated and stamped and in case of alterations, should be properly authenticated.
5. There should be no discrepancy in the weight mentioned in the invoice and the weight listed in other documents.
6. The drafts/bills of exchange should be complete and correct in all respect.

7.5 EXPORT IMPORT BANK OF INDIA (EXIM BANK)

The EXIM bank was set up on January 1, 1982 as the apex institution providing finance and refinance in connection with the foreign trade of the country. It took over the operations of the international finance wing of the IDBI. The objectives of this bank are clearly set out as, *granting loans and advances in India solely or jointly with commercial banks* and *other financial bodies to persons exporting or importing or intending to export from India, goods and services including export of turnkey projects, joint ventures and civil construction services*. It's other objectives include improving of bilateral trade relations with other countries, eliminating payment risks for importers, streamlined processing and quick turnaround. EXIM's offices are spread across India and in select locations of the world. EXIM became a self-sustaining, self-funding agency in 2007, (though the loans remain backed by the government). Recently the bank has raised $1 billion through the sale of 10 year bonds to global investors (ET 7.1.20).

7.5.1 Functions of EXIM Bank

1. Financing of exports and imports of goods and services not only into India but also in third countries.
2. Provision of financial assistance for exports/imports of machinery and equipment on lease basis.
3. Extension of financial help for facilitating joint ventures.
4. Granting lines of credit (LOCs). LOC is an effective market tool as well as a means of diversification for Indian exports. It is a risk free, non-recourse export option available to Indian exporters for export promotion. LOC helps them to enter new geographies or expand their business in existing export markets without any payment risks from overseas importers. LOCs are granted to governments, financial institutions and other organizations in foreign countries to enable persons in those countries to import from India, goods including turnkey projects, services including consultancy services. 37 LOCs have been extended to five neighbourhood countries—Bangladesh, Maldives, Myanmar, Nepal and Sri Lanka worth $14.27 billion covering 162 projects across sectors like roads, railways, power, telecom, ports and shipping, health, education and aviation. Another $14.07 worth of LOCs have been extended to countries in Africa (TOI 25.7.22).

5. Issuing bid bonds or guarantees and other similar facilities in India or abroad solely or jointly with commercial banks on behalf of persons exporting or intending to export from India.

7.5.2 Assistance Provided by EXIM Bank

There are two types of assistance provided by the EXIM bank, namely, funded and non-funded.

Funded assistance: Funded assistance involves financial outflow. It is provided to Indian exporters to enable them to operate in international markets. It includes provisions of medium term credit to exporters, investment finance for equity participation in joint ventures abroad, technology and consultancy services as well as pre-shipment finance for export of capital goods. Under this scheme, loans are also provided to foreign governments, companies and financial institutions for purchase of capital goods and services from India, as well as re-lending facilities for overseas banks to enable them to provide term finance for import of goods from India. Loans for export bills rediscounting and refinance of export credit are also provided to Indian banks.

Non-funded assistance: Non-funded operations include various types of guarantees in association with Indian commercial banks, on behalf of Indian exporters/contractors in favour of their overseas counterparts. These guarantees are given to Indian project exporters to secure and facilitate execution of export contracts in the form of bid bonds, advance payments and performance guarantees and guarantees for raising finance abroad.

7.6 EXPORT CREDIT GUARANTEE CORPORATION OF INDIA (ECGC)

Is essentially an export promotion organization. It started as the export risk insurance corporation (ERIC) in 1957 which was transformed into export credit and guarantee corporation limited (ECGC) in 1964. The corporation's name was changed to the present export credit guarantee corporation of India (ECGC) in 1983. It is wholly owned company of the government of India which is administered on commercial lines and works on a *no profit, no loss* basis. It is the fifth largest credit insurer of the world in terms of coverage of national exports. It is managed by a Board of Directors comprising representatives of government, Reserve Bank of India, the banking sector and insurance and exporting firms. It was set up with the twin objectives of providing export credit insurance and export credit guarantees, so that the exporter is offered financial protection, and also that his financial standing vis-à-vis his bank is strengthened.

The ECGC provides a range of credit risk insurance covers to exporters against loss in export of goods and services. It also provides overseas investment insurance to Indian companies investing in joint ventures abroad in the form of equity or loan. Insurance protection against payments risk is also granted to exporters. Export credit insurance is designed to protect exporters from the consequences of political and commercial payment risks, and to enable them to expand their overseas business without fear of loss. As already observed, political risks include outbreaks of war/civil war, insurgency, change in government policy, such as ban on certain imports, devaluation of currency, which can result in blockages and delay of delivery of the exports. Commercial risks include bankruptcy and protracted default of buyers. The degree of risk involved in export business is supposed to be higher than that in the domestic market. ECGC helps by providing information regarding different countries with it's own ratings. It also provides guidance for activities related to exports and information regarding credit worthiness of overseas buyers.

However, ECGC's commission rates are lower than those charged by the banks and insurance companies. In fact the rates of premium charged by ECGC are the lowest in the world and vary between 4–7%. They are dependent on the grades on which countries have been classified on basis of commercial and political risks.

Export credit guarantee: These are financial guarantees issued to banks to cover their advances to exporters both at the pre-shipment and post-shipment stages. Since the banks get protection against losses, they are encouraged to make advances to the exporters. Financial guarantees include packing credit guarantee, post-shipment export guarantee, export finance guarantee and export production finance guarantee. The non-financial guarantees are export performance guarantee, transfer guarantee and investment insurance guarantee.

The policies issued by ECGC can be broadly classified into four groups, viz., (i) standard policy, (ii) specific policies, (iii) financial guarantees, and (iv) special schemes.

1. *Standard policy:* It is ideally suited to cover risks in respect of goods exported on short-term (i.e., less than or equal to 180 days) credit. It covers both commercial and political risks from the date of shipment.
2. *Specific policies:* These cover risks arising from deferred terms of payments, including construction work and turnkey project as well as other services rendered outside India.
3. *Financial guarantees:* The guarantees cover risks to banks when they extend financial support at pre-shipment and post-shipment stages.
4. *Special schemes:*
    - Transfer guarantees protect banks that add confirmation of LC opened by the foreign bank.

- Insurance cover for buyer's credit.
- Exchange fluctuation risk insurance.

ECGC also has an overseas investment risk insurance to protect Indian overseas investment as well as dividends and interest available thereon. Investment can be either in the form of cash or export of capital goods and services. However, it does not cover risks arising out of disputes in respect of inferior quality of goods or those arising out of exchange rate fluctuations.

KEY TERMS

Bill discounting Receiving payment on a bill of exchange prior to its maturity by surrendering the bill for face value less applicable interest for the time remaining to maturity.

Bill of lading A document which represents ownership of goods in transit.

Devaluation The reduction, by the authorities, in the exchange value of a country's currency in terms of other currencies as a matter of policy.

FOB (Freight on Board or Free on Board) A shipment term to indicate whether it is the seller or buyer who is liable for goods that are damaged or destroyed during shipping, e.g. FOB, origin means it is the buyer who is liable.

LIBOR (London Interbank Offered Rate) It is a global benchmark interest rate at which banks lend to and borrow from one another in the interbank market. It is usually used for pricing of interest rate swaps, currency rate swaps as well as mortgages.

Turnkey Project It is a delivery method under which a contractor works with a project owner under a single contract to complete all stages of a project from detail engineering through construction.

REVIEW QUESTIONS

7.1 Explain the nature of export finance.

7.2 Highlight the precautions that a banker must take while extending pre-shipment credit.

7.3 Examine the role of EXIM bank in boosting India's foreign trade.

7.4 Write short notes on
 (i) Risks in export finance
 (ii) Running Account facility
 (iii) Lines of credit (LOCs)

7.5 Discuss the objectives for which the Export Credit Guarantee Corporation has been established.

8

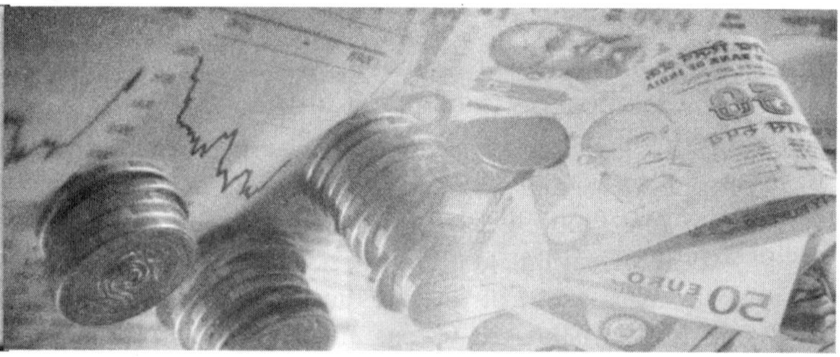

Annual Report and Balance Sheet of a Bank

Learning Objectives

After going through this chapter we will be able to:

- Understand the importance and contents of an annual report.
- Learn about bank audit.
- Know about the balance sheet of a commercial bank.
- Describe the liabilities and assets of a bank.

The business of banking is like other businesses, i.e., to earn profit. Unlike manufacturing firms which organize raw material machinery, land and labour to produce goods/services which are then marketed to earn profits, banks earn profits by borrowing funds at a relatively low interest rate, and lending or investing these funds at a higher rate. In recent years along with these funding activities, fees generated from non-funding activities through other services provided by banks, e.g., mutual funds, insurance, forfeiting, loan syndication, underwriting, etc. have become significant contributors to profits.

8.1 DISTINGUISHING FEATURES OF BANKING BUSINESS

While it is true that the objective of every business is profit maximization, for banks this has to be balanced with certain social objectives. There are certain other differences also in case of operations of ordinary commercial concerns and those of a bank. A bank works under certain liquidity constraints as it has to maintain cash reserves as per the directions of the Reserve Bank of India. Banks do not enjoy total freedom in investment of their funds for another reason also, i.e., to comply with the priority sector lending norms. A bank does not have to report any opening or closing levels of stocks like other commercial concerns as it does not deal in goods. Cash deposits in a bank are the liability of a bank but for a commercial concern, cash deposited by them in a bank is their asset. An important feature of bank accounts is that the entry of every transaction has to be made on the same day and that too within banking hours so that the bank books reflect the balances on that day and they may be verified. For preparation of accounts the provisions relating to preparation and audit of financial accounts as laid down in the Banking Regulation Act, 1949, have to be followed. The provisions of the Company Act, 2013, are also applicable in so far as they are not in contravention of the provisions of the Banking Regulation Act, 1949.

In view of the fact that banks largely deal in other peoples' money and that they are at the heart of the financial system, the importance of a viable, sound and safe banking system cannot be overemphasized. As a result there is an imperative need that banks function with utmost prudence, diligence and care so that the confidence of their shareholders and the public at large is not abused. For the same reason very efficient system of internal checks and controls becomes a pre-requisite.

8.2 ANNUAL REPORT

The annual report of the bank presents all relevant operational and financial information to the shareholders, government and other stakeholders. It is a statutory requirement for all joint stock companies including banks to hold an annual general meeting once a year, and file an annual report with the registrar of companies and send one copy each to all its shareholders. It also has to file three copies of the balance sheet and auditors report with the Reserve Bank of India.

An annual report is a reflection of the company's philosophy, policies, achievements and shortcomings. The annual report gives general information regarding the name(s) of the chairman/MD, chief executive officer and all the directors, the bankers and auditors of the company, registered office, date, time and venue of the annual general meeting. It also gives a summary of the financial operations as well as its assets and liabilities. An annual report comprises two parts.

Part I: It includes

- Notice of the meeting of the shareholders.

- Directors' Report. The chairman of the company presents the Directors' report which usually highlights the company's achievements in the given macro and micro-environment, new initiatives/products/technology, etc. proposed to be used, constraints if any faced by the company, future plans for modernization, diversification, etc.
- The company's philosophy that describes how the company does business, is delineated in a separate section.
- Social responsibility report. It has initiatives for environment conservation and corporate social responsibility. Since banks do not manufacture goods, therefore, treatment of effluents is not relevant. However, most banks do conduct a number of social outreach programmes for education, training, etc. for the poor and underprivileged sectors of the society.
- Corporate Governance report. Corporate governance deals with conducting the affairs of the organization with integrity, transparency and commitment to principles of good governance. It has to be certified that all mandatory requirement as stipulated by Securities and Exchange Board of India (SEBI) have been complied with.
- Declaration of dividend (if any) is provided.
- Retirement, reappointment of existing directors or appointment of new directors.
- For the sake of uniformity and transparency in reporting, banks are also supposed to give details of their non-performing assets (NPAs). NPAs are those assets which have remained unpaid for a period of 90 days. They are further categorized as sub-standard, doubtful and loss.

Part II: The second part of the report deals with performance highlights of the organization.

- It includes a balance sheet, a profit and loss account, cash flow statement and other statements and explanatory material that are an integral part of the financial statements.
- An auditors' report certifying that the financial statements together present a true and fair view of the company's affairs, and are in compliance with existing accounting standards, applicable laws and regulations.
- Disclosure norms as per the RBI banks in their Annual Report have to disclose about their capital adequacy, asset quality, liquidity, earning aspects and penalties, if any, imposed on them by the regulator.

8.3 BALANCE SHEET OF A COMMERCIAL BANK

One of the best ways to learn about a business's creditworthiness and financial strength is through perusal of its balance sheet. Balance sheet is one of the three fundamental financial statements (other two being the Income statement and Cash-flow statement). It is used by financial analysts for accounting purposes as well as financial modelling. A balance sheet is a statement of assets and liabilities of a business firm at a particular point of time. It throws light on the financial health or otherwise of the enterprise. Assets are economic resources of a firm, such as land, buildings, machinery, equipment, accounts receivable (i.e., amounts owned by customers), etc. Liabilities are economic obligations of a definite or reasonably certain amount to be paid in the future. These include amounts payable to creditors, loans, wages, taxes, salaries, etc.

The financial statements of banks and other manufacturing and trading companies show many differences—for a bank the equity base is very low and financial leverage is very high. The proportion of fixed assets is very low as unlike manufacturing or trading organizations, a bank does not have to invest in plant and machinery or stock. Also, the operating leverage (ratio of fixed cost to total cost) is very low. The sources of funds are primarily short term in nature, payable on demand or with short-term maturity, a high proportion of bank funds are invested in loans and advances or investments all of which are subject to interest rate volatility.

For learning about the business of banking, one can study a typical bank's balance sheet. It will give an account of the bank's assets and liabilities.

Another way of viewing a balance sheet is as a statement of the sources and uses of bank funds. Banks obtain funds in the form of deposits (fixed, savings and current) by borrowing from other banks (RBI, commercial banks, etc.) and by obtaining equity funds from the owners (i.e., the shareholders of the bank) through the capital account. All these constitute the liabilities of the bank. Banks use these funds to grant loans, invest in securities, purchase equipment and hold cash items such as currency and deposits in other banks. All these are the assets of the bank. Figure 8.1 depicts sources and uses of funds:

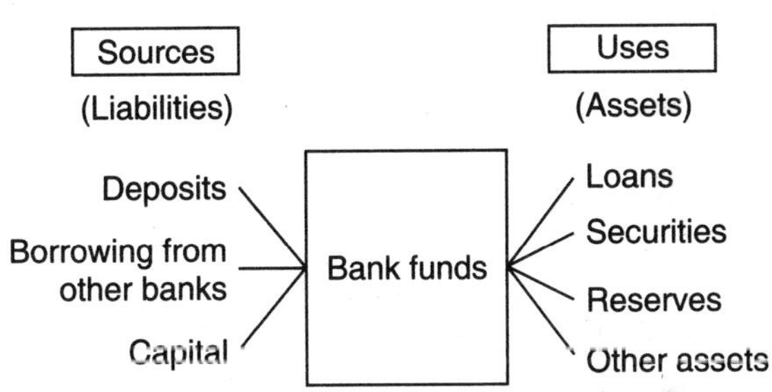

Figure 8.1 Sources and uses of commercial bank funds.

8.4 STATUTORY REQUIREMENTS FOR BALANCE SHEET

Every banking company has to comply with Accounting Standards as notified under the Company's (Accounting Standards) rules, 2006. Banks have to follow norms laid down for Income recognition, Asset classification and Provisioning.

According to section 29 of the Banking Regulation Act, 1949, at the expiration of each calendar year (or at the expiration of a period of twelve months ending with such date as the Central Government may, by notification in the official gazette, specify in this behalf), every banking company incorporated in India, in respect of all business transacted by it, and every banking company incorporated outside India, in respect of all business transacted through its branches in India, shall prepare with reference to that year or period, as the case may be, a balance sheet and profit and loss account as on the last working day of the year or the period, as the case may be, in the forms set out in the third schedule or as near thereto as circumstances admit.

The balance sheet and profit and loss account shall be signed:

(i) in the case of a banking company incorporated in India, by the manager or the principal officer of the company. Where there are more than three directors of the company, by at least three of those directors. Where there are not more than three directors, by all the directors, and

(ii) in the case of a banking company incorporated outside India by the manager or agent of the principal office of the company in India.

8.4.1 Audit

The balance sheet and profit and loss account prepared in accordance with section 29 shall be audited by a person duly qualified under any law for the time being in force to be an auditor of companies. The appointment of an auditor for a bank has to be made with the prior approval of the RBI and their remuneration has to be fixed by the RBI in consultation with the Central government. Since a bank deals in money and the number of transactions is colossal, to minimize the chances of fraud a bank's accounting system should be devised in such a manner that there is a continuous built-in-system of audit and accounts.

If the Reserve Bank is of opinion that audit is necessary in the interest of the public or the banking company or its depositors, it may, at any time order a special audit of the banking company's accounts, for any such transaction or class of transactions or for some specific period or periods as it deems necessary. The RBI may through its order either appoint a person duly qualified under any law for the time being in force to be an auditor of companies or direct the auditor of the banking company himself to conduct such special audit. In banks concurrent audit is done by the bank auditor besides the statutory auditor.

8.4.2 Publication and Filing of Accounts (Section 30)

The accounts and balance sheet referred to in section 29 together with the auditor's report shall be published in the prescribed manner, and three copies thereof shall be furnished as returns to the Reserve Bank within three months from the end of the period to which they refer.

A banking company which furnishes its accounts and balance sheet in accordance with the provisions of section 31 shall send three copies of such accounts, balance sheet and the auditor's report to the Registrar.

It is mandatory for all banking companies incorporated outside India that before the first Monday in August of any year in which it has carried on business, it must display a copy of its last audited Balance Sheet and Profit and Loss Account prepared under section 29, in a conspicuous place in its principal office and every branch office in India. These should be kept on display until they are replaced by a copy of the subsequent Balance Sheet and Profit and Loss Account.

8.4.3 Format of the Balance Sheet of a Bank

The balance sheet of a commercial bank like any other balance sheet comprises two sides; conventionally the left side shows liabilities and capital, while the right side shows assets. A bank's assets are indications of what the bank owns or the claims that the bank has on external (non-bank) entities: individuals, firms, governments, etc. A bank's liabilities are indications of what the bank owes as claims which are held by external entities of the bank. The net worth or capital is calculated by subtracting total liabilities from total assets.

$$\text{Assets} - \text{Liabilities} = \text{Net worth}$$

or

$$\text{Assets} = \text{Liabilities} + \text{Net worth}$$

The balance sheet should reflect a true and fair picture of the financial position of the bank. Any form of window dressing, short provisioning, miscalculation of NPAs, under reporting, incorrect computation of risk weightage, capitalisation of expenses or deliberate inflation of assets or reduction of liabilities can invite penal action against the bank.

The format of a balance sheet according to schedule III (section 29) of the Banking Regulation Act, 1949 is given below in Table 8.1.

Table 8.1 Format of a Balance Sheet of a Commercial Bank

SCHEDULE III

(Section 29)

FORM A

FORM OF BALANCE SHEET

Capital and liabilities	₹ P.	₹ P.	*Property and assets*	₹ P.	₹ P.
1. Capital (i) Authorised capital (ii) Subscribed capital (iii) Amount called up less calls unpaid Of (iii) above, held by (a) Individuals (b) Cooperative institutions (c) State government			1. Cash In hand and with Reserve Bank		
2. Reserve fund and other reserves (i) Statutory reserve (ii) Agricultural (credit stabilization fund) (iii) Building fund (iv) Dividend equalisation fund (v) Special bad debts reserve (vi) Bad and doubtful debts reserve (vii) Investment depreciation reserve (viii) Other funds and reserves (to be specified)			2. Balances with other banks: (i) Current deposits (ii) Savings bank deposits (iii) Fixed deposits		
3. Principal/subsidiary state partnership fund account For share capital of: (i) Central Cooperative banks (ii) Primary agricultural credit societies (iii) Other societies			3. Money at call and short notice		
4. Deposits and other accounts (i) Fixed deposits (ii) Saving bank deposit (iii) Current deposits (iv) Money at call and short notice			4. Investments (i) in central and state government securities (ii) Other trustee securities (iii) Shares in cooperative institutions other than in item (5) below (iv) Other investments (to be specified)		
5. Borrowings (i) From the Reserve Bank of India (a) Short-term loans, cash credits and overdrafts@ (b) Medium-term loans@ (c) Long-term loans@ (ii) From the State Bank of India (a) Short-term loans, cash credits and overdrafts@ (b) Medium-term loans@ (c) Long-term loans@ (iii) From the state government (a) Short-term loans@ (b) Medium-term loans@ (c) Long-term loans@ (iv) Loans from other securities			5. Investment out of the principal/subsidiary state partnership fund In share of: (i) Central cooperative banks (ii) Primary agricultural credit societies (iii) Other societies		
			6. Advances: (i) Short-term loans, cash credits overdrafts and bills discounted# (ii) Medium-term loans# (iii) Long-term loans#		
			7. Interest receivable of which overdue considered bad and doubtful of recovery		
			8. Bill receivable being bills for collection (As per contra)		
			9. Branch adjustments		
			10. Premises less depreciation		
			11. Furniture and fixtures less depreciation		
			12. Other assets (to be specified)		
			13. Non-banking assets acquired in satisfaction of claims (stating mode of valuation)		
			14. Profit and loss		

(*Contd.*)

Table 8.1 Format of a Balance Sheet of a Commercial Bank (*Contd.*)

SCHEDULE III
(Section 29)

FORM A
FORM OF BALANCE SHEET

Capital and liabilities	₹ P.	₹ P.	*Property and assets*	₹ P.	₹ P.
6. Bills for collection being bills receivable as per contra					
7. Branch adjustments					
8. Overdue interest reserve					
9. Interest payable					
10. Other liabilities					
(i) Bills payable					
(ii) Unclaimed dividends					
(iii) Suspense					
(iv) Sundries					
11. Profit and loss					
Profit as per last balance sheet					
Less appropriations					
Add profit for the year brought from the profit and loss account					
TOTAL			TOTAL		
Contingent liabilities					
(i) Outstanding liabilities for guarantees issued					
(ii) Others					
TOTAL					

Note:

* Of which secured against
(a) Government and other approved securities
(b) Other tangible securities including borrowings against gold and gold ornaments repledge of goods, mortgage or land, etc.

\# Of the advances, amount overdue. Considered bad and doubtful of recovery

@ Of which secured against:
(a) Government other approved securities;
(b) Other tangible securities.

8.5 LIABILITIES AND ASSETS OF A BANK

Many institutions offer financial services. It is the taking of deposits and granting of loans that single out a bank from other financial institutions. Deposits are liabilities for banks, which must be managed if the bank is to maximize profits. Likewise they need to manage the assets created by lending. The liabilities and assets of a bank are explained below.

8.5.1 Liabilities of a Bank

A liability is an obligation as a result of a pass event. Its settlement results in outflow of resources. Liabilities of a commercial bank are claims on the bank. They represent the amounts which are due from the bank to its shareholders, depositors, etc. Bank liabilities are the funds that banks obtain and the debts they incur, primarily to make loans and purchase securities. The major components of the liabilities of a bank are as follows:

Capital: Capital and reserves together they constitute owned funds of a bank. What the customer regards as an asset, the same bank deposit is a liability for the bank as the customer gains claim over them. The paid up share capital implies the liability of the bank to its shareholders. It is the amount actually received by the bank out of the total subscribed capital. Adequate share capital is considered as a source of strength for the bank as it provides confidence to the depositors about the solvency of the bank.

Reserve fund: Reserves are created out of the undistributed profits which are retained over a period of years by the bank. At least 20 per cent of profits before declaration of dividend has to be transferred to the reserve fund. Creation of reserve fund is a statutory requirement in most of the countries of the world. Reserve requirements limit the portion of the bank's funds that it can use to give loans and purchase securities. Banks build up reserves to strengthen their financial position and also to meet unforeseen liabilities or unexpected losses. Reserve fund, together with capital represents the capital structure or net worth of the bank. **Net worth** is a residual term that is calculated by subtracting total liabilities from total assets.

Deposits: Deposits constitute the major sources of funds for banks. A bank raises deposits from households, corporates and the government. What the customer regards as an asset, the same bank deposit is a liability for the bank as the customer gains claim over them. Banks get funds from investment and these are indirectly the source of its income. Banks keep a certain percentage of its time and demand deposits in cash and after meeting the liquidity requirement, they lend the remaining amount on interest. Indian banks accept two main types of deposit, demand deposits and term deposits. Demand deposits, as the name suggests, are repayable on demand and term deposits are repayable after the expiry of a particular period. The prosperity, growth and goodwill of the bank depend upon the amount of these deposits. Fixed deposits have specific maturity and so can be used by bank to earn income. Demand deposits can be further subdivided into current and savings. Current deposits are chequeable accounts with no restriction on the number of withdrawals. It is possible to obtain clean or secured overdraft on these accounts. Saving deposits are more liquid than fixed deposits as money can be withdrawn when needed, though some banks restrict the number of withdrawals per-month or per-quarter.

Borrowing from other sources: In case of need, banks can borrow from the Reserve Bank of India, other commercial banks, development banks, non-bank financial intermediaries like LIC, UTI, GIC, etc. Secured loans are obtained on the basis of some recognized securities whereas unsecured loans are out of its reserve funds lying with the central bank. In the balance sheet, borrowings have to be showed as 'borrowings from India' and 'borrowings outside India'.

Other liabilities: Other liabilities include bills payable, bills sent for collection, acceptance, endorsement, etc. The amounts of all such bills are shown on the liability side of the balance sheet.

Contingent liabilities: Contingent liabilities are those liabilities which may arise in future but cannot be determined accurately, e.g., guarantee given on behalf of others, outstanding forward exchange contracts, etc. A contingent liability is an off-balance sheet item. In good times for banks contingent liabilities can generate substantial income but if the counter party does not honour his commitment, then these contingent liabilities can convert into a fund-based liability for bank.

Profit or loss: Profit is unallocated surplus or retained earnings of the year after paying tax and dividends to shareholders. As shareholders have claim over the bank's profit, it is shown as a liability. In case of loss, the figure will be shown on the assets side.

Others: Provisions made for income tax, bad debts, depreciation, etc. come under this head.

8.5.2 Assets of a Bank

Like all other business firms banks also strive for profit. Commercial banks use their funds primarily to purchase income earning assets, mainly loans and investments. These assets are shown in the balance sheet of the bank in decreasing order of the liquidity. The major assets of the bank include:

Cash: Cash in hand and cash balances with the Reserve Bank of India are the most liquid assets of a bank. Cash assets provide bank funds to meet reserve requirements and the liquidity to meet the withdrawals of deposits and to accommodate new loan demand. Maintaining of cash reserve ratio with RBI is a statutory requirement for the banks.

Money at call and short notice: This is the money lent by the banks to other banks, bill brokers, discount houses and other financial institutions for a very short period of time varying from 1 to 14 days. When these funds are repayable on demand without prior notice, it is called **money at call**. On the other hand, if some prior notice is required, it is known as **money at short notice**. In the balance sheet, both are shown as a single item on the asset side. Banks charge very low rate of interest on these. If the cash position continues to remain comfortable, these loans may be renewed day after day.

Loans and advances: Loans and advances are the bank's earning assets. The interests earned from these assets generate the bulk of commercial bank revenues. Loans may be demand loans or term loans which may be repayable in single or in many instalments. Advances are usually made in the form of cash credit and overdraft.

Investments/securities: Commercial banks use funds for investment in various types of securities like the gilt edged securities of the central and state government as well as shares and debentures of corporate undertakings. The securities issued by government are safe from the risk of default though they are subject to risk from change in rate of interest. These securities include treasury bill, treasury deposit certificates and postal obligations such as national savings certificate, etc. The long-term investments have the greatest profitability.

Bills receivable: Bills receivable and other credit instruments accepted by the commercial banks on behalf of their customers are also shown on the asset side of the balance sheet. The reason is that the bank has a claim on the payee, on whose behalf it has accepted the bills. Thus, the same amount appears on assets as well as liabilities sides of the balance sheet of the bank.

Other assets: These include the physical assets of a bank like the bank premises, furniture, computers, machines equipment, etc. These also include the collaterals which the bank has repossessed from the borrowers in default.

The balance sheet reports the summary of an entity's assets and liabilities at a given point of time. It is typically used by investors, lenders and creditors to estimate the liquidity of the business. However, to make their company look more financially secure than it actually is companies often use **Off-Balance Sheet reporting**. Off-balance sheet items refer to those assets and liabilities of the company that do not appear on the balance sheet. This accounting practice is frequently used for sheltering company's financial statements from the impact of large asset ownership and it's corresponding liability as they are usually funded with debt financing. But too much debt financing can make a company less desirable to investors and lenders. Using off-balance sheet method of reporting makes helps a business to maintain appealing leverage ratios. It is most commonly used for operating leases, leaseback agreements and accounts receivable, letters of credit, derivatives. Often companies set up special-purpose vehicles (SPVs) that have their own balance sheets and companies place the off-balance items on the SPV's balance sheet. It's pertinent to note that companies have to disclose these and other financial arrangements in the notes to their financial statements.

KEY TERMS

Loan syndication Agreement between two or more lending institutions to provide a credit facility top a borrower using common loan documents.

Underwriting When banks guarantee the purchase of stocks, bonds, etc. and assume liability in case of loss.

Continuous audit It is an internal process that examines accounting practices, risk controls, compliance, information technology systems and business procedures on an ongoing basis. It is designed to automate error checking and data verification in real time.

Leverage The ratio of a company's loan capital (debt) to it's equity (share) capital.

Leverage ratio or debt-equity ratio = Long term debt/owner's equity. Lower the debt ratio, stronger is the financial position of the company.

REVIEW QUESTIONS

8.1 Explain the need and contents of an annual report of a bank.

8.2 Briefly outline the sources and uses of bank funds.

8.3 Describe the balance sheet of a bank and prepare an imaginary balance sheet in order of permanence.

8.4 Explain the various assets and liabilities of a bank.

8.5 Write short notes on:
- (i) Publication and filing of accounts
- (ii) Audit of bank accounts
- (iii) Off-balance sheet items

9

Project and Working Capital Finance

Learning Objectives

After going through this chapter we will be able to:

- Understand the meaning of project finance.
- Know the parameters for project appraisal.
- Describe the operating cycle of working capital.
- Explain the factors affecting working capital.
- Understand working capital ratios.

A project entails commitment of various managerial, financial, technical, human and other resources which are pooled together in an organization to achieve some specific purpose. It usually has to be executed in a specified time frame and is undertaken to provide goods and services.

As projects deploy huge investments any uninformed/hasty decision can have grave consequences both for the banks/funding institutions which may be saddled with NPAs as well as for the owners/promoters of the project. The mounting industrial sickness can prove alarming for the economy as well. In view of the high stakes for lenders, borrowers and the nation at large, it becomes all the more imperative that project finance must be undertaken most judiciously by ensuring the right blend of managerial and financial acumen to ensure the most effective allocation and utilization of resources, which result in financial and competitive gains for the organization. The demand for credit could be for starting a new project or for expanding an existing one. Credit appraisal is comparatively easier in the latter case as the borrower has a track record of last two—three years which can help in predicting future performance. For a new venture if similar products are already available in the market, estimates can be made. But for a completely new product the risk is high and a more diligent appraisal will need to be made.

The borrower can be an individual, a proprietorship or partnership firm, a public or private limited company, government, etc. While granting finance, the banker should keep in mind that the liabilities of different borrowers are different—while individuals, sole proprietors and partnership firms (unless it's a Limited Liability Partnership) have unlimited liability, the others have limited liability. It is also imperative to check whether a charge on assets has been created for a previous loan.

9.1 PROJECT FINANCE

Every project involves certain financial outlay which can be referred to as project finance. A credit facility can be for either fund-based facility, like term loan or working capital loan, or it could be for a non-fund based facility—generally for Letter of Credit, bank guarantee, deferred payment guarantee, etc. The appraisal process is likely to be different for both. Project finance has traditionally been the domain of developmental institutions, as it employs deployment of funds for the medium to long-term period. Now, even the commercial banks have started providing project finance along with working capital funds. If the project requires huge amounts of capital, e.g., if they are for gas exploration, mining or for setting up of steel or fertilizer plants, and so on, then usually a consortium of companies is formed which collectively finance the project and share the risks. Part of the capital comes from equity participation and part from lender or lessors. The debt and equity used to finance the project are paid back from the cash flow generated by the project.

Finance is required to assemble various inputs of the project like land, labour, machinery, raw materials, etc. Financial planning is based on the financial appraisal of the project, i.e., ascertainment of total long-term and short-term financing requirements, choosing the sources of finance, at the most reasonable cost and at the appropriate time. Apart from the amount, source, cost and time, decisions regarding determination of capital structure, i.e., debt-equity ratio, credit policy, contingencies, and so on also have to be taken.

Different stages of the project require different kind of funding, e.g., at the initial stage *seed finance* is required for conducting feasibility studies to prove that the concept is viable. *Start-up capital* is needed to get the company organized and operational. Then finance is needed for expansion and growth.

Availability of adequate and timely credit continues to be a matter of grave concern for the entrepreneur. Credit provided for creation of fixed assets like land, building, plant and machinery is called **long-term capital** or **fixed capital** and credit provided for day-to-day running expenditure like raw materials, electricity, water, wages, salaries, etc. is called **short-term capital** or **working capital**. Various sources can be tapped by an entrepreneur depending on their need. Table 9.1 lists the main sources of funds for long and short-term requirements.

Table 9.1 Sources of Funds

Long-term	*Short-term*
Owner's capital equity	Bank borrowings (loans, overdrafts, etc.)
Term loans from financial institutions	Deposits from friends/relatives
Deposits or loans given by owners/partners	Sundry creditors
Hire purchase or leasing facility by NBFC	Advances from customers
Loan syndication/consortium financing	Factoring

The banker should ensure that on receiving the proposal for loan, the bank should move fast in processing and sanctioning the same as any delay on their part might jeopardize the viability of the project.

9.2 PROJECT APPRAISAL

The first step towards financing of a project is the making of the project report. A project report is a detailed report of all the aspects of an investment proposal including the nature of goods or services to be produced, its likely market demand the proposed location of the plant, the technology to be used, the estimated cost and returns, etc. The project report which is prepared by the borrower has to be appraised. Project appraisal is a prerequisite for funding. Though the project may appear to be most desirable on paper but its viability from the point of view of technical viability, financial feasibility, market potential, management appraisal, environmental and ecological implications, etc. have to be systematically reviewed and assessed. The general appraisals which have to be conducted are briefly explained hereinafter.

9.2.1 Technical Appraisal

Technical feasibility analysis is primarily conducted to ensure that the project is technically sound. All the cost estimates flow from this appraisal and form the basis for studying the financial and economic feasibility of the project. It examines the project idea/concept, the manufacturing processes, plant and machinery as well as other equipment and know-how, etc. proposed to be used. Whether the technology is obsolete or too advanced, whether it is indigenously available or has to be imported, the technical transfer arrangement if any, availability of personnel with high technical competency, etc. are other areas which have to be studied.

9.2.2 Financial Appraisal

It involves assessment of the cost and profitability of a project. An assessment of total financial requirements including those for fixed capital, working capital as well as establishment costs, etc. has to be made. The sources from where the funds have to be obtained have to be identified. The cost of funds has to be calculated and projected rate of returns have to be estimated. Only if the project is able to service debt and satisfy return expectations it will be considered financially viable.

9.2.3 Market Appraisal

Market appraisal helps to assess the market potential of the proposed product/service. Realistic estimate of market demand, supply gaps, competition both direct and from substitutes, existing as well as potential, has to be made, export market too should be examined. Consumer behaviour, pricing policies and distribution channels have to be studied and identified. Until the project appears to have a positive market forecast all efforts in organizing the project will be wasted.

9.2.4 Management Appraisal

The character or willingness of the borrower the reputation and goodwill, vigour and enthusiasm are all very important aspects for the success of the venture. The educational, technical qualifications and experience of the borrower/managerial team are other important factors which have to be kept in mind. If the management is not efficient, effective, reliable or credible, then the chances of success of the business become remote.

9.2.5 Environmental Appraisal

Environmental and ecological appraisal has become a very important part of project appraisal. Any damage to the environment as a result of technology used or waste/effluents not being managed properly needs to be examined. Substitute raw materials, eco-friendly technology should be explored. Minimization of emission or renewable uses for waste materials are other aspects merit serious attention. In many countries including India, there are legal provisions regarding environmental norms which have to be adhered to.

When the above feasibility parameters produce a positive result only then the funding agencies will consider grant of finance for the project.

A project is considered viable when the cash flow generated from the project is adequate enough to service the funding arranged by the project owners. The financing institution has to satisfy itself on all the above accounts—in other words that there is a market demand for the proposed goods/services to be manufactured/supplied, availability of technical know-how for the manufacturing process, economical cost of the product, self-sustainability of the project, and availability of an efficient and competent management team.

9.3 WORKING CAPITAL

Working capital is the life blood of a business organization. Proper working capital management is a prerequisite for the uninterrupted functioning of a firm. If this is not properly managed, then it can have serious consequences for the business which might come to a halt if there is a liquidity crunch. Working capital is the amount of funds required by an enterprise to finance its day-to-day business operations. It is that part of the total capital which is employed in short-term assets such as raw materials, accounts receivable, inventory, etc. In other words it signifies investment in current assets which rotate during the operating cycle and keep the business running.

Working capital is also defined as the excess of current assets over current liabilities. Current assets include cash and bank balances, receivables, inventory, prepaid expenses, etc. These assets are converted into cash within the accounting period (one year) as a result of routine business operations. Current liabilities are the debts of the firms which have to be repaid during the current accounting period. These include creditors, outstanding expenses, short-term borrowings, advances received against sales, taxes and dividends payable, etc.

9.3.1 Operating Cycle

The acquisition of raw materials and the final cash realization always involves a certain time gap. For a manufacturing unit the period between the materials ordering stage to conversion of sales into cash is referred to as the operating cycle. Trading concerns have a shorter operating cycle comprising the procurement of goods from the market which ends with the realization of cash from creditors after the sale of goods. Manufacturing concerns, on the other hand, have a longer operating cycle beginning with procurement of raw materials, processing stage, finished goods inventory stage to sales and conversion of bills receivable into cash.

Working capital is required as production, sales, receipt of payment and realization do not take place simultaneously. Hence, there is mismatch between cash inflows and outflows. Working capital is required to fill this gap and ensure that there is no liquidity problem and the resultant dislocations.

This is depicted in Figure 9.1 here.

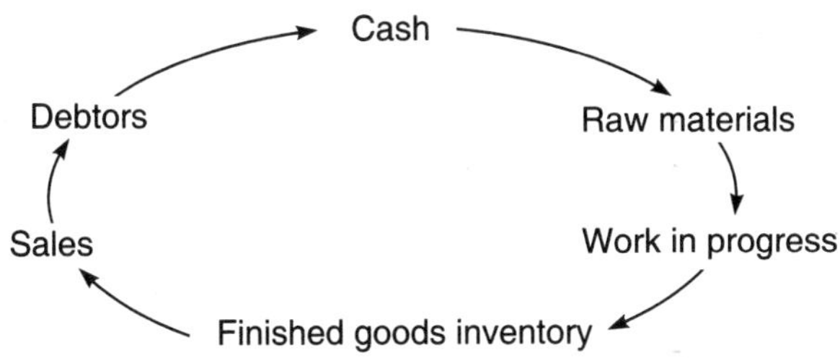

Figure 9.1 Operating cycle interpretation of working capital.

9.3.2 Types of Working Capital

Working capital may be permanent or fluctuating, gross or net.

Permanent working capital: Permanent working capital is the amount needed to produce goods and services at the lowest point of demand. It is that part of working capital that gets locked up with the investment decision and is realized only after the liquidation of the concern. This is financed out of long-term funds.

Fluctuating working capital: The part of working capital that fluctuates with the level of business activity is called **fluctuating** or **circulating working capital**. Its sources are trade creditors, bank overdrafts, bills discounting and the like.

Gross working capital: Gross working capital means the **total value of current assets**. Current assets are the assets, which are converted into cash within a period of one year. These include cash in hand, cash at bank, stock or inventory, bills receivable or short-term investments. Gross working capital is a financial concept. It does not reveal the true financial position of an enterprise.

Net working capital: Net working capital implies the excess of current assets over current liabilities. Current liabilities are those liabilities, which have to be paid off within the accounting year or one year. These include claims of outsiders such as creditors, bills payable and outstanding expenses. Current liabilities are sources of funds in the sense that these finance current assets. The net working capital may be either positive or negative. If the current assets are more than the current liabilities, then there is a positive working capital balance. If the current liabilities exceed the current assets, then the net working capital will be negative. The net working capital concept indicates the liquidity position of the firm. It tells how much current assets will be left after paying off current liabilities.

Net working capital = Current assets – Current liabilities

9.3.3 Factors Affecting Working Capital

There are no set rules to determine the working capital requirements of firms. Numerous factors influence working capital needs of firms ranging from the type of business, the prevailing macro and micro-economic conditions, nature of technology employed, etc. The degree of importance of factors also changes for a firm over time. Therefore, an analysis of relevant factors should be made in order to determine total investment in working capital. The following is the description of factors, which generally influence the working capital requirements of firms:

Nature of business: The nature of business influences the working capital requirements of a firm. The requirement for investment in fixed assets is nominal for trading and financial firms. However, they require large sums of money to be invested in working capital. Retailers, for instance, must invest in huge inventories of different variety of goods to satisfy their customers. Public utilities, hospitality industries, etc. have comparatively very limited need for working capital as they supply services which generate cash sales daily. Manufacturing concerns, on the other hand, produce products and their working capital requirements fall in between the two extreme requirements of trading firms and public utilities.

Business cycle fluctuations: The amount of working capital of a concern is also influenced by the cyclical demand for its goods. Demand usually increases during boom conditions, necessitating the need for larger cash requirements. On the other hand, not much investment in working capital is required during recessive conditions.

Seasonal operations: Working capital requirements also vary for those businesses which are seasonal in nature with more working capital is required during peak season for maintaining higher inventories and *vice versa*.

Nature of technology employed and length of the production cycle: All businesses which use modern machinery and sophisticated technology require higher investment in fixed capital. As the production process is not labour intensive the wage bill is low. This reduces the level of working capital requirements. But if the production cycle is either labour intensive or long, then a higher level of working capital will be required.

Credit policy: Finished goods are sold on cash as well as on credit basis. If the component of cash sales is higher, then comparatively less working capital is needed. If on the other hand, sales are dominated by credit transactions, then more working capital is required. If the credit period is longer, more working capital is needed and *vice versa*. Many a times, the nature of sales also depend to a large extent on the practice prevailing in the industry.

Cash requirements: Need for cash to meet the operating expenses like wages, rent, taxes, transportation charges, etc. also exercises an influence on the amount of working capital.

Terms of buying: Terms of purchases also influence the need for working capital. If a company purchases raw materials and other services on credit basis, it will require less investment in working capital. But if a concern purchases raw materials on cash basis its requirement of working capital will be higher.

Sales turnover: If the sales turnover is high it means cash flow is faster. There is no need for more working capital since the amount is available from the sales of goods, which can be ploughed back into business.

9.3.4 Working Capital Ratios

The following ratios are used for efficient management of working capital:

Working capital to sales ratio: This ratio helps to measure the efficiency of the utilization of net working capital. It is computed by dividing working capital by sales. Any proposed increase in sales should be matched by adequate working capital.

Inventory turnover ratio: The effectiveness and efficiency of the inventory management is indicated by this ratio. It indicates how speedily the inventory is turned into accounts receivable through sales. A lower ratio implies a more efficiently managed inventory and *vice versa.*

Current ratio: It is a ratio between the current assets and current liabilities. If the current assets are larger than the current liabilities this reflects the short-term financial strength of a business concern in meeting its current liabilities without default. A good ratio is 2:1 as it indicates the firms ability to meet its current liabilities by disposing of its current assets at half its value in case of need.

Quick ratio: This is similar to the current ratio except that the inventories are excluded in the current assets. It measures the short-term liquidity of a business concern. Quick ratio of 1:1 is generally considered excellent.

9.3.5 Procedure for Assessment of Working Capital Requirements

The following methods are generally followed for assessing working capital requirement of a firm:

Turnover method: Under this, the working capital is assessed as minimum 25 per cent of the sales turnover, which is financed by way of bank finance at minimum of 20 per cent and the borrower's contribution at 5 per cent of the projected sales.

Traditional method: This method takes the length of the operating cycle and the size of the sales into account. The level of working capital would be the sum total of anticipated current assets and also reasonable level of other assets.

Cash budget method: As per this method, monthly cash inflow and outflow statement is prepared and the gap between the two becomes the basis for sanction of credit limit.

KEY TERMS

Collateral Something pledged as security for repayment of loan which can be forfeited in the event of default.

Consortium financing Under this the banks formally, agree to join together to meet the working capital requirements of the borrowing concerns.

Debt-equity ratio It is a measure of the relative contribution of the creditors and shareholders or owners in the capital employed in business. It is the ratio of long-term debt and equity capital.

Factoring Refers to the sale of receivables to a financial institution usually on a non-recourse basis.

Lessors The party which through a contract of lease grants the other party, i.e., the lessee, the right to use an asset in return for periodic payments.

Limited Liability Partnership (LLP) The Limited Liability firm has a separate legal entity. It is liable to the full extent of it's assets, but the liability of the partners is limited to the extent of their capital contribution to the LLP.

Unlimited liability Full legal responsibility is assumed by proprietors and partners for all loans and debts and if needed then owner's/partner's personal assets can be seized and sold for repayment of debt.

REVIEW QUESTIONS

9.1 What do you understand by project appraisal? Explain the various parameters used to appraise a project.

9.2 Describe the operating cycle of working capital.

9.3 How would you access the working capital requirement of a hosiery concern exporting T-shirts to Europe?

9.4 Write short notes on
- (i) Project Finance
- (ii) Net working capital
- (iii) Working capital ratios

10

Banking Legislation

Learning Objectives

After going through this chapter we will be able to:

- Explain the need for regulation of the banking sector.
- Describe the schedules to the Reserve Bank of India Act, 1934.
- Understand main provisions of the Reserve Bank of India Act, 1934.
- Explain the provisions of Banking Regulation Act, 1949 and Amendments of 2012, 2017 and 2020 to the Act.

Banks deal substantially in other people's money. Any non-judicious use of these funds, or their misappropriation in any manner can have very grave repercussions. Banks are also used as an instrument by governments to give shape to their monetary and fiscal policies—the deployment of funds into priority sector or opening up of more branches in rural districts, bank lending rates, the statutory liquidity ratio (SLR) are all examples of the above. As a result, the preservation of the safety and soundness of the banking sector has come to occupy centre stage.

The unplanned and uncontrolled growth of banks in pre-Independent India led to rampant failures. 87 banks during 1913–1917 and another 373 banks during 1922–1932, completely shattered public confidence in banks. More recently, the spate of failures of cooperative banks in Gujarat and failure of the Yes bank in the private sector, have again highlighted the need for control and regulation. With the liberalization of the Indian economy and the subsequent banking sector reforms, the above needs have been reinforced. Legislation was thus extremely important for the twin purposes of protecting the interest of depositors, shareholders, stockholders and confidence of the public at large as well as for the smooth functioning of the monetary and financial system. In view of the important role banks play and the way their branch networks are woven into the social and economic fabric of the nation, there is a vital need of regulating the sector.

During the early 20th century, banking was carried on mostly by joint stock company banks, most of which had insufficient knowledge of banking principles and practices. The unorganized money market was also strong, and there was non-existence of a central bank, though the three presidency banks, namely, the Bank of Bengal (estd. 1806), Bank of Bombay (estd. 1840) and Bank of Calcutta (estd. 1842) performed some functions of a central bank like issuing of bank notes (till 1862) and managing treasury business of the government. The Imperial Bank of India which was formed in 1921 by the amalgamation of these three banks functioned primarily as a commercial bank, though it was entrusted with certain central banking functions for complete control over banking activities and as an instrument for economic development of the nation. A strong need was felt for a central bank as well as centralized organized banking system for a money market as well as need to guard the interests of the stockholders and depositors. The RBI Act was passed in 1934 for performing the role of a central bank, and Banking Regulation Act was passed in 1949 for regulation of banking in India. An overview of both these Acts is discussed in Sections 10.1 and 10.2.

10.1 THE RESERVE BANK OF INDIA ACT, 1934

The Establishment

The RBI was established on April 1, 1935 under the RBI Act of 1934. It performs all the traditional functions of a central bank which prior to its nationalization in 1949 were performed by the Imperial Bank of India. Originally, it was a shareholder bank which was taken over by the Central Government under the Reserve Bank (transfer of public ownership) Act, 1948. It had a paid-up capital of ₹5 crore.

Head Office

The central office of RBI is in Mumbai since its inception. There are 22 regional offices, most of them in state capitals.

Preamble

The preamble prescribes the objective as to regulate the issue of bank notes and keeping of reserves with a view to secure monetary stability, and generally to operate the currency and credit system of the country to its advantage.

The RBI Act consists of five chapters and five schedules. A brief outlines of these chapters are discussed followed by a summary of main provisions of the Act.

Chapter I Preliminary: It gives a short title, extent and commencement as well as some definitions. The Act may be called the **Reserve Bank of India Act, 1934**, and extends to the whole of India. It will come into force at once and remaining provisions will come into force on such dates as notified in the official Gazette in India. It gives a number of definitions including that of the Bank, Bank for International Settlement as well as Export-Import Bank, National Housing Bank, Small Industries Development Bank of India, Scheduled Bank, State Financial Corporation, State Bank, Cooperative Bank, etc.

Chapter II Incorporation, capital, management and business: It encompasses the establishment and incorporation of the bank, provisions regarding share capital, offices, branches and agencies as well as composition, functions and meetings of its central board, local boards, as well as terms like disqualification, removal, etc. of directors. Sections 14–16 have been repealed and Sections 17–19 deal with the business which is to be transacted and which may not be transacted by the bank.

Chapter III Central banking functions: This chapter outlines banks obligations and right to transact government business, right to issue bank notes, their denomination, form as well as reissue, recovery and issue of special bank notes. The assets and liabilities of issue department, cash reserve ratios of scheduled banks, publication of consolidated statements by bank, and so on are also mentioned in this chapter.

Cash Reserve Ratio (CRR)

Under Section 42 of the RBI Act, 1934, every scheduled bank is under a statutory obligation to keep a cash reserve with the RBI. It is required to maintain an average daily balance equal to at least 3 per cent and up to a maximum of 20 per cent of its net demand and time liabilities. Average daily balance means the average of balances held at the close of business on each day of the fortnight. When the RBI wants to tighten credit control, it increases the CRR and thus absorbs the excess liquidity. However, if it wants to expand credit and injects liquidity, then it lowers the CRR. The CRR was at its peak at 15 per cent during 1994–95. But currently (i.e., in June 2012) it stands at 4.5 per cent.

Chapter IIIA Collection and furnishing of credit information: Provisions regarding the power of the bank to collect credit information, procedure for furnishing information and prohibited information are outlined in this chapter.

Chapter IIIB Provisions relating to non-banking institutions receiving deposits and financial institutions: This chapter does not apply to state bank or its subsidiaries or a banking company as defined in section 5 of Banking Regulation Act, 1949. It lays down requirement for registration and net owned fund, reserve fund as well as maintenance of percentage of assets. It also outlines the banks power to call for, and to collect information for non-banking institutions. The powers and duties of auditors are also laid down in Chapter IIIB.

Chapter IIIC Prohibition of acceptance of deposits by unincorporated bodies: This chapter specifies the deposits which are not to be accepted in certain cases and lays down power to issue search warrants.

Chapter IIID Regulation of transactions in derivatives, money market instruments or securities: It gives the definition of derivatives, money market instruments, repo and securities as well as specified transactions in derivatives.

Chapter IV General provisions: This chapter gives general provisions regarding contribution of Central Government to reserve funds, national, rural, industrial and housing credit, appointment, powers and duties of auditors, exemption of banks from income tax and super tax, delegation of powers, liquidation of the bank, etc.

Chapter V Penalties: This chapter lays down penalties for any person, directors, auditor and company whoever makes a wrong statement wilfully, whether in any application, declaration, return, advertisement, book, account, document, etc.

Any default in complying with regulation of this Act is also punishable.

Schedules: The Act also has five schedules, namely, the first schedule, which specifies areas where local boards are to be constituted. The second schedule which lays down provisions for scheduled banks. The third, fourth and fifth schedules have been repealed. of the Act is given in Table 10.1.

Table 10.1 Summary of Main Provisions of Reserve Bank of India Act, 1934

Section	*Provision*
2(e)	Scheduled bank means a bank whose name is included in the 2nd schedule of RBI Act, 1934.
17	Defines various types of business—acceptance of deposit without interest from central/state government, any other person/institution, purchase/sale of foreign exchange, securities, rediscounting of bills/ promissory notes, government loans, etc.
19	Business which RBI may not transact
20	As a banker to government, RBI transacts government business and manages public debt of the Central Government

(*Contd.*)

Table 10.1 Summary of Main Provisions of Reserve Bank of India Act, 1934 (*Contd.*)

Section	*Provision*
22	Sole right to issue bank notes
24	Denomination of notes—2, 5, 10, 20, 50, 100, 500, 1,000, 5,000, 10,000, any denomination may be discontinued. Like ₹2 and ₹5 notes have been continued.
26	Bank notes issued by RBI shall be legal tender and guaranteed by Central Government
29	Bank note shall be exempted from stamp duty under Indian Stamp Act
33	Assets of issue department of RBI shall consist of gold coins, gold bullion and foreign securities not at anytime be less than ₹200 crore, of which gold coin and gold bullion not less than ₹115 crore
42	Cash reserve ratio (CRR) of scheduled bank to be kept with RBI as prescribed.
42(c)	RBI can add or delete the name of any bank in 2nd schedule
43	Publication of fortnightly consolidated statements showing aggregate liabilities and asset of SCBs
45	Power of RBI to collect credit information
45(H)	Regulations relating to non-bank finance companies
48	Exemption to RBI from paying income tax or super tax
49	Announcement/publication of bank rate, i.e., the standard rate at which the RBI is prepared to buy or rediscount bills of exchange or other eligible commercial papers

10.2 THE BANKING REGULATION ACT, 1949

The Banking Regulation Act provides the legal framework for the regulation of the baking system by the Reserve Bank of India. As a result, for the first time, banking came to be organized on certain universal parameters.

This Banking Regulation Act consolidates the law relating to banking and provides for the nature of transactions which can be carried out by banks in India, the control over management, suspension and winding up of banking companies and penalties for violating provisions of the Act. Initially, the banking companies came under the purview of the Companies Act. The primary objective of company law is to safeguard the interest of the stockholder and that of banking legislation is the protection of the interest of the depositor. Therefore, it was felt that separate legislation was necessary for the regulation of banking in India. As a result the Banking Regulation Act was passed in 1949 (initially it was called the **Banking Companies Act**). The Act contains following five parts:

Part I Preliminary

Part II Business of banking companies

Part IIA Control over management

Part IIB Prohibition of certain activities in relation to banking companies

Part IIC Acquisition of the undertakings of banking companies in certain cases

Part III Suspension of business and winding-up of banking companies

Part IIIA Special provisions for speedy disposal of winding-up proceedings

Part IIIB Provisions relating to certain operations of banking companies

Part IV Miscellaneous

Part V Application of the Act to cooperative banks

Part I Preliminary: This part gives the short title to the Act which extends to the whole of India. Application of other laws like Companies Act is not barred. The Act has a very limited application to cooperative societies in certain cases. It also defines a banking company's demand and time liabilities, secured and unsecured loans, managing agents, managing directors, sponsored and subsidiary banks, regional rural banks, etc.

Part II Business of banking companies: Specifies the businesses in which the bank may and must not engage, prohibition on trading rules regarding directors and chairman, restriction on commission and brokerage, loans and advances. Nature of subsidiary companies, requirement as to minimum paid-up capital and reserves, accounts, balance sheets, licensing and auditing.

Part III Suspension of business and winding-up of banking companies: This part contains provisions for suspension of business, winding-up by High Court, power to dispense with meetings with creditors, preferential payment to depositors, etc.

Part IV Miscellaneous: This part lays down penalties for officers, application for fines, special provisions for private banking companies, change of name or alternation of memorandum, power of central government to make rules, etc.

Part V Application of the Act to cooperative banks: It defines a cooperative bank, a cooperative credit society, a multistate cooperative society. Any dispute regarding their primary object or principal business is referred to and determined by the RBI. It also lays down requirements as to minimum paid-up capital and reserves.

The Act also contains five schedules:

Schedule I
Schedule II
Schedule III
Schedule IV
Schedule V

The summary of main provisions of Banking Regulation Act, 1949, is given in Table 10.2.

Table 10.2 Summary of Main Provisions of Banking Regulation Act, 1949

Section	*Provision*
5b	Banking means accepting for the purpose of lending or investment, of deposits of money from public, repayable on demand or otherwise and withdrawable by cheque, draft order or otherwise.
5c	Banking company means any company which transacts the business of banking.
5e	Transact banking business in India.
5f	Demand liabilities must be met on demand and those which are not demand liabilities are time liabilities.
6.1	Banking business includes accepting of deposits, borrowing and lending money, dealing in bills, buying/selling of foreign exchanges, lockers, issuing of letter of credit, travellers' cheques, mortgages, insurance business and acting as trustee, etc.
6.2	Restriction on carrying on any other business apart from the above.
7	Use of the word bank, banking or banking company in the name of all banking companies which are carrying on business of banking in India.
8	Restrictions on business of trading of goods.
10	Management—prohibitions on employment like Chairman, Director, etc.
11 & 12	Paid-up capital and reserves for foreign banks minimum ₹15 lakh but in cities of Mumbai and Kolkata minimum ₹20 lakh. For domestic banks not less than ₹5 lakh.
15	Prohibits payment of dividend by any bank until all of its capitalized expenses have been completely written off.
18	Cash reserve—non-scheduled banks to maintain 3 per cent of the demand and time liabilities as cash reserves.
19	Banks can form subsidiary company for certain purposes.
21	RBI has power to determine policy for advances (such as purpose, margin, extent, rate of interest, etc.)
21A	Rate of interest charged by banks are not subject to scrutiny by Courts with effect from 15th February, 1984.
22	Contains provisions regarding licensing of banking companies.
23	Branch licensing: Restrictions on opening new and transfer of existing place of business.

Table 10.2 Summary of Main Provisions of Banking Regulation Act, 1949 (*Contd.*)

Section	*Provision*
24	Statutory liquidity ratio—Every bank to maintain a percentage of its demand and time liabilities by way of cash, gold, unencumbered securities 25–40 per cent as on last Friday of 2nd preceding fortnight. CRR is maintained as a cash reserve, whereas SLR is maintained in liquid near cash instruments, for example, government securities and other approved securities. While the aim of CRR is to take care of immediate liquidity needs, SLR has twin objectives: those of liquidity and profitability. An increase in SLR will contract the money supply and vice versa. Currently (June 2012) the SLR stands at 24 per cent.
26	Deposits which remain unclaimed must returned within 30 days of close of each calendar year to RBI.
29	Every bank has to publish its balance sheet.
30-I	Balance sheet has to be audited by qualified auditors.
31	Balance sheet and auditors report to be submitted within three months from the end of the period to which they refer.
35	RBI is authorized to undertake inspection of banks and give appropriate directions.
36	RBI has powers to terminate the services of any chairman and employee.
45	RBI can apply to Central Government for suspension of business by a banking company and prepare a scheme of reconstitution or amalgamation.
45Y	Preservation of records in accordance with Central Government directors.
45	Nomination facilities on bank deposits and lockers.
47A	RBI can impose penalty for various kinds of violations.
49A	Other than a banking company/RBI/SBI, no person can accept deposits of money withdrawable by cheque.
52	Power of Central Government to make rules for all matters.

10.3 THE BANKING REGULATION LAWS (AMENDMENT ACT), 2012

The Banking Regulation Law (Amendment Act), 2012 was passed with a view to strengthen the RBI's regulatory powers.

10.3.1 Salient Features

1. **New bank licenses and greater supervisory oversight:** The Act will enable the RBI to issue new bank licenses to corporate houses. The RBI will now have the power not only to remove a Director or Officer of a recalcitrant banking company but if need be, to supersede the entire board in public interest, and appoint

an administrator to run the bank for a period not exceeding 12 months. This amendment will also empower the RBI to impose higher rates of monetary penalties on a bank which disobeys rules and directives or gives false information.

2. **Power to Inspect:** The RBI will have power to call for, and inspect information and returns from the associate and group companies of the banking companies if it so desires. This will provide greater supervisory oversight to the RBI to grant licenses to industrial houses for setting up new banks. The RBI can also impose penal interest on a bank if it fails to maintain the prescribed minimum amount of Cash Reserve Ratio (CRR) on any given day.
3. **Acquisition of Shares and Voting Rights:** An acquisition of 5 percent or more shares or voting rights will from now on require the RBI's prior approval. It shall be empowered to impose such conditions as it deems fit in this regard.
4. **Unclaimed Bank Accounts:** RBI will have the power to transfer the money lying in unclaimed bank accounts—these are those bank accounts, which have not been operated by the account holder for more than 10 years. The monies lying in these accounts will be transferred to the "Depositor Education and Awareness Fund", which will be managed by a committee appointed by the RBI. In the event of the return of the account holder, the money shall be returned to him by the bank, with interest.

10.4 AMENDMENTS RELATED TO PRIVATE AND PUBLIC SECTOR BANKS

10.4.1 Revised Voting Rights

Private Sector Banks: The cap on voting rights in private banks has been raised from 10 to 26 percent. However, a single shareholder cannot exercise voting rights in excess of 15% of the total voting rights of the shareholders (ET 28.2.2020).

Public Sector Banks: This amendment also enables the government to raise voting rights in PSBs, such as the State Bank of India, from 1 to 10 percent. The voting rights will be made proportional to the number of shares held by shareholders and this provision will hopefully attract foreign institutional investors.

10.4.2 Issue of Bonus Shares by Public Sector Banks

With the passing of this amendment all nationalised banks will now be able to raise capital through 'bonus' and 'rights' issue. PSBs will be able to increase or decrease the authorised capital as per need, with approval from the government and the RBI without being limited by the ceiling of a maximum of ₹30 billion under the Banking Companies (Acquisitions and Transfer of Undertakings) Act of 1970 and 1980.

10.4.3 Mergers and Acquisitions

The Competition Commission of India (CCI) will approve all Mergers and Acquisitions (M&A) in banks. However, for those banks which are in trouble, the RBI will have the final authority.

10.4.4 Stamp Duty for Foreign Banks

To provide a thrust to expansion of operations of foreign banks in India, they will now be allowed to convert their Indian operations into local subsidiaries or transfer shareholding to a holding company of the bank without paying stamp duty.

10.5 BANKING LAWS (AMENDMENT ACT) 2017

The downturn in the Indian economy during the last five years has led to surplus capacity in many industries especially in the steel, infrastructure, power and textile sectors, thus impairing their debt servicing capacity. Consequently, NPAs running into trillions of rupees were chocking the Indian banking system. So, it became imperative for the RBI to intervene in order to take urgent measures for their speedy resolution. The Banking Law (Amendment Act) 2017 was passed to make provisions for handling cases related to stressed assets or NPAs of banks.

10.5.1 Salient Provisions

1. Insolvency Proceedings—The central government can authorize RBI to start insolvency proceedings to resolve specific stressed assets under the Insolvency and Bankruptcy Code 2016.
2. Issue directions to banks for resolution of stressed assets from time to time.
3. The RBI can form a committee to advice banks on such resolutions. It can also appoint or approve members of such committee.
4. All the above provisions are applicable to SBI and RRBs.
5. Punitive Powers—The RBI will also be granted some punitive powers to ensure that banks act quickly on these bad loans.
6. The Amended Act hopes to correct the common perception amongst the banks and investors that the government takes an implicit guarantee to bear the cost of defaults and losses.

7. The RBI will also help bankers overcome concerns about their decisions being probed by vigilance agencies—an apprehension that acts as a hindrance in functioning of banks.

The RBI's December Financial Stability Report 2016 states that large borrowers, i.e. those debtors to whom lenders have an exposure of at least ₹5 crore, account for 56% of bank debt. In India, the NPA problem is mostly confined to these 50 large loan defaulters. With the help of this ordinance the RBI can effectively ask banks to focus on 40–50 big corporate defaulters to reach a settlement as part of the package. It is hoped that this would help to solve the crisis quickly.

10.6 BANKING REGULATION (AMENDMENT BILL) 2020

Co-operative banks were hitherto exempted from several provisions of the Banking Regulation Act, 1949. To prevent such catastrophes in future which resulted because of the crisis in Punjab and Maharashtra Co-operative Bank (PMC) crisis this bill was passed to expand RBI's regulatory control over co-operative banks in terms of management, capital, audit and liquidation.

10.6.1 Salient Features

1. With prior approval of the RBI, co-operative banks can now raise capital from members or other persons residing within the bank's area of operations.
2. The RBI can lay down conditions and prescribe qualifications for appointment of Chairman of co-operative banks. If the conditions are not met the RBI can remove such chairman and appoint a suitable person instead.
3. The RBI can also reconstitute the Board of Directors if it feels that it lacks sufficient number of qualified members—not less than 51% of members should have specialised knowledge or practical experience in areas such as accountancy, banking, law or any other.
4. If need be the RBI can even supersede the Board of Directors of the co-operative bank after consultation with the state government.
5. The bill allows RBI to undertake reconstruction or amalgamation of a bank without imposing a moratorium.
6. Audit will have to be conducted at par with commercial banks and RBI's prior approval shall be required for appointment, re-appointment or removal of auditor.
7. Certain provisions applicable to commercial banks for winding up and speedy disposal of such proceedings will now be applicable to co-operative banks

KEY TERMS

Amalgamation Combination of two or more companies into a new identity. Neither of the company survives, a completely new entity is formed.

Diligence Degree of attention or care expected of a person in a given situation.

Funding activities These are a bank's core activities—loans and advances, which generate income.

Non-funding activities New income generating products and services introduced by banks. Like mutual funds, credit cards, insurance, bank guarantee.

Prudence Careful management, using sound economical judgment.

Winding Up Process of liquidation of a company.

REVIEW QUESTIONS

10.1 Explain the need for regulation of the banking sector.

10.2 Describe the main provisions of the Reserve Bank of India Act, 1934.

10.3 Write a note on the importance of the Banking Regulation Act, 1949. Highlight its main provisions.

10.4 Explain the following:

- (i) Unclaimed bank accounts
- (ii) Cash Reserve Ratio (CRR)
- (iii) Recent amendments to the Banking Regulation Act, 1949
    - (a) 2012
    - (b) 2017
    - (c) 2020

11

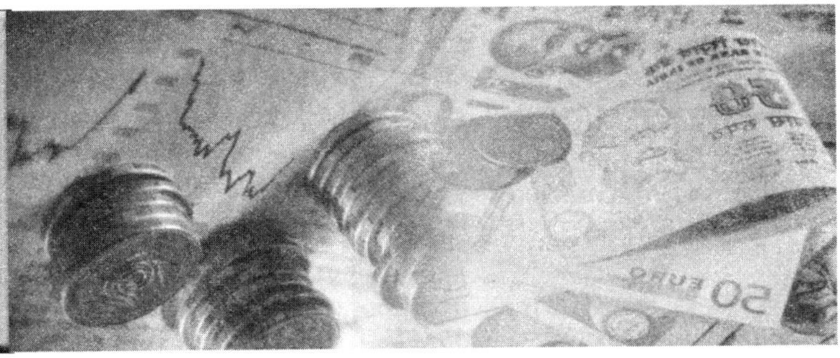

Banking Sector Reforms and NPAs

Learning Objectives

After going through this chapter we will be able to:

- Understand the rationale of banking sector reforms.
- Identify major reforms introduced in 1991.
- Describe the later phases of reforms based on the Bassel II and Bassel III recommendations.
- Understand the meaning and implications of Non-Performing Assets (NPAs).
- Know the basis for asset classification.

The resources of banks constitute a substantial portion of financial resources in a developing economy. Any weakness in the banking system shall threaten the financial stability of the country. Also, economic reforms in the real sectors of economy will fail to realize their full potential without a parallel reform in the financial sector. The problem of South-east Asian and Latin American countries, the recessionary trends in the Japanese economy provide ample proof of how a weak banking sector can undermine confidence in macro-economic policies.

11.1 RATIONALE OF BANKING SECTOR REFORMS

For a very long time banks, in India were subjected to a highly regulated environment characterized by an administered interest rate structure, quantitative restrictions on credit flows, high reserve requirements under cash reserve ratio (CRR) and pre-emption of significant proportion of lendable resources for the priority sectors under statutory liquidity ratio (SLR). As a result, banks in India were characterized by low efficiency and productivity. Overstaffing and union pressure added to their woes. Banking regulations as to liquidity, rate of interest to be charged and norms for priority sector lending resulted in banks reeling under bad debts, defaults and mounting NPAs.

The process of globalization of Indian economy has created an environment where the financial services system has to be cost-effective, customer oriented and technology based. Banking sector has been undergoing drastic metamorphosis where the need for a stable, efficient, resilient and vibrant banking system has come to occupy centre stage. The increasing levels of deregulation, stiff competition and the technology revolution have placed numerous demands on banks. The banking sector reforms are aimed at enhancing the productivity, efficiency and competitiveness of the banking industry.

The main thrust of the economic reforms was on the removal of structural bottlenecks, introduction of new players and instruments, introduction of free pricing of financial assets, relaxation of quantitative restrictions, improvement in trading, clearing and settlement practices, promotion of institutional infrastructure and ensuring technological upgradation. However, while deregulation has opened up new vistas for banks to augment revenues, it has also created intense competition accompanied with high risks.

11.1.1 Pre-reform Era

Before the opening up of the Indian economy and the advent of the banking sector reforms, the Indian banking sector was plagued by the following deficiencies:

- (i) Imposition of stringent regulations by the RBI
- (ii) Low productivity and efficiency of public sector banks
- (iii) Deteriorating portfolio quality, mounting bad debts and increasing NPAs due to government regulations, political interference and poor monitoring
- (iv) Poor quality of customer service
- (v) Inferior work technology
- (vi) Inability to face competition

It was on account of the deterioration in the financial health, integrity, autonomy, flexibility and vibrancy in the financial sector that reforms became imperative. In these circumstances that the first Narasimham Committee was set up in 1991 to suggest remedial measures for strengthening the banking system encompassing banking policy, institutional structure, supervisory system, legislative and technological changes.

Basel Committee I In 1988, Basel Committee on Banking Supervision published the Capital Accord. This focused on credit risk to strengthen the soundness and stability of the banking system. It prescribed a minimum capital adequacy ratio of 8% of the total risk-weighted assets. The RBI also implemented the guidelines on capital measures and capital standards as given by the committee on banking regulations and supervisory practices though it prescribed a minimum capital adequacy ratio of 9%.

11.1.2 First Phase of Banking Sector Reforms

Narasimham Committe I (1991)

This phase included the following:

(i) A phased reduction in SLR and CRR to 25 per cent and 10 per cent, respectively.

(ii) Deregulation of interest rates of deposits and advances of all cooperative banks and banks allowed to set their own interest rates on post-shipment export credit in rupees.

(iii) Transparent guidelines for private sector banks. Modification of balance sheet and profit and loss account to disclose more information.

(iv) Direct access to capital markets for public sector banks with profitable operations.

(v) Liberalized branch licensing policy wherein the option of opening or closing branches, other than rural branches should be left to the commercial judgment of individual banks and more licences for private sector banks.

(vi) No further nationalization for banks and no difference in treatment between public sector banks and private sector banks.

(vii) Setting up of debt recovery tribunals to ensure quick recovery of debts.

(viii) Prudential norms for income recognition, classification of assets and provisioning for bad debts.

(ix) Asset reconstruction fund (ARF) should be created to take over bad debts of the banks on discount and leave a clean balance sheet. The level of discount being determined by independent auditors on the basis of clearly defined guidelines.

(x) Limit of priority sector advances set at 40 per cent of total advances.

(xi) Capital adequacy norms—BIS norms on capital adequacy should be achieved and attain a capital adequacy ratio (CAR) of 8 per cent by 1998.

(xii) Speedy computerization of the banking system.

The financial system reforms initiated during 1991–92 are based on twin principles of operational flexibility and functional autonomy so as to continuously enhance efficiency, productivity and profitability of the financial institutions. It aimed at providing a diversified, efficient and competitive financial sector with ultimate objective of improving the allocative efficiency of available resources, increasing the return on investments and promoting an accelerated growth of real sector of the economy.

It was hoped that introduction of reforms will help to develop a market-oriented, competitive, world-integrated, diversified, autonomous and transparent financial system. It would also bring about the effectiveness, accountability, profitability, vibrancy, professionalizm and depoliticization in the financial sector as well as promote competition, free entry and exit for institutions and that the market players would create level playing fields. Reforms also tried to ensure that the rationalization of interest rates structures occurs, that interest rates are flexible, market-determined or market-related.

11.1.3 Second Phase of Banking Sector Reforms

Narasimham Committee II (1998)

In the initial phase of reforms, the focus of reforms was on the scheduled commercial banks, given their systemic importance. In the last few years, however, the reform process has become increasingly broad-based encompassing other institutions such as RRBs, Urban Cooperative banks, FIs and NBFCs.

After evaluation of the performance of the banking sector after the introduction of reforms the second Narasimham Committee gave its report in 1998, and made further suggestions and the following major recommendations:

(i) The banks should reduce the average level of net NPAs for all banks to below 5 per cent.

(ii) An asset is classified as doubtful if it is in the substandard category for 18 months in the first instance, the period was subsequently reduced to 12 months in 2005.

(iii) For banks with a high NPA portfolio, all loan assets in the doubtful and loss categories should be transferred to an asset reconstruction company (ARC) and issue swap bonds to the banks.

(iv) Adoption of international practices by introduction of norms of 90 days in a phased manner.

(v) Greater attention to be paid to asset liability management to avoid mismatch.

(vi) Banks should be encouraged to adopt statistical risk management techniques.

(vii) Interest rates on deposits and advances of all cooperative banks to be deregulated.

(viii) Prudential norms for income recognition, classification of assets and provisioning for bad debts for commercial banks, regional rural banks and financial institutions.

(ix) Banks were required to make their balance sheets fully transparent and make full disclosures in keeping with International Accounts Standards Committee.

(x) Freedom to open, shift and swap branches as well as to open extension counters given to banks.

(xi) Banking ombudsman scheme was introduced in 1995 to look into and resolve customers' grievances.

(xii) The developmental financial institutions should convert themselves to banks.

The capital adequacy guidelines recommended by the Basel Committee II called **Accord II** were also adopted for implementation from March 31, 2007. The revised accord takes into account both market and operational risks (and not just the credit risks which were the focus of Basel I accord), reinforced by a three pillar approach—minimum capital requirement, supervisory review and market discipline, to enhance the stability and soundness of the financial system. Under this, the banks capital requirements will be more closely aligned with the underlying risks in their balance sheets and thus help to promote stronger risk management. In particular, the banks will adopt the standardized approach for credit risk and the basic indicator approach for operational risk. The proposed Basel II Accord hopes to strengthen banks and other financial institutions so they are more resilient to withstand periods of economic and financial stress. Indian banks will have to raise ₹6,00,000 crore in external capital over the next 8 years till the year 2018, besides lowering their leveraging capacity.

The Basel Committee released a New Basel Capital Accord in January 2001 which contain three mutually reinforcing pillars. In India these Basel III recommendations are in force since 1.1.2013. The three pillars of this accord are:

Pillar I: Minimum capital requirements The definition of capital remains the same as Basel I however, the mechanism of calculating risk-weighted assets is significantly different. In India, the minimum capital specified by RBI is 9%.

Pillar II: Supervisory review process The second pillar provides for supervisory review of the bank's capital adequacy and internal risk measurement process. National supervisors will be responsible for ensuring that the bank's internal processes will enable them to take care of all existing and potential risks and capital adequacy requirements.

Pillar III: Market discipline This is intended to act as a compliment the above two pillars. Market participants should be able to asses a bank's risk profile and level of capitalization through increased disclosures.

11.2 NON-PERFORMING ASSETS (NPA)

Simply put, Non-Performing Assets are those that cease to generate income for the bank. The enormity of the problems can be gauged from the following figures—in 2018 NPAs stood at ₹10.4 trillion which was 11.2% of the advances given. PSBs accounted for 90% of the total NPAs. 10 Indian banks under reported their NPAs to the tune of ₹24,000 crores. PNB had NPAs of ₹2,167 crores (MINT 3.12.19). From 2011 to 2014 the banks helped promoters not to default on loans by giving them fresh loans, but from 2015 banks were forced to recognize their bad loans (MINT 9.5.22).

The Narasimham Committee (1991) after studying the financial system felt that the prevalent accounting and disclosure practices did not always reflect the true state of affairs of banks and financial institutions. It identified NPA as one of the possible causes/effects of the malfunctioning of the public sector banks (PSBs). NPAs are those categories of assets (advances, bills discounted, overdraft, cash credits, etc.) which cease to generate income for the bank. The basis for treating a credit facility as non-performing is as follows:

1. Where the interest on instalments on a term loan remains overdue for a period of more than 90 days.
2. Any bill which remains overdue for a period of 90 days.
3. Any amount due on any other loan which remains overdue for a period of 90 days.
4. Any cash credit/overdraft which remains out of order for a period of 90 days.

A loan granted for short duration crops will be treated as an NPA if any instalment or interest thereon remains unpaid for two crop seasons. For a long duration crop the above period would be one crop season beyond the due date.

(**Note:** The period of 90 days was 180 days before March 31, 2004).

11.2.1 Asset Classification

In order to quantify the NPA problem, Narasimham Committee (1991) made it mandatory on the part of the banks to publish annually the magnitude of NPAs. Banks in India are required to categorize NPAs on the basis of (i) the period for which the asset has remained non-performing and (ii) the realizability of the dues. The Committee suggested a classification of assets into the following broad categories according to the quality of the assets:

Standard: Standard asset is one which does not carry more than normal risk attached to the business and which does not disclose any problems.

Sub-standard: Sub-standard asset is one which has been classified as NPA for a period not exceeding 12 months (with effect from March 31, 2005). In case of these assets the current net worth of the borrower or guarantor is not enough to ensure recovery of debt in full—in other words, there is a distinct possibility of the bank suffering some loss.

Doubtful: A doubtful asset is one which has remained NPA for a period exceeding 12 months (with effect from March 31, 2005). These have the weaknesses of sub-standard assets and in addition collection in full seems highly questionable according to the available information.

Loss asset: A loss asset is one where loss has been identified by the bank or internal or external auditors or the RBI inspectors, but the amount has not been written off, wholly or partly. Such asset is considered uncollectible and of little value (less than 10 per cent) though there may be some salvage or recovery value.

11.2.2 Implications of NPA Accounts

NPAs reduce profits in absolute terms and profitability in percentage terms.

These NPAs do not generate any income and, on the contrary, banks are required to maintain capital funds for their provisioning.

Banks also have to incur higher administrative expenses to maintain these accounts. High levels of NPAs also lower the image of the bank as it is perceived to be less efficient.

Banks cannot credit income to their profit and loss account to the debit of loan account unless recovery thereof takes place.

Interest or other charges already debited but not recovered have to be provided for and provision on the amount of gross NPAs also has to be made.

All loan accounts of the borrower would be treated as NPA, if one account is NPA.

11.2.3 Management of NPAs

Provisioning Norms

Banks have to classify assets as sub-standard, doubtful and loss depending upon the chances of realization of amount from the security of these assets and make adequate provisions for these.

Standard Assets: A general provisions of minimum of 0.4 per cent to 1 per cent on global loan portfolios is to be made. Different sectors can attract lower or higher provisions within these norms, e.g., the agricultural and SME sector would have a provision of 0.25 per cent.

Sub-standard Assets: A general provision of 10 per cent is made of total outstanding (irrespective of ECGC guarantee cover and securities available). Another 10 per cent provision will have to be made on the 'unsecured exposures' identified as sub-standard.

Banks in India have been able to contain their NPAs to just two per cent to their net advances in spite of adopting 90 days delinquency norms. This has been possible because of use of treasury profits by banks.

Recovery and management of NPAs has significantly strengthened the lenders' ability to enforce its right to collateral under the Securitization and Reconstruction of Financial Assets and Enforcement of Security Interest (SARFAESI) Act, 2002. The corporate debt restructuring (CDR) system has also emerged as a time bound and transparent mechanism for arriving at a consensual financial arrangement between the creditor and the borrower. The Credit Information Companies Act, 2005, enables sharing of credit information which helps in reducing transactional costs of banks in extending credit to small and medium borrowers which again translates into lower NPAs.

Lok Adalats for outstanding balance of up to ₹20 lakh by way of a compromise settlement can be an effective and speedy method.

Debt Recovery Tribunal (DRT): So far 29 DRTs have been made, however, they have not been able to deliver very good results.

One time settlement scheme was also started in 1999–2000 and then again in 2004.

Insolvency and Bankruptcy Code: The Insolvency and Bankruptcy Code, 2016 was set up with the objective of providing a consolidated framework for insolvency resolution in a time bound manner for individuals, partnership firms and companies. The resolution process is expected to quicken. For banks the RBI will continue its control over the quality of assets and make changes in the provisioning requirements where ever needed, with a higher proportion of provisions going to make the bank books better. Till September 2020 approval of 277 resolution plans with realizable amount of ₹1.9 lakh crore had been given (TOI 16.3.21).

Credit Risk Management: Credit risk management involves credit appraisals and monetary accountability by performing various analysis on profit and loss accounts.

Asset Reconstruction Company: A company engaged in financial asset reconstruction, such as securitization, takeover of management, sale of assets charged, etc.

Current Trends

In December 2021, the NPAs showed some improvement and stood at ₹7.7 trillion or around 6.4% of the total advances. Some of the contributing factors for this were—bad loans being written off after four years, the recurrent recapitalization of PSBs by the government, the recovery of a few bad loans and banks being put under PCA framework by the RBI. The setting up of a bad bank to acquire risky and illiquid assets will also help to clean up the balance sheet of a company. Accountability of middle and senior level management is also very important. PSBs especially need to come up with proper guidance and framework for appointments to senior level positions and corporate governance. Government has infused ₹3.2 lakh crore in PSBs in last six years and the banks themselves have raised 2.8 lakh crore through equity and bonds and a further ₹36,226 crores by selling non-core assets (TOI 16.3.21). Nearly 9.55% of education loans of PSBs have been categorized as NPAs, probably due to job and income loss after the Covid pandemic. This category has witnessed higher NPAs than housing and retail loans which were between 1.6% and 6.91% in financial year 2019–2020 (HT 16.3.21).

KEY TERMS

Asset reconstruction company It is a specialized financial institution that buys NPAs or bad loans from banks and financial institutions and helps them to clean up their balance sheets.

BIS (Bank for International Settlement) It is the world's oldest international financial organization set up in 1930 in Basel, Switzerland. It serves as a bank for Central Banks for many countries and aims at fostering international monetary and financial co-operation.

Capital adequacy ratio (CAR) The statutory minimum reserves of capital which a bank or other financial institution must have available to handle a certain amount of losses, before being at risk for becoming insolvent. It is reported as a percentage of a bank's risk-weighted credit exposures.

CRR (Cash reserve ratio) CRR is the ratio of bank's cash reserve balances with RBI with reference to the bank's net demand and time liabilities to ensure the liquidity and solvency.

Portfolio A set or group or combination of securities held by an investor.

Prudential Exercising sound judgment, managing carefully and economically without being rash.

SLR (Statutory liquidity ratio) Every banking company is required to maintain an amount which shall not at the close of business on any day be less than 25 per cent of the total of its demand and time liabilities. This is called **statutory liquidity ratio**.

REVIEW QUESTIONS

11.1 Explain the rationale of banking sector reforms.

11.2 Critically appraise the important banking sector reforms that have been implemented till date.

11.3 Give a summary of recommendations of 2nd Narasimham Committee.

11.4 Classify NPAs according to their quality. Critically examine the measures taken to reduce such assets.

11.5 Write short notes on:

(i) Three pillars of Basel III

(ii) Implication of NPAs

(iii) Sub-standard Assets

12

Practical Banking

Learning Objectives

After going through this chapter we will be able to:

- Define a cheque, including a cheque in the electronic form and a truncated cheque.
- Know what is a demand draft and a pay order.
- Understand what is meant by Magnetic Ink Character Reading (MICR) and Core Banking Solution (CBS).
- Know what is crossing and bouncing of cheques.
- Learn about Demat Accounts, KYC norms, Deposit Insurance and Credit Guarantee Corporation.
- Explain the functioning of Banking Ombudsman.

In the recent past the way banking business is conducted has undergone a sea change. For instance the concept of performing banking functions during banking hours on working days no longer holds true as most banking activities can be performed 24 × 7, 365 days of the year. With the introduction of internet banking, ECS, RTGS and NEFT systems of settlement money can be quickly and securely transferred from one bank to another. A cheque no longer refers to a paper cheque only as an electronic cheque can be used for all banking transactions. Even the concept of a customer of a particular branch of a bank no longer holds true after the introduction of the CBS system as one can operate their account from any branch of their bank irrespective of the city or state.

For conducting day-to-day banking operations on understanding of the practical aspects of banking is very essential.

12.1 CHEQUE

During the last few decades more and more people in India have become a part of the formal money market and are increasingly using cheques as a mode of payment. Receiving and making payments through cheques provides convenience, safety and security. A **cheque** is written on a serially numbered, printed leaf which is issued in the form of a **cheque book** by the banker to the customer. A cheque directs the banker to make the payment of the sum mentioned therein according to the instructions of the customer who issues it. However, since 2003, now a cheque in the electronic form and the image of a truncated cheque is also included.

According to Section 6 of the Amendments to the Negotiable Instruments Act, 1881—"A cheque is a bill of exchange drawn on a specified banker and not expressed to be payable otherwise than on demand and it includes the electronic image of a truncated cheque and a cheque in the electronic form.

(a) "a cheque in the electronic form" means a cheque which contains the exact mirror image of a paper cheque, and is generated, written and signed in a secure system ensuring the minimum safety standards with the use of digital signature (with or without biometrics signature) and asymmetric crypto system;

(b) "a truncated cheque" means a cheque which is truncated during the course of a clearing cycle, either by the clearing house or by the bank whether paying or receiving payment, immediately on generation of an electronic image for transmission, substituting the further physical movement of the cheque in writing. The characteristics of truncated cheque are as follows:

   (i) The electronic image will replace the physical cheque.

   (ii) When the banks concerned and the clearing house create an electronic image of a cheque. It is called **truncation of the cheque**.

   (iii) From the point and time of truncation the physical cheque will be substituted by the truncated cheque. This is done during the course of a clearing cycle to reduce the time taken in realizing its payment.

   (iv) The paper cheque is retained by the bank/clearing house after truncation.

Always first a physical paper cheque is prepared then its electronic image is created by scanning it and digital signature of the drawer is added to the electronic image to make it secure.

12.2 MAGNETIC INK CHARACTER READING (MICR) CHEQUES/DRAFTS

To overcome problems associated with manual processing the Reserve Bank of India has introduced mechanized cheque processing system using Magnetic Ink Character Recognition (MICR) technology. This has standardized and streamlined operations and, hence, drastically reduced the time taken for clearance and collection of cheques, drafts and other payment instruments. MICR instruments are made of special quality paper and printing specifications. There is a code line at the bottom containing information printed in magnetic ink which when placed under MICR equipment, allows for instant readability and identification. The following information is contained in the code line:

1. The first six numbers indicate the serial number of the cheque.
2. Next three numbers indicate the city code, e.g., for New Delhi the city code is 1100, for Mumbai 2200 for Kolkata 3300 and Chennai 4400.
3. The next three numbers indicate the bank code.
4. The last three numbers indicate the branch code. After some space there is a number of transaction code, e.g., whether the transaction is for saving or current account. This number is of two digits for all cheques except Government of India cheques drawn on the RBI which have a three digit code.
5. The last field represents the amount field and consists of 13 digits.

12.3 CORE BANKING SOLUTION (CBS) SYSTEM

Core Banking Solution refers to networking of all branches of a bank which enables a customer to operate their accounts from anywhere. Before introduction of this system a customer could withdraw/deposit money only in the account he had opened in a particular branch of a bank and from nowhere else, e.g., a person who had an account with the Connaught Place Branch of a bank could operate it only from that branch. But with the CBS system a customer is not hampered by any geographical limitation and can operate from any branch of his bank whether local or national. Though there is no limitation on the deposits which can be made but usually a maximum limit of ₹50,000 is imposed on withdrawals which can be made from any other branch of the bank.

12.4 ESSENTIAL FEATURES OF A CHEQUE

Unconditional written order: A cheque is always an unconditional order by the maker directing his bank to make payment. It is always payable on demand. It is made in writing and that too in ink not in pencil so that alterations cannot be made.

Parties to a cheque: The maker of the cheque is called the **drawer** and the person to whom it is made payable is called the **payee**. Sometimes the drawer and payee might be the same person, e.g., in the case of a **self** cheque. The bank on whom the cheque is drawn is called the **drawee** and the **paying banker**. If a customer receives a cheque drawn on another bank and gives it to his bank to receive that money then the banker who is so deputed is called a **collecting banker**.

The bank issues a cheque book to its customer which usually contains ten or twenty leaves. These cheque leaves are serially numbered and made on special paper and have **MICR** marking.

Date of the cheque: A cheque contains the date on which the cheque is issued. If the date on the cheque is a future date, e.g., a cheque issued on 25th March carries the date of 1st of April it is called a **post-dated cheque**. Such a cheque cannot be encashed till the date mentioned in the cheque, i.e., in the above example only on or after the 1st of April. The validity of a cheque used to be six months from the date of issue which from the 1st of April 2012 has now been reduced to three months. In the above example, the cheque can be withdrawn till the 1st of July after which the cheque will become a **stale** cheque and will no longer remain valid.

Amount: The amount which has to be withdrawal of deposited of the cheque has to be mentioned both in words and figures and the two should tally.

Signature: At the time of opening of the account of a customer his/her specimen signatures are maintained in the bank records. The signature of the drawer of the cheque must tally with the specimen signature of the customer with the bank.

If the above conditions are fulfilled, i.e., the cheque is properly drawn and valid and there is sufficient money in the account of the customer, then the banker is legally bound to honour the cheque. If the banker refuses to do so and wrongfully dishonours the cheque, then he is liable to compensate the drawer for any loss that the latter might incur.

A specimen of a cheque is given in Figure 12.1.

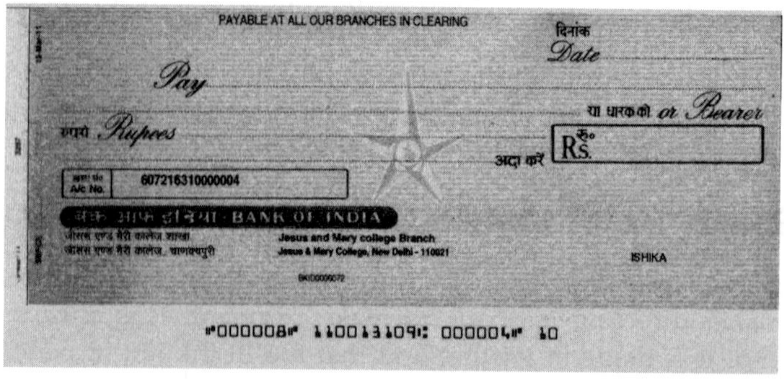

Figure 12.1 Specimen of a cheque.

12.5 BANK DRAFTS/PAY ORDER, BANKER'S CHEQUE

A bank draft also commonly known as a **DD** is a mode of payment. It is issued by a bank and it is made payable at any of its own branches or the branch of any other bank. These are prepaid instruments, i.e., the account holder has to make the payment first and only then the draft is issued. Hence, they are very secure, e.g., if Rajat, a student of Delhi wants to apply for an MBA Programme in Mumbai, he has the option of making the payment for the prospectus, admission form, etc. through a cheque issued in the name of that educational institute or he can do so through a DD. If he sends a cheque, the institute bears the risk of the cheque being dishonoured as well as the risk of it falling into the hands of unscrupulous person who might encash it. If, however, Rajat gets a DD made he will first have to pay the amount he has to send with some commission charges to his bank in Delhi, along with a written request for issuing a DD in favour of that institute's bank in Mumbai. Since the amount has already been paid by Rajat and it is payable only to that particular bank the above risks are taken care of.

12.5.1 Pay Order/Banker's Cheques

If the demand draft is issued by the bank on any of its local branch, then it is called a pay order or sometimes **banker's cheque**, e.g., a pay order issued by a bank in New Delhi will be payable in New Delhi and the NCR, if it is issued in Mumbai it will be payable in Mumbai.

12.5.2 Crossing of Cheques

Crossing is an instruction given to the banker by the customer as to how payment is to be made. A cheque may be an **open cheque** or a **crossed cheque**. In case of an open cheque, payment is made across the counter in the bank. If such a cheque gets lost or is stolen and falls into wrong hands, then there is a risk that payment will not be made to the right person. Thus, to minimize risk people prefer to issue crossed cheques. Crossing is an instruction to the paying banker not to make the payment across the counter, instead he should credit the amount into the account of the payee. Both cheques and drafts can be crossed. Crossing may be either general or special.

General crossing: General crossing consists of drawing two transverse parallel lines with or without the words 'and company' or not negotiable. The lines are drawn on the face of the cheque. They are transverse and not drawn in a vertical or horizontal manner. A specimen or general crossing is given in Figure 12.1.

The effect of such a crossing is that the amount mentioned in the cheque will not be paid in cash across the counter but will be credited into the payee's account.

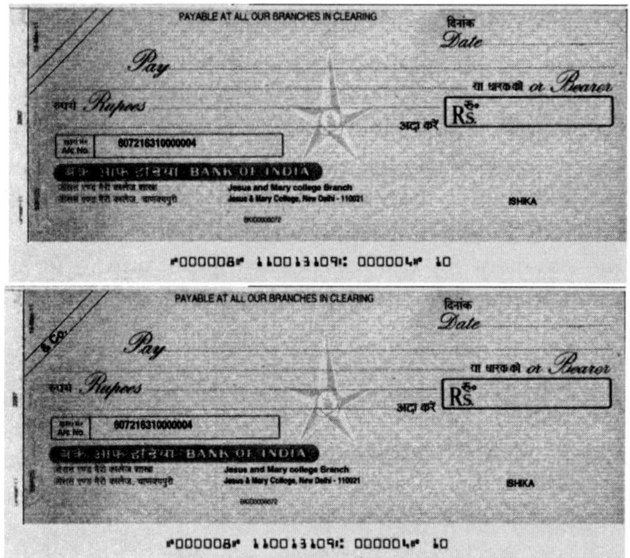

Figure 12.2 Specimen of general crossing.

Special crossing: In a case of special crossing, the name of the banker is written across the face of the cheque either with or without the words 'Not Negotiable'. The drawing of two transverse parallel lines is optional and not a pre-requisite. Special crossing is a direction to the paying banker to honour the cheque only if it is presented through the bank whose name is mentioned in the crossing. A specimen of special crossing is given in Figure 12.3.

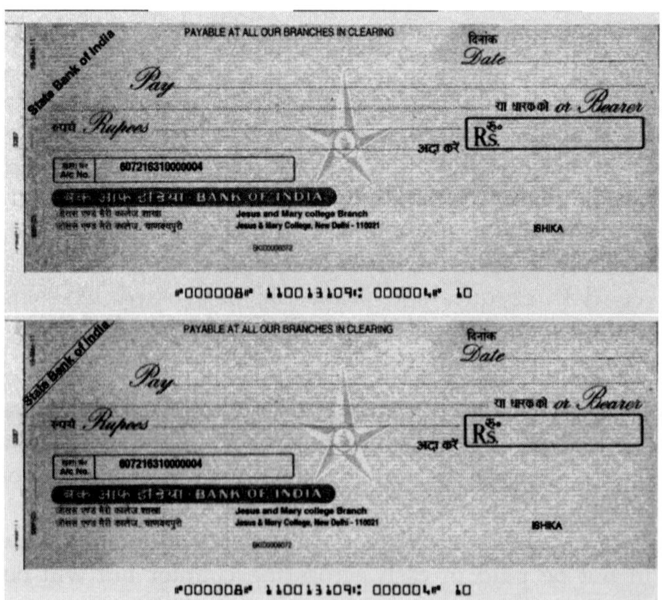

Figure 12.3 Specimen of special crossing.

Not negotiable crossing: If the words 'not negotiable' are written on the face of the cheque whether in a general crossing or a special crossing is means that though the cheque can be transferred further but the feature of negotiability will be taken away, i.e., the transferee (the person to whom the cheque is transferred) will get the same title as the transferor. Figure 12.4 presents a veiw of not negotiable crossing.

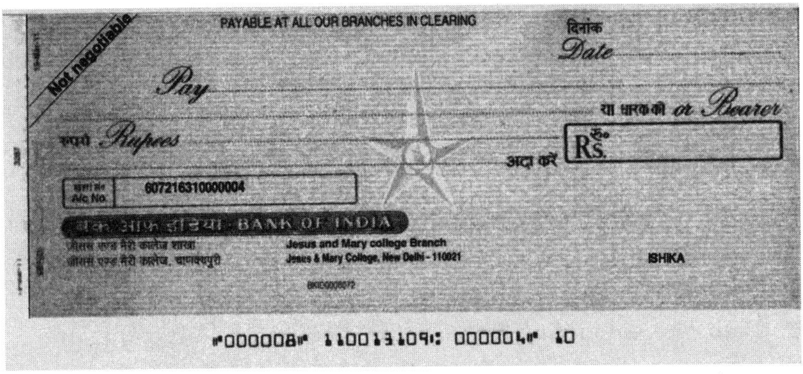

Figure 12.4 Specimen of not negotiable crossing.

Restrictive crossing: In this case, the words 'Account payee' are added either to general or special crossing. In this case, the amount of the cheque has to be credited to the account of the payee only. So for all practical purposes the further transfer of the cheque is restricted. Figure 12.5 shows an example of restrictive crossing.

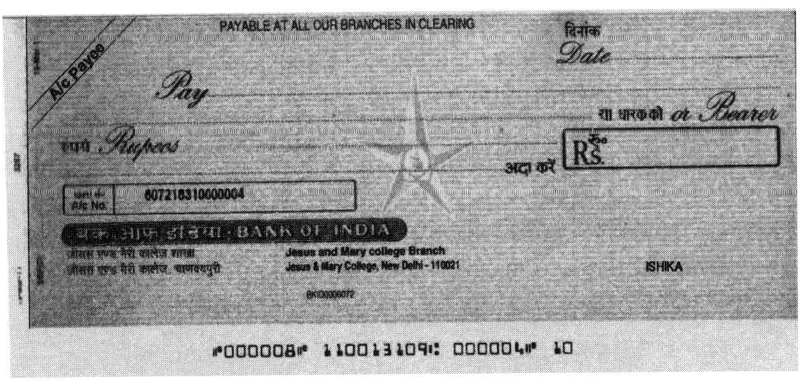

Figure 12.5 Specimen of restrictive crossing.

12.5.3 Bouncing of Cheques

A cheque becomes due for payment on or after the date mentioned on it till the time it is valid. Before issusing a cheque the drawer of the cheque must ensure that there are sufficient funds in his account. When the payee of a cheque presents the cheque to his bank for collection but the cheque is returned to him on account of insufficiency of funds standing to the credit of the drawer, the cheque is said to be **bounced**. If a cheque bounces, then according to Sections 138 to 142 of the Negotiable Instruments Law (Amendment) Act, 1988, the drawer is punishable.

There are more than 33 lakh cheque-bounce cases pending in different courts which are clogging the system. The supreme court has ordered setting up of special courts headed by retired judicial officers exclusively to deal with such cases. As a pilot project 25 such courts will be set up in five districts of Maharashtra, Rajasthan, Gujarat, Delhi and UP where pendency of cheque-bounce cases is the highest (TOI 11.3.21).

12.5.4 Punishment for Bouncing of Cheques

If the cheque of a drawer bounces because of insufficiency of funds, he can be punished in the following manner:

1. With imprisonment extending up to a period of one year, or
2. With fine amounting to twice the amount of the cheque, or
3. With both.

The above punishment is given only if the following conditions are satisfied:

1. The cheque should have been dishonoured due to insufficiency of funds and not because of any other reason like wrong date or mismatch of amount in figures and words or signature, etc.
2. The payment for which the cheque was issued should have been a legally enforceable debt or liability in whole or part and not for any other purpose. For example, if the payee receives the cheque as a gift and it bounces, then the drawer cannot be punished.
3. The cheque should have been presented to the bank within its period of validity.
4. The payee or holder should have made a demand for payment by giving a notice to the drawer within 15 days of receipt of information about the return of the cheque.
5. The drawer should have failed to make the payment before the expiry of 15 days from the receipt of the said notice.
6. The payee or holder of the dishonoured cheque should have made a written complaint within one month of cause of action arising of Section 138.

12.6 KNOW YOUR CUSTOMER (KYC)

In today's date high level technology is being used in almost all banking transactions. Fraudsters and miscreants have also changed their modus operandi and are resorting to technology driven criminal activities for fraud, forgery and cheating. It has become imperative for a bank to verify the identity of a customer and the risks involved in opening an account for him.

To prevent the misuse of the banking system for perpetration of frauds or laundering of money derived from criminal activity, banks are required to be very vigilant in opening of new customer account and follow the KYC guidelines very strictly.

The following four elements should be kept in mind for formulating the KYC policies by a bank:

- Customer acceptance policy
- Customer identification policy
- Monitoring of transactions
- Risk management

As per RBI guidelines for KYC, a customer has been defined as:

- A person or entity that maintains an account/or has a business relationship with the bank.
- One on whose behalf the account is maintained (i.e. the beneficial owner).
- Beneficiaries of transactions conducted by professional intermediaries, such as stock brokers, chartered accountants or solicitors, as permitted under law; and
- Any person or entity connected with a financial transaction, which can pose significant reputational or other risks to the bank like a wire transfer or issue of a high value demand draft as a single transaction.

An introductory reference should be given by the individual or body corporate at the time of opening an account by an existing customer of the bank. The following information has to be filled in the prescribed form:

Name of the applicant/s, their address both temporary and permanent, date of birth for individuals, occupation/nature of business. Names of person/s having cheque signing authority for Firms and Companies, address of their registered office. A copy of the partnership Deed of Firms and Articles of Association and Memorandum of Association of a company, as the case maybe, have to be submitted. The properly filled form has to be submitted along with photographs and specimen signatures. Banks must ensure that their customers are genuinely those whom they claim to be. For instance, for individuals, proof of address can be verified from valid driving license, utility bills, property tax return, voter register card, etc. A copy of the their PAN Card has to be submitted, which is both a proof of identity and income. The bank also have to prepare and maintain documentation on their customers relationship and transactions to maintain the KYC relationship and for prevention of money laundering.

Records of these transactions have to be retained for at least five years. Especial care should be taken for high value transactions and dormant accounts.

12.7 DEMATERIALISATION (DEMAT ACCOUNTS)

Demat account is an account that is used to hold shares and securities in electronic format. Dematerialisation is the process of converting physical shares into electronic form. This was made mandatory in 1996. Holding shares in electronic form reduces the risk of theft, damage and malpractices which were quite easy when shares and securities were held in physical form. When shares were transferred by post fraudsters could intercept them and sell them to unauthorised persons. The bonafide shareholders were put to enormous difficulties in getting duplicate shares issued form companies and could do so only after filling indemnity bonds and fulfilling other formalities like placing advertisements in newspapers etc.

Another driving factor for dematerialization was the stupendous growth in volume of trade in shares and securities. An idea of the volume of trade can be gauged from the fact that a total of 34.6 million new investors flocked to the bourses in the last year—this was a jump of 63% from the previous year (TOI 1.5.22). If these shares had been held in physical form the settlement process would have been very time consuming and exerted tremendous pressure on stock exchanges. It would also have been an impediment in the healthy growth of capital market.

All these factors contributed to the concept of dematerialization of shares and securities and opening up of demat accounts.

The bank of the customer with whom he opens a demat account is called a Depository Participant (DP). Through their DP they can open their demat account with either of the two depositories set up in the country—National Security Depository Limited (NSDL) or the Central Depository Services Limited (CDSL). The banker DP acts an agent of NSDL or CDSL. For every purchase of shares and securities the demat account of the customer gets credited, and with every sale it gets debited. The bank acting as DP earns considerable amount of fees and commission from these accounts and transactions. Also, for opening a demat account the customer is required to open an account in the bank whether savings or current, in this manner the customer base of the bank also increases- this can be gauged from the fact that India closed FY22 with 89.7 million demat accounts—a total of 34.6 million new investors.

12.8 DEPOSIT INSURANCE AND CREDIT GUARANTEE CORPORATION (DICGC)

The Deposit Insurance and Credit Guarantee Corporation is a wholly owned subsidiary of RBI which provides insurance cover on bank deposits.

The DICGC Act was passed in 1961 to provide for an establishment of a corporation for the purpose of insurance of deposits and guaranteeing of credit facilities and for other matters connected there with or incidental thereto.

It covers the principal amount and interest thereon in all deposit accounts whether savings, current, recurring or fixed. All commercial banks including branches of foreign banks, Local Area banks, Regional Rural banks and Co-operative banks are covered by this scheme. For a very long time the limit of the principal amount and interest there on was limited to ₹1 lakh but this limit has been raised to ₹5 lakh on 4.2.2020. For calculating this limit, the amount all the accounts of the customer will be taken into account whether they are in the same or different banks.

Previously, in practice it used to take 8–10 years for a customer to get their money from the stressed bank as they were paid only after liquidation of the bank was completed. With this amendment quicker relief will be provided to depositors of stressed banks as money will be paid within 90 days of RBI placing a bank under moratorium. 98.3% of all deposit accounts and 50.9% of deposits by value will be covered by this scheme. The cost of this insurance is borne by the banks. It has been raised from 10 paise per ₹100 to 12 paise per 100 now.

In October 2022, DICGC will be making payments up to ₹5 lakh, to 17 eligible Co-operative banks. Several restrictions including on withdrawals had been imposed on these banks in view of their deteriorating financial positions. Of the 17, eight are in Maharashtra, four in Uttar Pradesh, and one each in New Delhi, Andhra Pradesh and West Bengal (TOI 22.8.22).

12.9 BANKING OMBUDSMAN SCHEME, 2006

Many times the bank's customers have to face a lot of harassment while trying to get their grievances addressed by their banks. The RBI introduced Banking Ombudsman Scheme under Section 35A of the Banking Regulation Act, 1949 with effect from 1995. It has been revised from time to time. It is a quasi-judicial authority functioning under the supervision of the RBI. This scheme provides a speedy and inexpensive forum to bank customers for resolution of their complaints relating to certain services rendered by banks. This scheme covers all Scheduled Commercial Banks, RRBs and Schedule Primary Co-operative Banks. The RBI appoints the banking ombudsman who is a senior official to look into and redress customer's complaints against deficiency in certain banking services. So far fifteen banking ombudsmen have been appointed by the RBI with their offices being located mostly in state capitals. They can receive and consider any complaint relating to the following deficiency in banking services including Internet banking.

- If the bank does not pay or inordinately delays the payment or collection of cheques, drafts, bills, pay orders, inward remittances.

- If the bank does not follow RBI guidelines for ATM/Debit Cards/ Credit Card operations or the applicable rates of interest or any other guidelines issued by RBI from time to time.
- Complaints from NRIs regarding remittances from abroad, deposits or any other matter.
- Non-adherence to the fair practices code as adopted by the bank or those issued by Banking Codes and Standards Board of India.
- Failure to honour guarantee or letter of credit commitments.
- Forcible closure of deposit accounts without giving sufficient reason or proper notice.
- Refusal to close or delay in closing of an account.
- Delays in sanction, disbursement or disposal of loan applications.
- Delays in receipt of export proceeds, handling export bills, etc. for exporters, provided the said complaint pertains to the banks operation in India
- Any other matter relating to the violations of directives issued by the RBI in relation to banking or other services.
- The complaint has already been settled earlier through the banking ombudsman proceedings.

Bank customers were mis-sold own and third party products. Till 2017 the RBI was reluctant to take its role as a protector of retail customers seriously. But now RBI has allowed such customers who have been mis-sold products to approach the banking ombudsman.

The banking ombudsman will consider the complaint only if the following conditions are fulfilled:

1. The subject matter is within their ambit.
2. The complaint should not be frivolous or vexatious.
3. The customer has first approached the bank for redressal of his grievance.
4. The complaint should be made within one year from the date on which the customer had received the reply of the bank or if no reply has been received then within one month and one year from the date of the representation to the bank.

Fee and compensation: No fee is charged for either filing or resolving customer's complaints by the banking ombudsman. The amount of compensation granted to a customer is limited to the amount directly arising out of the act or omission of the banker or ₹10 lakh whichever is lower.

If a customer is dissatisfied with the banking ombudsman decision they can approach the appellate authority who is generally a Deputy Governor of the RBI. The concerned bank too has the option to do the same if it feels the need.

KEY TERMS

Bill of exchange A bill of exchange is an instrument in writing containing an unconditional order, signed by the maker, directing a certain person to pay a certain sum of money only to, or to the order of a certain person or to be bearer of the instrument.

Negotiable instruments A negotiable instrument is one which is easily transferable and the bona fide transferee who receives it for value, always gets a good title. According to Section 13 of Negotiable Instrument Act, 1881, a negotiable instrument means a promissory notes, bill of exchange or a cheque payable either to order or bearer.

Payable on demand A cheque has to be honoured by the banker immediately when it is presented. It has no days of grace which a bill of exchange enjoys.

Truncated Cheque When an electronic cheque image is substituted for the physical cheque in a clearing cycle.

Unconditional order For issuing a cheque no condition can be imposed, e.g., 'Pay Dhruv the sum of Rupees Ten Thousand only after he wins the cricket match'.

REVIEW QUESTIONS

12.1 Define a cheque and explain its essential features.

12.2 Differentiate between
- (i) Post-dated cheque and stale cheque.
- (ii) Demand draft and pay order.
- (iii) General crossing and special crossing.

12.3 Write short notes on
- (i) Importance of KYC norms
- (ii) Role and importance of Deposit Insurance and Credit Guarantee Corporation(DICGC)
- (iii) Bouncing of cheques
- (iv) Dematerialisation of shares

12.4 Explain the need for a banking ombudsman. How does it help bank customers in settling their grievances?

13

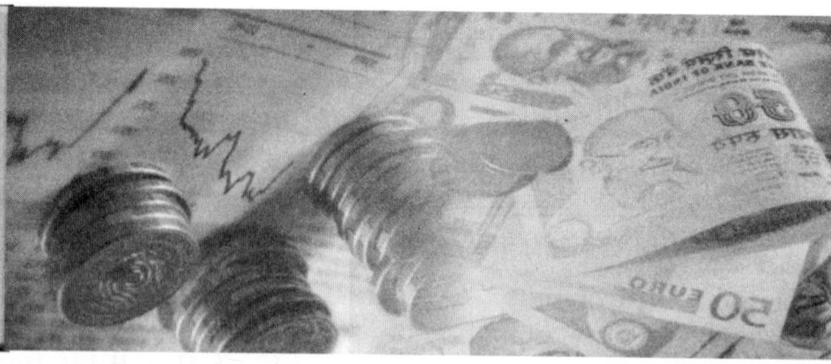

Risk Management: An Overview

Learning Objectives

After going through this chapter we will be able to:

- Define the concept of risk management.
- Explain the importance of risk management.
- Describe the concept of risk.
- Explain the concept of business risks.
- Explain the nature and causes of business risks.
- Describe different types of business risks.
- Discuss the various methods of handling risks.
- Summarize the fundamentals of enterprise risk management.

Traditionally, the concept of *risk management* has been considered synonymous with *insurance*. It has evolved with the business complexity, encompassing business risks so as to provide a platform for an organization's decision-making process. Bearing of risk is an essential element of the business in the sense that every business undertaking is faced with multitude of risks, inherent in business and is inevitable. Business decision making, in general, is based on assumptions, expectations, estimates and forecasts of future indeterminate events. Thus, risk management can be seen as the task of handling and controlling risks requiring management to take preventive and corrective measures. It is an integrated process of delineating specific areas of risk, developing a comprehensive plan, integrating the plan and conducting ongoing evaluation.

Risk management involves the following steps:

1. Identification of risk
2. Evaluation of risk
3. Selecting the appropriate device of handling the risk
4. Executing the decision
5. Aftermath and evaluation, i.e., performance appraisal

13.1 IMPORTANCE OF RISK MANAGEMENT

Both human and business life, are full of risks of various kinds as a consequence of uncertainties surrounding the future. Managing risk is significant in ensuring social, political and economic development of a country. The importance of risk management can be discussed as follows:

1. For developing appropriate business policies and strategies
2. For effective management of resources
3. For evaluating and appraising events that can have a bearing on the operations of the business
4. For qualitative and quantitative assessment of such risks with a view to assist top management make effective decisions concerning innovation, expansion and growth of the business
5. For developing plans and procedures to minimize, handle and manage such risks and ensuring smooth functioning of the business
6. For avoiding costs, disruptions and inefficiencies, thereby ensuring maximization of stockholders' wealth. The significance of risk management lies in the fact that it helps the business organizations to tackle all those risks which can threaten the assets or earning capacity of the business.

This brings us to the questions, what is meant by *risks*? what are the various types of *risks*?, and what are their causes? The following sections would attempt to find answers to these questions. Blessed with enormous thinking power, human beings are quick to react and distinguish between good and bad situations, although the reaction often depends on an individual's own perception. However, all human beings constantly desire and strive for situations that match their expectations, and want to avoid the adverse ones, giving rise to the argot called **risk!**

13.2 THE CONCEPT OF RISK

Different people have defined risks, differently. However, in most of the definitions the term *risk* includes exposure to adverse situations:

Macmillan dictionary: It defines *risk* as: *The possibility that something unpleasant or dangerous might happen".*[1]

E.J. Vaughan: refers to the term *risk* as: *A condition in which there is a possibility of an adverse deviation from a desired outcome that is expected or hoped for.*[2]

S.E. Harrinton and G.R. Niehaus: state that *At its most general level, risk is used to describe any situation where there is uncertainty about what outcome will occur. Life is obviously risky.*[3]

Life Insurance Corporation of India: It defines the term risk as: *A condition where there is a possibility of an adverse deviation from a desired outcome that is expected or hoped for; there is no requirement that the possibility be immeasurable, only that it must exist.*

The concept of risk may also be explained as the possibility of unfavourable results following any occurrence. Risks arise due to uncertainties, although many a times, the term *uncertainty* is confused with *risk*. Uncertainty refers to a situation where the outcome or result can only be estimated but not predicted with precision. Uncertainty is a subjective phenomenon, a concept based on an individual's own perception, thereby implying different degrees to different individuals. Decisions under uncertain situations thus are obviously very difficult and depend not only upon an individual's skills, power of judgment but to a great extent upon luck too. Thus, unlike risk, uncertainty is not calculable and consequently not insurable, although it is uncertainty which is the major cause of risk. Uncertainty is a state of mind, and contains an element of doubt as it is based on lack of knowledge about what will or what will not happen in the future.

The concept of risk may also be distinguished from the concept of *perils* and *hazards*. Peril, in the literary sense, means a serious and immediate danger. It refers to the cause of loss or a happening causing a loss. For example, fire can cause loss of human lives besides damaging assets and buildings. Windstorm, hail, etc. also cause losses in different ways while theft, burglary and robbery cause direct financial loss to the sufferer.

Hazards, on the other hand, refer to the conditions that increase the severity of loss or the conditions affecting perils. For example, fall in *sensex*, (a peril) may cause loss to the business, but in certain cases it may cause a fatal heart attack or mental breakdown to the business-owner (here it would be a hazard).

---

[1] *Macmillan English Dictionary*, Macmillan Publishers, p. 1227, 2002.

[2] Vaughan, Emmet J., *Risk Management*, John Wiley & Sons, Inc., p. 8, 1997.

[3] Harrington, S.E. and G.R. Niehaus, *Risk Management and Insurance*, McGraw-Hill, p. 7, 1999.

Hazards can be classified into the following categories:

(i) Physical hazards include those physical conditions, which may aggravate the probability of loss caused by any peril. For example, storing crackers in a congested commercial complex, with no fire-fighting arrangements.

(ii) Moral hazards refer to the increase in the severity of loss resulting from dishonesty of a person. A typical case of moral hazards is the person who destroys his own insured asset and tries to make profit out of exaggerated claims.

(iii) Morale hazards emerge from an attitude of carelessness or indifference towards the cause of loss merely because it is insured for. It reflects the mental condition of individuals affecting their willingness to cooperate such as rash driving, poor maintenance of machinery, etc.

Thus, peril is used for the loss-producing events and hazards for an aggravating factor magnifying the impact of loss. Here it is important for us to understand the concept of loss, and also to draw a clear distinction between the term *loss* and the term *chance of loss*. Loss, in the literary sense, means the act of losing something or someone or the disadvantage that results from losing something. It is, in other words, that portion of the deterioration in value for which no compensation has been received. The chance of loss, on the other hand, refers to the frequency of occurrence of loss, that is, the probability of loss.

13.3 MEANING OF BUSINESS RISKS

Risk is an inherent part of any business. In fact, it is that element which differentiates business from other economic activities, leading to uncertainty. This is because every business is directed towards the future which itself is uncertain, unpredictable. Every business aims at profits, but many a times it is forced to face losses because it has practically no control over several factors affecting profits, e.g., changes in consumer's tastes, fashions and demand, technology, degree of competition, government policies, and so on.

Thus, conceptually the terms *risk* and *business risks* are not basically different. Business risk is a subset of the generic expression risk. Thus, it is the risk applicable to the business situations. The term, *business risk* implies risk in the objective sense.

13.4 NATURE OF BUSINESS RISKS

Risk, an essential element of business: Risk is inherent in every business, and bearing of risk is a fundamental condition of business. In fact, profit earned by an entrepreneur is the reward for undertaking risk. Business risk is universal. It is an inevitable, unavoidable part of business.

Business risks are caused due to uncertainties: Business decisions are concerned with future which cannot be predicted with 100 per cent accuracy. Business operates in, interacts with, and is thus influenced by an ever-changing environment. For example, uncertainties like changes in demand, prices, fashion, government policies, technology and natural calamities, cause risks in business.

Business risks vary according to the nature and size of business: All businesses do not face the same type of risk or the degree of risk. Generally speaking, larger the scale of business operation, greater is the risk. The level of risk also depends on the nature of the business. For example, a business influenced by changes in fashion or demand faces a high degree of risk. Location and time are other factors affecting business risks.

Profit is the reward for risk bearing: *No risk, no gain* is a well-known business quote. Moreover, as stated earlier, greater the risk inherent in a business, higher is the chance of profit. Profit is the return earned by a businessman for bearing risk.

Evaluation of business risk is very difficult: It is extremely difficult to evaluate, measure or calculate business risk accurately. This is because business risk arises due to many factors related to the environment in which the business exists. The impact of these factors varies from business to business. For example, terms of sale, competence of management, degree of competition are some of the factors causing business risk.

Business risk cannot be eliminated: No business can absolutely avoid risk. This is because every decision taken by a businessman is a calculated risk. With efficient management and accuracy in calculations, however, the adverse effect of business risk can be minimized to a great extent.

13.5 CAUSES OF BUSINESS RISKS

There are different types of business risks which are caused by various factors. The causes of business risk may be classified into the following categories:

Natural causes: Risks caused by the actions of nature are called **natural risks**. Human beings have no control over the nature, and at the same time it is very difficult to forecast natural calamities with certainty. Unforeseen natural events like earthquake, famine, tsunami, cyclone, tornado and excessive heat or cold, cause heavy losses to individuals and business.

Political causes: Political causes include change in government, political stability, changes in government policies, price regulations, unfavourable economic policies, communal violence and such other political changes affect profit margins of business enterprises.

Social causes: Changes in the social environment and in consumer behaviour cause risk to the business. For example, changes in fashion, changes in the tastes and preferences of the target customers, changes in the lifestyles, changes in the income patterns of consumers and changes in social values, affect the profit earning ability of business.

Economic causes: Increase in the cost of raw materials and other factors of production due to inflation, increase in the rate of interest, reduction in demand due to economic recession, severe competition, trade cycles, etc. are some of the economic factors causing business risks.

Managerial causes: Success or failure of the business, ultimately depends on the efficiency and competence of its management. For example, inaccurate estimation of demand by management, inefficient handling of the business and disharmony between management and workers cause risk to the business.

Competitive causes: Unforeseen increase in the level of competition can threaten not only the growth and expansion but also the survival of business. Competitive causes of business risks include entry of a very large number of business enterprises in the same line of business activity, and influx of multinational companies adversely affecting the market shares of the domestic companies.

Technological causes: Advancement in production and distribution technologies may render the old technology as obsolete causing severe financial losses to organizations carrying on with old technology. New models of cars have drastically brought down the prices of old models. Similarly, development of supercomputer has made the old models of computers obsolete.

13.6 TYPES OF BUSINESS RISKS

The distinction between various categories of business risks can be discussed as follows:

13.6.1 Pure Risks and Speculative Risks

Pure risk refers to a chance of loss without any possibility of gain to the individual. For example, when a fire breaks out, it can only cause losses and no gain. Similarly, where a car is insured against the contingency of an accident, the insurance company is liable to compensate the loss, if the accident occurs; but if the accident does not occur, the insured obviously does not get any benefit or gain.

Speculative risk on the other hand, implies a situation which involves not only the chance of loss but also a possibility of gain as well. For example, investment in stock market may bring either gain or loss to the investor. Similarly, a business innovation may result either in increased profits or heavy losses to the business. Other examples of speculative risk include changes in demand, price fluctuations, changes in fashion and tastes, and so on.

The distinguishing characteristics of pure and speculative risks are discussed in the Table 13.1.

Table 13.1 Differences between 'Pure Risks' and 'Speculative Risks'

Pure risks	*Speculative risks*
Pure risks are inherent in business. They cannot be avoided. One can at best try to minimize their adverse impact.	Speculative risks are deliberately assumed by entrepreneur with the expectation and in the hope of making profits.
Pure risks may or may not cause losses but they never cause gains.	The element of gain is inherent in some business situations. Accordingly, speculative risks may cause either loss or gain.
Pure risks are generally insured for.	Speculative risks cannot be insured.
An entrepreneur may avoid insure or simply assume the pure risk.	An entrepreneur may reduce, avoid or shift the speculative risk to others.

Pure risks may further be classified into the following categories (Figure 13.1):

Figure 13.1 Classification of 'pure risks'.

Personal risks: Risks that directly affect the earning capacity of individuals are called **personal risks**. Personal risks include

Premature death. Death of the earning member, who made no provisions for financial obligations, affects the financial status of the family.

Old age. Risk that an individual may not be able to earn his livelihood in old age or may have insufficient income at the age of retirement, is a pure risk of personal nature.

Sickness or disability. Poor health or disability affects the earning capacity of individuals.

Unemployment. Unemployment is a personal risk resulting in financial insecurity to the unemployed and his dependents.

Property risks: Property risks include the possibility of loss of property, the use of the property or income from the property. For example, immovable property like land and building may get damaged due to floods, earthquake or fire. Personal assets like appliances may be stolen or destroyed due to fire. Losses due to property risks may be direct or indirect. A direct loss is the apparent physical loss or damage to the property while an indirect loss is a financial loss consequently to the loss of income from the property, non-availability of the property for use or expenses incurred to render the damaged property usable. For example, a house destroyed due to earthquake is a direct loss and the rent income earned by the owner is an indirect loss.

Liability risks: Liability risks arise due to intentional or unintentional injury caused to the persons or damages to their properties or due to loots or invasion of the rights of others for which one is liable to pay damages or compensation. Liability risks generally arise from the legal provisions. Liability under the Workman's Compensation Act or other labour laws in India are typical examples of pure, liability risks.

13.6.2 Internal and External Risks

Internal risks are caused by the internal events associated with the working of a business enterprise. However, forces belonging to the external environment affecting the particular business enterprise cause external risks. Worker's strike, breakdown of machinery, carelessness or dishonesty of employees, disharmony in worker-management relationship are examples of the internal risks adversely affecting the working of an enterprise and likely to cause losses. On the other hand, changes in the market conditions, distribution, production technology and political environment; natural calamities; social unrest are some risks external to the business enterprise, but affecting its profit-earning capacity. Internal risks can be controlled, to a great extent, through efficient handling whereas external risks cannot be controlled or can be controlled with great difficulty by the management.

13.6.3 Fundamental and Particular Risks

General or group risks, which affect the economy or a large section of the population at the macro level are called fundamental risks. They are the consequence of factors beyond the control of individuals who suffer the losses. Thus, it is society and not an individual who is expected to deal with such risks. They are impersonal in origin, and are not caused by the fault of any particular individual and may be caused by economic, social, cultural, political and natural factors. Earthquake, floods, war, inflation and unemployment are the examples of fundamental risks.

Particular risks are personal in origin. They are caused by the fault of particular individuals. They cause losses only to a few individuals. Such risks are expected to be dealt with by individuals rather than the society. For example, the burning of a house, burning of a factory, bank robbery, burglary, theft, murder of a manager, etc. are particular risks.

13.6.4 Static and Dynamic Risks

Static risks are those risks which would occur irrespective of any changes in the economy. Such risks result in destruction of an asset or change in its possession. They are a consequence of human factors like dishonesty of workers, natural calamities, etc. Static risks cannot be a source of gain to society. These risks are more or less predictable as they have the tendency to occur at regular intervals of time. As such, static risks can be insured for.

Dynamic risks are a consequence of changes in the economic environment. These are less predictable than static risks as they do not have a defined pattern of occurrence. For example, price level changes, technology changes, changes in consumer tastes, income and output, etc. may cause financial loss to business enterprise. Dynamic risks are the result of adjustments to misallocation of resources, and thus bring gains to the society in the long run. Unlike static risks, dynamic risks are not covered by insurance.

13.6.5 Financial and Non-financial Risks

Risky situations, likely to cause financial losses are referred to as financial risks. On the other hand, when the possibility of a financial loss does not exist, the situation involves a kind of risk which is non-financial. Financial risks are more particular, i.e., personal in nature.

13.6.6 Insurable and Non-insurable Risks

Insurable risks are *pure* risks which can be predicted and the chances of their occurrence too can be determined. These risks imply a situation involving the chance of loss or no loss. These risks can be shifted through various types of insurance policies, covering the risk. For example, life insurance, marine insurance, fire insurance, automobile insurance, credit insurance, personal accident insurance, burglary insurance, etc.

Non-insurable risks are those risks, which cannot be covered or shifted through insurance. The likelihood of occurrence of these risks cannot be determined. These risks cannot be predicted with any degree of accuracy. These risks are speculative in nature. They refer to uncertainties that are caused due to lack of business entrepreneurship and lack of mental presence. They cannot be forecasted and thus, cannot be insured. They are non-insurable risks. For example, changes in demand, changes in supply, changes in fashion, price fluctuations, etc.

The essential requisites of insurable risks are as follows:

(i) The risk to be insurable must arise out of the ordinary course of business, must be accidental or occur by chance and not created artificially.

(ii) The risk must be a common one, in the sense, that there must be a large number of units, which are likely to face the risk, so that spreading it at a nominal cost is justified.

(iii) There must be an element of uncertainty regarding the chances of occurrence of the risk and also the time of its occurrence.

(iv) The loss caused by the risk must be predictable and measurable with a fair degree of accuracy.

(v) The party must have genuine interest in the avoidance of risk.

(vi) The risk must be capable of causing substantial loss or damage although not necessarily be catastrophic.

13.7 METHODS OF HANDLING RISKS

Human beings have the natural tendency to dream of a brighter, more prosperous future and protect oneself from adverse situations. Perhaps, the greatest fear that man can ever have is the fear of shattered dreams. But then, future is uncertain and life is obviously risky. Risks cannot be completely eliminated. However, sensible handling of risks can help in minimizing the negative consequences of various risks. Risks can be handled by adopting any of the following methods:

13.7.1 Avoiding Risks

One can avoid risk by avoiding the causes of risk. Avoidance of risk is a preventive method of handling risk. Of course, *prevention is better than cure*, but it can be counter-productive when used as a technique to deal with risk. A person or an organization may avoid getting involved in the action that may give rise to risks, particularly when the potential results or gains are not considered to be worthy of the risk. This itself gives rise to the risk of losing an opportunity to gain. For example, a businessman fearing the risk of survival may not attempt to develop a new product and prefer to follow the leaders in the industry. This may ensure survival of his business, but surely not maximization of economic gains.

Risk may also be avoided by adopting a safer alternative, an out of harm's way to a risky proposition. But, it may not always be possible to avoid risks, particularly when no alternatives are available. For example, a person may travel less frequently by air in order to avoid the risk of dying in a plane crash. He would then be required to adopt alternative mode of travel; which might be much riskier.

13.7.2 Reducing Risks

It is not always possible or viable to avoid risks. Such risks can be abridged by concentrated efforts of risk management. Loss prevention and control is a commonly applied method of reducing risks. Actions that reduce the expected cost of losses by reducing the frequency of losses and/or the acuteness of losses that occur are termed as **methods of loss control** or alternatively, **methods of risk control**. Actions that largely affect the frequency with which the losses occur are referred to as *loss prevention methods* while those which influence the acuteness of losses that occur are referred to as *loss reduction methods*.

EXAMPLES

- Losses from theft, shoplifting, etc. can be minimized by giving effective training to the employees and by employing burglary alarms, night watchman and safety vaults.
- Losses from fire can be completely reduced by constructing a fireproof building or by not smoking in a factory producing inflammable items.
- Proper safety testing of an automobile reduces the chances of accidental loss as well as the severity of loss, both in terms of damage to the automobile and the injuries suffered by the passengers travelling in it.
- Losses from bad debts can be dealt with through careful screening of customers and prompt collection of outstanding debts.

13.7.3 Shifting Risks (or Transferring Risks)

There are several risks which can neither be avoided nor even reduced. However, attempt can be made to shift or transfer such risks to those who are willing to bear the risks, through various methods such as:

Hedging: Hedging is the process of entering simultaneously into two contracts of an opposite, but equivalent nature (one in the spot or cash market and the other in the future market) to protect against losses due to fluctuations in commodity prices. Risk transfer, in this case, is accomplished by buying and selling for future delivery, whereby the dealer is protected against the risk of decline or increase in market price of the product between the time it is bought and the time of selling it.

However, hedging is not a foolproof method of transferring risks because prices in spot and future market may not change in the same proportion.

Underwriting: A public company issuing shares and debentures faces the risk of loss due to under-subscription of its issue. In case of the first issue made by the public company, it is legally required to raise the *minimum subscription*. Failure to do so will lead to winding up of the company. This risk can be shifted to an underwriter. Underwriting is an agreement entered into between the promoters of a public company and underwriters, whereby the underwriters undertake to buy the securities not subscribed to by the public, in consideration of a specified commission.

Subcontracting: Long-term contracts requiring specialized services of several experts involve the risk of increase in prices of inputs. These risks are best tackled through subcontracting some operations and processes in the contract. For example, building contractors generally engage subcontractors for plumbing, electric wiring, woodwork, etc.

Sharing or spreading risks: Company form of business ownership and joint ventures are the typical examples of sharing or spreading risks. In the company form, investment of a large number of persons is pooled and thereby the risk is spread over a large number of shareholders. Each shareholder contributes a small amount towards the capital of the company called SHARES and bears a limited liability or risk. Thus, the risk of business loss is shared by a large number of shareholders defined by and limited to the extent of the shareholder's contribution to the company's capital.

Joint ventures are formed between business allies undertaking technical or financial ventures that involve high degree of risk. The risks get spread over the partners in the joint venture who share such risks.

Insurance: Insurance is a social device whereby the risks of individual entities are shifted or transferred to an insurer who, agrees for a consideration called the PREMIUM, to assume to a specified extent, losses suffered by the insured.

Assuming risks: Failure of finding any better alternative of handling the risk may compel the businessman to assume risk. Risk may be assumed voluntarily or otherwise. For example, if the cost of preventing or reducing the risk is very high and the chance of loss is not considered worth the cost of insurance, risk may be assumed. Sometimes a person failing to foresee the possibility of occurrence of loss, makes no plans of handling the risk. Such a person, when exposed to the risk, has no way but to bear the loss.

13.8 ENTERPRISE RISK MANAGEMENT

Enterprise risk management (ERM) may be defined as the management of the various risks that an enterprise is constantly exposed to. As a result of the recent advancements in technology and the growing need for globalization, there has been a significant improvement in the field of corporate risk management. ERM is a move towards a more defined and formalized risk management. It is commonly believed that managerial decision-making based on an integrated approach produces better results than the piecemeal approach. It has been recommended that the process of identifying and appraising the various types of risks that a firm is exposed to is valuable because the process provides managers with a better understanding of their business and the events that can potentially hinder the firm's strategic objectives. Thus, a significant benefit of ERM is that the organizations will be able to make improved decisions because of a better understanding of the firm's risk. It is imperative thus, for all the organizations concerned with corporate governance to employ an all-embracing risk assessment process and adopt suitable risk management policies.

An important aspect of ERM is identifying risk exposures. A business organization may be exposed to various types of risks depending upon the nature of its business. The following methods can be carried out by the business organizations for identification of risks:

1. Assessing the probable changes in the environment that can affect the working of the organization
2. Evaluating the probable impact of risks on the organization's resources based on their size, value, type, accessibility, portability and location
3. Identifying, in particular, the risks that may be difficult to measure, with low probability of occurrence, but rather high in terms of their consequences

13.8.1 Role of CRO in ERM

The growing need towards an integrated approach to risk management has forced companies to assign specific responsibilities to the Chief Risk Officer to smooth the progress of ERM. The role of CRO in ERM includes

1. Formation of risk management information systems (RMIS)
2. Building up of risk information database through an uninterrupted process of documentation and reporting
3. Communication of risk management strategy to various levels of management
4. Training of the working team associated with the ERM
5. Frequent evaluation of ERM strategies

13.8.2 ERM in Insurance

Business organizations exposed to high degrees of risks and endeavouring to reduce the catastrophic effects of such risks find ERM as one of the best approaches for the purpose. ERM can be an effective tool for the insurance companies, particularly in the following domains:

Handling of exposures: With the help of ERM, an insurer is able to identify, gauge and lessen disastrous effects of risks, for instance, a natural disaster affecting several types of insurance, the primary and reinsurance sectors, the underwriting operations and the investment operations.

Situation analysis: ERM can also help insurers in managing radical events through such techniques as worst-case analysis.

Disaster response: ERM based structural simulation modelling allows insurers to quickly evaluate alternative financial responses to a disaster, whether the event creates a short-term emergency that requires an immediate infusion of capital or whether it creates a short-term opportunity such as capital restructuring.[4]

Asset liability management: ERM skills help insurance companies to optimize asset liability management (ALM) and achieve their dual goal of solvency and profitability.

Relationship management: Continuous interaction with shareholders, regulators and the analysts being the basis of ERM helps organizations develop competent relationship management.

KEY TERMS

Business risk 'Risk' applicable to business situations.

CRO Chief Risk Officer responsible for an enterprise's risk management.

Hazards Conditions or factors affecting severity of loss.

Hedging A method of transferring risk of losses due to fluctuations in prices.

Peril Cause of loss.

Pure risk Insurable risks that cause only losses and no gains.

Risk management The task of handling and controlling risks.

RMIS Risk Management Information Systems are Software Tools used for effective risk management.

---

[4] Miccolis, Jarry, *ERM and September 11, Treasury management*, ICFAI Press, January 2002, pp. 55–58.

Speculative risk Non-insurable risks that may cause either loss or gain.

Uncertainty Incalculable event that is not insurable.

Underwriting Agreement to buy the unsubscribed securities of a company.

REVIEW QUESTIONS

13.1 What do you understand by the risk management? Explain the importance of risk management.

13.2 Explain the concept of risk.

13.3 What do you mean by business risk? What are the causes of business risk?

13.4 What are the various types of business risk? Suggest some methods of handling different risks.

13.5 Write short notes on

(i) Enterprise risk management

(ii) Role of chief risk officer

(iii) ERM in insurance

14

Introduction to Insurance

Learning Objectives

After going through this chapter we will be able to:

- Understand the meaning and nature of insurance.
- Discuss the purpose of insurance.
- Explain the need to get insured.
- Discuss the benefits of insurance.
- Describe the functions of insurance.
- Understand the elements of an insurable risk.
- Discuss the importance of insurance.
- Explain the principles of insurance.
- Discuss the nature of insurance contract.
- Understand the fundamentals of insurability.
- Describe the classification of insurance
- Describe the insurance terminologies/definitions.

The basic philosophy of insurance is a cooperative device by which the loss likely to be caused by an uncertain event is spread over a number of persons who are exposed to it and who propose to insure themselves against such an event. The essence of insurance is the elimination of risk and substitution of certainty for uncertainty. Insurance helps in replacing risk with known costs—the costs of buying and maintaining insurance policies. Thus, insurance is not only an important aid to industry and commerce but also provides great benefits to the society as a whole.

The term *insurance* has been defined in both financial and legal sense:

In Financial Sense

The term *insurance* may be defined in the financial sense as: *A social device providing financial compensation for the consequences of adversity, the payments being made from the accumulated contributions of all parties participating in the arrangement. The essence of insurance thus, is collective bearing of risks as it involves pooling of risk.*

In Legal Sense

A contract of insurance may be defined as: *A contract under which the insurer (insurance company) in consideration of a sum of money paid (premium) by the insured (the person whose risk is insured) agrees to:*

(i) make good the loss suffered by the insured against a specific risk (for which the insurance is effected), or

(ii) to pay a prefixed amount to the insured or his/her beneficiaries on the happening of a specified event.

Thus, insurance is a contract between the insurer and the insured requiring all the essentials of a valid contract according to the law of contracts. The instrument containing the contract of insurance is called a **policy**.

14.1 CHARACTERISTICS OF INSURANCE

The characteristics of insurance that emerge from the above definitions of insurance are as follows:

- **Insurance is a cooperative device:** Insurance is the result of the cooperation of a large number of persons voluntarily agreeing to share the monetary loss arising due to the common risk insured by them.
- **Insurance is preceded by evaluation of the risk:** The amount charged on insurance, termed **premium**, is based on the evaluation of the risk or probability of loss. Higher the probability of loss, higher is the rate of premium to be charged.
- **The amount of compensation is contingent on the extent of the loss:** In insurance, the amount of compensation payable by the insurer depends on the extent of the loss occurred due to the insured risk except in the case of life insurance where a defined sum is paid due to the certainty of the occurrence of the insured risk.
- **Contractual relationship between the insured and the insurer:** Insurance creates a contractual relationship between the

insured and the insurer. The essential requisites of a valid contract must be complied with for a contract of insurance to be legally enforceable.

- **A contract of insurance is a contract of indemnity:** The payment of compensation in the case of insurance is conditional on the occurrence of the loss with the exception of life insurance as the contingency insured, that is, death or expiry of the term, is sure to take place and the insured amount accordingly is certainly paid.
- **Insurance is a means of converting uncertainty into certainty:** Insurance helps in converting uncertainty into certainty by insuring assets, properties and lives and improving the welfare of the society. Insurance is non-speculative and therefore, is not gambling.

14.2 INSURANCE: PURPOSE AND NEED

The purpose of insurance as a method of transferring risk is to provide economic protection against the losses that may be incurred due to uncertain predicaments caused by disability, death of an earning family member or economic losses. The events that cause losses may or may not occur during the operative time of the contract of insurance. People, therefore, opt for insurance purely for the reasons of uncertainties in life. Insurance gives the insured a kind of peace of mind as he is assured of making up the loss in the event of such uncertainties in life. The insurance of business organizations is essential in the sense that if adverse happenings are not guarded, they may affect the business as well as the business owner in person and his personal assets. This would adversely affect the financial well-being of the business owner and endanger the survival and growth of the business. Thus, insurance is of vital importance in the day-to-day business and social activities.

The purpose and need of insurance lies in the services it provides to the society and business organizations as discussed hereinafter.

Reduction in worries. Efficiencies are improved when the tensions and fears involving the risks are shifted to the insurer.

Reimbursement of losses. The financial status of individuals and business organizations remains unaffected by the losses caused by the risks insured for.

Opportunity for investment. Life insurance contracts provide double benefit of—protection and investment because the event insured against is sure to happen. In fact, life insurance investment offers attractive return.

Credit enhancement: Businessmen enjoy better credit standing as the risks are transferred to the insurance company.

Opportunity for employment. Insurance companies are playing a vital role in tackling the problem of unemployment in the country by offering employment opportunities to many people. As a result, there are large number of people working as insurance agents, professionals, etc.

Indeed, the subject of Insurance has come a long way from the earlier times when it was originally conceived only as a risk-covering medium for short periods of time covering temporary risk situations such as sea voyages. Though covering of risk may still be seen as the main purpose of insurance, but today it is being growingly acknowledged as a useful tool for a number of situations, including the following:

Temporary needs/threats. Life insurance policies provide for replacement of income on death, personal accident, etc.

Regular savings. People seeking financial independence for their family, go for life insurance schemes offering attractive returns on savings. Insurance provides funds for meeting various needs like children's education, marriage, and so on.

Investment. Put simply, the building up of savings while safeguarding it from the ravages of inflation. Unlike regular saving products, investment products are traditionally lump sum investments, where the individual generally makes a one off payment.

Retirement. Provision for later years becomes increasingly necessary, especially in a changing cultural and social environment. One can buy a suitable insurance policy which will provide periodical payments in one's old age.

14.3 BENEFITS OF INSURANCE

The following are some of the benefits of insurance:

Shifting of risks: Insurance is a social device whereby individuals and businessmen shift specific risks to the insurer under a contract of insurance. This helps the businessmen to concentrate their attention on important business issues.

Providing pecuniary security: Insurance gives a sense of security to the policyholder. In the event of loss or damage to the insured property, he is indemnified to the extent of the actual loss and his financial condition remains unaffected by the loss/damage. In life insurance, a life policy grants pecuniary protection to the dependents, where the policyholder dies before the date of maturity of the policy, and to the policyholder where he survives till the maturity of the policy.

Assuring expected profits: An insured businessman or policyholder can enjoy normal expected profits as he would not be required to make provisions or allocate funds for meeting future contingencies.

Safeguarding interest of consumers: As the businessman is duly insured against the risks that can cause losses, and he can hope for a normal profit margin, he need not maintain large reserves of funds to meet the consequences of unforeseen, uncertain occurrence of losses. This enables him to charge lower prices and protect the interests of consumers.

Improving credit standing: Insurance has the effect of improving credit standing of businessman as the assets which are insured are easily accepted as security for loans by commercial banks and financial institutions. Life policy is a valuable asset, and one can raise an emergency loan against it.

Providing investment opportunity: A life insurance contract provides not only protection but also investment opportunity such as pension in old age. It is a contingent contract and not a contract of indemnity. In case of life insurance, the payment is guaranteed and in most of the policies, bonuses are also paid along with the guaranteed amount.

Encouraging savings: It is particularly true for life insurance. The insured person must regularly save out of his current income an amount equal to the premium to be paid. The policy gets elapsed if the premium is not paid on time. Thus, life insurance is a compulsory form of saving.

Capital formation: Insurance companies mobilize the savings of community through collection of premiums and invest these savings in productive channels. As institutional investors, these companies provide funds for financing economic development plans. Thus, insurance serves as an agency of capital formation.

Generating employment opportunities: With the growth of insurance business, the insurance companies are creating more and more employment opportunities.

Promoting social welfare: Policies like old-age pension scheme; policies in respect of education of children or marriage of children provide a sense of security to the poor policyholder, ensuring social welfare.

Helps controlling inflation: Insurance extracts the money in supply through collection of premium amounts from all the policy-holders. These funds when provided for production narrow down the inflationary gap.

14.4 FUNCTIONS OF INSURANCE

The functions of insurance may be discussed as follows:

Diffusion of risks: Insurance may not be able to avoid uncertainties associated with life, in general and business in particular, but it is able to diffuse the impact of the occurrence of loss by equitably distributing the loss over large number of policyholders. For example, in the case of fire insurance, all the policyholders pay premiums, but all of them do not suffer losses caused by fire. Only those who actually suffer the loss are compensated out of the common pool.

Providing protection: The main function of insurance is to provide protection against risk of loss. The insurance policy covers the risk of loss. The insured person is indemnified for the actual loss suffered by him. Insurance thus provides financial protection to the insured. Life insurance policies may also be used as collateral security for raising loans.

Encouragement of savings: Insurance not only provides protection against risks but also a number of other incentives which encourage people to insure. Since regularity and punctuality of payment of premium is a prerequisite for keeping the policy in force, the insured feels compelled to save.

Promotion of efficiency and motivation: Insurance has contributed greatly in the advancement of industry and trade. The large-scale industrial and commercial organizations that exist today are the result of the various services provided by the insurance companies. With the elimination of worries and uncertainty of risks, businessmen feel motivated and encouraged to take risks to enhance their profit-earning. This also helps in improving their efficiencies.

Prevention of losses: The insurance companies help in prevention of losses as they join hands with those institutions which are engaged in loss-prevention measures. The reduction in losses means that the insurance companies would be required to pay lesser compensations to the assured and manage to accumulate more savings, which, in turn, will assist in reducing the premium.

Providing funds for investment: Insurance provides not only protection but also capital to the society. Usually, accumulated funds through savings in the form of insurance premia are invested in economic development plans or productivity projects. The vast economic reservoir built up by the insurance sector, furnishes a good means of capital formation in the country.

Solution to social problems: One of the most important functions of insurance is to take care of many social problems. At present, we have insurance against industrial injuries, road accidents, old age, disability or death, etc. In the absence of insurance, the businessmen and individuals will have to provide for all such risks. With no or little savings for investment, no economic growth would be possible. Thus, insurance is of great service to the society as a whole, and acts as a good means of solving many social problems.

14.5 IMPORTANCE OF INSURANCE

In a dynamic world that we are all living in today, economies are changing at a very fast pace. Future is extremely uncertain, unpredictable and immeasurable. There are obvious risks for an individual as well as business organizations. Insurance has been universally accepted as the most important method of handling various kinds of risks and is indispensable in the following respects:

1. Insurance provides protection against the possible occurrence of uncertain events like losses due to fire, floods, lightning, etc. The insurer compensates the insured for the loss arising from the risk insured against.
2. Insurance is a device for eliminating risks and sharing the losses. All the policyholders who regularly pay for the loss, which may or may not happen, share the burden of the loss. Thus, the loss suffered by a person is spread over the whole of insured community.
3. Insurance is a cooperative method of spreading risks. Insurance cannot prevent occurrence of contingencies that are insured, but surely reduce the impact of the loss by spreading it over to a large number of policyholders.
4. Insurance makes for uninterrupted business operations and facilitates international trade. A businessman is free of worries associated with the risks that are insured.
5. Insurance serves as an agency of capital formation. As institutional investors, insurance companies provide funds to the government and public, and contribute in the economic development of the country.

14.6 PRINCIPLES OF INSURANCE

The fundamental principles of insurance are enumerated as follows:

14.6.1 Principle of Insurable Interest

Insurable interest means that the person opting for insurance must have pecuniary interest in the property he is going to get insured, and will suffer financial loss on the occurrence of the insured event. This is one of the essential requirements of any insurance contract. Therefore, a person can go for insurance of only those properties where he stands to benefit by the safety of the property, and will suffer loss, damage or injury in case of destruction or damage to the property. A purely emotional interest is not an insurable interest. Insurable interest is of a financial nature. Thus, if we want to insure Qutab Minar or Red Fort, we will not be allowed to do so as these are public properties but we, as an individual, do not have any pecuniary interest in these properties. No contract of insurance can be valid without insurable interests as it would amount to speculation. The owner of a property has absolute insurance interest. When a person insures a property, what is insured therein, is his financial interest in that property. The insurable interest must exist both at the time of the proposal and at the time of claims in the case of fire insurance; at the time of the proposal in the case of life insurance and at the time of claims in the case of marine insurance. The principle of insurable interest may be created either out of legal obligation or by contract or custom; or by own choice of owners, mortgagors, lessors, trustees and tenants. For example, all of us have an insurable interest in the assets owned by us, e.g., car, watch. But we have no insurable interest in the assets belonging to our employer.

14.6.2 Principle of Utmost Good Faith (Uberrimae Fidei)

Like other contracts, the insurance contract must also be based on good faith. If the insurance contract is obtained by way of fraud, concealment of facts or misrepresentation, it is void. Accordingly, it is the inherent duty of both parties to the insurance contract, to make full and fair disclosure of all material facts relating to the subject-matter of proposed insurance. The duty of disclosure is absolute and positive. Thus, the principle of utmost good faith is equally applicable to both the parties. However, the onus of making a full disclosure of all material facts usually rests primarily upon the insured. For example, in case of life insurance, the insured must reveal the true age and details of the existing illnesses/diseases. Similarly, in case of the insurance of a building against fire, the insured must disclose the details of the goods stored, particularly, whether such goods are of hazardous nature.

14.6.3 Principle of Indemnity

The insurance contract should always be a contract of indemnity only and nothing more. According to this principle, the insurance contract should be such that in case of loss due to the eventualities mentioned in the contract, the insured should be neither better-off nor worse-off after receiving the insured amount. This means that on the happening of an event insured against, the insured should be placed by the insurer in the same pecuniary (monetary) position that he/she occupied immediately before the event. The main object of this principle is to ensure that the insured is not able to use this contract for speculation or gambling. That is, under no circumstances the insured is allowed to benefit more than the loss suffered by him. The exceptions to the rule are found in life policies, personal accident policies, agreed value policies in marine insurance and valuables, and reinstatement policies like in engineering policies. These are also contracts of indemnity, but by a special application of the principle, the measure of indemnity is decided at the time of entering into the contract itself, and in the event of loss, the insured can recover the actual amount of loss (on providing valid proof of actual loss) not exceeding the amount of the policy. In the case of life insurance, however, there is no question of actual loss. This is logical in the sense that life cannot be indemnified, thus if a person dies, then under the contract of life insurance the sum assured will be paid by the insurer. These contracts are not insurance but assurance contracts.

14.6.4 Principle of Subrogation

Subrogation, in general, means the legal right of one person, having indemnified the other in a contractual obligation to do so; that is, to stand in the place of another and avail all the rights and remedies of the other, whether enforced or not.

The principle of subrogation entitles the insurance company to step into the shoes of the insured after indemnifying him for the loss. That is, the insurer acquires every right of the insured after settling the claims of the insured in respect of the covered loss. The condition of subrogation is a corollary to the principle of indemnity. A loss may occur accidentally or by the action or negligence of third party (not workmen). For instance, in case of property insurance, the property owner, who may have suffered damage due to the deliberate action of a third party, has a right to take legal action against the offending third party to recover the loss/damage or proceed under the insurance policy. However, he cannot have the benefit under both the alternatives because a contract of insurance is a contract of indemnity. If the insured opts to recover the loss under the insurance policy, which is faster and does not involve litigation, he will legally surrender his rights against the third parties in favour of the insurers. The insurer on the other hand, would get only such rights which are available to the insured. He cannot be allowed to recover more than what the insured could have recovered. Life insurance policies are of course an exception to this principle. Subrogation applies only to the contracts of indemnity. For example, where an insured vehicle is damaged due to the negligence of a third party, the insurer can take legal action against the third party to recover the cost of repairs paid by him to the insured.

14.6.5 Principle of Contribution

Contribution condition is a corollary to the principle of indemnity. The principle of contribution applies in cases of double insurance. It implies that when a property is insured for the same risk with two or more insurers, the different insurers will contribute to the total payment in proportion to the amount assured by each. The principle of contribution does not apply in case of life insurance. Moreover, the right of contribution is subject to the following conditions:

(i) The same subject-matter is insured under different policies.
(ii) The policies are in force at the time of loss.
(iii) The policies cover the same period during which the loss occurred.
(iv) One of the insurers has paid to the insured more than his share of the loss.

14.6.6 Principle of Causa Proxima

According to the principle of causa proxima, the insurer is liable only for those losses which have been most closely and directly caused by the peril insured against. It is always the duty of the insured to prove that the loss arose out of the insured peril, which is proximate. Under this principle, the insurers are not liable for remote causes that are not insured against. It is not the first cause sparking-off a series of events, but the last cause directly responsible for the loss which determines whether the insurer is liable or not. Thus, the principle is significant only in those cases where the loss is caused by a series of events. For instance, in a marine policy, the goods were insured against damage by sea-water. Some rats on board made a hole in the bottom of the ship causing sea-water to pour into the ship and damage the goods. Here, the proximate cause of loss is sea water, which is covered by the policy and the holes made by the rats is a remote cause. Therefore, the insured can recover damages from the insurer.

14.6.7 Principle of Mitigation of Loss

On the occurrence of the event covered by the insurance policy, it is the duty of the insured to take all the possible steps to mitigate or minimize the loss to the subject-matter of insurance. He is expected to act in the same manner in which he would have acted in the absence of the insurance contract, and do everything that a man of ordinary prudence would do under the circumstances to save the insured property. Otherwise, the insurer can refuse to compensate him for the loss caused due to his negligence. On the other hand, the insured has the right to recover the losses suffered by him in taking steps to reduce the loss.

14.7 NATURE OF INSURANCE CONTRACT

A contract of insurance is a form of contract under which the insurer agrees in consideration of payment of premium to make good the loss suffered by the insured against a specified risk such as fire or any other contingency or compensates him on the happening of a specified event such as accident or death. Insurance contracts other than life insurance are contracts of indemnity. A contract of life insurance is a contingent agreement. The general principles of law as defined in the law of contracts apply to the contract of insurance. The contract of insurance, in other words, must fulfil the essentials of a valid agreement. There must be valid offer and acceptance and free consent. The parties must be competent to contract. The purpose must be legal, and there must be lawful consideration. From the social point of view, insurance is a device by which the loss likely to be caused by an uncertain event is spread over a number of persons who are exposed to it and who propose to insure themselves against such an event. Insurance is thus a cooperative way of spreading risks.

14.7.1 Salient Features of a Contract of Insurance

The salient features of a contract of insurance may be summed up as follows:

Essential requisites of a contract. Every contract of insurance must fulfil all the requirements of a valid contract as laid down in the Indian Contract Act.

Utmost good faith. It is the duty of the insured to disclose all material facts concerning the subject-matter of insurance so that the insurer must be in a position to accurately determine the risk undertaken by him.

Insurability of risk. The risk that is being insured must fulfil all the requirements of insurability as only insurable risks can be legitimately covered. Most importantly, the insured must have insurable interest in the subject-matter of insurance.

Indemnification. A contract of insurance (other than life, personal accident and sickness) is a contract of indemnity under which the insurer agrees to indemnify the insured for any loss suffered by him on the happening of the event insured against. This implies that the mechanism of insurance should not be misapplied for making profits.

14.8 TYPES OF INSURANCE CONTRACTS

Insurance contracts may be classified into the following four categories, on the basis of the nature of the event that is insured:

Personal insurance: This includes life, accident, health and sickness insurance. In this contract, the insurer agrees to pay a predetermined sum of money, on the happening of the event, such as reaching a certain age or death, whichever is earlier. This is so because the actual loss cannot be calculated or measured in case of human life.

Property insurance: This includes all such contracts where the subject matter of insurance is property of any kind. In this case, the insurer agrees to pay the actual loss of property insured under a policy. This includes fire, marine, motor and miscellaneous insurance.

Liability insurance: Where a person is liable to a third person in accordance with the provisions of law or to his employee under the provisions of an act, the liability towards such payments can be covered under liability insurance. Workmen's compensation insurance and third party insurance are examples in this case.

Guarantee insurance: It is an agreement whereby the insurer agrees to indemnify the insured for a fixed amount against loss arising through dishonesty or fraud or a breach of contract. Fidelity insurance and credit insurance are examples in this case.

14.9 FUNDAMENTALS OF INSURABILITY

A risk can be insured if and only if it satisfies the following essential requisites:

1. There must be sufficiently large number of people exposed to a common risk who would be willing to pay for getting the risk insured. Only then would it be possible for the insurer to predict the risk and estimate the extent of the loss. The cost of the loss is accordingly determined which, in turn, is the basis of determination of the rate of premium to be charged.
2. The losses caused by the risk should not only be fairly predictable, but also measurable in monetary terms. Emotional losses are not, therefore, insurable.
3. The probability of occurrence of loss, which is the result of the risk to be insured, should also be capable of statistical measurement. Otherwise there is no possibility of insurance of the risk.
4. There should be some defined pattern of occurrence of the event insured, which should also be predictable. Naturally, if the event is non-random or the loss has occurred in the past, there is no question of insurance.
5. The losses should not be catastrophic, in the sense that all the units in the homogeneous group should not be exposed to the adverse event and suffer the loss simultaneously.
6. The rate of premium should not be very high. It should be affordable for every class of insured.

14.10 INSURANCE CONTRACT VS. WAGERING AGREEMENT

An agreement between two parties by which one promises to pay money or money's worth on the happening of some uncertain event in consideration of the other party's promise to pay if the event does not happen is called a **wagering agreement**. Thus, if A and B enter into an agreement that A shall pay B ₹10,000 if Indian hockey team wins the match, and that B shall pay A the same amount if it does not win, it is a wagering agreement. It is important to understand that the event may be uncertain either because it is to happen in future or if it has already happened, the parties are uncertain and express opposite views regarding the event.

It is sometimes said that a contract of insurance whether it is marine, fire or life very closely appears like a wagering agreement. Table 14.1 depicts the distinction between insurance contracts and wagering agreements:

Table 14.1 Differences between Insurance Contracts and Wagering Agreements

Insurance contract	*Wagering agreement*
Contracts of insurance are based on the basic principle of insurable interest. An insured/assured cannot get insurance without having insurable interest in the subject-matter of insurance.	The insurable interest is not essential for a wagering agreement. Parties are interested in knowing about the event only for the purpose of winning or losing.
Contracts of insurance are contracts of indemnity (with the exception of life insurance). The insured is indemnified for the actual loss suffered by him and not more than that.	In a wagering agreement the amount to be paid is pre-decided by the parties to the agreement. There is no question of indemnity as no risk is covered.
Contracts of insurance are valid contracts and thus legally enforceable. Both parties to the contract can take legal action against non-performance.	Wagering agreements have been expressly declared to be void in India. In fact, in the states of Maharashtra and Gujarat they have been declared to be illegal. Neither party has any legal remedy against non-performance.
Contracts of insurance are based upon the principles of good faith, i.e., both parties to the contract must make full disclosure of material facts. Otherwise there would be no binding contract.	There is no question of disclosure of material facts by either of the parties in a wagering agreement.
Assessment of risks and determination of premium is on the basis of scientific methods and actuarial calculations.	No such calculations are made in the case of wagering agreements. A wagering agreement is just a gamble.

14.11 ASSURANCE VS. INSURANCE

The two terms *assurance* and *insurance* have often been used interchangeably and treated as synonyms, but a fine distinction between the two concepts is required for a better understanding of the subject of insurance. Assurance is used in those contracts which guarantee the payment of a certain sum on the happening of a specified event, that is bound to happen sooner or later. In life policies, for instance, there is absolute certainty regarding the happening of the event, and the only uncertainty is about the time of occurrence of the event. Thus, life policies come under assurance. Under life policies, the insurer is required to pay the fixed amount agreed upon in advance in the event of death or on the expiry of the period of the policy. The term *assurance,* therefore, refers to contingent contracts or contracts of guarantee. Insurance, on the other hand, envisages the happening of certain events, stipulated in the contract, which are not surely expected but which may happen. Insurance contracts are contracts of indemnity under which the insurer, in consideration of a sum of money, undertakes to compensate the insured for the loss suffered by him due to the happening of a specified event such as accident in case of accident insurance, illness in case of health insurance, destruction of property in case of fire insurance, damaging of goods in case of marine insurance, and so on. In such events, there is absolute uncertainty. The time of occurrence as also the severity of the loss caused by the occurrence of the event are uncertain. Thus, insurance refers to those risks which are contingent in nature as fire, marine or accident.

14.12 GAMBLING VS. INSURANCE

Gambling cannot be insured. Insurance is based on a contractual relationship between the insurer and the insured. The contract of insurance must fulfil the essential conditions of a valid contract in accordance with the requirements of the law of contracts. One of the basic requirements for a valid contract is that the object of the agreement must be legally enforceable. Law prohibits the use of insurance for gambling purposes. Covering of gambling activities through insurance would only give a boost to a serious social evil. Insurance against risks of gambling would put the gambler in a win-win situation, as he will never stand to lose. This is because if it is head, he wins and if it is tails, he still is not a loser as in this case he would get compensated by the insurance company. In general, the insurance premium includes the charge for the losses and the expenses of providing the services of insurance and, therefore, the premium charged from the insured must be more than the mathematically calculated value of the potential loss. But, the risk of gambling is rather enjoyable for the gambler, and he is unlikely to pay the premium needed for transferring the risk being enjoyed. In short, gambling and insurance are not analogous except that they share one common factor—they both deal with risk. While insurance is a method of transferring risks, gambling initiates the problem of risk. Moreover, gambling deals with speculative risk. The act of gambling may cause losses or gains while insurance deals with pure risks. There may be loss, or no loss but there is no chance of gains in pure risks.

14.13 CLASSIFICATION OF INSURANCE

Everybody faces risks of various kinds. Different risks cause different types of losses. Risks may be insurable or non-insurable. Insurance companies offer various kinds of insurance policies to cover various kinds of risks and providing security against various losses. Depending on the subject-matter, insurance may be classified into two broad categories:

Life insurance: Life insurance is a contract whereby the insurer in consideration of a premium paid either as lump sum or as periodical instalments, undertakes to pay, either on the death of the insured or on the expiry of specified number of years whichever is earlier, an annuity or a specified amount. For example, whole-life plans, endowment assurance plans, pension plans, unit linked plan.

Non-life insurance: Non-life insurance is a contract whereby the insurer in consideration of a premium paid by the insured agrees to indemnify him for the financial loss suffered by him due to an adverse event which is covered by the terms of the policy.

Non-life insurance may be classified further into general insurance and miscellaneous insurance. Again, depending on the subject-matter, there are the four kinds of **general insurance:**

Marine insurance. Marine insurance is a contract of insurance under which the insurer undertakes to indemnify the insured, in the manner and to the extent thereby agreed, against marine losses incidental to marine adventure. For example, loss or damages to the ship, cargo, freight, vessels or any other subject of a marine adventure. Accordingly, there are various types of marine policies like voyage policies, valued policies, hull insurance, time policies, cargo insurance, freight insurance, etc.

Fire insurance. Fire insurance is a contract under which the insurer agrees to indemnify the insured, in return for payment of a premium in lump sum or by instalments, losses suffered by him due to destruction of or damage to the insured property, caused by fire during an agreed period of time.

Personal accident insurance. Personal accident insurance is a contract under which the insurer undertakes to pay a specified amount of money on the death or disability of the insured on account of an accident.

Motor vehicle insurance. Under this type of insurance a personal or commercial vehicle is insured against loss or damage to the vehicle due to accident or theft, personal injury or death of the owner or passenger due to accident or damages payable to third parties by the owner of the vehicle for accidents.

Non-life insurance, in addition to general insurance includes other miscellaneous insurance. Some of the types of **miscellaneous insurance** are discussed here:

Fidelity guarantee insurance. This is the type of contract of insurance and also a contract of guarantee to which general principles of insurance apply. Fidelity guarantee does not mean the guarantee of the employee's honesty. But it guarantees the employer for any damages or loss resulting from the employee's dishonesty or disloyalty.

Crop insurance. A contract of crop insurance is a contract to provide a measure of financial support to farmers in the event of a crop failure due to drought or floods.

Burglary insurance. A burglary policy provides protection against loss or damage caused by theft, larceny, burglary, housebreaking and acts of such nature.

Cattle insurance. Cattle insurance is a contract of insurance whereby a sum of money is secured to the insured in the event of death of animals like bulls, buffaloes, cows and heifers.

Cash in transit insurance. This type of insurance compensates the insured against loss of money or cash stolen from his business premises or while it is being carried from or to the bank.

The following chart portrays the classification of insurance (Figure 14.1):

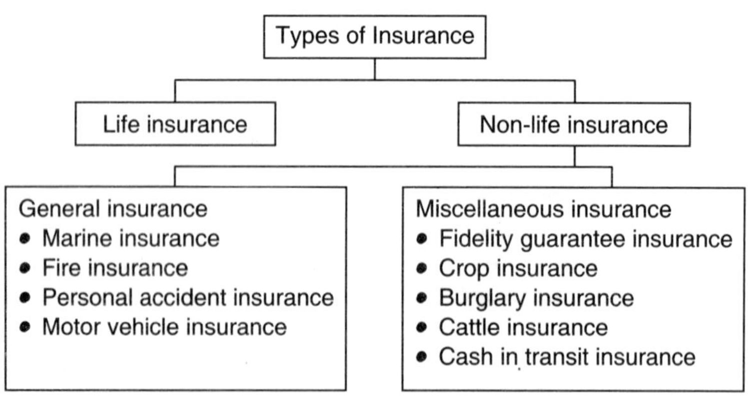

Figure 14.1 Classification of insurance.

ILLUSTRATIONS

14.1 A applied for a life insurance policy for ₹2 lakh, disclosing all the necessary information in the proposal form. However, before the acceptance of proposal by the insurance company, A was taken ill with pneumonia. The proposal was accepted by the insurer the following day. The company learnt about his illness after two days of A's demise due to pneumonia. Is the insurance company liable to pay?

Ans: A contract of insurance is a contract of absolute good faith. Thus, the insurer is entitled to get notice of any material alteration in the risk between the time of the proposal and its acceptance.

Here, such a notice was not given, and therefore, there was a breach of good faith. The insurer is, therefore, not liable for making payment.

14.2 The cargo on a ship was insured against loss arising on account of sea-water. Some rats on the ship caused a hole in the bottom of the ship resulting in entry of sea-water into the ship and resulting in loss to the cargo. The insurance company refuses to pay the money on the ground that loss was caused on account of rats; which was not an insured peril. Is the insurance company liable?

Ans: The insurer is liable to compensate the insured for any loss that occurs on account of a sea peril insured against provided such peril is the proximate cause of loss.

In the above case, the rats were a remote cause of loss and sea-water, a proximate one. Since loss on account of sea-water is an insured peril, the insurer is liable to pay for the loss.

14.3 A's goods in a warehouse were insured against fire with B's Insurance Company. The goods were burnt and A recovered the full value of ₹5 lakh from the insurance company. Subsequently A also sued the warehouse keeper and recovered a sum of ₹5 lakh from him. Can A retain this money?

Ans: According to doctrine of subrogation in contracts of indemnity an insured cannot be allowed to make any profit from an insurance claim. He cannot take benefit of an insurance policy as well as any other alternative rights or remedies.

On the basis of the principle of subrogation, in the above case, A must return the sum of ₹5 lakh to the insurance company.

14.4 A ship was insured for ₹20 lakh, though its declared value was ₹25 lakh. In a collision with another ship, the insured ship was completely lost. The insurer paid the insured amount of ₹20 lakh. But later, the insurer recovered a sum of ₹30 lakh from the owner of the ship responsible for collision. Can the insurer retain the sum received?

Ans: The doctrine of subrogation entitles the insurer to all alternative rights and remedies available to the insurer against a third party. However, it is to be noted that subrogation of the insurer extends to the value insured and no more than that. The insurer can retain only ₹20 lakh.

14.5 A contracted to build a shop for B for ₹5 lakh. All the materials were to be supplied by B. Can A get the materials insured during the period of construction?

Ans: Yes, A can get the materials insured because he has an insurable interest in the subject matter, as he would suffer financial loss on the destruction of the materials.

INSURANCE TERMINOLOGIES

Actual cash value The measure of property insurance loss. Usually defined as the cost of replacing the destroyed property with new property, minus an allowance for depreciation.

All-risk insurance A generic term for insurance that covers all risks except those explicitly excluded.

Annuity A contract that provides an income for a stated period or for a person's lifetime.

Assurance The term used for life insurance contracts.

Automobile liability coverage Automobile insurance policy that protects against claims for legal liability arising out of automobile accidents. Provides legal defence and pays sums necessary to settle claims against the insured person.

Automobile collision coverage The part of an automobile insurance policy that pays for collision damage to the insured auto.

Automobile comprehensive coverage The part of an automobile insurance policy that pays for loss or damage to the insured automobile other than the loss or damage caused by collision.

Automatic premium loan A provision under life insurance policy authorizing the insurer to use the policy's loan value to pay any premium not paid by the end of the grace period.

Beneficiary The person named in the insurance policy to receive the proceeds of a life insurance policy upon the death of the insured person.

Binder A binder is only a temporary insurance contract (written or oral) that remains in effect until replaced by a regular policy.

Cash surrender value The sum payable to a policyholder who discontinues a life insurance policy.

Casualty Insurance Insurance policy covering losses caused by injury to others or damage to property of others.

Coverage The protection provided by insurance.

Credit life insurance A term life insurance that covers repayment of a loan in the event of death of the borrower.

Deductible clause A provision, which defines the specific amount of loss that, if exceeded, will trigger insurance coverage.

Dividend A part of premium that is returned. It is the difference between the premium charged and the amount needed to cover the company's operations and payments on claims.

Endowment insurance Life insurance plan whereby the amount of insurance becomes payable to the insured if he or she is living on the maturity date stated in the policy, or to a beneficiary if the insured dies before that date.

Exclusions Provisions that are explicitly excluded from the coverage provided by an insurance policy.

Expiration date The date when an insurance policy ends.

Grace period A specified period of time after the date the premium is due, during which a policy remains in force even though the premium has not been paid.

Group insurance An Insurance plan that covers a number of individuals under a single contract. It is typically issued to an employer for the benefit of employees.

Guaranteed insurability A provision in a life insurance policy permitting the purchase of additional insurance at stated times irrespective of the condition of the insured person's health.

Incontestable clause A policy provision that prevents the insurer from challenging or contesting claims after a specified period of coverage, irrespective of any misstatements made by the applicant.

Insurance rate The price of insurance per unit of coverage.

Insured A person or organization that is protected or covered by insurance.

Insurer An insurance company or other organization that provides cover or insurance.

Liability insurance An insurance policy that provides cover against claims for legal liability. Provides legal defence and pays sums necessary to settle claims against the insured.

Limit of liability The maximum amount that an insurer is liable to pay in the event of a covered loss.

Limited payment whole-life Whole-life insurance policy for which premiums are payable for a specified number of years.

Loss An event, contingency or circumstance for which insurance may pay.

Medical payments coverage A type of insurance cover that pays for medical and funeral expenses without regard to liability.

Named peril insurance Any insurance policy that specifies the perils (risks) it covers.

No-fault system A system in which compensation for injuries on the basis of fault (tort liability) is not legally available.

Non-participating insurance Insurance policies on which no policy dividends are payable.

Non-forfeiture options Alternatives available to a policy owner who stops payment of premium on a policy of insurance.

Participating insurance Insurance policies on which dividends are payable.

Permanent life insurance Any type of individual life insurance that develops a cash value.

Policy loan A loan offered by a life insurance company to a policy owner on the security of a policy's cash surrender value.

Replacement cost The cost of replacing damaged or destroyed property with new property, without deduction of depreciation.

Risk The cause of a possible loss, which is also referred to as peril.

Settlement options The claims-settlement alternatives, other than immediate payment in cash, in which a life insurance beneficiary may choose to have policy benefits paid.

Stock insurance company A corporate insuring organization owned by stockholders.

Straight life insurance Life insurance on which premiums are payable for the whole life.

Term life insurance Life insurance plan in which the insurance amount becomes payable to a beneficiary when the insured dies within a specified period. If the insured is living at the end of the period, the policy expires without value.

Underwriting The process of determining which losses to insure and how to insure them.

Uninsured motorists coverage A type of automobile insurance that pays the damages that insured persons are legally entitled to collect from uninsured motorists.

Waiting period In disability income insurance, waiting period refers to the period of time between the beginning of a disability and the period when the policy's income payments begin. In group insurance, it refers to the period an employee must work for a firm in order to qualify for coverage.

Waiver of premium A provision in life or health insurance policy stating that premiums will not be charged, if the insured becomes totally and permanently disabled.

Whole life insurance Life insurance policy in which the insurance amount is payable to a beneficiary at the death of the policyholder, whenever it may occur. Premiums may be payable for a specified number of years (limited payment life insurance) or for life (straight life insurance).

KEY TERMS

Contract Agreement between two or more parties enforceable by law. Thus, Contract = Agreement + Enforceability by law.

Contribution Sharing of loss by insurers, who are liable for the same risk.

Indemnity Compensation for the actual loss not exceeding the amount of policy.

Policyholder The entity or person, who pays premium and owns an insurance policy. This is usually the insured, but it may also be a relative of the insured, a partnership, or a corporation. Also called a **policy owner**.

Premium The price of an insurance policy, or consideration paid by the insured to the insurer for the risk covered under the policy.

Subrogation A principle of law providing that once insurer has paid for a loss, the insurer receives the policyholder's rights to recover from any third party who caused the loss.

REVIEW QUESTIONS

14.1 Define the concept of *insurance*. Briefly explain the purpose and need of getting insured for an individual and a business firm.

14.2 Explain various functions of insurance.

14.3 Write a note on the characteristics and importance of insurance.

14.4 Write short notes on
- (i) Principle of insurable interest
- (ii) Principle of utmost good faith
- (iii) Principle of indemnity
- (iv) Principle of subrogation
- (v) Principle of contribution
- (vi) Principle of causa proxima and principle of mitigation of loss.

14.5 What is a contract of insurance? What are the various types of insurance contracts?

14.6 What are the various requisites of insurability of risks?

14.7 Explain the various kinds of life insurance contracts.

14.8 Explain the various kinds of non-life insurance contracts.

14.9 Distinguish between
- (i) Insurance contracts and wagering contracts
- (ii) Assurance and insurance
- (iii) Gambling and insurance

14.10 Define—all-risk insurance; non-forfeiture options; automatic premium loan; deductible clause; limit of liability; settlement options; underwriting; term life insurance.

14.11 Write short notes on

(i) Fidelity guarantee insurance

(ii) Burglary insurance

(iii) Cash in transit insurance

(iv) Marine insurance

(v) Motor vehicle insurance

15

Life Insurance

Learning Objectives

After going through this chapter we will be able to:

- Explain the meaning of life insurance.
- Differentiate between life insurance and non-life insurance.
- Describe the essential features of life insurance.
- Understand the advantages of life insurance.
- Discuss the importance of life insurance.
- Describe the various types of life insurance plans.

The Insurance Act, 1938, defines life insurance business as the business of effecting contracts of insurance upon human life, including any contract whereby the payment of money is assured on death (except death by accident only) or the happening of any event insured by the contract. In other words, a life insurance contract is a contract in which the insurer in consideration of a certain premium either in lump sum or other periodical payments, agrees to pay to the assured or to the person for whose benefits the policy is taken, an agreed sum of money on the death of the insured or on the expiry of a specified period of time, whichever is earlier. Thus, under a whole-life assurance, the policy money is payable at the death of the assured and under an endowment policy, the money is payable on the maturity of the policy or on his death, in case if that occurs earlier. In case of life insurance the payment is certain. The event insured against is sure to happen, though the time of its occurrence is uncertain. Life insurance contracts are contingent contracts, while non-life insurance contracts are contracts of indemnity. That is why, life insurance is known as life assurance and not insurance.

The life insurance and non-life insurance contracts differ in important respects. These differences are discussed here:

(i) There is complete sureness as to the occurrence of the event insured against in life insurance. The only ambiguity is about the timing of the happening of the event insured, i.e., death. The insurer, thus, is committed to compensate the insured. In the case of non-life insurance, however, the event insured against may or may not occur, and the insurer is under no obligation to compensate the insured.

(ii) The contract of life insurance is not a contract of indemnity. That is, the principle of indemnity does not apply to life insurance contracts. The insurance may be for any amount for which no proof of actual loss is needed. This is because the loss of human life cannot be calculated in terms of money. All non-life insurance contracts are the contracts of indemnity and as such, the assured can only recover the actual loss subject to the maximum amount of the policy.

(iii) In case of non-life insurance, the insurable interest of the assured in the subject-matter of insurance must be calculable in monetary terms. This, however, is not possible in life insurance. Moreover, the insurable interest must be present both at the time of contract as well as at the time of loss in fire insurance, but only at the time of loss in marine insurance. In life insurance such interest is required to be established only at the time of the contract.

(iv) Non-life insurance contracts are twelve-monthly, that is, annual contracts. They provide cover for a specified period or for a particular voyage as in the case of marine insurance. The life insurance contract is always a long-term contract.

15.1 ESSENTIAL FEATURES OF LIFE ASSURANCE

The following are the essential features of a valid contract of life insurance:

Elements of a valid contract: Since life insurance establishes a contractual relationship between the insured and the insurer, the contract of insurance must contain the essential elements of a valid contract in accordance with the provisions of the Indian Contract Act, 1872.

Insurable interest: A person cannot insure the life of any other unless he has an insurable interest in it. The insurable interest must exist at the time of the contract of insurance. The risk against this policy is the death of the insured.

Insurable interest exists in the following cases:

- A person has unlimited insurable interest in his own life.
- A husband is presumed to have insurable interest in his wife's life and vice versa.
- A surety has insurable interest in the life of the principal debtor to the extent of his claim.
- A father (or a mother) has insurable interest in the life of his/her son or daughter on whom he/she is dependent. Similarly, a son has insurable interest in the life of his parents.
- A creditor has insurable interest in the life of the debtor, to the extent of the debt.
- A partner has insurable interest in the life of his co-partner(s).

Utmost good faith: Insurance contracts are contracts of uberrimae fidei, i.e., based on utmost good faith. The doctrine of disclosing all the material facts is embodied in this important principle which applies to all the forms of insurance. At the time of taking a policy, policyholder should ensure that all questions in the proposal form are correctly answered. Any misrepresentation, non-disclosure or fraud in any document leading to the acceptance of the risk would render the insurance contract null and void. Thus, both, the insured as well as the insurer, is bound to disclose all the material facts and figures known to one but unknown to the other. For example, age, income, education, occupation, health, family size, etc. are some of the material facts that should be disclosed at the time of entering into the contract.

Warranties: Warranties are an important feature of life insurance contract, and are the basis of the contract. In case of an untrue statement by the insured, whether regarding material or non-material facts and figures, the contract shall become null and void and the insurer would be entitled to forfeit the premium paid by him.

Assignment and nomination: Both assignment and nomination are the essential features of life insurance policy. Assignment of a life policy means transferring the rights of the assured in respect of the policy to the assignee. In the case of the nomination, a person is merely named to collect the amount to be paid by the insurer on the death of the assured, but the rights of the assured are not transferred.

Certainty of the event: In life assurance policy, the insurer has to pay the insured amount one day or other because the death of the assured or his reaching a particular age is certain to happen.

Premium: The premium is the price paid by the insured for the risk of loss undertaken by the insurer. In the case of the insurance, premium is usually required to be paid in cash and advance payment of the premium is a precondition to a binding contract of insurance. In life insurance, the premium is calculated on the average rate of mortality, and the premium is payable till the maturity of the policy or until death of the insured.

Terms of policy: An insurance policy specifies the nature of risk insured for, the terms and conditions of insurance as also the time-period it covers. A life insurance policy may cover a specified number of years or the balance of the insured life.

15.2 ADVANTAGES OF LIFE ASSURANCE

Protection: Savings through life insurance guarantee full protection against risk of death of the saver. Also, in case of demise, life insurance assures payment of the entire amount assured (with bonuses wherever applicable) whereas in other savings schemes, only the amount saved (with interest) is payable.

Aids thrift: Life insurance encourages *thrift*. It allows long-term savings since payments can be made effortlessly because of the *easy instalment* facility built into the scheme (premium payment for insurance is either monthly, quarterly, half yearly or yearly). For example, the salary saving scheme popularly known as SSS, presents a convenient method of paying premium each month by deduction from one's salary. In this case, the employer directly pays the deducted premium to LIC. The salary saving scheme is ideal for any association or enterprise subject to specified terms and conditions.

Enhances creditworthiness: In case of insurance, it is easy to acquire loans on the sole security of any policy that has acquired loan value. Besides, a life insurance policy is also generally accepted as security, even for a commercial loan.

Tax relief: Life insurance is the best way to have the benefit of tax deductions on income tax and wealth tax. This is available for amounts paid by way of premium for life insurance subject to income tax rates in force. Assesses can also avail of provisions in the law for tax relief. In such cases, the assured in effect pays a lower premium for insurance than otherwise.

Provides liquidity: A policy that has a suitable insurance plan or a combination of different plans can be effectively used to meet certain monetary needs that may arise from time-to-time. Children's education, start-in-life or marriage provision or even periodical needs for cash over a stretch of time can be less stressful with the help of these policies. Alternatively, policy money can be made available at the time of one's retirement from service and used for any specific purpose such as purchase of a house or for other investments. Also, loans are granted to policyholders for housebuilding or for purchase of flats (subject to certain conditions).

15.3 TYPES OF LIFE INSURANCE PLANS

Life insurance is a contract providing for payment of a sum of money to the person assured or to his nominee, on the happening of certain events. Various insurance companies offer a large number of life insurance policies. This is because of the fact that everyone of us has different aspirations in life. The ways of life of all individuals being different, the needs and expectations of each person are different from that of the others. Thus, the insurance needs and requirements obviously vary from individual to individual. Life Insurance Corporation of India has made available a number of insurance plans/policies, providing various benefits and offering appropriate options to tone with the requirements of different parties or individuals.

The leading life insurance plans/policies offered by Life Insurance Corporation of India can be classified into the following categories:[1]

15.3.1 Whole Life Plans

The ordinary whole life policy: A typical whole life policy runs as long as the policyholder is alive. In other words, the policyholder is covered for the entire life of the policyholder and that is why they are termed **whole life policies**. The premium in this case is the lowest as it is to be paid till death of the policyholder. The policy moneys and the bonuses are payable only to the nominee upon the death of the policyholder. The policyholder is not entitled to any money during his or her own lifetime. In other words, there is no survival benefit in case of whole life policies making them somewhat rigid and inflexible. These policies are suitable only in a few, very specific cases and are primarily devised to create an estate for the heirs of the policyholder. Such plans are beneficial for people with meagre income whose dependents need maximum monetary security or those who are eligible for a sizeable pension during their retired life as whole life policy shall cover the risk of death taking place and, therefore, the pension coming to an end after retirement. In such a case a whole life policy serves as financial protection to the family for the early loss of pension.

However, considering the increased longevity of the Indian population, the corporation has amended the above provision, thereby providing for payment of sum assured plus bonuses in the form of maturity claim on completion of 80 years age or on expiry of term of 40 years from the

---

[1] *Source:* www.licindia.com.

date of commencement of the policy whichever is later. The premiums under the policy are payable upto age 80 years of the policyholder or for a term of 35 years whichever is later. If the payment of premium ceases after 3 years, a paid-up policy for such reduced sum assured will be automatically secured provided the reduced sum assured exclusive of any attached bonus is not less than ₹250. Such reduced paid-up policy is not entitled to participate in the bonus declared thereafter, but the bonuses already declared on the policy will remain attach, provided the policy is converted into a paid-up policy after the premiums are paid for 5 years.

The whole life policy—limited payment: This is the best form of life assurance for family provision since it enables the life assured to pay all the premiums during the ordinarily vigorous and most productive years of life. He need not pay any premium in the later stages of life if and when his conditions might become adverse. That is, premiums are payable for a limited period, selected by the assured but sum assured is payable only on death of the assured.

The whole life policy—single premium: This policy is considered to be the best form of life assurance for family provisions as the premiums are generally paid by the assured during the most active, productive years of his life. The life assured is relieved from the compulsion of making payments of premiums later in life when they might become a financial burden.

The above policies are 'with-profit' policies and do not cease to participate in profits after completion of the premium-paying period but continue to share in the periodical bonus distribution until the death of the life assured. If the policyholder pays at least 3 years' premiums and then discontinues paying any more premiums, a reduced paid-up assurance policy comes into force. Such a reduced paid-up policy will not be entitled to participate in the profits declared thereafter, but the bonus as already declared on the policy will remain attached to the policy. The minimum premium-paying period under this policy is 5 years and the maximum period is 55 years.

Jeevan Umang: LIC's Jeevan Umang plan offers a combination of income and protection to your family. This plan provides for annual survival benefits from the end of the premium paying term till maturity and a lump sum payment at the time of maturity or on death of the policyholder during the policy term. Additionally, this plan also takes care of liquidity needs through loan facility. On death of the Life Assured during the policy term before the commencement of Risk return of premium/s paid without interest shall be payable, provided all due premiums have been paid. However, if death occurs after the commencement of risk, death benefit shall not be less than 105% of all the premiums paid as on date of death. On the life assured surviving to the end of the premium paying term, provided all due premiums have been paid, a survival benefit equal to 8% of basic sum assured shall be payable each year. The first survival benefit payment is payable at the end of premium paying term and thereafter on completion of each subsequent year till the life assured survives or till the policy anniversary prior to the date of maturity, whichever is earlier. On the life assured surviving to the end of the policy term, provided all due premiums have been paid, sum assured on maturity along with vested simple reversionary bonuses and final additional bonus, if any, shall be payable. The policy also participates in profits of the Corporation during the policy term. The minimum basic sum assured under the policy is ₹2,00,000 while there is no limit on the maximum basic sum assured. The basic sum assured shall be in multiples of ₹25,000. The premium paying term may be 15, 20, 25 and 30 years but the policy term is (100 minus age at entry) years. While the minimum age at entry may be 90 days (completed), the maximum age at entry can be 55 years (nearest birthday). Besides, the minimum age at the end of premium paying term should be 30 years (nearest birthday) but the maximum age at the end of premium paying term may be 70 years (nearest birthday).

15.3.2 Endowment Assurance Plans

The pure endowment assurance policy: Endowment assurance policies cover the risk for a specified period at the end of which the sum assured is paid back to the policyholder together with all the bonuses accumulated during the term of the policy. This feature of the payment of the endowment to the policyholder upon the completion of the policy's term or to the nominee on the policyholder's death if it occurs during the term period has made endowment policies very popular. Moderate premiums, high bonus, high liquidity and being savings oriented are some of the important features of the policy. These policies do not make provisions for the family of the life assured in event of his early death but also assures a lump sum at a desired age. The lump sum can be reinvested to provide an annuity during the remainder of his life or in any other way considered suitable at that time. As compared to whole life policies, the premium rates for endowment policies are higher and the bonus rates lower. The premiums are usually payable for the selected term of years or until death if it occurs during the term period. Being an endowment assurance policy, this plan is apt for people of all ages and social groups who wish to protect their families from a financial setback that may occur owing to their demise. In case the policyholder becomes totally and permanently disabled due to an accident before reaching the age of 70 and the policy is in full force, he will not be required to pay further premiums, and the policy will continue to be in force.

The endowment assurance policy—limited payment: Just as in the case of limited payment whole life policies, here, too the payment of premium can be limited either to a single payment or to a term shorter than the policy. The endowment is, however, payable only at the end of the policy term or on death of the policyholder if it takes place earlier. If payment of the premiums ceases after at least three years' premiums have been paid, a free paid-up policy for an amount bearing the same proportion to the sum assured as the number of premiums actually paid, bears to the number stipulated for in the policy, will be automatically secured provided the reduced sum assured, exclusive of any attached bonus, is not less than ₹250. Such reduced paid-up policy will not be entitled to participate in the profits declared thereafter, but such bonus as has already been declared on the policy, will remain attached hereto.

1. **LIC's Bima Jyoti Plan**

   Key Features of LIC Bima Jyoti Plan are:

   - The plan offers alternative premium payment options such as yearly, half-yearly, quarterly, and monthly.
   - The loan facility is also available under LIC's Bima Jyoti policy.
   - The policy term of the plan varies from 15 years to 20 years such that for a 20-year policy, the premium payment term will be 15 years and for 15 years, premium paying term (PPT) will be 10 years.
   - It also offers the facility of buying plans online as well as offline.
   - In case of dissatisfaction with the policy's terms and conditions, the company has the provision to return the premium paid.
   - Where the policyholder dies before the "Risk Commencement Date", all the premiums paid will be returned to the nominee. However, any extra premium charged or rider premiums will not be paid. And if the policyholder dies after the "Risk Commencement Date", the nominee shalll get the Sum Assured on Death.
   - On reaching the date of maturity, the policyholder shall receive sum assured + all guaranteed additions accumulated till date.
   - The policyholder is eligible to get a loan against this policy once it acquires a Surrender Value, which will be after 3 full years of premiums have been paid.

2. **LIC's Bima Ratna:** LIC's Bima Ratna is non-linked, non-participating, individual, savings and life insurance plan.

   Here are the key features of the plan:

   - In case of unfortunate death of the life insured, his/her family members or nominee would get the sum insured which would be higher of the following:

- 125% of basic sum assured
- 7 times of annualized premium
- 105% of the total premiums paid excluding any rider premium paid

- In the case of minor aged below 8 years, being the insured, on death before commencement of the risk, only the premium amount paid would be refunded as death benefit.
- Guaranteed Additions are offered under this plan which is payable as follows:
  - 1st to 5th year of the policy – ₹50 per every 1,000 thousand sum assured (5%)
  - 6th to 10th year of the policy – ₹55 per every 1,000 thousand sum assured (5.5%)
  - 11th to 25th year of the policy – ₹60 per every 1,000 thousand sum assured (6%)
  - And in case of death of the life insured, guaranteed additions would be paid for a full year in that year.
- In case of survival of life insured, maturity benefit would be paid which is equal to "Sum Assured on Maturity" along with Guaranteed Additions. Sum Assured on Maturity would be equal to 50% of Basic Sum Assured.
- Minimum age of entry to the plan is 5 years for a 15 year policy and 90 days for 20 and 25 year policy.
- Maximum age of entry is 55 years for a 15 year policy and 50 years for 20 and 25 year tenure policy.
- Maximum age of maturity is 70 years.
- While the minimum basic sum assured is ₹5 Lakhs, there is no maximum basic sum assured limit. However, it should be in multiples of ₹25,000.
- Policy term would be 15 years, 20 years and 25 years.
- Premium paying term for the policy is 11 years for 15 year policy term, 16 years for 21 year policy term and 20 years for the 25 year policy term. Premiums can be paid either monthly, quarterly, half yearly or yearly or through monthly salary deductions.

3. **LIC's Dhan Sanchay:** LIC's Dhan Sanchay is a newly launched non-linked, non-participating, individual life insurance savings Plan. Offers a combination of savings and protection at the same time and provides financial support to the family in the event of an unfortunate death of the life assured during the policy term.

Key Features of LIC's Dhan Sanchay Plan are:

- It is an endowment plan which provides a dual benefit of protection and savings.
- The policy provides guaranteed income during the payout period from the date of maturity.
- The plan may be bought offline and online as well.
- Loan facility too is available under LIC Dhan Sanchay plan.
- The plan provides the option to take death benefit in installments and maturity benefit in lump sum.
- Rider benefits are available with this plan.
- Tax benefit is also available under this plan.
- If death occurs during the policy term after the date of commencement of risk but before the date of maturity, then sum assured on death will be payable to the nominee as per the policy terms and conditions.
- If Life Assured survived the entire policy term then he/she will receive the maturity benefit which will be payable in the form of Guaranteed Income Benefit and Guaranteed Terminal Benefit.
- Guaranteed Income Benefit is payable in advance during the Payout Period from the date of maturity and thereafter, based on the Payout Mode opted for by the Policyholder.
- Guaranteed Terminal Benefit (GTB) shall be payable as a lump sum payment along with the last installment of Guaranteed Income Benefit (GIB) and the policy will terminate.

4. **LIC's Jeevan Labh:** LIC's Jeevan Labh is a limited premium paying, non-linked, with-profits endowment plan which offers a combination of protection and savings. This plan provides financial support for the family in case of unfortunate death of the policyholder any time before maturity and a lump sum amount at the time of maturity for the surviving policyholder. This plan also takes care of liquidity needs through its loan facility. In case of death during the policy term, provided all due premiums have been paid, death benefit, defined as sum of "sum assured on death", being higher of 10 times of annualised premium or absolute amount assured to be paid on death, vested simple reversionary bonuses and final additional bonus, if any, shall be payable. On maturity of the policy, an amount equal to basic sum assured, along with vested simple reversionary bonuses and final additional bonus, if any, shall be payable in lump sum on survival to the end of the policy term provided all due premiums have been paid. The

policy also participates in profits of the Corporation and shall be entitled to receive Simple Reversionary Bonuses declared as per the experience of the Corporation, provided the policy is in full force. Final (Additional) Bonus may also be declared under the policy in the year when the policy results into a claim either by death or maturity.

5. **Single Premium Endowment Plan:** LIC's Single Premium Endowment Plan is a participating non-linked savings cum protection plan, in which premium is paid in lump sum at the outset of the policy. This combination provides financial protection against death during the term of the policy with the provision of payment of lump-sum at the end of the selected policy term in case of the life assured's survival. This plan also takes care of liquidity needs through its loan facility.

6. **New Endowment Plan:** LIC's New Endowment Plan is a participating non-linked plan offering a combination of protection and saving features. This combination provides financial support for the family of the deceased policyholder any time before maturity and a lump sum amount at the time of maturity for the policyholders surviving the term of the policy. This plan also takes care of liquidity needs of the policyholder through its loan facility. In case of death during the policy term provided all due premiums have been paid '**sum assured on death'** being higher of basic sum assured or 10 times of annualised premium. and vested simple reversionary bonuses and final additional bonus, if any, shall be payable. This death benefit shall not be less than 105% of all the premiums paid as on date of death. **On maturity,** basic sum assured along with vested simple reversionary bonuses and final additional bonus, if any, shall be payable in lump sum provided all due premiums have been paid.

7. **New Jeevan Anand Plan:** LIC's New Jeevan Anand Plan is a participating non-linked plan which offers an attractive combination of protection and savings. This combination provides financial protection against death throughout the lifetime of the policyholder with the provision of payment of lump sum at the end of the selected policy term in case of life assured's survival.

   Provided all due premiums have been paid, on death during the policy term, death benefit, defined as sum of sum assured on death and vested simple reversionary bonuses and final additional bonus, if any, shall be payable. Sum assured on death has been defined as higher of 125% of Basic Sum Assured or 10 times of annualised premium. However, death benefit shall not be less than 105% of all the premiums paid as on date of death. At the end of policy term, basic sum assured, along with vested simple reversionary bonuses and final additional bonus, if any, shall be payable in lump sum. The policy is entitled to participate in profits of the Corporation and receive simple reversionary bonuses declared as per the experience of the Corporation during policy term provided the policy is in full force.

8. **LIC's Jeevan Lakshya:** LIC's Jeevan Lakshya is a participating non-linked plan which provides for annual income benefit that may help to take care of the needs of the family. The policy is primarily meant for the benefit of children, in case of death of the policyholder any time before maturity of the policy and a lump sum amount is paid at the time of maturity regardless of the survival of the policyholder. This plan also takes care of liquidity needs through its loan facility. The minimum sum assured under the policy is required to be ₹1,00,000 with no limit on the maximum sum assured. Further, the basic sum assured can be in multiples of ₹10,000 only. Policy term can vary from 13 to 25 years. The minimum age at entry must be 18 years (completed) while the maximum cannot exceed 50 years (nearest birthday). In case of the death of the policyholder within the policy term, a Sum Assured on Death plus simple reversionary bonuses and the final additional bonus (if any) will be provided. The Death Benefit shall not be less than 105% of all the premiums paid as on date of death. Provided all the premiums have been paid in full and the policyholder has survived till the end of the policy term, the maturity benefit will encompass the Sum Assured on Maturity plus the vested simple reversionary benefits and the final additional bonus, if any. The Sum Assured on Maturity is the same as the basic sum assured.

9. **Aadhaar Shila:** LIC's Aadhaar Shila Plan offers a combination of protection and savings. This plan is exclusively designed for female lives having Aadhaar Card issued by UIDAI (Unique Identification Authority of India). This plan provides financial support for the family in case of unfortunate death of the policyholder any time before maturity and a lump sum amount at the time of maturity for the surviving policyholder. In addition, this plan also takes care of liquidity needs through its 'Auto Cover' as well as loan facility. Basic sum assured under the policy may range between from ₹75,000 and ₹3,00,000. The policy term can be anywhere between 10 to 20 years. In case of the death of the policyholder before the end of the policy term, the nominee will receive the highest of the Basic Sum Assured, 10 times the Annualised Premium or 105% of all premiums paid till date of death. On the life assured surviving to the end of the policy term, provided all due premiums have been paid, 'sum assured on maturity' along with 'loyalty addition', if any, shall be payable.

10. **Aadhaar Stambh:** LIC's Aadhaar Stambh Plan offers a combination of protection and savings. It is similar to LIC's Aadhaar Shila Plan except that this plan is *exclusively designed for male lives* having Aadhaar Card issued by UIDAI (Unique Identification Authority of India). This plan provides financial support for the family in case of unfortunate death of the policyholder any time before maturity and a lump sum amount at the time of maturity for the surviving policyholder. In addition, this plan also takes care of liquidity needs through its Auto Cover as well as loan facility. On death of the Life Assured during first five years of the policy term provided all due premiums have been paid 'sum assured on death' shall be payable. On death after completion of five policy years but before the date of maturity: "sum assured on death" and loyalty addition, if any, shall be payable. The death benefit shall not be less than 105% of all the premiums paid as on date of death. Premiums referred above shall not include any taxes, extra amount chargeable under the policy due to underwriting decision and rider premiums, if any. On the life assured surviving to the end of the policy term, provided all due premiums have been paid, 'sum assured on maturity, i.e., the basic sum assured along with loyalty addition, if any, shall be payable.

15.3.3 Term Assurance Plans

Term assurance plans cover only the risk during the selected term period. This term can vary between 5 and 40 years depending upon the insurance company. For example, the LIC provides term insurance for a period of 5–35 years, whereas other private insurance companies like HDFC standard life insurance and ICICI prudential life insurance provide term plans of 10–40 years tenure. If the policyholder survives the term, the risk cover comes to an end. And, if he dies within the term of insurance, the dependents would receive the full insurance cover amount known as **sum assured**. That is, the sum assured is payable only in the event of death of the assured before the expiry of the specified term.

LIC's Tech-Term: It is a non-linked, without profit, pure protection "online term assurance policy" which provides financial protection to the insured's family in case of his/her unfortunate demise. This plan is available through online application process only and no intermediaries are involved. It is a pure term insurance plan and thus involve no investment angle. The sum assured is paid to the nominee in case if the policyholder passes away during the policy term. But nothing is paid if the policyholder survives the policy term. The minimum sum assured under the policy is fixed at ₹50 lacs but there is no limit on the maximum sum assured. The minimum age of the insured at entry must be 18 years and the maximum age at entry should not exceed 65 years. The maximum age at exit is fixed at 80 years. The minimum policy term for on-line tech-term assurance policy is 10 years while the maximum policy term can be 40 years. The policy provides for differential premium rates for smokers and non-smokers. The policy offers an option to add accidental death benefit rider. It may be emphasised that only Indian nationals can apply for the policy. OCI (overseas citizen of India) or PIO (person of Indian origin) cannot apply for this policy. NRIs can purchase the policy during their stay in India.

Jeevan Amar: LIC's Jeevan Amar plan is a non-linked, without profit, pure protection plan. Being a pure protection plan, it offers life cover to the policyholder at an affordable price and ensures financial support for the family in case of unfortunate death of the policyholder during the policy term. The plan offers the flexibility to choose from two death benefit options—(i) level sum assured and (ii) increasing sum assured. Under this plan, there are two categories of premium rates—(i) non-smoker rates and (ii) smoker rates. Also lower premium rates on the policy are available for female proposers. The plan offers the option to choose from single, regular and limited premium payment options. The policyholder also enjoys the flexibility to choose death benefit payment either as a lump sum payment and/or in instalments.

LIC's Saral Jeevan Bima: LIC Saral Jeevan Bima policy plan is a non-linked, non-participating, individual, and pure risk life insurance plan that offers financial support and assistance to the insured policyholder's family in case of his/her unanticipated death during the policy tenure.

The salient features of LIC's Saral Jeevan Bima Plan are:

- This plan offers policyholders to choose from various premium payment options—Single-Premium, Regular Premium, and Limited Premium Payment.
- The policy can be purchased online as well as offline.
- The policy offers a rebate on the higher sum assured.
- No surrender value is applicable under this policy.
- No loan facility is available under this policy.
- If the policyholder fails to pay the premiums within the grace period then the policy will lapse. A lapsed policy may be revived within a period of 5 consecutive years from the date of the first unpaid premium but before the date of maturity.
- Minimum entry age under the policy is 18 years while the maximum entry age is 65 years.
- The maximum maturity age under the policy is 70 years.
- The minimum amount of sum assured is required to be ₹5 lakhs while the maximum is fixed at ₹25 lakhs.
- One can avail of the tax benefit towards the premiums paid for this policy in accordance with the provisions of the Income Tax Act.

15.3.4 Money Back Plans

Unlike ordinary endowment insurance plans where the survival benefits are payable only at the end of the endowment period, money back policies provide for periodic payments of partial survival benefits during the term of the policy, so long as the policy holder is alive. A distinguishing feature of money back policies is that in the event of death at any time within the policy term, the death claim amount comprises full sum assured without deducting any of the survival benefit amounts, which may have already been paid as money back components. Similarly, the bonus is also calculated on the full sum assured.

1. **Bima Shree:** LIC's Bima Shree plan is a with-profit, limited premium payment, non-linked, money-back life insurance policy. The policy serves as a savings-cum-protection instrument. The Bima Shree plan is specially catered towards high net-worth individuals. In the event of the policyholder's death during the policy term, this policy will provide financial support to the concerned individual's beneficiaries. In addition to offering a maturity benefit along with loyalty additions, and accrued guaranteed additions payable at the completion of the policy term, periodic payouts in the form of survival benefits, amounting to a percentage of the basic sum assured is also payable on certain pre-specified policy years. In case if the policyholder succumbs to an untimely death during the first five policy years, the death sum assured and accrued guaranteed additions will be paid. But if the individual passes away after 5 years, the death sum assured, loyalty additions, and accrued guaranteed additions will be paid as the death benefit under the policy. Policyholders can opt for this policy with a policy term of 14 years, 16 years, 18 years, or 20 years. In order to purchase this policy, the minimum age of the life assured should be 8 years while the maximum age at entry can range between 45 years and 55 years, based on the policy term opted for. The maximum age of the policyholder at maturity of the policy cannot exceed 69 years. To buy this policy, one must opt for a minimum sum assured of ₹10 lakh. Once the policy has acquired a surrender value, the policyholder can avail a loan against the policy.

2. **Jeevan Shiromani:** Jeevan Shiromani Plan offered by LIC is a with-profit, non-linked, limited premium payment, money-back life insurance policy that serves as a savings instrument, besides offering protection benefits to the policyholder. This policy is specifically designed to cater to the needs of high net-worth individuals. A unique benefit of this policy is that it comes with an inbuilt critical illness benefit. Thus, if the policyholder happens to be diagnosed with any critical illness that is specified in the policy brochure,

the insurer will offer a certain payout to the policyholder. The policy offers financial protection to the policyholder's dependents in case of an untimely eventuality. The policy also offers regular payouts in the form of survival benefits and a maturity benefit at the completion of the policy term. If the life assured dies within 5 years of purchasing the policy, death sum assured along with the accrued guaranteed additions is paid to the nominee but if death occurs after the first five policy-years, the nominee is paid death sum assured, loyalty additions, and accrued guaranteed additions. The minimum age at entry for procuring Jeevan Shiromani plan, is 18 years and the maximum age at entry shall vary based on the policy-term selected. Minimum sum assured under the plan is fixed at ₹1 crore. Policyholders can choose a tenure of 14 years, 16 years, 18 years, or 20 years for the policy.

3. **New Money Back Plans—20 years; 25 years:** LIC's New Money Back Plan 20 years and New Money Back Plan 25 years are participating non-linked plans which offer an attractive combination of protection against death throughout the term of the plan along with the periodic payment on survival at specified durations during the term. This unique combination provides financial support for the family of the deceased policyholder any time before maturity and lump sum amount at the time of maturity for the surviving policyholders. These plans also takes care of liquidity needs by providing loan facility.

   Unlike ordinary endowment insurance plans where the survival benefits are payable only at the end of the endowment period, these schemes provides for periodic payments of partial survival benefits during the term of the policy, of course so long as the policy holder is alive. In the case of a 20-year Money Back Policy, 20 per cent of the sum assured becomes payable each after 5, 10, 15 years, and the balance of 40 per cent plus the accrued bonus become payable at the 20th year. For a Money Back Policy of 25 years, 15 per cent of the sum assured becomes payable each after 5, 10, 15 and 20 years, and the balance 40 per cent plus the accrued bonus become payable at the 25th year.

4. **New Bima Bachat:** It is a money back policy which requires the policyholder to pay premium only once at the outset of the policy, the amount of premium being dependent on the duration of the policy taken. Life insurance under the policy is available till the date of maturity. The person applying for the policy should have completed 15 years and should not be older than 66 years. The policy will mature when the person is 75 years old. The minimum sum that needs to be assured is ₹35,000 for policy term 9 years; ₹50,000 for policy term 12 years; ₹70,000 for policy term 15 years

and there is no limit on the amount that can be assured. 15 per cent of the sum assured is paid at the end of the 3rd, 6th, 9th and 12th years, depending on the term of the policy. Full sum assured is payable on the death of the policyholder during the term of the policy. Bima Bachat is the only money back policy that offers a loan facility.

5. **New Children's Money Back Plan:** This is a participating non-linked money back plan. This plan is specially designed to meet the educational, marriage and other needs of growing children through Survival Benefits. In addition, it provides for the risk cover on the life of child during the policy term and a number of survival benefits on surviving to the end of the specified durations. The plan can be purchased by any of the parent or grand-parent for a child aged 0 to 12 years. On the Life assured surviving the stipulated date of maturity, provided the policy is in full force, Sum Assured on Maturity (which is 40% of the Basic Sum Assured) along with vested Simple Reversionary Bonuses and Final Additional Bonus, if any, shall be payable. On the Assured surviving the policy anniversary coinciding with or immediately following the completion of ages 18 years, 20 years and 22 years, 20% of the Basic Sum Assured on each occasion shall be payable, provided the policy is in full force. The policy shall participate in profits of the Corporation and shall be entitled to receive Simple Reversionary Bonuses declared as per the experience of the Corporation, provided the policy is in full force.

6. **Jeevan Tarun:** LIC's Jeevan Tarun is a participating non-linked limited premium payment plan which offers an attractive combination of protection and saving features for children. This plan is specially designed to meet the educational and other needs of growing children through annual survival benefit payments from ages 20 to 24 years and maturity benefit at the age of 25 years. It is a flexible plan wherein at proposal stage the proposer can choose the proportion of survival benefits to be availed during the term of the policy as per the following four options:

Options	*Survival Benefit*	*Maturity Benefit*
Option 1	No survival benefit	100% of Sum Assured
Option 2	5% of Sum Assured every year for 5 years	75% of Sum Assured
Option 3	10% of Sum Assured every year for 5 years	50% of Sum Assured
Option 4	15% of Sum Assured every year for 5 years	25% of Sum Assured

7. **LIC's Dhan Rekha: Dhan Rekha** insurance plan from LIC is a non-linked, non-participating, individual savings money back plan that offers an attractive benefit of protection as well as savings. In the case of the policyholder's untimely death during the policy term, this plan provides financial support to the policyholder's family. LIC Dhan Rekha also provides liquidity by way of a loan facility.

   Some of the prominent features of LIC's Dhan Rekha plan are:

   - It is an individual, non-linked, non-participating, savings, and money-back plan.
   - This plan comes with a single premium option and a limited premium payment plan.
   - This plan provides a loan facility to meet liquidity needs of the policyholder.
   - The plan comes with riders, however, an additional charge is required to avail the benefit.
   - Premiums can be paid on a yearly, half-yearly, quarterly, or monthly basis, or through salary deductions.
   - From the date of the first unpaid premium, a grace period of 30 days for yearly, half-yearly, or quarterly premiums and 15 days for monthly payments will be permitted.
   - The policy can be surrendered by the policyholder at any moment throughout the policy term if it is paid with a single premium. The policyholder can surrender the policy at any point throughout the policy term if two full years' premiums have been paid under limited premium payment.
   - If the policyholder is dissatisfied with the policy's "Terms and Conditions," the policy may be returned to the company within 15 days (30 days in the event of an online transaction) of receiving the policy bond, citing the reasons for the return.
   - Minimum basic sum required to be assured under the policy is ₹2,00,000 and there is no limit to the maximum basic sum assured.
   - Minimum entry age for policy term 20 years is 8 years; for policy term 30 years is 3 years; and, for policy term 40 years is 90 days.
   - Maximum entry age for single premium is 40 to 60 years and for limited premium option is 35 to 55 years.
   - The "Sum Assured on Death" plus Accrued Guaranteed Additions is payable on death during the policy period after the date of commencement of risk. For a single premium

payment, the policyholder will receive 125% of the basic sum assured as the "Sum Assured on Death". Whereas, for limited premium payment, the policyholder will receive 125% of the basic sum assured or 7 times the yearly premium as the "Sum Assured on Death".

- A specific percentage of the basic sum assured is paid if the life assured survives for each of the stated durations during the policy period, provided the policy is in force.
- If the life assured survives the given date of maturity while the policy is in force, the "Sum Assured on Maturity" will be paid, along with any Accrued Guaranteed Additions.

15.3.5 Micro Insurance Plans

Micro Insurance Plans offered by LIC of India are a perfect blend of insurance and investment. The Micro Insurance Plans offered by LIC include the following:

1. **LIC's New Jeevan Mangal:** This is a protection plan with an in-built accident benefit rider which provides double risk cover in case of death due to accident.

   Features and benefits of LIC's New Jeevan Mangal are:

   - The minimum entry age is 18 years while the maximum is fixed at 60 years.
   - The policy term ranges from 10 to 15 years for regular premium payment.
   - The minimum instalment premium is ₹15.
   - Minimum sum assured under the policy is ₹10,000 whereas the maximum is ₹50,000.
   - On death during the policy term, the sum assured shall be payable to the nominee.
   - Maturity benefit is paid at the end of the policy term.
   - Accidental benefit rider is also offered with this plan.

2. **LIC's Bhagya Lakshmi Plan:** LIC's Bhagya Lakshmi Plan is a non-participating limited payment protection plan. A sum equal to 110% of total amount of premiums is paid on maturity.

   Features and benefits of LIC's Bhagya Lakshmi Plan are:

   - The minimum age at entry to the policy is 18 years while the maximum is fixed at 55 years.
   - The minimum premium paying term is 5 years and the maximum is 13 years.

- The minimum sum assured under the policy is ₹20,000 and the maximum is ₹50,000.
- On survival of the policyholder up to the date of maturity, sum assured becomes payable which is equal to 110% of the total amount of premiums paid during the term of the insurance contract.
- If the insured dies during the policy term, then the sum assured is payable to the nominee.

3. **Aam Aadmi Bima Yojana:** This plan was approved by the Ministry of Finance of India and merged with Aam Aadmi Bima Yojana and Janashree Bima Yojana.

   Features and benefits of this plan are as follows:

   - The minimum entry age is 18 years and the maximum is fixed at 59 years.
   - The minimum premium amount payable is ₹200 per month.
   - Sum assured is paid if the member dies during the policy term.
   - A free add-on benefit, in the form of scholarship benefit is offered to 2 children studying between 9th and 12th Standard. ₹100 is paid under the plan every month.
   - Moreover, benefit will also be provided for total or partial disability caused due to accident to the members of the plan.

4. **LIC's Micro Bachat Plan:** LIC's Micro Bachat Plan aims to provide financial support to the policyholder's family in case of his death during the term of the policy. It also guarantees a lump sum amount for the surviving policyholder at the time of policy maturity.

   Features of LIC's Micro Bachat Plan are discussed below:

   - Minimum age is 18 years, and the maximum age is 55 years as per the last birthday.
   - The maximum age as per the last birthday should not exceed 70 years.
   - The policy term ranges from 10–15 years
   - The premium paying term is the same as the policy term.
   - The minimum basic sum assured (available in multiples of ₹5000) is ₹50,000 while the maximum is fixed at ₹2,00,000.

There are two main benefits that a policyholder can avail of under the LIC Micro Bachat Policy. These are:

1. **Death Benefits:** In the event of the policyholder's death during the first five years of the policy's term, the sum assured on Death

will be payable provided that all premiums due have been duly paid. And, in the event of the policyholder's death occurring after completion of the first five years but before the policy term ends, the sum assured on death will be payable, along with any loyalty additions.

2. **Maturity Benefit:** In the event that the policyholder survives till the end of the policy term, the sum assured on maturity will be payable, provided all due premiums have been paid by the policyholder. Loyalty benefit, if any, is added to the Sum Assured.

3. **Loyalty Addition:** Loyalty additions in case of maturity or death claim under this Policy *will* be payable only if the premiums have been paid for five years and the policy has completed five years and the policy is in force.

   Loyalty additions for either paid up or surrendered policies will be payable if five policy years are completed with five years premiums paid and maturity paid-up sum assured is ₹50,000 or more.

15.3.6 Pension/Annuity Plans

These plans are a form of investment that one makes, either in a single lump sum or through instalments paid over a certain number of years, in return for which you receive back a specific sum every year, every half-year or every month, either for life or for a fixed number of years, which is why they are also called **annuity plans**. These policies are most suited for senior citizens and those planning a secure future.

1. **LIC's Jeevan Akshay—VII:** The main features of the LIC Jeevan Akshay VII plan are as follows:
   - LIC Jeevan Akshay VII Plan is an annuity plan with different options to suit different financial needs of the policyholder.
   - It can be purchased both offline and online.
   - A free look period of 15 days is attached to this plan if the policy is purchased offline and if it is purchased online, then one gets 30 days. If one is not satisfied with the policy terms & conditions, the policy can be returned by the policyholder.
   - The policy offers loan facility. The loan facility is open after 3 months of completion of the policy. In few cases, the loan facility may be open after the expiry of the look-up period. However, the loan facility is offered only for specific annuity options.
   - The surrender option is also made available under this policy.
   - The policy also offers an option of lump sum payment.

2. **LIC's Saral Pension**

Features of LIC's Saral Pension are:

- LIC's Saral Pension plan is a standard pension plan which is issued as per the guidelines issued by IRDA.
- Saral pension plan is a non-linked, non-participating, single premium, individual immediate annuity plan.
- This is a single premium lump sum pension plan where one can get an immediate pension income.
- The minimum purchase price is based on the minimum annuity that is opted.
- There is no maximum purchase price limit on the plan.
- Minimum age of entry to the plan is 40 years while the maximum age of entry is 80 years.
- The annuity is payable either monthly, quarterly, half yearly or yearly.
- One can surrender the pension plan after 6 months based on prescribed terms and conditions.
- It comes with two annuity options: Option I: Life Annuity with Return of 100% of Purchase Price; Option II: Joint Life Last Survivor Annuity with Return of 100% of Purchase Price on death of the last survivor.

3. **Pradhan Mantri Vaya Vandana Yojana:** Pradhan Mantri Vaya Vandana Yojana (PMVVY) is a pension scheme issued by LIC and is designed for citizens above the age of 60 years. Under this plan, the guaranteed rates of pension for policies sold during a year are reviewed and decided at the beginning of each year by the Ministry of Finance, Government of India. For the first financial year, i.e. upto 31st March 2021, the scheme has decided to provide an assured pension of 7.40% p.a. payable monthly.

Features and benefits of PMVVY policy are as follows:

- If the policyholder survives during the policy term of 10 years, then the pension amount in arrears, that is, at the end of each period as per mode chosen is paid to the policyholder. However, the total amount of purchase price under this plan cannot exceed more than ₹15 lakhs.
- In the event of the death of the pensioner during the policy term, the purchase price of this policy is refunded to policyholder's nominee/beneficiary.
- If the pensioner survives upto the stipulated date of maturity, then the purchase price of this policy along with the final pension installment is refunded back to the pensioner.

- This plan also offers the benefit of loan facility. The policyholder can avail loan against this policy after completing 3 policy years. The maximum loan that can be availed is equal to 75% of the purchase price.

4. **LIC's New Jeevan Shanti:** LIC's Jeevan Shanti policy is a non-linked and non-participating plan. It provides different options to the insured. Within an immediate annuity plan, a total of 10 options are available, out of which 2 options are available for life cover. Alternatively, within a deferred annuity plan, 2 options are available that provide adequate cover against any risk that the policyholder might come across in life.

The primary objective of LIC's Jeevan Shanti plan is to offer various insurance options to the potential customers. When it comes to the returns, the same can be availed instantly within an immediate annuity plan. The time of returns can be chosen in the case of a deferred annuity plan. In addition, an individual can either withdraw the pension immediately or delay the same with returns.

LIC's Jeevan Shanti is a Single Premium Annuity Plan. This plan can be used to secure fixed payouts at regular intervals for the rest of policyholder's life. Under this plan the policyholder pays a Single Premium (also called the 'Purchase Price') to purchase an Annuity. LIC will then pay the policyholder regular amounts for the rest of his/her life. One can receive these regular payouts on monthly, quarterly, half-yearly or annual basis. This regular payout amount is called an Annuity. There are 2 options in this plan—Immediate Annuity and Deferred Annuity. Collectively there are 12 options to receive the regular annuity payments.

Some of the benefits of buying LIC Jeevan Shanti plan are explained below:

- **Ease of Buying:** Any individual can buy the LIC Jeevan Shanti plan both online as well as offline.
- **Assured Returns:** When an individual opts for a deferred annuity plan, assured returns are guaranteed.
- **Multiple Alternatives:** The LIC Jeevan Shanti policy offers both immediate and deferred annuity plans, wherein the insured can pick from the several options available within the policy.
- **Guaranteed Income:** While investing in such plans, the policyholder will receive a regular monthly income. The policyholder will receive this income for a lifetime.
- **The Flexibility of Annuity Payment:** Notwithstanding the plan one takes, the annuity payments can be made as per convenience

at various intervals. Annuity payments may be made on a monthly, quarterly, half-yearly, or yearly basis.

- **Loan Facility:** Loan facility can be availed under the plan after the completion of one year.
- **Surrender Value:** The policy can be surrendered within three months of the purchase of policy.
- **Free Lookup Period:** The LIC Jeevan Shanti Plan has a free lookup period of 15 days. Within this period, the policyholder can return the policy if not satisfied with the terms and conditions of the policy.
- **Tax Benefits:** The Tax benefits as per Section 80C of the Income Tax Act, can be availed of. The one-time premium, which is paid, will be recovered when the tax is being paid.

15.3.7 Unit Plans

Unit plans are investment plans for those who realise the worth of hard-earned money. These plans help you see your savings yield rich benefits and help you save tax even if you don't have consistent income.

LIC's New Endowment Plus: LIC's New Endowment Plus is a unit linked non-participating endowment assurance plan which offers investment as well as insurance cover during the term of the policy. This plan is specially designed to provide a good combination of protection and long term savings along with greater flexibility to build a better life and to realise one's dreams. Under this policy, the investment risk in investment portfolio is borne by the policyholder. The linked insurance products do not offer any liquidity during the first five years of the contract. The policyholders will not be able to surrender/withdraw the amounts invested in linked insurance products completely or partially till the end of fifth year. On death before the date of commencement of risk, an amount equal to the policyholder's fund value shall be payable. And, on death after the date of commencement of risk an amount equal to the higher of basic sum assured or policyholder's fund value shall be payable. On life assured surviving the date of maturity provided the policy is in force, an amount equal to policyholder's fund value shall be payable.

LIC's Nivesh Plus: Below are mentioned some of the key characteristics of LIC's Nivesh Plus Plan:

- The LIC company will invest a part of the premium amount of the policyholder in unit funds, from which he/she will have four investment fund options to choose from. These four options are Balanced Funds, Growth Funds, Secured Funds, and Bond Funds.

- At the time of policy commencement, policy seekers have two options for their basic sum assured amount.
- Jeevan Nivesh Plus Plan from LIC permits a client to switch his fund unit in the middle of his policy term if he so desires. This functionality does, however, come with some terms that should be carefully read.
- After the policy has been in force for five years, the life guaranteed can partially withdraw his units under the Jeevan Nivesh Plan LIC. In the event of minors, partial withdrawals will be permitted only until life assured has reached the age of eighteen years. Partial withdrawals can be made in either a definite amount or a fixed number of units.
- Those who purchased the policy offline have a 15-day free look period, while those who purchased Nivesh Plus online have a 30-day free look period. If the insured is not satisfied with the plan's terms during this time, he or she can return the policy to the company.
- Policyholders of the Nivesh Plus Plan from LIC have the option of receiving their death benefit in a lump sum or instalments. If the life assured dies later, his nominee is compensated in the same way.

The plan offers the following benefits to the policyholder:

- If the life assured dies during the policy term, the nominee would get a death benefit from the LIC's Nivesh Plus Plan.
- The insured is paid an amount equivalent to the Unit Fund Value if the policyholder lives to the end of the Nivesh Plus LIC's maturity period. This is termed as the maturity benefit.
- The LIC's Linked Accidental Death Benefit is an additional rider option available with the Jeevan Nivesh Plan. This rider benefit can be added at any point throughout the plan's life cycle or on the policy's anniversary. The benefits under this additional rider option will be available until the plan's maturity or policy anniversary.

LIC's SIIP Plan: LIC's SIIP plan is a unit linked plan which offers potential to grow one's money besides offering life cover as well. Being a unit linked plan, it offers growth potential if invested over a long period of time. The performance of the funds the money is invested in determines the overall returns of the investment. This plan also has tax savings advantage built into it. The prospective policyholder has to decide on the amount of money he/she wants to invest on a monthly basis (investment can be made in annual, quarterly, half-yearly or single mode also). Thereafter the term of the policy may be selected between 10 to 25 years. Based on the premium amount and the applicant's age, his/her life cover gets decided automatically. The money which is paid is invested in the funds of the investor's choice. Based on the amount invested and the choice of funds, the policyholder will be allocated units of these funds. The value of these funds depends on the NAV which are declared on a daily basis. Thus, one can keep track of one's investment and performance from Day 1.

KEY TERMS

Assignment Method of transferring the assured's rights under a policy to another party or assignee.

Contingent contracts Contracts to do or not to do something, if some event, collateral to such contract, does or does not happen.

Nomination Declaration of the name of a person to whom the insured amount shall be payable in the event of death before the date of maturity of the policy.

Premium The amount of money or consideration charged by insurance company for any insurance coverage.

Term assurance Policy that covers the risk of life for a specified period of time.

Uberrimae fidei Contracts based on principle of utmost good faith.

Warranty Undertaking by the insured that certain conditions shall be fulfilled or that certain statements are true.

Whole life assurance Policy that covers the risk of life for whole life until death.

REVIEW QUESTIONS

15.1 Explain the meaning of life assurance. What are the advantages of life assurance?

15.2 Explain the features of a contract of life assurance.

15.3 Describe the endowment assurance plans offered by the LIC of India.

15.4 Explain the various kinds of life policies.

15.5 Explain the following:
- (i) Endowment policy
- (ii) Money back policy
- (iii) Unit plans
- (iv) Annuity policy
- (v) Whole life policy

15.6 Describe LIC's leading Micro-insurance plans.

15.7 Describe the features of some of the term assurance plans.

15.8 Explain the features and benefits of the following insurance plans:

(i) Jeevan Umang

(ii) Pradhan Mantri Vaya Vandana Yojana

(iii) Aam Aadmi Bima Yojana

(iv) New Jeevan Mangal Plan

(v) Jeevan Tarun

16

Fire Insurance

Learning Objectives

After going through this chapter we will be able to:

- Discuss the need and importance of fire insurance.
- Understand the nature of fire insurance contracts.
- Explain the principles of fire insurance.
- Discuss the salient features of various fire insurance policies.
- Briefly explain fire insurance claims settlement procedure.

Fire insurance is defined under the provisions of the Insurance Act, 1938, as the business of effecting, otherwise than incidentally to some other class of insurance business, contracts of insurance against loss by or incidental to fire or other occurrence customarily included among the risks insured against in fire insurance policies. Under a contract of fire insurance the insurer, in consideration of a sum of money paid by the insured either in lump sum or in fixed instalments, accepts to indemnify the insured against the consequences of fire, or the loss or injury as arising therefrom during a fixed period and up to a certain sum. Fire insurance thus, is a contract of indemnity wherein the insurer undertakes to indemnify the insured against financial loss or damage to property caused directly as a result of fire anytime during an agreed period of time.
The fire insurance policy document contains

1. The written contract between the insurer and the insured setting forth the terms and conditions under which the insurance is issued.

2. The particulars of the property insured, risks and hazards covered, the sum assured, the cost or the rate of premium and the period.

The contract contained in the policy-document of the fire insurance is usually for a period of one year. Thereafter, the contract may be renewed every year. The risk under the fire policy commences from the time the cover note or the deposit receipt or the interim protection note is given and continues for the term covered by the terms of the contract as laid down in the insurance policy document. However, certain number of days is generally allowed as grace period within which a fire policy may be renewed after the cessation of the term. In such a case, if a fire occurs during this period, the insured would be entitled to recover damages. But the grace period would be allowed only when the insured has the intention to renew the policy, failing which, the policy expires on the last day of the period fixed up for the policy. Sometimes, it is expressly stipulated in the policy that unless the renewal premium is paid and the renewal risk is accepted the insurance would expire. In such a case, the insured would not be entitled to recover the loss where a fire occurs after the expiration of the term, and before the acceptance of the proposal for further insurance by the fire insurance company.

The term *fire* in a contract of fire insurance means the production of light and heat by combustion. Combustion occurs only at the actual ignition point. Hence, there is no fire without ignition. Loss or damage that occurs in an attempt to put out the fire is also insured and covered in the fire insurance contract. However, fire caused by earthquakes, riots, civil tumult, alien enemy, insurgence, etc. are not covered by way of fire policies.

For example, three shops, A, B and C, in a row at a market place were damaged. Shop A fell to the ground due to an earthquake as a result of which fire broke out and spread to shop B consequently, an explosion occurred due to which, shop C was completely destroyed. The liability of the insurer for the damages suffered by the owner of shop C under the fire insurance policy was debated and it was held that in such a case where explosion actually causes ignition to spread into fire, the loss would be taken as a loss by fire and the insurer is liable.

It may be noted that though fire risks do not cover losses caused only by explosion but generally, fire insurance policies do cover losses caused by explosion, incidental to fire unless even that is specifically excluded.

Any kind of property, movable or immovable having a pecuniary value can be insured against fire. Fire insurance contracts being governed by tariff, the property that is being insured must accordingly be described. Insurable properties include

1. Buildings
2. Electrical installation in buildings
3. Contents of buildings such as machinery, plant and equipment, accessories, etc.

4. Goods (raw materials, work in progress, semi-finished goods, finished goods, packaging materials) in factories and godowns
5. Goods in open
6. Contents in dwellings, shops, hotels, etc.
7. Furniture, fixture and fittings
8. Pipelines (including contents) located inside or outside the compound, etc.

16.1 SCOPE OF FIRE INSURANCE[1]

Fire insurance business in India is governed by the All India Fire Tariff that lays down the terms of coverage, the premium rates and the conditions of the fire policy. The risks covered under fire insurance are as follows:

1. **Fire:** Destruction or damage to the insured property as a direct consequence of fire is certainly covered but its fermentation, natural heating or spontaneous combustion in undergoing heating or drying process cannot be considered as damage due to fire. Correspondingly, paints or chemicals in a factory undergoing heat treatment and consequently damaged by fire are not covered.
2. **Lightning:** Lightning may cause fire damage or other types of damage such as a roof broken by a falling chimney struck by lightning or cracks in a building due to lightning strike. Both fire and other forms of damage caused by lightning are covered.
3. **Explosion/implosion:** An explosion may cause fire damage. Explosion may be defined as a sudden, violent burst with a loud noise. This is caused inside a vessel when the pressure within the vessel exceeds the atmospheric pressure acting externally on the surface. Implosion means bursting inward or collapse. This takes place when external pressure exceeds the internal pressure. This policy, however, does not cover destruction or damage caused to the boilers in which heat is generated.
4. **Aircraft damage:** The loss/damage to property by fire or otherwise, directly caused by aircraft and other aerial devices and/or articles dropped therefrom, are covered. However, destruction or damage resulting from pressure waves caused by aircraft travelling at supersonic speed is not covered.
5. **Riot, strike, malicious and terrorism damage:** Any loss or physical damage to the insured property directly caused by any kind of terrorist activity or by the action of lawful authorities in suppressing such damages or minimising its consequences is covered.

---
[1] www.insuremagic.com

6. **Storm, cyclone, typhoon, tempest, hurricane, tornado, flood and inundation:** The various types of natural disturbances that are accompanied by thunder or strong winds or heavy rainfall are covered.
7. **Impact damage:** Damage resulting from the impact of any rail/ road vehicle or animal by direct contact with insured property is covered.
8. **Subsidence and landslide including rockslide:** Destruction or damage caused by subsidence of any part of the site on which the property stands or landslide/rockslide is covered.
9. **Bursting and/or overflowing of water tanks, apparatus and pipes:** Loss or damage to property by water or otherwise due to bursting or accidental overflowing of water tanks, apparatus and pipes is covered.
10. **Missile testing operations:** Destruction or damage due to impact or otherwise from trajectory/projectiles in connection with missile testing operations by the insured or any other person is covered.
11. **Leakage from automatic sprinkler installations:** Damage caused by water accidentally discharged or leaked out from automatic sprinkler installations in the premises of the insured is covered.
12. **Bush fire:** This covers damage caused by burning, whether accidental or otherwise of bush and jungles and the clearing of lands by fire. However, destruction/damage caused by forest fire is excluded.

16.2 FIRE INSURANCE: UNDERLYING PRINCIPLES

The following underlying principles are essential for a valid contract of fire insurance:

Principle of indemnity: The purpose of this principle is to put the insured, to the extent possible, in the same financial position after the suffering of the loss that he was in, immediately before the loss occured. The insured can recover only the amount of actual loss subject to the sum assured.

Principle of insurable interest: In fire insurance, the insurable interest must exist both at the time of effecting the insurance as well as at the time of the loss. The insurable interest may be legal or equitable and may arise under a contract of purchase or sale.

The following are believed to have insurable interest in the subject-matter in the context of fire insurance:

- Owner
- Executor

- Trustee
- Mortgagee
- Pledgee
- Bailee
- Person in lawful possession of the property
- Tenants, liable to pay rent after a fire
- Insurer
- Commi ssion agent, where the agency is coupled with interest

However, the extent to which a person would be allowed to get the property insured is limited to the extent of his/her financial stake in that property.

Principle of good faith: All contracts of fire insurance are contracts of *uberrimae fidei*, that is, a contract based on unconditional good faith. This principle requires the insured to make full and detailed disclosure of all material facts that may have a bearing on the decision of the insurer to accept or reject the proposal and in determining the rates of premium to be charged. Hence, for a valid fire insurance contract the description of the property should be correctly given, as also any other information that may be required. Information pertaining to the class of goods and articles that are kept on the premises or in the surrounding neighbourhood, wherever sought, should be accurately supplied.

Principle of causa proxima: In a fire insurance contract, only losses resulting from fire or some other related cause, being the proximate cause of loss are covered. However, where the fire is caused by the insured himself or with his connivance or by the operation of a peril expressly excluded under the policy like earthquake, the loss will not be covered and the insurer will not be liable to indemnify the insured.

Principles of subrogation and contribution: All fire insurance contracts are based on the principle of subrogation whereby the insurer, after paying compensation to the insured, becomes entitled to claim all the rights of the insured against third parties who may be proved to be responsible, directly or indirectly, for that loss.

Fire insurance contracts are also governed by the principle of contribution, which provides that where the subject-matter has been insured with more than one insurer, each insurer has to meet the loss only rateably. If he has paid more than his share of loss, he is entitled to recover the excess amount paid by him from his co-insurers.

16.3 TYPES OF FIRE POLICIES

Some of the commonly offered fire insurance policies are discussed hereinafter:

Specific policy: A specific policy is one where the insurer undertakes to make good the loss only upto the amount specified in the policy, regardless of the actual value of the property. For example, a house worth ₹20,00,000 is insured for ₹10,00,000. The house gets destroyed because of fire and the actual loss is estimated to be ₹15,00,000. Under a specific fire insurance policy, the insured can recover the actual loss where the actual loss is equal to or less than the value of the policy, but in case if the actual loss is more than the sum insured, the insured would be entitled to recover only the amount of policy. Thus, in this case too, the insured can claim only the amount of the policy being less than the actual loss.

Valued policy: A valued policy is usually taken where it is not easy to ascertain the value of the property. For example, it is not easy to determine the value of works of art, antiques, pictures, sculptures, etc. The value of such articles or valuable possessions is declared by the insured and is mentioned in the policy. In the case of total loss in the valued policy the insurer undertakes to pay the value of the property as mentioned in the policy, or the declared value, irrespective of its actual or market value. Thus, this type of policy flouts the basic principle of indemnity. However, such policies are not very common in fire insurance.

Average policy: Under an average policy the insured is penalized for under insurance of the property. This kind of fire policy contains an *average clause*. In other words, the insured is entitled to only such proportion of the loss as the value of the insured part of the property bears to the actual value of the property. The insured is expected to personally assume the risk to the extent of under insurance. Thus, an average clause is relevant only in cases of under insurance and partial loss. For example, if a property, which is worth of ₹8,00,000 is insured for ₹6,00,000 and the actual loss as a result of fire is ₹4,00,000, then the liability of the insurer in settlement of claim to be paid will be calculated as follows:

$$\text{Claim Amount} = \frac{\text{Amount insured}}{\text{Actual value of property}} \times \text{Actual loss}$$

That is,

$$\frac{6,00,000}{8,00,000} \times 4,00,000 = 3,00,000$$

The average clause, however, applies only in cases of underinsurance and partial loss, that is, where it is proved that the loss suffered by the insured is less than the sum insured. But where there is total loss or the loss is more than the sum insured, the insured amount will be paid. For instance, in the above example, if the entire property was lost, then the insured amount would have been claimed.

Floating policy: A floating policy is taken to cover loss on goods, which are lying in different places and the stock of which is almost continuously fluctuating. The volume of goods changes with each transaction of sale or purchase making it difficult for the owner to specify the quantity in each place and take a policy for a specific amount. In such cases, the owner usually prefers to take out only one floating policy, against one premium, instead of separate specific policies for all his goods, some of which may be in stores or warehouses, others in railway stations, shops, etc. Under the floating policy the insured is required to declare only the total value of the risk and not separate values in separate risks.

Reinstatement policy: This policy is issued to cover damages/losses suffered in respect of buildings; plant and machinery; furniture, fixtures and fittings, etc. Under this policy, instead of paying compensation to the insured for the property destroyed, the insurer undertakes to pay the cost of reinstating or replacing the property.

Comprehensive policy: Comprehensive policy is also termed as *all insurance policy*. This is because it provides protection not only against the risk of fire but also consequential risks. It does not, of course, mean that the comprehensive policy covers every type of risk but it definitely covers losses caused by fire coalescing with the risk against burglary, riot, civil commotion, theft, damage from pest, lightning. Such policies are not common in India.

Consequential loss policy: Under this policy the insurer undertakes to indemnify the insured for the financial loss or loss of profits, suffered due to dislocation of his business as a consequence of fire. That is why consequential loss policy is also known as *loss of profit policy*. Loss of goods or property damaged, loss of net profits, interruption in business after fire, outstanding expenses (interest on debenture, salaries, rent on building, etc.) and prepaid expenses are some examples of losses covered under the policy. Since such substantial losses are otherwise not covered under the ordinary fire policy, the loss so suffered is separately calculated from the loss directly suffered as a result of fire.

Declaration policy: Declaration policy is taken in respect of stock of inventory (stock of raw material, stock of work-in-progress and stock of finished goods) of the policyholder. Since the levels of stock, which are subject to frequent fluctuations in value or in volume, present a special problem for insurance, the businessman takes a policy for a maximum amount considered to be at risk and the premium is paid accordingly. On a fixed date of every month or for a specified period, the policyholder declares the amount of stock covered under the policy to the insurance company. The annual premium is determined on the average of these declarations.

Adjustable policy: The adjustable policy is granted to remove the disadvantages of declaration policy. This policy covers the fluctuating stock of the insured businessman allowing him the freedom to vary at his option. The premium varies with the variation of the stock. This is issued for a definite period on the existing stock. The premium is calculated in the regular manner and is paid in full at the beginning of the policy. The insured is liable to inform the insurer about every variation in the stock immediately. The moment the insurer receives the information regarding variation in the stock, the policy is suitably ratified and the premium adjusted on a pro-rata basis. The policy amount too changes from time to time.

Sprinklers leakage policy: This policy covers the loss arising out of water leakage from sprinklers that are set up to extinguish fire.

16.4 ASSIGNMENT OF FIRE POLICY

According to the English Common Law, fire insurance contracts are contracts of a personal nature, and therefore, can be assigned only with the consent of the insurer or the insurance company. A policy of fire insurance does not pass with the sale or assignment of the property on which it is affected. Transfer or assignment only with the approval of the insurance company would bestow a valid right to the assignee.

The Transfer of Property Act u/s 135 A provides for only an endorsement or any other writing for assigning an immovable property which has been insured against fire. Notice is only needed to make the insurer liable to the assignee in case if the insurer pays the claim amount to the insured after receiving notice of the assignment. This notice is not necessary for validating the assignment of a fire policy.

16.5 SETTLEMENT OF CLAIMS

The first step required of the insured in case of an outbreak of fire is to give notice to the insurance company and submit proofs and details of losses. For this the insured has to furnish all plans, documents, invoices, proofs and other relevant facts needed by the insurer. Fire policies generally incorporate a clause requiring notice to be furnished within a specified time (usually 15 days) from the date of occurrence of the loss due to fire. This clause must be firmly complied with. The claim to be made out should be for the exact value of the goods damaged or destroyed by fire. In case of partly destroyed or damaged goods, separate detailed particulars regarding their value *in good condition* and *in damaged condition* must be made out and delivered to the insurance company. The basis of claim in the case of damaged buildings is the cost of repairs of the damage.

ILLUSTRATIONS

16.1 Potato bags kept in a warehouse were insured against fire. The potatoes were fouled by heat due to the closing of the ventilators of the warehouse. Explain the liability of the insurance company.

Ans: The insurance company faces no liability in this case as the loss is not directly caused by fire. The loss by heating alone is not loss by fire.

16.2 Some insured goods, kept in a godown, were partially destroyed by fire and the insured was duly compensated by the insurer for the loss. The insurer then sued the godown keeper and recovered a sum of ten thousand rupees from him. The insured claimed payment of even this amount from the insurer. Is he entitled?

Ans: No, the insured is not entitled as he cannot be allowed to make a gain out of a contract of fire insurance. It is a contract of indemnity.

16.3 Mr. Bose gets his house worth ₹40 lakh insured for ₹30 lakh against loss due to fire. The fire policy contains an average clause. The house is destroyed by fire and the actual loss is estimated at ₹24 lakh. How much can Mr. Bose recover by way of compensation from the insurance company?

Ans: In case of an average policy

$$\text{Claim Amount} = \frac{\text{Amount insured}}{\text{Actual value of property}} \times \text{Actual loss}$$

Thus, A can recover the loss amount of ₹18 lakh from the insurance company.

16.4 A property worth ₹3 crore was insured against fire for only ₹2 crore. The average clause was attached in the policy. The house was completely destroyed by fire. The insured claimed the whole of the insured amount. The insurer declined to pay on grounds of the "average clause". Comment.

Ans: The "average clause" applies only in cases of partial loss and not in cases of total loss. In the above case, the property is absolutely lost. Therefore, the insured is entitled to recover the whole insured amount.

KEY TERMS

Assignment Transfer of the right of property in somebody else's name.

Average clause Condition defining insurer's liability in case of under insurance and partial loss.

Consequential loss Loss due to interruptions or dislocation of business as a result of fine.

Endorsement Alterations or additions in the policy terms.

REVIEW QUESTIONS

16.1 Define fire insurance contract. Elucidate the characteristics of a fire insurance contract.

16.2 Discuss the various kinds of fire policies.

16.3 Fire insurance is a personal contract, comment.

16.4 What is the effect of average clause in a fire policy?

16.5 What is the meaning of fire in a fire insurance policy? What is the subject-matter of fire insurance?

16.6 Draw a distinction between declaration policy and adjustable policy.

16.7 "A fire insurance is a contract of indemnity". Comment.

16.8 Elaborate on the scope of fire insurance.

16.9 Write short notes on

(i) Insurable interest in a fire insurance policy

(ii) Specific policy

(iii) Floating policy

(iv) Declaration policy

(v) Double insurance

17

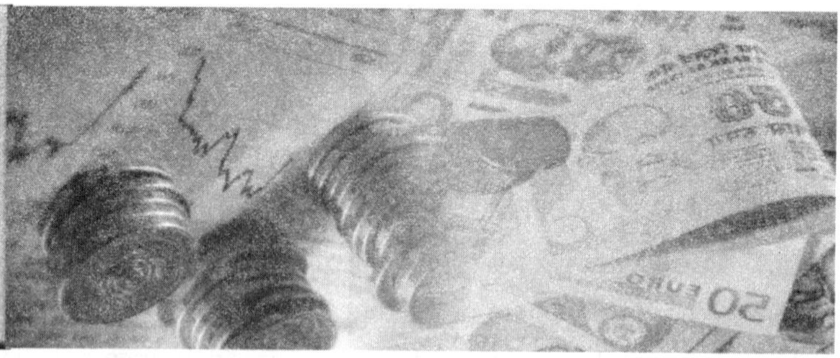

Marine Insurance

Learning Objectives

After going through this chapter we will be able to:

- Understand the concept of marine insurance.
- Explain the scope of marine insurance.
- Discuss the nature of marine insurance contracts.
- Describe the fundamental principles of marine insurance.
- Describe the different types of marine insurance policies.
- Understand the various types of losses covered by marine insurance.
- Explain the important clauses of marine insurance.

Marine insurance, in its modern form, was introduced by the British insurers with the establishment of the first company known as the **Sun Insurance Office Ltd**. being set up in Kolkata (then Calcutta) in 1710. Subsequently, many more insurance companies from different parts of the world entered into the business of marine insurance. The subsidiaries of the General Insurance Corporation of India, namely, New India Assurance, National Insurance, Oriental Insurance and United India Insurance conduct marine insurance business in India.

The inexorableness of marine insurance can be analyzed by the fact that though not legally bound, yet every shipowner and shipping merchant gets their property insured against losses or damages associated with maritime venture. The rationale for marine insurance is the enormous capital loss that the modern ships are, otherwise exposed to. No single shipping corporation can survive if it has to bear the liability arising out of such huge damage/loss. Moreover, the banks and other financial institutions providing nearly all the financial resources required for the purposes of marine adventure also insist on insurance as collateral security.

17.1 THE SCOPE OF MARINE INSURANCE

The scope of marine insurance has extremely widened over time. Though the expression generally applies to the risks associated with the transportation of goods by sea, the scope of marine insurance extends to a mixture of broad property coverage, divided between land risks (inland marine) and sea risks (ocean marine). Ocean marine insurance refers not only to the insurance of ships but also includes the insurance of hulls, the cargo and liabilities likely to be faced by shipowners and operators. Marine insurance also covers the insurance of wharves, ports/harbours, container terminals, oil platforms, drilling rigs, etc. In general, marine insurance can be classified into the following three categories:

Hull insurance: Hull insurance involving the insurance of ships including vessel-machinery, refers to the marine insurance policy whereby insured is indemnified for losses as a result of loss or damage to the ship. The perils usually covered under hull insurance include stranding, sinking, fire and collision. The hull insurance also comprises the construction risk when the vessel is under construction.

Cargo insurance: Goods and commodities transported by sea is the subject-matter of cargo insurance. It covers the multitude of risks associated with the trans-shipment of goods by sea or air in international trade. The terms and conditions of cargo insurance will be based on the provision of the insurance contract. Cargo insurance offers two alternatives—the special policy to cover specific risks like sinking of the vessel or piracy or *all risks* with reference to a particular deal, and the open cargo policy to cover the cargo warehouse to warehouse, thus, providing insurance against risks that are related to land transportation as well.

Freight insurance: Freight may be referred to as the charges paid for the conveyance of goods or the fee charged for the carriage of goods in the vessel. Freight may be received in advance or after the goods reach the destination. Where the freight is received in advance, no risk is involved, but in case if freight is to be paid later, there is always the fear that the goods will not reach the destination port safely. In case if the vessel is destroyed in route, the freight would also be lost along with the vessel. That is why, it is a normal practice to buy freight insurance policy along with every hull insurance policy.

Liability insurance: Liability insurance, also known as **protection and indemnity insurance (P&I)**, is designed to provide protection to the vessel-owners against liabilities for damages to docks, cargo, illness or injury to the passengers or crew, and the consequent fines and penalties payable by the ship-owner.

17.2 MARINE INSURANCE CONTRACTS

Marine Insurance Act, 1963, defines a contract as *an agreement whereby the insurer undertakes to indemnify the assured, in the manner and to the extent thereby agreed, against losses incidental to marine adventure.* Marine insurance contracts may also be defined to cover loss or damage to vessels, cargo or freight.

The document containing the contract of marine insurance as entered into, between the insurer and the assured is called a **marine policy** or **sea policy**. The consideration for the policy is called the **premium**. The insurer in marine insurance is known as the **underwriter**. The insured may be cargo-owner or a ship-owner or a receiver of freight. The subject-matter of marine insurance, that is, the insurable property may include any ship, goods or other movables exposed to nautical perils.

The term *marine adventure* in the context of marine insurance denotes

1. An insurable property exposed to marine perils
2. The earning or acquisition of any freight, commission, profit or other financial benefit, or the security for any advances, loans or disbursement endangered by the exposure of insurable property to maritime perils
3. Any liability to a third party, which may be insured by the owner of, or any other person interested in or responsible for, insurable property by reason of maritime perils.

Nautical/maritime/marine perils, also called as **perils of the sea**, mean all those perils that are consequential or incidental to sea journey. Perils of the sea include collisions, war perils, captures, jettisons, barratry, etc. and any other perils which are either of the like kind or may be designated by the policy. The term *perils of the sea* refers only to inadvertent, unpremeditated accidents or casualties of the sea. It does not include the typical action of the winds and waves. Losses caused because of collision against a sunken rock or collision with another ship or losses caused due to holes made at the bottom of a ship by rats, which allowed sea water to enter the ship and damage the cargo, etc. are some examples of perils of the sea.

17.3 FUNDAMENTAL PRINCIPLES OF MARINE INSURANCE

The marine insurance is based on the following fundamental principles:

17.3.1 Non-life Contract

A marine insurance policy involves an agreement between the insured and the marine insurance company, also known as **underwriter**. In order to be legally enforceable, the policy must comply with all the essentials of a valid contract, that is, offer, acceptance, agreement, competent parties, free consent, lawful consideration and legal object. The consideration or premium is ascertained on the basis of proper appraisal of the proposal. It is to be paid at the time of the contract.

17.3.2 Insurable Interest

The insured must have an insurable interest in the subject-matter of insurance. This is required to be established at the time of occurrence of the loss. Thus, it is not compulsory that insurable interest must exist at the time of affecting the contract of insurance.

The following parties are said to have insurable interest in the context of marine insurance:

(i) Ship/cargo-owner
(ii) Master and crew (only to the extent of their wages)
(iii) Mortgager/mortgagee
(iv) A creditor who has advanced money on a ship or cargo (to the extent of his interest in such a ship or cargo)
(v) Person who has paid advance freight (where freight is recoverable on loss)
(vi) Shippers and their agents
(vii) Trustee
(viii) Bailee
(ix) Assignee of the bill of lading
(x) Insurer—he can reinsure

17.3.3 Utmost Good Faith

Marine insurance is a contract of uberrimae fidei or a contract of utmost good faith. The insured must disclose all such relevant facts to the insurer, which are likely to affect his inclination or willingness to undertake the risk. According to section 19 of the Marine Insurance Act 1963, if any party does not observe utmost good faith, the other party may avoid the contract. In addition, under section 22 of the Act, every material representation that is made by the insured to the insurer during negotiations for the contract and before the contract is concluded, must be true. If it is found to be untrue, the insurer may avoid the contract. Moreover, if either party does not disclose complete facts, the other party can avoid the contract.

17.3.4 Contract of Indemnity

Marine insurance contracts are contracts of indemnity wherein the underwriter agrees to indemnify the insured against losses by sea risks to the extent of the amount insured. As a result the insured can recover only the actual loss suffered. He will not be allowed to make a profit of his loss. The insured in return for this undertaking pays an agreed amount known as the **premium**.

17.3.5 Principles of Subrogation and Contribution

Marine insurance contracts are based on the principles of subrogation and contribution. According to the principle of subrogation, after compensating the insured's loss on agreed basis, the insurer steps into the shoes of the insured and becomes entitled to all the rights and remedies available to the insured against third persons.

The doctrine of contribution also applies in such cases of marine insurance, where the subject-matter has been insured with more than one insurer. Each insurer contributes to the loss proportionately and meets only the rateable proportion of the actual loss. If he has paid more than his share of loss, he is entitled to recover the excess amount paid from other co-insurers of the policy.

17.3.6 Principle of Warranty

A warranty means a stipulation or condition, the breach of which entitles the insurers to completely avoid the policy. The principle of warranty applies even though the breach arises through circumstances beyond the control of the warrantor.

Warranties are of two kinds—express and implied. These are discussed hereinafter.

Express warranties: These are warranties expressly included in or written upon the policy or contained in some document referred to in the policy.

Express warranties generally include the following:

- The ship is safe on a particular day.
- The ship and goods are non-aligned and shall continue to be so.
- The ship will proceed to its destination without any deviation.
- The ship will sail on or before a particular day.

Implied warranties: These are warranties, which are implied in every marine insurance contract except when they are expressly excluded.

Some of the implied warranties are explained as follows:

Seaworthiness of the ship. A voyage policy includes a warranty of seaworthiness by the insured ensuring that the ship concerned is fit for the voyage on which it is sailing in every respect. This warranty is to be given by the insured at the time of affecting the insurance.

The warranty of seaworthiness implies that

- The ship is sound as regards her hull
- The paraphernalia is sufficient, fully equipped and manned
- The ship would not be overloaded
- If the voyage is to be performed in stages, the ship must be seaworthy at the commencement of each stage
- Seaworthiness also include cargoworthiness. It must be fit to carry the cargo
- Legality of the voyage
- Proper documentation of the ship

Non-deviation warranty. In the case of a voyage policy where a voyage is contemplated between any two given ports there is an implied warranty of non-deviation on the part of the insured, by which the insured is supposed to give an undertaking, that he shall take the usual route taken by navigators, and shall not deviate therefrom except in cases where it is excusable by the law. Thus, deviation means change of the prescribed route or where no route is prescribed by the policy, change of the usual or customary route. If the ship, without lawful excuse, deviates from the voyage contemplated by the policy, the insurer is discharged from liability as from the time of deviation. The intention to deviate is immaterial. There must be deviation in fact to discharge the insurer from his liability under the contract. It is immaterial in such a case that the ship may have regained its route before any loss occurs.

Examples of such deviations include

- Where the course of the voyage is clearly specified in the policy, but that course is departed from.
- Where the course of the voyage is not clearly specified in the policy, but the normal and regular course is departed from.
- Sometimes several ports of discharge are specified in the policy. In such cases, the ship must proceed to those ports of discharge in the exact order as designated by the policy, and where it does not, there is a deviation.
- Where the policy is to ports of discharge within a given area, which are not named, the ship must proceed to them in their geographical order, if it does not, there is a deviation.

However, the insurer continues to remain liable under certain cases of deviation. For instance, where the voyage is to be completed in phases, seaworthiness of the ship must be ensured at the commencement of each phase. Seaworthiness also includes cargoworthiness, that is, it must be fit to carry the cargo.

17.4 MARINE INSURANCE POLICIES

Marine insurance policies cover various kinds of risks associated with trans-shipment of goods. Based on the needs of trade and industry and the requirements of the Marine Insurance Act, the following types of policies are issued:

Voyage policy: The voyage policy is issued to cover risks involved in a particular transit from a particular point to another. The cover ceases upon the ship reaching the town of destination. The risks covered by this policy are determined by the places covered in the specific trip. For example, Mumbai to Singapore; Mumbai to London. Such a policy is generally used for cargo insurance. Though it may sometimes be used for freight insurance, but rarely for hull insurance. While the basic policy document contains general conditions, the scope of cover and exceptions/ special exclusions are added by distinct clauses, which are known as institute cargo clauses (ICC).

Time policy: The purpose of this policy is to give cover for a specified period of time, say, for example, noon, Ist Jan. 2007 to noon, 1st Jan. 2008. This is usually taken for one year. The policy also provides cover while the vessel is under construction. Risks in the case of construction are covered for more than 12 months. Time policies are common in the case of hull insurance except in those cases where an owner prefers to insure his ship for each separate voyage under voyage policy.

Voyage and time policy or mixed policy: Voyage and time policy (also called mixed policy) is a combination of voyage and time policy. This policy covers the risk during a particular voyage for a specified period. For example, a vessel may be insured for voyages between Mumbai to London for a period of one year.

Valued policy: This policy specifies the agreed value of the subject-matter insured, which may not necessarily be the actual value of the subject-matter. This agreed value is referred to as the insured value. Once the value has been agreed, it cannot be recommenced except where an evidence of deceitful purpose is established, otherwise it remains binding on both parties. These policies are not very common.

Unvalued policy: In an unvalued policy, the value of the subject-matter that is insured is not specified at the time of effecting insurance. It is taken for a specified amount and the insurable value is settled at the time of occurrence of loss. The insurer's liability is limited only upto the actual loss incurred to the sum insured. It is also known as open policy.

Floating policy: This policy provides another method of obtaining a long-term contract for goods insurance, which may be used instead of or in addition to an open-cover. Under a floating (or open) policy the terms and conditions of insurance contract are settled as usual except that the name(s) of the ship(s) is (are) to be defined by subsequent declaration(s). This policy is a valid marine policy in all respects and fully complies with the requirements of the Marine Insurance Act. The declaration may be made by endorsement on the policy or in any other customary manner. Unless otherwise provided in the policy, the declaration encompassing all the consignments within the terms of the policy along with their genuine values must be made in the order of shipment. When the total amount declared exhausts, the amount of the policy issued too is said to have *run-off* or *fully declared*. Then the assured has to fix up another policy.

Wagering policy: This policy, although void in law, is issued without requiring the policyholder to establish any insurable interest in the subject-matter of insurance. Whenever a policy contains words like *policy proof of interest* (PPI) or *interest or no interest,* it is called a wagering policy.

Construction risk policy or builder's risk policy: This is designed to cover the risks incidental to the building of a vessel usually giving cover from the time of laying the keel to the completion of trails and handing over the vessel to the owners. Marine cum erection insurance policy is a marine policy, which is taken as a part of builder's risk. In the ordinary marine (cargo) policy, the cover ends once the goods are delivered at the site of erection. But it is not feasible to examine internal damages to the consignment immediately on delivery and such losses emerge only at the time of erection. Such losses that are caused by transit risks are covered under the marine policy and erection policy, wherein each of the two policies bear 50 per cent of the cost of damage. This is possible only if both marine policy and erection policy is taken from the same insurers.

Annual/open cover policy: The purpose of open cover policy is to provide marine insurance in advance with an added benefit of an all time cover. This policy is most popular amongst regular importers and exporters who prefer some kind of *blanket insurance* and also want to avoid the effects of rapidly fluctuating rates. Open cover is a means of achieving this objective. Where a business involves regular dispatch of goods throughout the year, and the quantity can be reasonably estimated in advance, an annual policy with an open cover can be obtained on the basis of estimated annual dispatches. An open cover is an agreement between the assured and his underwriters whereby the assured agrees to declare, and the underwriter to accept, all shipments being covered by the annual/open cover policy during the specified time-period. Premiums collected in advance will be adjusted at the end of the year. A certificate of insurance is issued for each declaration duly stamped for appropriate value and the certificate will be negotiable. The policy, however, is not negotiable.

Declaration policy: A declaration policy is issued as a substitute to annual policy. This policy is taken for a fixed amount such that each dispatch that is to be insured for transportation risks is declared, in accordance with the insurance contract and accounted until the sum insured is exhausted. The policy can be extended for additional amount.

Port risk policy: This policy provides cover for a specified period to a ship/cargo-owner against the risks likely to be suffered due to the ship/ cargo being on a port as contrast to voyage risks.

Duty policy: The unique feature of custom duty policy is that it is a typical indemnity policy wherein the insured is entitled to be paid the actual amount of loss of custom duty as a consequence of loss or damage to the consignment. The policy must be taken before the vessel reaches the port of destination.

17.5 TYPES OF MARINE LOSSES

The losses covered under marine insurance policies can be classified into the following categories:

17.5.1 Total Loss

A total loss occurs where the subject-matter of insurance ceases to be in its original form or where it is completely devastated and is thus absolutely lost to its owner. A total loss may either be an actual total loss or a constructive total loss.

Actual total loss can occur in any form. It may mean physical destruction, e.g., loss due to fire, ship found missing, etc. or it may imply loss of shape or character of the subject-matter as, for instance, when the cargo no more match the original description with which the cargo was insured. Irreversible deprivation of ownership of goods or vessel is yet another form of total loss, e.g., capturing of the ship, or fraudulent disposal of the goods by the captain or crew.

A constructive total loss occurs when the subject-matter of insurance/ property insured is not absolutely destroyed but it is so severely damaged that the cost of repairing it or attempting to recover it is likely to far exceed the value of the property that would be revived. In such a case, it is preferable to simply abandon the destroyed property. The important concept to grasp for now is that, most of the marine insurance policies provide that the whole amount of insurance is payable in the event of either an actual or a constructive total loss.

17.5.2 Partial Loss

In marine insurance, a partial loss of vessel or cargo is called an **average**. A partial loss occurs when the subject-matter of insurance is partially destroyed or damaged. Partial loss may further be classified into—general average and particular average.

Average, in marine insurance means *loss* and *particular average* means *partial loss* while *general average* refers to *the sacrifices made during extreme conditions for the purpose of rescuing the ship and the cargo from being damaged.* The consequent loss has to be shouldered by all parties having an interest or stake in the marine adventure. The general average clause in a marine insurance policy requires the insurers of various interests to willingly share the cost of losses incurred to save the vessel from complete destruction provided the act was voluntary, necessary and successful. Typical example of general average is the act of jettison, which means throwing part of the cargo or equipment of the vessel overboard to lighten the load and save the vessel. The owner of the jettisoned goods is entitled to a general average, i.e., the loss is shared by the vessel-owners and the cargo-owners, proportionately.

Particular average refers to the loss that occurs as a result of damage fortuitously caused by the perils insured for. The loss arising thus, is borne by the underwriter who insured the item that is damaged, e.g., if a ship is damaged due to bad weather the loss incurred is a particular average loss. A particular average is a partial loss that is to be borne by only a particular party. A damaged property would imply general average only if it was sacrificed in order to save the entire venture or was damaged as an outcome of the action to save. If this aspect is absent, the damage is a particular average. An example of particular average is damage to the vessel and cargo on the vessel caused by fire.

Marine insurance policies do not cover losses or damages resulting from strikes, riots, civil commotions, war, etc. These risks can be, and frequently are, insured through use of endorsements for additional premiums.

17.6 IMPORTANT CLAUSES OF MARINE INSURANCE

Though the basic policies of marine insurance carry defined features and are issued as such along with standard clauses but certain specific clauses may also be included to cater to the individual requirements of the insured. These special clauses are included in the basic policy in accordance with the terms and conditions of the contract. Some of the important clauses of marine insurance are briefly explained here.

Waiver clause: This clause is included in the policy to safeguard the interest of the insured and maintain that no act of the insured or the insurer meant to save, retrieve or preserve the insured subject-matter, shall be taken to imply that either the insured intends to forgo the compensation or that the insurer accepts the act as abandonment of the policy.

Sue and labour clause: The sue and labour clause authorizes the insured to take all possible steps to prevent or mitigate the loss or to protect the insured subject-matter in the event of danger. The insured is entitled to recover the expenses that may have been incurred for this purpose from the insurer.

Valuation clause: This clause states the value of the subject-matter of insurance as settled upon between both the parties to the insurance contract.

Touch and stay clause: Under this clause, the ship is allowed to touch and stay only at such ports and in such order as has been specified in the policy. Except in extreme circumstances, when it is essential to save the ship or the lives on board, any departure from the route mentioned in the policy or the ordinary trade route followed, will be considered as deviation.

Lost or not lost clause: This clause is used in marine insurance under which the insurer is liable to pay even if the insured loss has occurred prior to the effective date of the insurance. However, the insurer is not liable where the policyholder had knowledge about the loss at the time when the insurance was bought. This clause covers the risks between the issue of the policy and the shipment of the goods.

Inchmaree clause: This clause covers the loss or damage caused to the ship or machinery as a result of negligence of the master of the ship or due to explosives or underlying defect in the machinery or the hull.

F.P.A. and F.A.A. clause: The F.P.A. (free of particular average) clause alleviates the insurer of liability arising from particular average while in case of F.A.A. (free of all average) clause, the insurer is relieved from both particular average liability as well as general average liability.

Warehouse to warehouse clause: This clause provides cover to the cargo from the time they are dispatched from the consignor's warehouse until their delivery at the consignee's warehouse at the port of destination.

Running down clause: This clause is used in hull insurance to cover the risk of damage arising out of collision between two ships holding insurer liable to pay compensation to the owner of the damaged ship.

Free of capture and seizure clause: Under this clause, the insurer is relieved from the liability of indemnifying the insured for the loss arising due to the capture and seizure of the vessel. The insured can insure such an abnormal risk. It is also covered under the war risks policy.

At and from clause: This clause, usually used in voyage policies, covers the subject-matter insured while it is lying at the port of departure and until they reach the final port of destination. If the policy incorporates only the word *from* instead of *at and from*, the policy would cover the risk only from the time of departure of the ship.

Barratry clause: This clause covers losses incurred by the ship owner or the cargo owner due to wilful conduct of the master or crew of the ship.

Jettison clause: *Jettison* denotes an act of throwing overboard a part of the ship's cargo in order to reduce the weight of the vessel and/or to save other goods. Under this clause, all interested parties collectively compensate the loss suffered by owner(s) of jettisoned goods as a result of such acts.

Continuation clause: With this clause the vessel is allowed to continue and complete its voyage even after the policy period has run out. This clause is generally incorporated in a time policy. The insured is required to give a prior notice for this and deposit a monthly pro-rate premium.

ILLUSTRATIONS

17.1 A ship carrying eatables was insured against losses caused by collision. On voyage, the ship got delayed because of collision. As a result, the eatables were spoiled. What is the extent of insurer's liability for the loss?

Ans: Here, the proximate cause of loss is not collision that is insured for. Instead the loss has been caused because of the ship getting delayed. The insurer, therefore, is not liable to indemnify the loss suffered by the insured.

17.2 A, the owner of a ship by fraudulently representing the ship to be seaworthy induces 'B' an underwriter to insure the ship. Can 'B' obtain the cancellation of the policy?

Ans: A contract of insurance is a contract of 'Uberrimae fidei', that is, 'absolute good faith'. It is, therefore, expected from the insured to disclose all facts regarding the subject-matter of insurance correctly to the insurer. On account of the above reasons, B can obtain cancellation of the policy.

KEY TERMS

Barratry Losses due to deliberate conduct of the owner or crew of the ship.

General average Rateably borne or shared loss due to voluntary sacrifice or expenditure incurred in time of peril.

Inchmaree Damages due to negligence of the master of the ship or due to explosives or underlying defect in machinery or the hull.

Jettison An act of throwing overboard ship's cargo to reduce the vessel's weight.

Ocean marine insurance Insurance to protect against losses in respect of or damages to goods or vessel at sea.

Particular average Partial loss caused by an insured peril.

Warranty Statement by the insured person promising to do or not to do a particular thing.

REVIEW QUESTIONS

17.1 Define a contract of marine insurance. What are its essential features?

17.2 Define the term warranty in connection with marine insurance contract. What are express and implied warranties?

17.3 Write a note on marine losses.

17.4 What do you mean by perils of the sea? Discuss the scope of marine insurance.

17.5 Describe the different kinds of marine insurance policies.

17.6 Define the important clauses of marine insurance contracts.

17.7 Write short notes on

(i) Voyage policy

(ii) Floating policy

(iii) Wagering policy

(iv) Valued policy

(v) F.P.A. and F.A.A.

18

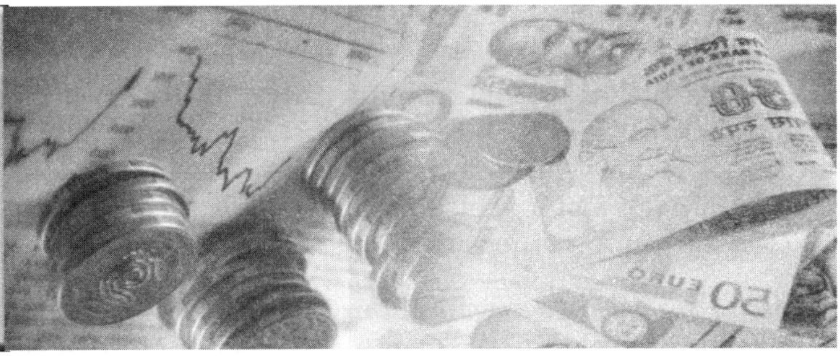

Motor Vehicle Insurance

Learning Objectives

After going through this chapter we will be able to:

- Understand the nature of motor vehicle insurance.
- Explain the provisions of the motor vehicles act.
- Describe the kinds of motor vehicles insurance policies.
- Explain the procedure for effecting motor vehicle insurance.
- Discuss claims settlement procedure under motor vehicle insurance.

Motor vehicle insurance, which emerged in the United Kingdom, has now assumed great importance throughout the world as is evident by the fact that it accounts for a major share of the mixed premium income of insurance companies. Motor vehicle insurance is required not only to cover risks towards the owner and the vehicle but also to cover the financial liability that may arise from an accident injuring a third party. In the absence of insurance, a person would have to pay an exorbitant sum to the other party towards the cost of repairs of his/her vehicle besides huge amounts being spent on own vehicle. The expenses may further shootup if the accident involves hospitalisation too. Thus, motor vehicle insurance is indeed essential.

In India, the Motor Vehicles Act, 1938 was enacted with the objective of safeguarding the financial interests of the persons who were injured/ killed or suffered damages due to the negligence of the motorists and/ or such other risks associated with the use of motor vehicles. The Act was amended in 1988, making it mandatory for the motorists to insure against the risk of liability to third parties. However, it must clearly be understood that it is the insurance of third party liability arising out of the use of motor vehicles in public places, which is compulsory and not the insurance of motor vehicles against risk.

The relevant provisions of the Motor Vehicles Act include

Necessity for insurance against third party risks: Section 146 provides that no person shall use, except as a passenger or cause or allow any other person to use, a motor vehicle in a public place unless affecting a policy of insurance in accordance with the provisions of the Act.

Insurance of motor vehicles carrying hazardous goods: The Act also provides for mandatory insurance in the case of a motor vehicle carrying or meant to carry dangerous or hazardous goods (as defined in the Environment Protection Act). There shall also be a policy of insurance under the Public Liability Act, 1991.

Consequences of driving uninsured vehicle: According to section 196, whoever drives a motor vehicle or causes/allows a motor vehicle to be driven in violation of the provisions of section 146 of the Motor Vehicles Act, shall be punishable with imprisonment or with fine or with both.

18.1 TAXONOMY OF MOTOR VEHICLES

For the purpose of insurance, motor vehicles may be classified into

1. Private cars (the ones which are not used for commercial purposes)
2. Motorcycles and motor scooters
3. Commercial vehicles. Commercial vehicles further consist of
   - (i) Goods-carrying vehicles
   - (ii) Passengers-carrying vehicles like motorised riskshaws, taxis, buses, etc.
   - (iii) Miscellaneous vehicles like ambulances, cinema film recording and publicity vans, mobile dispensaries, garbage-dumping trucks, fire tenders, etc.

18.2 KINDS OF MOTOR VEHICLE INSURANCE POLICIES

To cover the losses arising in respect of motor vehicles, the following different kinds of policies are issued under motor vehicles insurance:

18.2.1 Act/Liability Policy

This policy aims at complying with the requirements of Motor Vehicles

Act, 1988, and is issued by the insurance companies to cover *act risks*. The Act provides for compulsory insurance of motor vehicles in relation to liabilities arising out of the use of motor vehicles in a public place. As per the provisions of Motor Vehicles Act, all the vehicles plying in the territorial limits of India must possess an act policy at all times. The violation is punishable with fine, etc. as per Motor Vehicles Act (as prevalent at the time of detection). The All India Motor Tariff governs motor insurance business in India. According to the tariff, all classes of vehicles use two types of policy forms. They are form A and form B. Form A, or what is commonly known as act policy, covers *act liability*, which is a compulsory requirement of the Motor Vehicles Act. No vehicle can be used without this minimum insurance cover. Use without such insurance is a penal offence. In case a vehicle is purchased under hire purchase agreement, the financiers insist upon a comprehensive policy to take care of their interest as collateral security.

The following liabilities can be covered under the policy:

(i) Unlimited liability towards third party bodily injury.

(ii) Liabilities towards damage to the property of third parties. As per requirements of the Motor Vehicles Act, while compensation for personal injuries to third parties is unlimited, property damage is limited (in the case of commercial vehicles it is limited to ₹6,000 only). This limit can be enhanced on payment of additional premium.

(iii) Unlimited liability towards bodily injury of passengers of the vehicle.

(iv) Liability towards employees of the owner of the vehicle while travelling in or using it, against bodily injury, to the extent required under the Employees Compensation Act.

18.2.2 Third Party Policy

This policy provides insurance against the liabilities towards third parties suffering loss pertaining to the damage of property/personal injury/death. In addition, the policy may also include fire, theft risks and legal liability to persons employed in connection with the operation and/or maintenance and/or loading/unloading of motor vehicles. Section 146 of the Motor Vehicles Act 1988, provides that no person shall use or allow any other person to use a motor vehicle in a public place, unless the vehicle is covered by the policy of insurance complying with the requirements of the Act. Section 147 of the Motor Vehicles Act 1988, requires that the policy must provide cover against liabilities incurred by the insured in respect of death or bodily injury to any person or damage to any property of a third party or against death or bodily injury to any passengers of a public service vehicle, caused by or arising out of the use of the vehicle in a public place.

18.2.3 Package/Comprehensive Policy

Also called **form 'B' Policy**, the package/comprehensive policy is an optional policy, which provides cover against own damage, losses and act liability. It is a package policy issued by the insurance companies for *comprehensive risks*. Unlike the form A/Act policy, which is identical for different classes of vehicles, the comprehensive policy cover differs for various classes of vehicles.

Comprehensive policy contains the following three sections:

(i) First section covers damage to the vehicles and covers the risks like fire, explosion, self-ignition and lightning; burglary, housebreaking and theft, riot, strike, malicious and terrorism, damage, earthquake flood, typhoon, etc.

(ii) Second section covers the insured liability to third parties.

(iii) Third section differs according to the class of the vehicles.

The following perils may be covered under the policy in accordance with the provisions of the tariff.

(i) Damage to vehicle by accidental external means, fire, lightning, explosion, self-ignition, burglary, housebreaking

(ii) Riot and strike, malicious acts and terrorist acts

(iii) Earthquake

(iv) Flood, inundation, cyclone, etc.

(v) Landslide/rockslide while in transit by rail, road, air, inland waterways, lift or elevator

Thus, the policy covers all the risks of liability policy as well as the loss or damage to insured vehicle.

Further, package policy can be restricted to loss or damage due to fire or theft or both fire and theft in combination with or without policy A. The rate of premium charged for *motor car* (i.e., personal vehicle) insurance would vary as follows:

(i) In case of Act/liability policy + fire, the premium is only 25 per cent of own damage premium + liability premium.

(ii) In case of Act/liability only policy + theft, the premium is only 30 per cent of own damage premium + Act/liability premium.

(iii) In case of liability only policy + fire and theft, the premium is 50 per cent of own damage premium + Act/liability premium.

Whereas, the rate of premium charged for commercial vehicle insurance would vary as follows:

(i) In case of Act/liability policy + fire or theft, the premium is only 25 per cent of own damage premium + Act/liability premium.

(ii) In case of Act/liability + fire and theft, the premium is 40 per cent of own damage premium + Act premium.

18.2.4 Garage Insurance Policy

Risks related to the motor vehicles standing in the motor garages or service stations are covered under the garage insurance policy.

18.2.5 Collision Insurance Policy

Damages and losses due to any collision or accident between two or more vehicles are covered under the collision insurance policy.

18.3 SERVICING OF MOTOR VEHICLE INSURANCE

The procedure for servicing of motor vehicle insurance policies involves the following steps:

Proposal forms: A proposal form is used as the means of communicating the offer to the insurance company for taking a motor insurance policy. It is also customary to indicate on the form a brief statement or the terms and conditions of insurance provided by the appropriate policy.

Rating of insurance: After selecting an appropriate policy, the proposal form elicits all information necessary to determine the amount of premium and underwriting. Some examples of rating are given here:

Private cars. Rates are determined on the basis of the cubic capacity (power of the engine) as given by manufacturer, insured estimated value and the zone of operation.

Goods carrying vehicles. The rate or amount of premium is determined on the basis of gross vehicle weight, i.e., the total weight of the vehicle and load certified by the registering authority.

Tariff rules: Some important regulations prescribed by the tariff include

- *Agreed value policies* are allowed only for vintage cars and not any other vehicle.
- Policies can be issued only in the name of the registered owner.
- In the absence of full details being available, the prescribed cover note, which incorporates certificate of insurance, should be used.
- Duplicate certificate can be issued when the original is defaced, lost or torn, etc. strictly in accordance with the procedure prescribed by the tariff.
- The tariff provides concessions, e.g., return of premium, restricted cover, etc. when the vehicle is laid up in a garage and not in use for a period of two consecutive years or more.

Policy form: On the issue of the policy, the cover note is cancelled and the formal policy form issued to the insured. The policy is not the contract itself, but the evidence of the contract.

Insurance term: The motor insurance policy is usually issued for one year but in certain cases the policy may also be issued for less than one year. However, the premium rate will be higher, e.g., the premium rate is three-fourths of annual premium for a six months policy.

Additional benefits: Thus, additional risks/benefits may be incorporated to the original policy on payment of extra premium provided the policy is still in force.

Change of vehicle: The insured vehicles can be sold of along with the policy. The term of policy will remain unchanged and the policy will continue upto the unexpired period with the purchaser of the vehicle. Likewise, the insured can replace another car under the same policy.

18.4 CLAIMS SETTLEMENT UNDER MOTOR VEHICLE INSURANCE

Motor vehicle insurance claims can be divided into the following types:

Claims for own damage: On receiving the notice regarding loss, the particulars of the policy and the vehicle are verified from the policy records. The loss is entered in the claim register and a claim form is issued to the insured for submission after completion accompanied with a detailed estimate of repair charges.

The damaged vehicle is inspected and a survey report giving the causes and extent of loss is submitted along with the copy of the policy, claim form and estimate cost of repairs by independent automobile surveyors appointed for the purpose.

Besides these the other documents required for claim settlement include police report, driving licence, registration certificate book, financial bill for repairs, receipted bill from the repairer, if paid by insured, fitness certificate and permit.

The insurance company determines the extent of its liability on the basis of survey report and other required claim documents and accordingly the loss is indemnified.

Claims for theft or total loss claims: Total losses arise where the vehicle is stolen and could not be traced by the police authorities till the settlement of the claim. These losses will have to be supported by a copy of the FIR lodged with police authorities immediately after the theft was detected. If the police authorities fail to recover the vehicle for theft claims, the insurance company determines the total loss on the basis of investigation or inspection with valid documents and the loss is indemnified.

Claims for third party: Section 165 of the Motor Vehicles Act, 1988, empowers the state government to set up motor accident claims tribunals, for regulating third party claims. On receiving the claim notice from the insured, or the third party or from the motor accident claims tribunals, the matter is handed over to an advocate. The insured is requested to submit full information relating to the accident along with certain other documents like police report, medical certificate, details of driver's prosecution, driving licence, death certificate, details of age, income, no. of dependents, etc.

On the basis of the written statements the matter is filed by the advocate with the motor accident claims tribunal (MACT), which determines the amount of claims to the third party.

KEY TERMS

Act liability Liability laid down under the provisions of the Motor Vehicles Act requiring compulsory insurance.

Automobile surveyors Persons appointed to assess the cause and extent of loss.

Proposal form Prescribed form used as written proposal for insurance and including the terms and conditions related to insurance.

Third party A person other than insured and the insurer.

REVIEW QUESTIONS

18.1 What do you mean by motor vehicle insurance?

18.2 Discuss the special features of motor vehicle insurance.

18.3 Briefly explain the salient features of various types of motor vehicle insurance policies.

18.4 What are the risks covered under motor insurance?

18.5 Elaborate on the procedure for effecting motor insurance.

18.6 Explain the settlement of insurance claims under motor vehicle insurance.

18.7 Write short notes on

(i) Third party policy

(ii) Act liability only

(iii) Comprehensive policy

(iv) Garage insurance policy

(v) Taxonomy of motor vehicles in connection with motor insurance

19

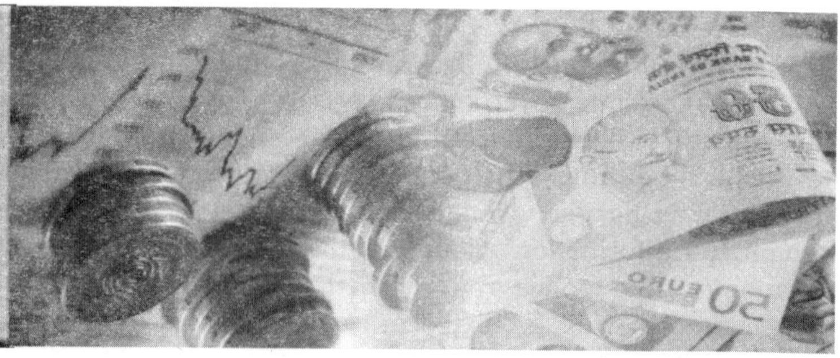

Health Insurance

Learning Objectives

After going through this chapter we will be able to:

- Understand the concept of health insurance.
- Explain the need for health insurance.
- Discuss health insurance schemes in india.
- Describe various types of health insurance policies.

The term 'Health Insurance' is commonly used to describe an insurance that pays for medical expenses. Health insurance also includes insurance covering disability or long-term nursing or custodial care needs. It is different from life insurance as regards the assurance of the payment of maturity amount and ability to renew the life insurance policy. Health insurance plans are a yearly contract and there is no compulsion on the customer to renew his policy again. Life insurance policies, on the other hand, require the customer to pay as long as the policy is in effect, until it matures. Health insurance may be provided in the form of a government-sponsored social insurance programme or by insurance companies and may be procured on a group basis or by individuals to protect themselves from high or unexpected health care expenses.

The concept of 'Health Insurance' was proposed by Hugh Chamberlen in 1694. 'Accidental Insurance' operating much like the modern disability insurance, began to be available in the late 19th century. The first employer-sponsored group disability policy was issued in 1911. Hospital and medical expenses policies were introduced during the first half of the 20th century.

Today, there are several modern health insurance programmes run by government-sponsored social insurance programmmes and by insurance companies.

A health insurance policy is a contract between an insurer and an individual or a group, in which the insurer undertakes to provide specified health insurance benefit to the insured in consideration of a fixed price called **premium** payable either in a lump sum or in instalments. Health insurance usually provides either direct payment or reimbursements for expenses associated with illnesses and injuries. The rate of premium charged and extent of cover provided by the health insurance depends on the specific policy bought under the insurance contract between the insured and the insurer.

In view of the increase in the cost of health care and treatment, health insurance is becoming increasingly essential in today's world. In India, nearly 80 per cent of the total health expenditure comes from self-paid category while the government's contribution is meagre 20–30 per cent. A majority of private hospitals are beyond the reach of a normal middle class family. Since it is impossible to foresee what may happen in the future and the cost of medical treatment being beyond the reach of the common man, even a healthy person today is aware of the need for a suitable health insurance policy to bank on, in case of any unforeseen medical exigency. Rising public consciousness for better health care and general yearning for better medicines and related health services has further contributed to the increasing demand for health insurance cover.

In general, the following factors are responsible for raising the demand for health insurance in India:

1. Human beings, in general, are facing serious health problems due to aggravation of environmental pollution.
2. Poisonous gases, various wastes including nuclear waste further are grave factors responsible for jeopardizing the well-being of life on earth.
3. Lifestyle changes have also lead to the spread of many diseases like AIDS endangering human life.
4. Difficulties in meeting the cost of medical treatment and hospitalization encourage people to go for health insurance.
5. Government policies and regulations in the form of taxation benefits have also helped in promoting health insurance.
6. Most companies, these days are providing the advantage of health insurance to its workforce, thus, boosting the demand for health insurance.

19.1 TYPES OF HEALTH INSURANCE POLICIES

The following are the fundamental policies issued by the insurance companies aiming at meeting the requirements of the general public:

Individual mediclaim or hospitalization benefit policy: An individual mediclaim or hospitalization benefit policy provides reimbursement (in Indian currency) of medical expenses incurred towards hospitalization (anywhere within India) in cases of sudden illness or accident and extends to pre-hospitalization of 30 days and post-hospitalization of 60 days. The cover also includes *domiciliary hospitalization,* which implies that a patient may get the medical treatment at home in cases where he/she is unfit to be moved to the hospital or where there is no accommodation in the specialist hospital on the condition that the treatment was for a period not less than 3 days and the sub-limits of sum insured towards domiciliary hospitalization are provided in the sum insured and premium schedules. The policy is available to any person in the age group of 5 to 80 years. However, children aged below 5 years but not below the age of 3 months can also be covered as long as one or both of the parents are covered at the same time. The policy carries some additional benefits and may be issued at insurance-premium discount on family package, cumulative bonus and health check. Besides, higher limits are permitted if the policy is in renewal for the preceding three years. The premium paid on the policy up to a maximum of ₹10,000 is totally exempt from income tax.

No cover is available under the policy in the following cases:

(i) Illness contracted within 30 days from the commencement of risk with the exception of accidental cases

(ii) Pre-existing diseases

(iii) Medical expenses incurred in respect of any treatment relating to pregnancy or childbirth; AIDS or similar kind of conditions; war or nuclear waste either directly or indirectly

(iv) Expenses incurred for the treatment of congenital internal diseases, fistula in anus, hydrocele, cataracts, piles, sinusitis and related disorders for 1st year of policy

Bhavishya arogya policy: This policy provides lifetime hospitalization and domiciliary hospitalization benefits to the insured, as a result of an accident or sickness, after the age of retirement, in consideration of his paying premiums upto that age to the insurer. The mode of premium payment can be either in lump sum or in equated annual installments. The policy is available to persons aged 25 to 55 years. The minimum sum to be insured under the policy has been fixed at ₹50,000 that can further be increased in multiples of ₹10,000 as a unit, at a premium load of 20 per cent and upto a maximum sum of ₹5 lakh. In case if the insured dies before the age of retirement, the policy even provides for refund of premium at a fixed scale being payable to the insured's nominee/assignee. In cases, where the policy is voluntarily cancelled, 75 per cent of the fixed scales applicable for death claims, may be refunded on the condition that there is no other claim under the policy.

Hospital cash daily allowance policy: Under this policy, the insurer undertakes to pay a daily allowance for every completed day of hospitalization in the event of insured person(s) being hospitalized due to sickness or accident. The number of days of hospitalization as well as the amount of daily allowance, which can be ₹500, ₹1,000 or ₹2,000 per day, shall be selected by the insured. The maximum number of days of hospitalization for which payment can be claimed under a specific policy is fixed up at 30/60 days. However, in case of ICU admission upto a maximum period of 7 days, double the agreed sum becomes payable. For such a purpose, a day would mean a period of 12 hours taken from the time of hospitalization but must include 0300 hours. No medical bills are required for admitting the claim, which is settled only on the basis of a discharge certificate. The policy can be taken by anyone in the age group of 3 months to 60 years with the provision of allowing additional cover to dependant spouse and any number of children in the age group of 3 months to 21 years. The policy carries tax benefit on premium amounts of upto ₹15,000 p.a. u/s 80D of IT Act.

Some of the cases not covered under the policy are:

- Hospitalization in cases of accidents due to drunken driving. But cases of cosmetic and plastic surgery resulting from accident are covered.
- Hospitalization expenses incurred during the initial 30 days of insurance.
- Treatment in cases of occupational diseases, sexual dysfunction, transsexual surgery, birth defects/congenital anomalies, hereditary diseases, pregnancy/childbirth even if it was a caesarian case.
- Hospitalization for dental treatment or dental surgery of any kind except due to accident.
- Medical treatment as a result of war/nuclear perils/defense operations requiring the use of arms as well as natural perils like avalanche, earthquake, volcanic eruptions, etc.
- Treatment carried out by an unqualified medical practitioner.
- Hospitalization in cases of officially acknowledged epidemics.
- Physiotherapy, weight reduction/improvement therapy, and so on.

Critical illness policy: This policy is designed to provide financial assistance in the event of the insured contracting any of the critical illnesses covered under the policy like first heart attack, bypass surgery, stroke, cancer, kidney failure, any major organ transplantation, multiple sclerosis, aorta graft surgery, primary pulmonary arterial hypertension and paralysis. The policy is available to persons in the age group of 6 to 59 years for a minimum sum assured of ₹50,000 and a maximum of ₹50,00,000. This plan is totally different from the rest of the plans because the benefits under this plan are paid in advance whereas in other medical insurance polices the expenses incurred are reimbursed as claim settlement. Even the claim procedure is quite simple requiring the insured to only submit the claim form along with a certificate from the specialist, authenticating occurrence of the critical illness. The payment under the policy becomes due as soon as the case of the life insured having contracted any of the covered illnesses is established provided he continues to live for at least 30 days after the diagnosis. The amount of premiums paid is exempt u/s 80D of IT Act.

Cases excluded from the policy include

- Pre-existing critical illness, for which treatment was recommended before the start of the policy period.
- Critical illnesses diagnosed within the first 90 days from the start of the policy period.
- Cases where the insured dies within 30 days of being diagnosed for the critical illness.
- Treatment of occupational diseases; HIV/AIDS infection.
- Illnesses traceable to pregnancy/childbirth, including caesarian cases, natural peril, war operations of the armed forces, invasion, terrorism, hostilities, rebellion, revolution, etc.

Health guard: Health guard policy offers cashless benefit and medical reimbursement for hospitalization expenses to the insured. Under this policy, the member/insured can avail of the cashless facility at various networked hospitals across India. The member may choose any other hospital besides the empanelled ones. In this case, the expenses incurred by him would be reimbursed within 14 working days from the date of submission of all the relevant documents. The policy covers relevant medical expenses incurred 60 days before and 90 days after hospitalization. Moreover the policy offers a cumulative bonus of 5 per cent to the sum assured against every claims-free year along with health check-up for maximum amount of ₹1,000 at the end of continuous four claims-free years. It also offers a family discount of 5 per cent on premiums. Premiums paid under the policy are eligible for tax rebate under section 80D of the IT Act. The policy is available to people in the age group of 5–75 years (the age at entry not exceeding 55 years). Children aged less than 5 years can also be insured provided the parents are concurrently insured.

The policy does not cover the following:

- Pre-existing diseases/injuries, congenital diseases, expenses incurred on the treatment of AIDS and related diseases
- Disease contracted during the first 30 days of commencement of the policy
- Treatment based on non-allopathic medicines and use of intoxicating drugs and alcohol
- Cosmetic/aesthetic/related treatment

However, certain diseases, for instance, hernia, cataract, piles, sinusitis, etc. can be covered only after a waiting period of 2 years.

Health shield: This is a medical insurance policy that is available to people in the age group of 90 days to 75 years, designed to cover all hospitalization expenses incurred on any sickness or accident provided that hospitalization is for a minimum period of 48 hours. However, some cases such as kidney stone removal, tonsillectomy, eye surgery, D&C and cataract, not requiring 48 hours hospitalization may also be covered under the policy. But cataract is covered only from the second year of insurance. The policy makes provision for the payment of pre-hospitalization expenses for 30 days and post-hospitalization expenses for 60 days. A single health shield insurance policy covering the spouse, dependent children and dependent parents can be taken, and the policy also offers a family discount of 10 per cent in case if three persons or more are insured. A cumulative bonus of 5 per cent upto a maximum limit of 50 per cent to the sum assured, without requiring any extra premium to be paid is also offered for every claims-free year. Premiums paid under the policy, subject to a maximum of ₹10,000, qualify for tax exemption under section 80D of the IT Act. Cash-less facilities, in cases of hospitalization in specified *networked* hospitals, can be availed subject to the policyholder obtaining pre-admission authorization from the insurer/insurer's TPA.

Jan arogya bima policy: This policy is quite similar to the individual mediclaim policy except that the cumulative bonus and mediclaim check up benefits are not included. The plan is designed to provide insurance benefit to the lower income segment of the society. As such it covers the expenses of hospitalization and domiciliary hospitalization upto ₹5,000 per person p.a. without any inner limits, for a meagre premium of ₹70 per adult and only ₹50 per dependent son/daughter aged not more than 25 years. The policy is available to persons in the age group of 5 years to 70 years. Children between the age of 3 months and 5 years can also be covered at the same time as under the policy if one or both the parents are covered. The policy also provides cover in case of pre-hospitalization of upto 30 days and post-hospitalization of upto 60 days. However, certain diseases are not provided any cover by the policy like any pre-existing disease, asthma, bronchitis, psychiatric or psychosomatic disorders, cataracts, hysterectomy, hernia, piles, etc.

Overseas mediclaim policy: The *overseas medical claim insurance* policy is particularly tailored to protect persons undertaking genuine overseas trips for business/holidays, studies or employment (sponsored by an Indian employer). The exceptional benefit of the policy is that premium is payable in Indian currency while claims abroad, are payable in foreign currency. The policy covers expenses for medical treatment taken by the insured person outside India as a direct result of an accident or bodily injury or illness/disease contracted during an overseas journey. The upper age limit for such a policy is generally 70 years and the lower limit is 5 years. Accompanying child from 1 month to 5 years can also be covered. No medical examination is usually required. However, persons travelling to USA/Canada and aged more than 40 years and those aged over 60 years and travelling to other countries have to undergo medical examination, and they are required to tender complete medical reports such as ECG and blood sugar test. Cases with indications of any heart ailment are also required to go for computerized tread mill stress test. Insurance, commences from the date of departure from India and terminates on arrival of the policyholder to India or on expiry of the period stipulated under the policy, whichever is earlier. Overseas medical claim policy is offered in the form of diverse plans. Plans A and B cover holiday and business travel. Plan A provides cover to persons travelling anywhere in the world excluding USA and Canada while plan B is meant for those travelling anywhere in the world including USA and Canada. Employment and study policy falls under plan C and D and is meant for the Indian citizens temporarily working or studying abroad while corporate frequent travellers policy is issued under Plan E. The insurance coverage limits under various plans range from US$ 50,000 to US$ 5,00,000. The period of cover under various plans too varies between 6 months and one year. The rate of premium would vary depending on the insurance period covered and the policyholder's age.

Jeevan Arogya (LIC): This is a unique non-linked health insurance plan launched by LIC, which provides health insurance cover against certain specified health risks. The plan offers the benefits of flexible premium payment options, increasing health cover every year, lump sum benefit irrespective of actual medical costs, flexible benefit limit to choose from and valuable financial protection in case of hospitalisation, surgery, etc.

A no claim benefit will also be paid provided there are no claims in respect of any insured covered under the policy during the period between date of commencement of policy and the next automatic renewal date or between two automatic renewal dates. Moreover, the principal insured (PI)), his/her spouse, children, insured's parents and parents-in-law can all be insured under one policy.

The minimum and maximum age at entry is as below:

	Minimum age at entry	*Maximum age at entry*
Self/spouse	18 years	65 years (last birthday)
Parents/parents-in-law	18 years	75 (last birthday)
Children	91 days	17 years (last birthday)

Health protection plus (LIC): This is a unique long-term health insurance plan launched by LIC that can combine health insurance covers for the entire family (husband, wife and the children). The salient features of the plan include hospital cash benefit (HCB) and major surgical benefit (MSB) along with a ULIP component (investment in the form of units) that is specifically designed to meet domiciliary treatment benefit (DTB)/ out-patient department (OPD) expenses for the insured members. Being a unit-linked insurance product, this plan is different from the traditional insurance products and is subject to risk factors. The premium paid in unit-linked life insurance policies is subject to investment risks associated with capital markets and the NAVs of the units may go up or down based on the performance of the fund and factors influencing the capital market and the insured is responsible for his/her decisions.

19.2 HEALTH INSURANCE SCHEMES IN INDIA

The various health insurance schemes in India can be broadly classified into the following:

Employer-administered health schemes: *Employer-administered health schemes* and the *reimbursement of health expenses by employers* are important instruments of health assurance in India. Several public sector undertakings, big industrial organizations and also defence services run their own dispensary and hospitals for the benefit of their employees. Even educational institutions, particularly universities too supply medical services to their employees. There are several medical-reimbursement plans being offered to the employees working in the private sector including commercial banks.

Government-based schemes: The central, state and local governments in India manage, finance and operate a vast network of hospitals, primary health centres, community health centres, dispensaries and speciality facilities that provide medical services throughout the country either free of cost or at a very nominal rate. These networks in conjunction with various other networks consisting of village health workers, maternal and child health programmes. Speciality disease prevention programmes have made a significant contribution in the country's primary health care system. The Central Government Health Scheme (CGHS) has made significant contribution in providing comprehensive medical care facilities to the government employees and their families. The Employees State Insurance Corporation (ESIC), a wholly government-owned enterprise, manages the Employees State Insurance Scheme (ESIS). It is an insurance system that offers both the cash and the medical benefits.

Besides this, certain non-governmental organizations (NGOs), for instance, child in need institute (CINI) also provide health facilities. Such voluntary and charitable organizations play a major role in creating awareness. Some of them also link up with key health insurers.

Market-based schemes: Besides GIC and LIC, there are many private insurance companies like Bajaj Allianz, ICICI, Oriental Insurance and

Royal Sundaram that offer a variety of health insurance policies. Some of the existing health insurance schemes currently available are individual/ family/group insurance schemes, senior citizens insurance schemes, long-term health care and insurance cover for specific diseases, etc. Some foreign companies entering the Indian insurance sector include Prudential, UK, New York Life, USA, AIG, USA.

KEY TERMS

CGHS Central Government Health Scheme providing medical facilities to government employees and their families.

Domiciliary hospitalization Treatment administered at home either on advice of the Doctor or due to non-availability of room in the hospital.

ESIS Employee State Insurance Scheme designed to provide protection to employees against loss of wages due to inability to work as a consequence of sickness or disability.

Health insurance Insurance providing cover for financial loss associated with illnesses and injuries and expenses incurred for the use of health related services.

Medical reimbursement Financing arrangement for compensation of medical expenses incurred.

Mediclaim Policy providing cover and reimbursing expenses incurred towards hospitalization.

NGO Non-governmental (voluntary and charitable) organization.

REVIEW QUESTIONS

19.1 Define health insurance. Explain the factors that are responsible for raising the demand for health insurance in India.

19.2 List the various health insurance systems in India. Comment on the performance of these systems.

19.3 Explain the salient features of any three basic health insurance policies.

19.4 Write short notes on

(i) Mediclaim policy of GIC
(ii) Bhavishya arogya policy
(iii) Videsh yatra mitra policy
(iv) Cancer policy
(v) Health shield policy
(vi) Jan arogya bima policy
(vii) Hospital cash daily allowance policy
(viii) Critical illness policy
(ix) Health protection plus

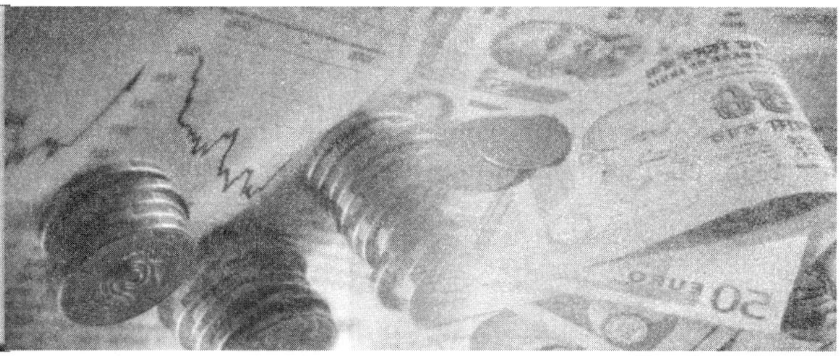

20 Miscellaneous Insurance

Learning Objectives

After going through this chapter we will be able to:

- Grasp the meaning of miscellaneous insurance.
- Understand the concept of fidelity guarantee insurance.
- Discuss the types of fidelity guarantee insurance policies.
- Define the meaning of property insurance.
- Know the concept of building insurance.
- Define the meaning of earthquake insurance.
- Appreciate the need for flood insurance.
- Understand the concept of burglary insurance.
- Describe types of burglary insurance policies.
- Elucidate the nature of cattle insurance.
- Explain the key features of engineering insurance policies.
- Summarize the concept of liability insurance.
- Comprehend the concept of crop insurance.

The term *miscellaneous insurance* encompasses a variety of insurance covers designed to meet the peculiar requirements of different individuals. Some of the miscellaneous insurance policies are discussed hereinafter.

20.1 FIDELITY GUARANTEE INSURANCE

Fidelity guarantee insurance provides a cover to the assured (employer) against losses arising through the fraud, or embezzlement on the part of the employees. The insurer undertakes to indemnify the assured upto a specified amount that is insured in consideration of payment of a specified amount of premium. This kind of insurance is normally taken up as a safeguard in cases where fresh and unproven employees are given positions of trust.

20.1.1 Fidelity Guarantee Insurance Policies

The following types of fidelity guarantee insurance policies are commonly offered:

Individual policy: Under this type of policy cover is provided only in a specific case. Thus, the policy is used where only one individual is to be guaranteed.

Collective policy: The policy embracing all employees falling within certain categories, or conversely, the whole staff, known as **collective policy** has become very popular with the employers.

Floating policy or floater: This is similar to the collective policy. Under a floating policy the names and duties of the employees to be covered are mentioned in a schedule but instead of distinct amounts of guarantee, a specified sum of guarantee is floated over the whole group of employees. A claim in respect of one employee will reduce the guarantee by the amount thereof until renewal of the policy.

Positions policy: This too is somewhat similar to a collective policy with the difference that instead of using names, the *position or rank* is guaranteed for a specified amount, so that the cover is not affected by any change in the person holding the position or rank. Moreover, the insurers' liability with regard to each position insured remains limited to the sum guaranteed for that position, not withstanding the number of persons acting in that position.

Blanket policy: A blanket policy covers the entire staff whatever be their names or positions. No details of the employees are required to be provided by the insured. Gigantic organizations with a large staff often go in for a blanket policy.

20.1.2 Rate of Premium

The rate of premium in the case of fidelity guarantee insurance depends upon the type of employment, position of the employee, the system of check and supervision. Under individual and collective policies, the rate of premium is proportionate to the amount guaranteed. The premium for a floating policy consists of a percentage charge and a per capita charge.

The percentage charge is applied on the amount guaranteed, and the per capita charge on the number of employees to be guaranteed.

20.1.3 Settlement of Claims

For the settlement of insurance claims under fidelity guarantee insurance, the surveyors conduct a detailed investigation into the circumstances of the loss. The investigation, which is generally entrusted to independent surveyors, (e.g., chartered accountants) is mainly based on the inspection of the books of accounts of the insured employer.

The claim amount under the policy and in the case of loss arising due to infidelity of an employee shall not exceed the amount of indemnity assured under the policy in respect of such employee.

20.2 PROPERTY INSURANCE

Property insurance provides insurance against fidelity, burglary and insolvency. Property insurance covers loss of property due to burglary, theft or housebreaking or any other criminal act.

20.3 BUILDING INSURANCE

Building insurance offers absolute coverage for damage to the insured. It provides a comprehensive package, designed to cover damages caused by various perils, as for instance, lightning, explosion/implosion, aircraft damage, riot, strike, malicious and terrorist damage, storm, typhoon, tempest, hurricane, tornado, flood and inundation, bursting and/or overflowing of water tanks, apparatus and pipes, missile testing operations, etc.

20.4 EARTHQUAKE INSURANCE

Earthquake insurance is a type of property insurance that covers damages to the property caused by an earthquake. Because of the practical difficulties involved, most of the policies falling in the category of *home insurance*, do not cover damages caused by earthquake. In India, people realized the need for an earthquake insurance plan only after facing the wrath caused by catastrophic earthquake that hit Gujarat a few years ago. Most of the houses and shops in the region were not insured, and the consequences were disastrous for every individual who suffered personal as well as financial loss. Indeed, insuring ones house is never taken up seriously except when disaster strikes. A comprehensive householders policy, covering damages caused as a consequence of various perils including earthquake has since then become very popular. A shopkeeper's policy too covers damages caused by a variety of perils. The insured is entitled to full reconstruction value in the event of loss due to the disaster insured for.

20.5 FLOOD INSURANCE

In India, flood insurance, commonly falls under the ordinary fire or special perils policy while in many other countries, it is covered as a part of the earthquake related natural perils in property insurance. Generally, the concept of flood insurance like earthquake insurance is not very common in India. While the need for earthquake insurance arose out of the ruinous consequences of the Gujarat earthquake, flood insurance is being seen as a way out to cover massive losses caused by floods only after experiencing the calamitous effects of 'tsunami'. However, Indian insurance companies are yet to work out whether tsunami should be categorized under floods or earthquakes. But the majority of them categorize it under *earthquake,* since a tsunami is a quake in the sea. However, the Indian insurance companies must be cautious when assigning this type of insurance because an earthquake strong enough to destroy one home will probably destroy hundreds of homes in the same area.

20.6 BURGLARY INSURANCE

Burglary insurance falls under the classification of insurance of property. Losses or damages of household goods and properties and personal effects due to theft, larceny, robbery, housebreaking and such similar acts are covered by burglary insurance policy. The policy is available to commercial establishments, factories, private premises, godowns, shops, etc.

20.6.1 Types of Policies

Burglary insurance covers losses or damage due to burglary and is available to commercial establishments, factories, godowns, shops, etc. The various types of burglary covers available are:

Business premises insurance policy: Risks of burglary and housebreaking alone are covered under business premises insurance policy. However, any theft without the use of violence and forced entry into the premises is not covered by the policy. A burglary insurance policy generally covers assets contained in a business premises, stocks owned, held in trust/commission and for which the insured is responsible, premises itself against damage (which is to be made good by the insured) and money, valuables, securities kept in a locked safe or cash box in locked steel cupboard.

Private residence insurance policy: This policy offers additional benefit of covering the risk arising out of theft besides the risk of loss due to burglary and housebreaking. The amount assured under this policy must represent the full value.

Jewellery and valuable insurance policy: This policy provides insurance against any loss or damage by any cause including fire, theft to the insured property, which may include jewellery, personal ornaments and other valuables. However, loss or damage caused by the consequence of war, act of foreign enemy, etc. is not covered by this policy.

All risk policy: This policy is usually taken to cover risks in respect of jewellery, high value possessions like works of art, paintings and such other items. All risks policy is suitable for covering any damage or loss by fire, burglary and theft, besides any other accident or casualty. The insurable value in such cases is determined on agreed value basis.

Money in transit insurance: *Money in transit* insurance provides insurance to the insured against any loss in the event of money or cash being stolen from his business premises or while it is being carried from, or to the bank. The scope of this insurance policy is important to any business as large sum of money are drawn from banks to meet routine expenses of business everyday.

The following may obtain cover under burglary insurance policy:

- Any individual whose property is exposed to risk of burglary
- One, which is liable for goods in trust/commission
- One who is liable to make good damage to premises

However, burglary insurance policies do not cover the following losses/ damages:

- Loss/damage to goods in trust/commission, jewellery, ornaments, title deeds, business—books except in cases where these are explicitly insured
- Losses that occurred due to shoplifting or damages caused by act involving insured or his family or members or employees
- Damages, which are recoverable under fire/plate glass insurance policy
- Losses due to war perils, riots, strikes, natural disasters, nuclear perils

20.7 CATTLE INSURANCE

A contract of cattle insurance is a contract whereby the insurer undertakes to pay an agreed sum of money to the assured in the event of death of animals like bulls, buffaloes, cows and heifers in consideration of a predetermined premium amount. Insurance is provided under the policy in the event of death of animals occurring during any period and if the animal is pregnant for less than four months, the indemnity will be restricted to 50 per cent of sum insured or market value, whichever is less. The risk of permanent total disability of the animal is also covered under the policy on payment of extra premium. The premium rates for different categories of animals are different.

The policy provides indemnity only in cases where death is caused by

1. Accident, which may be a result of fire, lightning, flood, inundation, storm, hurricane, earthquake, cyclone, tornado, tempest and famine
2. Diseases cropping up or contracted during the period of the policy
3. Surgical operations
4. Strikes and riots

In the event of death of animals, the policy is *agreed-value policy*; hence claim will be settled for 100 per cent of the sum assured. For this purpose, valuation of insurance is based on the market value of cattle, which is examined by veterinary doctors. The sum insured will not exceed 100 per cent of market value.

Moreover, the insured animals must be duly identified. The following methods may be applied:

1. Ear tag made of suitable materials be used
2. Natural identification and colour should be clearly noted in the proposal form
3. Photograph of animal may be insisted in case of high value animals
4. Death certificate
5. Veterinarian's report

The claim procedure involves immediate intimation to be sent to the insurers and furnishing of the following requirements:

1. Claim form (duly completed)
2. Death certificate on company's prescribed form (obtained from veterinarian)
3. Post-mortem examination report (wherever required)
4. Ear tag applied to the animal should be surrendered
5. Complete treatment chart (required only in case of permanent total disability claim)

All claims against cattle insurance policy would be lost in the following cases:

1. Malevolent or intentional injury or neglect, overloading, unskilful treatment or use of animal for purposes other than the ones stated in the policy without written approval of the company
2. Accidents occurring and/or diseases contracted before commencement of the risk

3. Theft and clandestine sale of the insured animal
4. Any accident, loss destruction, damage or legal liability, directly or indirectly caused or contributed by or arising from nuclear weapons
5. Consequential loss of any kind
6. Transporting of cattle by air and sea.

20.8 ENGINEERING INSURANCE

Also known as **machinery breakdown** or **plant all risks insurance**, the engineering insurance policy provides very broad cover for damage to electrical and mechanical machinery. It also covers losses/damages suffered by contractors and principals with respect to civil engineering projects like building, bridges, tunnels, etc.

20.8.1 Types of Policies

Various types of engineering insurance policies are:

Advance loss of profits insurance: This policy covers monetary losses due to delayed commissioning of the project as a result of a loss during construction/erection which is covered under a project insurance policy (MCE/EAR/CAR). The policy offers cover against loss of anticipated earnings/profits due to the delay in commissioning of the project following a loss covered under the project insurance policies.

Boiler and pressure plant insurance: A boiler policy insures damages to the boiler or other equipment described in the policy agreement or damage to other property of the insured. It also covers liability of the insured for intended or unintended injury to third parties or for damages to their property, owing to explosion or collapse of the boiler or other plant specified in the policy agreement. The policy covers loss or damage to power boilers, heating and domestic boilers and pressure vessels such as steam receivers and steam-jacketed pans as a result of the risks of explosion and collapse due to internal pressures, which are inherent in all such steam generating equipment.

The following types of damages and liabilities are covered under the policy:

- Damage to the boilers and other pressure plan except damage caused by fire
- Damage to encompassing property of the insured except when caused by fire
- Liability in consequence of the death or bodily injury to any person not being an employee of the insured or on account of damage to the property not belonging to the insured

Civil engineering completed risks insurance policy: This policy is a comprehensive insurance plan designed to protect owners and operators of civil engineering structures against loss or damage after the completion of the construction work, and the facilities have been taken over. This policy is generally taken to cover completed works such as runways, railway lines, bridges, flyovers, jetties, tunnels, dams, canals, harbours, dry docks, water pipe lines, irrigation systems, reservoirs, etc. Loss or damage due to fire, lightning, explosion, riot, strike, malicious damage impact by any rail, road or water-borne vehicle or animal, storm, cyclone, typhoon, hurricane, tornado, flood, landslide, rockslide, earthquake, etc. are covered under the policy. Further hazards depending on the location and type of risk can be included at an additional premium.

Machinery insurance policy: The policy provides cover against loss or damage to the plant and machinery due to sudden and unanticipated causes. The damage may occur as a result of

- Faulty material, design, construction or erection
- Vibration, mal-adjustment, mal-alignment
- Obstruction or entry of foreign bodies into the machine
- Electrical faults and failures
- Failure of connected machinery or protective devices
- Defective lubrication, loosening of parts, stress
- Lack of skill/carelessness of the operators
- Falling, impact, collision and so on.

Expenses incurred on the repair and restoration of damaged machinery like overtime, express freight, surrounding property, third party liability, additional customs duty, air freight, etc. can also be covered, but only on payment of required extra premium.

Industrial all risks insurance: *Industrial all risks insurance* policy is available to all the key industrial units (except petrochemical risks) having an overall sum insured of ₹100 crore and above in one or more locations.

Damages due to the perils covered by the following are insured under the policy:

- Burglary insurance policy
- Business interruption due to fire and special perils policy
- Machinery breakdown/boiler explosion/electronic equipment insurance
- Fire and special perils policy

However, losses due to the following reasons are not covered by the policy:

- Poor/defective workmanship, design and material
- Intrinsic defects, vice and normal wear and tear
- Wilful act, negligence, wars and nuclear risks
- Pollution, contamination, shrinkage, rust, corrosion, scratching and temperature changes
- Theft, fraud, dishonesty, inventory losses, shortage on delivery
- Collapse or cracking of buildings

Certain other covers like debris removal and escalation, which are otherwise available as additional benefits in case of fire policy, can also be included for the additional premium.

Contractors all risks insurance: This policy is designed to protect the interests of civil contractors and firms involved in construction activity against the damage or destruction of various civil engineering projects undertaken by them. The policy provides cover in case of various civil engineering construction works ranging from small buildings to massive dams, which are vulnerable to damage due to several causes during the entire period of construction, that is, from the time of commencement of works at site till the contract works are taken over or put into use.

The policy covers losses due to

- An act of God such as flood, earthquake, etc.
- Larceny and burglary, malevolent and terrorist damage
- Fire/lightning
- Collapse, conspiracy, collision
- Inadvertent damage during construction like dropping or falling, defective workmanship and material, lack of skill, negligence, malevolent act and human error

Additional cover to include expenses for clearance and removal of debris, damage to surrounding property, third party liability, escalation in costs additional customs duty are available on payment of additional premium.

20.9 LIABILITY INSURANCE

Liability insurance is designed to offer specific protection against third party claims. Payment, under liability insurance, however, is not made to the insured, but rather to the person who has actually suffered the loss and who is not a party to the insurance contract. A typical liability insurance policy does not cover damages caused intentionally. Contractual liability too is not covered under liability insurance policies. The legal costs of a defense are not affected by policy limits, which is a great advantage as such costs can be very high in certain cases.

20.10 CROP INSURANCE

Crop insurance is bought by agricultural producers or farmers, besides others who want to protect themselves against loss of their crops due to natural disasters like hail, drought and floods, or the loss of revenue due to declines in the prices of agricultural commodities.

In India, crop insurance falls under the Rashtriya Krishi Bima Yojana, which was introduced in 1999. The basic purpose of this scheme is to offer financial support to the farmers facing loss due to a natural disaster; to refurbish credit eligibility of farmers, who have suffered losses due to crop failure and to support and stimulate production of pulses and oilseeds in the country. The crops covered under the scheme include rice, wheat, millets, oil seeds, pulses, cotton, sugarcane and potato. The scheme is carried out in areas as defined through a notification by the Union Ministry of Agriculture. The problem with crop insurance in our country is that rural India, where it is needed most, is still not aware of it. A lot needs to be done on the front of crop insurance in India.

KEY TERMS

Embezzlement Fraudulently using or taking another's property or money entrusted to one's care.

Floater Policy under which a guaranteed amount is floated over a group of employees.

Freight Cost of transport of goods in bulk by truck, train, ship or aircraft.

Insolvency Financial inability to pay debts.

Inventory loss Loss of goods in stock.

Larceny Act of stealing personal property.

Perils Causes of loss or risks expressed as being covered by or excluded from a policy.

Surveyors Independent professionals appointed by insurers to assess the loss or damage on receipt of notice of loss or claim form.

REVIEW QUESTIONS

20.1 Explain the special features of fidelity guarantee insurance.

20.2 Write a note on the types of miscellaneous insurance.

20.3 What do you understand by (a) flood insurance (b) earthquake insurance?

20.4 What do you understand by engineering insurance? Discuss the various types of engineering insurance policies.

20.5 Explain the special features of cattle insurance.

20.6 Define burglary insurance. Describe the different types of burglary insurance policies.

20.7 Write a note on

(i) Property insurance

(ii) Building insurance

(iii) Earthquake insurance

(iv) Flood insurance

(v) Liability insurance

(vi) Crop insurance

(vii) Industrial all risks insurance

21

Reinsurance

Learning Objectives

After going through this chapter we will be able to:

- Understand the meaning and concept of reinsurance.
- Discuss the important reinsurance terminologies.
- Explain the characteristics of reinsurance.
- Describe the types of reinsurance.
- Discuss the concept of double insurance.
- Understand the meaning of over insurance.

Sometimes, the amount of total insurance is so high that it is extremely difficult for the insurer to bear the liability. In such a case, the insurance company may arrange with another insurer to insure a portion of the insured risk. This arrangement is known as **reinsurance**. The term *reinsurance,* therefore, is also termed as *insurance of insurance*. In other words, in the event of loss, if it is beyond the capacity of the original insurer to pay, then this reinsurance process is resorted to. The original insurer who transfers a part of the insurance contract is called the **reinsured** and the second insurer is called the **reinsurer**. Of course, the reinsured has to pay reinsurance premium for that portion of the risk, which is shifted to the second insurer. For example, if a property is insured for ₹40 lakh and the insurer on being satisfied as to the condition of the property has accepted the risk. Despite the insurance company's own limit of merely ₹25 lakh, it may arrange with another company to reinsure or to take up the portion of the risk that exceeds its limit of ₹25 lakh, so that if the property gets destroyed, the original insurer (insurance company) would pay ₹40 lakh to the insured, but would recover the amount under the reinsured agreement from the reinsurer.

21.1 CHARACTERISTICS OF REINSURANCE

The following are the important characteristics of reinsurance:

1. The purpose of reinsurance is to spread or share out the loss.
2. Reinsurance contract is made on the same terms and conditions that govern the original contract of insurance.
3. An original insurer has insurable interest upto the amount of the risk undertaken by him. Therefore, he can reinsure the subject-matter to that extent.
4. If the original insurance lapses for any reason, reinsurance may also be terminated.
5. On the occurrence of the loss, the original insurer has to pay the assured amount to the insured and only then he will be entitled to claim his share of the liability from the reinsurer.
6. In the absence of a legally accepted contract between the original party who has insured his subject-matter and the original insurer, the reinsurers are obviously, discharged.
7. The reinsurer is not liable to the original insured in the event of loss as there is no agreement between the two.

21.2 TYPES OF REINSURANCE

The contracts of reinsurance may broadly be classified as follows:

21.2.1 Proportional Reinsurance

Under this method, the reinsurance company (i.e., the ceding office) shares the aggregate claim liability with the reinsurer, within the scope of the agreement and irrespective of the size of the claim. The reinsurer will pay commission or brokerage to the ceding company or reinsurance broker at a specified percentage of the premium ceded. The method of proportional reinsurance may be based on

Quota method: Under this method, the reinsurance company shares such proportion of every risk as is stated in the agreement. If, for example, reinsurance is arranged on a 50 per cent basis, the reinsurer accepts half of each risk, obtains half the premiums, and bears half the claims while the leading company handles and holds the balance of 50 per cent.

Share surplus method: The amount for the reinsurance company, the scope of geographical area and class of business are all included under the agreement. When a risk is proposed, the reinsurance company has a free choice, within the liability specified in the agreement, as to how much it will retain for its own amount. If the sum insured is less than its normal retention level for that class of risk, it need not take reinsurance at all, i.e., it will retain all. Thus, the surplus of the risk alone may be reinsured.

21.2.2 Non-proportional Reinsurance

In these forms of covers, the ceding office and the reinsurers do not share each loss in fixed proportions, and may not share some losses at all. The ceding office will underwrite its retention as a form of first loss insurance, i.e., it will bear all losses up to a specified amount, and the reinsurers will deal with the balance of any loss exceeding this amount, with customarily, an upper limit. Premiums under non-proportional reinsurance are separately quoted by the reinsurer as a proportion of the total premium received by the ceding company for the particular class of business. Thus, there will be a deposit premium and adjustment premium at the end of the year.

The non-proportional method of reinsurance may be based on

Excess of loss method: Under this method the insurer decides the ceiling amount he is prepared to bear on any one loss and seeks reinsurance under an agreement whereby the reinsurers will be responsible for the amount of losses above the amount retained by the direct insurer.

Excess of loss ratio method: It does not deal with individual risks or individual events, but is designed to prevent wide fluctuations of the net claims ratio of a particular account over one financial year compared with another. The reinsurance is intended to protect the company from an abnormal experience and not just the normal year-to-year fluctuation.

Pools method: Under this method, the member companies accept to pool together all their business to a leading office and this leading office makes the payment. The losses and profits shall be distributed amongst member companies in accordance with their shares in the business.

Treaty method: Under this method, there is an agreement between the insurer and a reinsurer or a number of reinsurers, whereby each reinsurer is bound to accept a fixed share of every risk coming within the scope of the agreement.

Figure 21.1 depicts the classification of reinsurance contracts.

21.3 REINSURANCE VS. DOUBLE INSURANCE

When the subject-matter of insurance is insured with two or more insurers and the total sum insured exceeds the actual value of the subject-matter, it is called as **double insurance**. If the actual value of the subject-matter

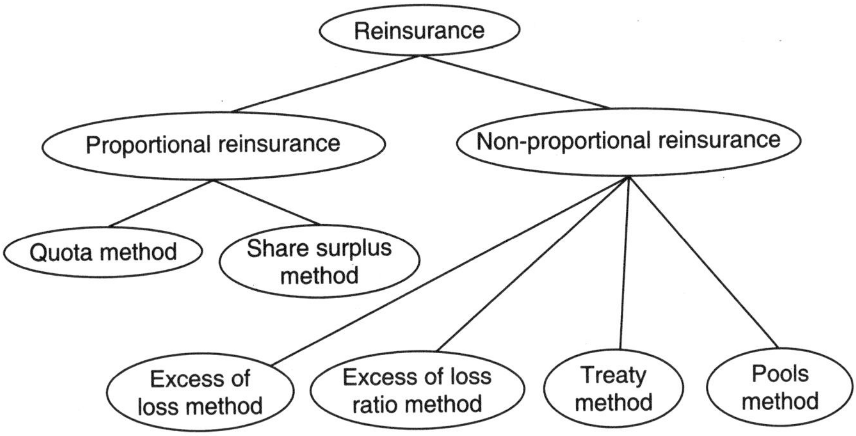

Figure 21.1 Types of reinsurance contracts.

is more than the total sum insured, it is not treated as double insurance, even if the insured has taken separate insurance policies with different insurers for the same subject-matter. For example, if a house worth ₹50 lakh is insured with A for ₹35 lakh and with B for ₹30 lakh, it is treated as double insurance because the total value of the subject-matter, i.e., total of all the policies exceeds the actual value of the house. Suppose if it is insured with A and B for ₹20 lakh each, there is no double insurance.

Table 21.1 can explain the differences between the two concepts:

Table 21.1 Difference between Reinsurance and Double Insurance

Reinsurance	*Double insurance*
The purpose of reinsurance is to spread the loss, i.e., when the risk is considered too great, get a part reinsured with another insurance company.	When the same risk and the same subject-matter are insured with more than one insurer, it is a case of double insurance.
Reinsurance does not affect the financial condition of the original insured. The reinsurance premium for the shifted risk is paid by the reinsured.	Total amount of all the policies, covering the risk, in case of double insurance, exceeds the actual value of the subject-matter.
The original insurer is able to transfer only a portion of the risk to the reinsurer.	The insurers enjoy the flexibility of adjusting the risks and contributions among themselves.
Reinsurance expires as soon as the original insurance lapses due to any reason.	There is no question of termination in the case of double insurance.
On the occurrence of loss, the original insurer has to pay the assured amount to the insured.	Assured can recover only upto the amount of the actual loss. If loss occurs, the assured may claim payment from the insurer in the order he selects.
Original insurer claims his share of liability from the reinsurer.	The assured can claim the full value on the original policies till his total loss is recovered.

21.4 OVER INSURANCE

It is a case of *over insurance,* when the value for which a subject-matter is insured is more than its actual value. Thus, the amount of insurance is the only measure of over insurance. It does not matter if the agreement of insurance is with only one insurer.

In the case of over insurance, different policies covering the same subject-matter are considered as one insurance. Thus, the assured can recover on the different policies, no more than their value but he may take legal action against insurer in respect of any of the policies, and claim from those, he so sued, to the full extent of his loss. Of course in such a case, the insurer so sued against the policy issued, can recover a chargeable sum by way of contribution from the insurers of the other policy.

21.5 ESSENTIALS OF A REINSURANCE PROGRAMME

The following provisions are laid under the IRDA regulations, 2000.

1. Reinsurance arrangements should be guided by the following objectives:
   (i) Expanding retention within the country,
   (ii) Developing enough capacity,
   (iii) Obtaining the best possible protection for the reinsurance costs incurred, and
   (iv) Simplifying the process of business management.
2. Every insurer shall uphold maximum retention corresponding to its financial strength and scale of business. The authority (i.e., IRDA) may require an insurer to justify its retention policy and may give such directions as considered necessary in order to ensure that the Indian insurer is not merely fronting for a foreign insurer.
3. Every insurer shall allow such proportion of the sum assured on each policy for different classes of insurance written in India to the Indian reinsurer as may be specified by the authority in accordance with the provisions of part IVA of the Insurance Act, 1938.
4. The reinsurance programme of every insurer shall commence from the beginning of every financial year, and every insurer shall put forward to the authority, his reinsurance programmes for the forthcoming year, 45 days before the commencement of the financial year.
5. Within 30 days of the commencement of the financial year, every insurer shall put on record with the authority a photocopy of every reinsurance treaty slip and excess of loss cover-note for that year together with the list of reinsurers and their shares in the reinsurance arrangement.

6. The authority may call for further information or clarification regarding the reinsurance programme of an insurer and may issue such directions as it considers necessary.
7. Insurers shall place their reinsurance business outside India with only those reinsurers who have over a period of the past five years counting from the year preceding for which the business has to be placed, enjoy approved rating standards. Placements with other reinsurers shall require the approval of the authority.
8. The Indian reinsurer shall organise domestic pools for reinsurance surpluses in fire, marine hull and other types of insurance in consultation with all insurers on such basis, limits and stipulations, which are fair to all insurers and assist in maintaining the retention of business within India. The arrangements so made shall be submitted to the authority for approval.
9. Surplus over and above the local reinsurance arrangements class-wise can be placed by the insurer separately with any of the reinsurers complying with sub-regulation (7) subject to a limit of 10 per cent of the total reinsurance premium ceded outside India being placed with any one reinsurer. Where it is required for a specialized insurance to cede a share in excess of such limit to any particular reinsurer, the insurer will have to obtain the specific approval of the authority giving reasons for such cession.
10. Every insurer shall offer a chance to other Indian insurers including the Indian reinsurer to participate in its facultative and treaty surpluses before placement of such cessions outside India.
11. The Indian reinsurer shall give back at least 50 per cent of the obligatory cessions received by it to the ceding insurers, at original terms and in addition to an overriding commission to the Indian reinsurer not exceeding 2.5 per cent.
12. Every insurer shall be required to submit to the authority data relating to its reinsurance transactions in such forms as the authority may specify, along with its annual accounts.
13. The insurers involved in the underwriting inward reinsurance business must have a well-defined underwriting policy that is carried on by persons with necessary knowledge and experience. The insurer shall file with the authority a note on its underwriting policy indicating the classes of business, geographical scope, underwriting limits and profit objective.
14. Every insurer must make outstanding claims provisions for every reinsurance arrangement accepted on the basis of loss information advices received from brokers/cedants and where such advices are not received, on an actuarial estimation basis.

21.6 IMPORTANT TERMS CONCERNING REINSURANCE

1. *Ceding insurer.* The insurer who obtains a guarantee (or places reinsurance). That is, the direct insurer.
2. *Ceding reinsurer.* A reinsurer who transfers (cedes) a portion of the underlying reinsurance.
3. *Cession.* The amount given off by way of reinsurance and therefore the amount accepted by the reinsurer.
4. *Direct insurer.* The insurer, who accepts the risk from the proposer and who, is directly responsible to the policyholder for the obligation undertaken.
5. *Facultative reinsurance.* Facultative reinsurance is the direct reinsurance of individual risks through the medium of a broker in precisely the same way as original insurances are placed.
6. *Line.* The amount of the retention of the direct insurer.
7. *Profit commission.* It is a percentage of the earned profits which the reinsurer agrees to return because the profit earned on business passing under a reinsurance treaty is deemed to be due to skill and care in the conduct of the business by the direct insurer.
8. *Reinsurance commission.* The amount paid by the reinsurer to the ceding company as a contribution to the acquisition and administration costs. It is calculated as a percentage of the premium received by reinsurer.
9. *Reinsurance policy.* The contracts of reinsurance except in fire practice where it is termed as guarantee or guarantee policy.
10. *Reinsurer.* The insurer who accepts a reinsurance from the direct insurer.
11. *Retention or holding.* The proportion of the risk, which the direct insurer holds on his own account.
12. *Retrocession.* A reinsurance of a reinsurance, i.e., where the reinsurer desires to reduce the limit of his liability in respect of business accepted.
13. *Underwriter.* (a) An insurance company that receives premium and in turn, accepts responsibility for the fulfilment of the policy contract; (b) The company employee who is responsible for assessment and selection of risks and determination of the terms for acceptance of the risks.

KEY TERMS

Agreement An accepted proposal that is agreement takes place with the communication of acceptance of an offer.

Brokerage The fee or commission received by a broker.

Retrocession Practice adopted by reinsurers to again reinsure their acceptance for spreading the risk further and protecting their own portfolio.

The authority The Insurance Regulatory and Development Authority (IRDA).

REVIEW QUESTIONS

21.1 What do you understand by reinsurance?

21.2 What are the characteristics of reinsurance?

21.3 Explain the various types of reinsurance.

21.4 What do you understand by double insurance?

21.5 Bring out the different types of non-proportional reinsurance.

21.6 What are the types of proportional reinsurance?

21.7 Write short notes on

(i) Double insurance

(ii) Over insurance

(iii) Surplus method of reinsurance

21.8 Explain the difference between reinsurance and double insurance.

22

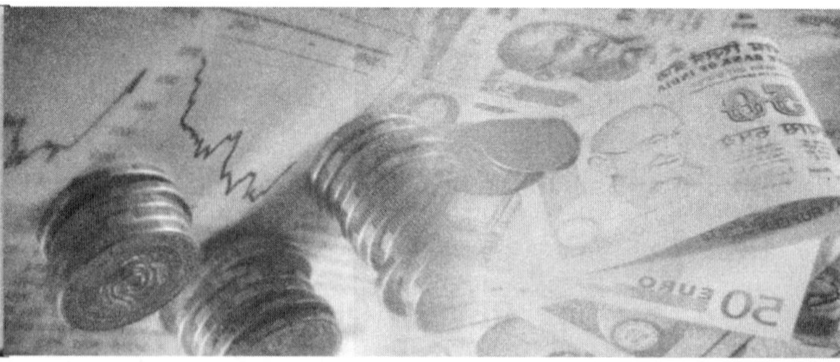

Insurance Pricing

Learning Objectives

After going through this chapter we will be able to:

- Understand the fundamentals of insurance pricing.
- Explain the objectives of insurance pricing.
- Discuss the various types of rating methods.
- Explain the methods of computing premiums for different types of policies.
- Be familiar with the role of different rate making entities.

Pricing of insurance products is different from the pricing of tangible products because it is difficult to determine the cost of inputs in the case of insurance products. It is problematic even when compared with other services, where the cost of providing the service can still be estimated with reasonable degree of accuracy. Moreover, in insurance transactions, the sales price (i.e., the premium) is collected before provision of stipulated services, that is, the payment of claims. Insurance is the business of buying risk. It is extremely difficult for an insurer to know at the time of selling a policy, as to what will be the realized cost of the policy because it depends upon whether or not the losses occur and if they do, how many and how large they will be. That is why, different people are charged different prices (premium) for policies providing the same kinds and amounts of insurance.

According to Harrington and Niehaus, *A fundamental principle of insurance pricing is that if insurers are to sell coverage willingly, they must receive premiums that (1) are sufficient to fund their expected claim costs and administrative costs and (2) provide an expected profit to compensate for the cost of obtaining the capital necessary to support the sale of coverage.*[1]

22.1 PRICING OBJECTIVES

Pricing of insurance products is an imperative subject in relation to the business of insurance. Insurance prices called premiums or rates are based on per unit of exposure. The insurance companies generally adopt comprehensive pricing strategy. However, in a competitive world, it is difficult to sell the product at statistically calculated prices. Moreover, the insurance companies are required to give incentives which leads to reduction in the realized prices. The non-life insurance business in India is considerably regulated by the Insurance Act, 1938 which empowers the tariff advisory committee (TAC) constituted under it, to control and regulate the rates as well as prescribe the terms and conditions offered by insurers in respect of general insurance business. These rates are based on statutory standards while all other products are non-tariff. Non-life insurance pricing is based on claims cost, business acquisition costs, management expenses, margin for fluctuations in claims experience and expected profits. These prices are obviously subject to wide fluctuations as the insurers make estimates based on past experiences, which are reviewed periodically. In contrast, life insurance pricing is less complicated and the prices do not change frequently. This is because, the determining factors for life insurance pricing, namely, mortality rate, expenses and interest rate are relatively stable.

Following are the general objectives of insurance pricing:

1. The rating system must generate sufficient premium income for the insurance company to be able to pay its claims and expenses; to give a reasonable rate of return to the investors of funds and to finance continuing growth and expansion.
2. The rate must not be unduly high as to allow abnormal gains to be earned by the insurer. The rate should be justifiable.
3. The rates must not be *inequitable*, in the sense that it should not be the same for heterogeneous buyers and must not be different for homogeneous buyers.
4. The rating system must be simple to understand.
5. The pricing system should not be very costly to use.
6. The rates should not be subject to too frequent changes, so that the public is not subjected to wide variation in costs year after year.
7. The mechanism should promote the reduction of losses by providing incentives to the insured to prevent losses.

---

[1] Harrington and Niehaus, *Risk Management & Insurance*, McGraw-Hill, p. 134.

22.2 LIFE INSURANCE PRICING ELEMENTS

The basic elements of 'life insurance pricing' are as follows:

Rate of death of large number of persons insured: The insured's occupation, age, life style, and medical history determine the mortality rates. The premium rates payable for life insurance are calculated on the basis of rate of deaths of very large number of persons insured, i.e., the experience of large number of cases is taken into consideration before deciding on mortality rate.

Administration cost and other expenses incurred by the insurer: All insurers incur certain expenditures or administrative costs related to the service provided. The administration cost incurred may depend on the frequency of payment of premium and the volume of records kept. If the premium is paid annually, cost is lesser as compared to quarterly, half yearly or monthly payments.

Income from investment of premium: Premium accumulated by the insurance company from various policyholders is again invested and the income earned on the same helps the insurance company to bear numerous expenses incurred and benefits awarded to policyholders.

The pricing of an insurance product calls for the estimation of claims costs and other business costs arising from the product and the estimation of investment income arising from the investment of the premium income related to the product. Pricing risk may ensue where the claims, costs or investment returns arising from the sale of a product are wrongly estimated.

Moreover, an insurer may incorporate on-going actuarial review and involvement in the pricing process and, where the insurer finds it appropriate, he can also undertake specific independent reviews of pricing for schemes and larger or more complex risks.

Accordingly, the insurer may also include the following elements concerning pricing in the risk management framework:

(i) Well-defined, suitable levels of delegation for approval of all relevant attributes of pricing;
(ii) Risk identification and assessment;
(iii) A procedure for the reflection of emerging experience in price adjustments;
(iv) Profit and loss analysis and price discounting authorities;
(v) A system for the insurer's product pricing to respond to competitive and other external environmental pressures;
(vi) A process to monitor deviations of actual price from the technical underwriting pricing;
(vii) Techniques for monitoring compliance with pricing policies and procedures.

22.3 INSURANCE RATING METHODS

Insurance rating methods determine the cost of the insurance products. In other words, an insurance rate is the price per unit of insurance and is a function of the cost of insurance. The basic rating methods include the following:

22.3.1 Judgement Rating

Judgement rating method is used when the proposed risk is so uncommon that very less or no quantitative data about similar risk is available. The rate is chiefly based on the underwriter's own opinion after evaluation of each exposure individually. In such cases class rate are difficult to be calculated since the loss exposures are extremely diverse and probable loss data are not available. Thus, each premium is exclusive and is based on the judgement of the person making it. Judgement rating is popularly used in ocean marine insurance and in some lines of inland marine insurance.

22.3.2 Class Rating

Class rating is the most commonly applied rating method in insurance business. In this case, risks are classified on the basis of some important characteristics. Insured risks belonging to the same class are charged the same rate per unit of exposure. The rate signifies the claims experience for the class as a whole. It is based on the assumption that future losses likely to be suffered by the insured will be generally determined by the same set of factors. The classifications and the respective rates being in the form of printed manuals, the rating method is also called **manual rating**.

The class rating decisions involve not only the decisions regarding the number of various risk classifications and rates to be taken into account but also the number of characteristics of the covered risks to be considered. These two decisions are inter-linked. The number of classifications are proportionate to the number of rating factors that are taken into account. That is, number of classifications increase with the increase in the number of factors.

Class rate is the product of the amount of incurred losses and loss adjustment expenses, and the number of exposure units. Incurred losses implies all losses paid during the accounting period, in addition to reserves created for the future payment of losses that have already occurred during the same period. The expenses incurred by the insurer in adjusting losses during the same accounting period are called the **loss adjustment expenses**.

Class rates are used in life insurance. In this case, rates are based on age, gender, physical fitness, lifestyle, habits, etc. Class rating method is also used in case of proprietary insurance, automobile insurance, workers compensation and health insurance.

22.3.3 Merit Rating

A variation of the class rating method is the *merit rating* method in which the class rate of a particular class of insured risk is altered on the basis of individual loss experience. It is based on the supposition that the loss experience of one insured will differ to a large extent from the loss experience of the other insured.

The different types of merit rating methods are discussed here-inafter:

Schedule rating: Under this method, each exposure is rated severally. Calculation of schedule rates involves the following steps:

- Analyze the risk in respect of the person or object insured, in order to understand the characteristics that are likely to cause losses or to avoid them
- Compare the risk with the usual or standard risk of its kind
- Make deductions for the anticipated characteristics of the risk from the standard rate, and additions for the adverse characteristics of the risk

However, there is a subjective element in the sense that additions to and subtractions from the standard rate are based upon the subjective opinion of the person responsible for rating.

Experience rating: Under this type of method, the class rate is modified on the basis of claim experience of a particular exposure. For this, comparison is drawn between the actual losses, in general, over a period of two or three years and the average risks, in the same class of risks. If the actual risk has been lower than the average risk, the rate is reduced. And, if the record for the actual risk is higher than the average risk, the rate is increased. Experience rating method is relevant only in cases of large risks involving many losses each year, as a matter of trend and is thus applied in large firms with reliable experience offering policies involving high premium amounts.

Retrospective rating: Unlike experience rating, retrospective rating is based on the current experience for which the policy contract contains a provision that final rates will be determined in retrospect. The policy contract specifies a range of maximum and minimum premium but the final premium is determined only after the expiry of the policy and depends upon the amount of losses incurred during the year. The insured is charged minimum premium for very small losses and maximum premium for very large losses. More often than not the final premium lies between maximum and minimum premium. Retrospective rating method encourages the insured to reduce losses and gain by paying lesser premium. This rating plan is usually applied to large liability and workers compensation policies.

22.4 CALCULATION OF PREMIUM

A rate is the price charged per unit of exposure or risk protection. Premium is the product of the predetermined rate and the number of units of exposure bought by the insured. It is calculated by multiplying the rate by the number of exposure units bought. The term *premium* may be classified into (i) *Net Premium* and (ii) *Gross Premium*. Net Premium may further be categorized into (a) *Net Single Premium*, and (b) *Net Level Premium*.

22.4.1 Net Single Premium

Net single premium, in general parlance, means the present monetary worth of the future death benefit. It is the lump sum premium amount, which together with the return/interest earned thereon, is precisely adequate to pay the claim-amount. Once the single premium is calculated it becomes the basis of calculating other premiums. Expenses of management and contingency costs do not form part of net single premium.

Net single premium calculation is generally based on the following assumptions:

- Premiums are paid in advance, at the beginning of the year of policy.
- Premiums amounts so collected are invested, at an assumed rate of interest, until required for the payment of claims. Even the returns on these invests are reinvested.
- Mortality rate is uniform throughout the year.
- Claims are paid only at the end of the period. All policies are of the same amount.

Calculation of net single premium involves the following procedure:

1. Define the constituents of a claim, which can be death, survival or both and also the period of payment of claims, which may be at the beginning, at the end, or at times, during the year.
2. Ascertain the number of insured, the duration of the policy, the plausible number of claims per year as well as the total value of claims per year.
3. Based on the number of years of interest involved and the present value of a rupee, determine the present value of the claim for each year. This calculation would help in finding out the present value of all future claims.
4. Calculate the net single premium by dividing the present value of future claims by number of insured persons, estimated to buy the policy. The net single premium, thus, is the present value of all claims.

Calculation of net single premium also varies with the nature of the policy as discussed here:

Term insurance policies: Under the term insurance contract, the insurer is liable to pay only if the life assured dies within the term specified in the contract. The premium is paid only once in a lump sum at the commencement of the policy. Death claims are paid at the end of the year in which the death occurred and not at the term-end. As the death can occur at any moment and the liability of the insurer to pay may arise on the occurrence of the death, the probability of death (calculated on the basis of mortality rate) in each year along with the present value of the claim for each year is taken into account for calculating the premium. The present value of the first year will be calculated for one year in the first year of insurance because if death occurs during the first year, the insurer can earn interest at least for one year. Similarly, in the second year of insurance, the present value of ₹1 is calculated for two years at a predetermined rate of return on investment, say, 5 per cent per annum.

Whole life policies: Payment of premium on whole life policies is to be made throughout the life of the assured and; the sum assured is paid by the insurer on the death of the insured to his beneficiary. The only difference between the term insurance policy and the whole life policy is that unlike the term insurance policy which is for limited number of years, the whole life policy continues for the entire life of the insured. The sum assured too is definitely paid. Only the time when it will be paid is uncertain. In most of the mortality tables life is presumed to continue upto 100 years. Thus, premium calculation starts from the date of commencement of risk to the 100th year. If a person has taken policy at the age of 35, the calculation will continue upto the 100th year.

The probability of death in each separate year will be multiplied by the face value of the policy and this amount is discounted by the present value for the period.

Pure endowment policy: Under the pure endowment policy, the insured amount becomes payable only if the holder survives a certain fixed period. Thus, the holder of 5 years pure endowment will be paid only when he is alive at the end of 5 years. In case if the insured dies during this period, the entire amount of premium paid is forfeited.

Net single premium = Probability of survival × Policy amount × Present value of ₹1 for the endowment period

Ordinary endowment policy. Under this policy payment of claim amount is certain as the policy amount is payable either at the survival of the term or at the death of the life assured, whichever is earlier. Death and survival being the basis of payment, the net premium is calculated on death and survival rate.

Double endowment policy. The only difference between ordinary endowment policy and the double endowment policy is that if the life assured survives up to the term, he is paid double the amount of the policy. Since the double of the policy amount is paid at the survival, one more premium on the basis of pure endowment is added to the premium of ordinary endowment policy.

Joint life policy: Under this policy payment of claim will be made at the first death of the assured lives. Here, the process of calculation will be the same as in the case of term insurance with only difference that the probability of death is compound one. The compound probability of death is calculated by multiplying the probability of death of each of the joint holders covered by the policy. The policy amount in case of last survival policy is payable only when all lives covered by the policy die. In this case, the compound probability of all policyholders is calculated. The calculation continues up to the youngest life's reaching to the highest age as per the mortality table. Thus,

Compound probability = Probability of death of one person
× Probability of death of other person

The calculation continues till the probability of death of even the last survivor.

Annuity policy: Under a contract of annuity, the insurer agrees to pay a stipulated amount to the insured, throughout his/her life or during their life for a fixed term, against a monetary consideration, i.e., premium, which is paid regularly over a period of time, forming a corpus with the insurer. The mode of payment may be annual, semi-annual, quarterly or monthly.

Annuities are of the following kinds:

Immediate annuity. Under the immediate annuity scheme, the payment of annuity starts from the date of first annuity period. The two kinds of immediate annuity are—life annuity, and term (temporary) annuity.

(i) In life annuity the payment of annuity shall continue up to the life of the insured. The cost of annuity depends upon his survival. Thus, the calculation is based upon the probability of survival.

(ii) The calculation of term annuity is on the same basis as for life annuity, with the basic difference that the calculation continues only up to a fixed period and not up to the completion of annuity mortality table as required in the case of life annuity.

Deferred annuity. Annuity payments under the deferred annuity policy start after a fixed period of time. Which may be called **deferred period** or **deferment period**. In view of the fact that the premium is received at the beginning of the contract while the payment starts only at the end of the deferment period, the present value too stands deferred with the deferment period. The survival rate is also calculated after the deferment period.

Minimum payment annuity. This annuity plan has the following features:

(i) It has the basic features of both, the term as well as life annuity. Notwithstanding the death of the insured, minimum annuity payments are definitely made for the agreed term.

(ii) Annuity amount is also paid after the specified term so long as the insured lives.

(iii) Up to the specified term period, the probability of survival is treated as one. This is because annuity payment is definite for the specified period. For the purpose of calculating annuity payment after the specified term, the actual probability of survival at that age is considered.

22.4.2 Net Level Premium

Unlike the net single premium, which is paid only at the commencement of the contract, the net level premium is paid periodically in accordance with the terms of the contract. Most people find it difficult to pay the premium amount in lump sum and prefer to pay for their insurance in instalment payments. Thus, the net level premium is generally considered to be more suitable than the net single premium. As observed above, the net single premium is the present value of all future claims. But then, the present value of all net level premiums is also equal to the sum total of the present values of all future claims. It can thereby be concluded that the present value of all net level premiums is equal to the net single premium. Therefore, if the present value of a unit level premium is calculated, the net single premium can be converted into level premium by determining the ratio between the net level premium and the net single premium. The ratio will differ according to the age of the insured at the commencement of the insurance contract, the nature of the policy and the duration of the policy. However, calculation of the ratio is comparatively easier for short-term policies, but it is rather difficult for whole life and endowment policies since the calculation involves very large number of years.

Net level premium may alternatively be calculated on the basis of annuity due principle. The annuity due for the same period and issued at the same age is exactly same as level premium. The premium, in both cases, is paid in the beginning of the period and is paid, usually so long as the assured is alive. Though the premium can also be paid only for a particular period like in the case of term and endowment policies. For acquiring life insurance, single premium is given and for annuity due, purchase price of the annuity due is given. Net purchase price of annuity due, which is issued at the particular age and for a specified period or up to life of the insured is equal to the net single premium payable for the life insurance issued at the same age and for the same period. Therefore, if the payment of periodical annuity due is determined, the level premium for the same period can readily be calculated.

22.4.3 Gross Premium

The gross premium is the premium charged by the insurer to be able to meet the expenses of insurance and pay the amount of claims. It depends upon the mortality rate, the assumed interest rate, the expenses and the bonus loading. The gross premium includes the net premium and loading. Loading refers to the amount added to the net premium to take care of other expenses, profit margin and also a margin towards contingencies. The amount required to pay bonuses on participating policies may also be included in loading. Thus, the sum total of pure premium, which covers expected losses and loss adjustment expenses, other operating expenses and contingency margin is called 'loading'. Gross premium is the actual premium required to be paid by the policyholders. It may also be referred to as the office premium.

Allocation of expenses: The business expenses included in the net premiums can be allocated either over various policies or over the period of the policy. For the purpose of equitable allocation, the expenses may be classified as follows:

1. Expenses varying with the size of the premium
2. Expenses varying with the amount of policy
3. Expenses, which are independent of both

Determination of percentage: It is also necessary for the insurer to determine the percentage or proportion in which the expenses vary with the premium. The percentage can be ascertained on the basis of the past experience. For instance, if the past experience shows that for a premium of ₹5 lakh, the insurer would be required to incur expenses worth ₹10 thousand it can be proved that the expenses varying with the premium will be 0.5 per cent of the premium amounts collected. The process can be extended to determine the percentage in relation to policy amount as well as to policy number and then the net premium can be loaded with these percentage or fixed sum for each policy.

22.5 METHODS OF LOADING

The following methods of loading may be applied:

Constant addition loading: This method presumes that all the expenses vary with the amount of the policy and therefore, a fixed amount per thousand of sum assured is loaded to the net premium.

Percentage addition loading: Under this method, a fixed percentage of net premium is added to the net premium. It assumes that all expenses vary according to the premium amount. Expenses varying with the policy amount, on the other hand, are completely ignored.

Modified percentage method: In this case, the loading consists of those expenses, which vary with net level premium for the given policies and also expenses that vary with net level premium of the whole life policy issued at the given age. Thus, it is an adaptation of the above two methods. However, it fails to relate the expenses according to their variations.

Constant and percentage addition method: Under this method, the loading includes a fixed amount per thousand of the sum assured, along with a fixed percentage of the net premium for the policy. The percentages are based on the past experience. The method seems to presume that the expenses vary either with the net premium or with the sum assured and ignores the fact that expenses may logical than the rest.

22.6 CLASSIFICATION OF EXPENSES

Proper understanding of the kind of expenses on the basis of their occurrence and equal distribution of these expenses every year is the most important requisite of equitable distribution of loading. This necessitates appropriate classification of expenses, as discussed here:

The initial expenses: Those expenses, which are incurred before the issue of the policy or at the time of issuing the policy are the initial expenses.

The recurring expenses: Expenses incurred every year during the entire duration of the policy are called **recurring expenses**. Some of them may be limited only up to the period of premium collection. For example, expenses incurred for issue of premium notices, premium receipts, etc.

The final expenses: The final expenses are the expenses that are incurred at the time of payment of claims or the surrender values. These expenses include the cost of approving the claims, the cost of correspondence, etc.

The general expenses: These include the fixed expenses, which represent the costs of the business taken as a whole. The accounting expenses, legal expenses, maintenance and establishment charges are important general expenses.

22.7 PAYMENT OF PREMIUM

The insured can pay premium in any of the following ways:

By cash, local cheque (subject to realisation of cheque) or demand draft at branch office. The DD and cheques or money orders may be sent by post. Premiums can be paid at any of the companies' branches that are networked.

Directly through the bank. On getting a standing instruction from the account holder the banks debit the account for the premium amount and send it vide a banker's cheque to the insurance company, on the due dates and months mentioned on the policy bond. Premium payment can also be made through ATMs of some specified banks.

Through internet. Payment of premiums can be made through internet, through service providers, viz., HDFC Bank, ICICI Bank, Times of Money, Bill Junction, UTI Bank, Bank of Punjab, Citibank, Corporation Bank, Federal Bank and Bill-Desk.

Through ECS. Premium payment can also be made through electronic clearing service (ECS) which has been launched at Mumbai, Hyderabad, Chennai, Kolkata, New Delhi, Kanpur, Bangalore, Vijaywada, Patna, Jaipur, Chandigarh, Trivandrum, Ahmedabad, Pune, Goa, Nagpur, Secunderabad and Visakhapatnam. A policyholder having an account in any Bank, which is a member of the local clearing house can opt for ECS debit to pay premiums.

22.7.1 Grace Period

Policyholder should pay the premiums on due dates. However, a grace period of not less than 30 days will be allowed for payment of yearly/half-yearly/quarterly premiums and 15 days for monthly premiums. When the days of grace expire on a Sunday or a public holiday, the premium may be paid on the following working day to keep the policy in force. If the premium is not paid before the expiry of the days of grace, the policy may lapse.

22.8 RATE MAKING

22.8.1 The Role of Actuaries

Actuaries are the financial wizards who play a pivotal role in the rate making process. They are responsible for performing actuarial analysis of insurance rates, rating procedures, rating plans and schedules of insurance companies. Being experienced and qualified, they render technical assistance to policy examiners and other technical staff regarding matters involving product design and pricing; review and analyses of insurance operations; reserves and underwriting procedures, and so on. They are required to perform the following functions:

(i) Conceiving new forms of insurance to cater to the changing needs of consumers.

(ii) Ascertaining the reserves required for meeting the future responsibilities and liabilities.

(iii) Evaluating the expenses and earnings and making suggestions for allocation of surpluses.

(iv) Investigating claims experiences in order to predict future claims and earnings.

(v) Communicating with the company officials, agents, policyholders, and regulatory authorities about company policies and practices.

Insurance Regulatory and Development Authority (appointed actuary) Regulations, 2000, provides that appointment of qualified actuary is mandatory for every life insurance company. As a result of this regulation, no life insurance company can carry on business of insurance without an *appointed actuary*, being appointed in accordance with the provision of the Act.

22.8.2 The Role of Professional Organizations

Professional organizations too play an important role in insurance pricing by performing the rating work for the insurance companies. Companies that do not have sufficient data of their own take advantage of the services provided by professional organizations. By working together and pooling their premium and loss data, they can develop more reliable rating information. Small companies also benefit from cooperative rate making.

KEY TERMS

Actuaries Experts responsible for the rate making process. They perform actuarial analysis of insurance rates and apply mathematical models to insurance problems in order to make financial provisions for the future.

Coverage The scope of protection provided under a contract of insurance.

Experience rating Rating method based on the expert's experience, whether actual or reconstructed.

Grace period A period of 15–30 days allowed as grace after the expiry of the due date for making payment of premium.

Operating expenses Routine expenses of conducting a business such as sales and administration.

Retrospective rating A variation of experience rating applied to determine the reinsurance rate and premium for a specified period based on the loss experience for that period.

REVIEW QUESTIONS

22.1 Distinguish between pricing of insurance products and pricing of other products. How are insurance prices determined?

22.2 What are the objectives of insurance pricing? \

22.3 What are the various assumptions underlying the calculation of premium?

22.4 What is rating? Briefly explain the various classes of rating.

22.5 Fair insurance rates fairly discriminate among the various policyholders. Comment.

22.6 Explain the methods of computing premiums for different types of policies and annuities.

22.7 What are the various methods of loading?

22.8 What is the role of actuaries and professional organizations in rate making?

22.9 Explain the significance of various insurance rating methods.

22.10 Write short notes on

(i) Net single premium

(ii) Net level premium

(iii) Insurance pricing elements

(iv) Payment of insurance premium

23

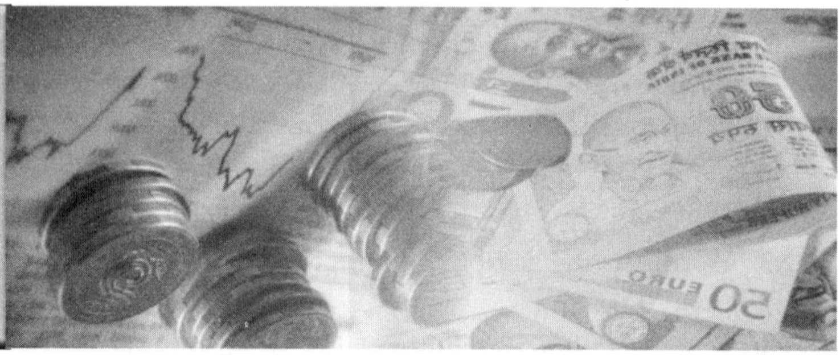

Underwriting

Learning Objectives

After going through this chapter we will be able to:

- Understand the concept of underwriting.
- Discuss the purposes and principles of underwriting.
- Elucidate the underwriting process.
- Describe the methods of rate determination.
- Discuss the different types of underwriters.
- Understand the role of agents in underwriting.

Underwriting is the function of evaluating the subject of insurance, which may be a person, property, profession, business, or other entity, and determining, on the basis of company's predetermined standards, whether to insure it or not. Underwriting thus, is the insurance function that is responsible for assessing and classifying the degree of risk a proposed insured or group represents and making a decision concerning coverage of that risk.[1] It is the foundation of the process leading to an insurance contract. The success of the insurance business depends on the precision with which the company's underwriter takes decisions to accept or reject applications and to determine the terms on which the risk is to be offered. *Underwriter* is the person who reviews and selects risks to be insured by the insurance company.

[1] Stone, Gene, *Insurance Company Operations*, LOMA 2000, p. 234.

23.1 PURPOSES AND PRINCIPLES OF UNDERWRITING

The underlying underwriting policy of the insurance company is the basis of the underwriting decisions involving selection of risks. The underwriting policy implemented by the insurance company is also called its underwriting philosophy or, in other words, the **fundamental principles of underwriting** followed by the insurance company. Unfavourable selection and continuity are indeed the basic underwriting principles, in the sense that the underwriter should be careful not to make an adverse selection of risks. In order to avoid losses, the rate of premium charged should be based on a careful evaluation of the basic risks in each case and must be affordable by the consumer. Otherwise, the consumer may be compelled to surrender the policy or the policy would lapse, causing serious detriment to the company. For the maintenance of insurance business, continuous renewal of the policy is essential.

The purposes of underwriting function are:

1. Underwriting must ensure reasonably accurate estimation of the risk in any insurance proposal. It should be based on cautious investigation of the factors which cause that risk, so that the premium charged is adequate from the point of view of the insurance company and at the same time, affordable to the consumer.
2. Another purpose of underwriting is to investigate and determine the factors responsible for any gap between the consumer's expectations and company's analysis affecting the demand for the insurance company's product.
3. Though underwriters are not directly responsible for the pricing of insurance products, but they make a significant contribution in the determination of insurance prices by appraising the degree of the risk, taking decisions whether to accept or reject the risk and then computing the price at which the risk would be acceptable.

23.2 THE UNDERWRITING PROCESS

The underwriting process generally involves the following steps:

23.2.1 Receiving Applications

The first step in the underwriting process is the appraisal of information by the life insurance company's underwriter. Most of the information required for the purpose is obtainable from the insurance application, collected usually by the agents working for the life insurance company. The information is categorized into

(i) The general information, which includes particulars such as name, age, address, date of birth, sex, income, marital status and occupation of the insured along with details about the insurance coverage such as type of policy, amount of insurance, name and relationship with the beneficiary.

(ii) Personal information, which includes information about family and personal history of the proposed insured.

(iii) The medical information, i.e., extensive information regarding present health of the insured as well as medical history of his/her family. Medical examination of the assured may also be sought by the insurance company in certain cases depending upon the age of the insured and the coverage amount of the policy.

(iv) The agent's report contains information about the proposer, his income and financial status, where the insured is an individual; financials of the business where the insured is a business organization, and both personal and financial statements in case of insured being a professional.

(v) A moral hazard report completed by a responsible officer of the insurer. The insurance companies generally have specified levels of officials whose reports are acceptable to appraise moral hazard.

23.2.2 Reviewing Application

The application in order to be acceptable must be duly executed and must also meet the insurance company's underwriting principles. At this point the company's underwriters would also determine whether any supplementary documentation is required and then take steps to procure the required additional information through appropriate sources. Where the information is not received within the specified time, the application may even be rejected. The most important aspect related to reviewing of the application involves determining whether the risk displays suitable insurable interest, essential for a valid contract of insurance or not. It is equally essential to ensure the insurability of the risk applied.

23.2.3 Assessing the Risk and Taking Underwriting Decision

After collecting the relevant information the underwriters appraise and categorize the risks, so that the premium for the policy is decided on the basis of primary and secondary factors in conjunction with the rates of premium set for a particular risk profile by the actuaries working for the company. The primary and secondary factors applied in an underwriting process depend to a great extent on the type of insurance being underwritten. For instance, in the case of life, health and disability insurance, the key factors would be age, sex, health, health history; nature of occupation, financial condition, personal habits and size of the policy, in the case of property insurance, type of the property, its value and other property features would be important factors in the underwriting decision. Similarly, in case of business operations related underwriting, type of business, its size, financial condition, etc. help the underwriter in taking underwriting decision.

On the basis of the above factors the underwriter may take any of the following decisions:

(i) Reject an application for insurance when it represents a risk that is unacceptable to the insurance company. A risk is unacceptable when it does not conform to the company's underwriting standards.

(ii) Issue a policy on a substandard basis when it involves a high risk as per the company's underwriting standards but is still not deemed to be completely outside its underwriting norms for that type of policy. In such a case the company may issue the policy with a higher premium than would be required for a standard policy; issue the policy with restricted benefits or issue the policy with certain prohibitions, that is, excluding certain provisions from the policy.

(iii) Issue a policy on a standard basis when it involves a risk that is within the normal, acceptable boundaries of the company's underwriting standards for that type of policy.

(iv) Issue a policy on a preferred basis when it involves the lowest category of risk as per the company's underwriting standards. The insurance company offers lowest possible rates of premium, within the limitations of the relevant insurance regulations, for covering such a risk.

23.2.4 Policy Writing

Policy writing is the function of recording details of the policy in a register for further reference in the future. Each accepted proposal is recorded in the register only after it is consecutively numbered and a review slip is prepared. Separate files are maintained for each proposal in which the review slip and details of other particulars are kept. However, these days, insurance companies have adopted computerized systems for recording the policyholders' particulars, details regarding premium payment and other necessary information regarding the policy.

23.2.5 Issue of Acceptance Letter and First Premium Receipt

When the underwriters decide to accept the proposal (application) made to the company through a duly executed proposal form, the company must communicate such acceptance of the proposal through the issue of acceptance letter to the proposer. The first premium receipt is issued on the payment of premium by the proposer.

23.3 METHODS OF RATE DETERMINATION

The function of underwriting and pricing in insurance business are closely linked. The function of underwriting involves the determination of the risks that are acceptable to the insurance business in order to meet market-competition and proposing the appropriate rate of premium for the coverage. While the pricing function in the business of insurance is concerned with the analysis of the commercial performance and profitability of the insurance products, evaluation of potential risk factors and the assessment of alternative pricing strategies, that is, fixing the rates of premium for the risks to be covered.

Within the legal constraints, the underwriters are free to use any method to determine rates. The various alternative methods of rate determination include the following:

23.3.1 Judgement Rating

Under judgement rating method, the underwriter relies on his own knowledge and experience and the advice of the medical referee and actuaries to determine the rate for each applicant. Thus, the effectiveness of this rating method depends on the underwriter's analytical abilities. No specified rates are generally applied as this sort of rating is usually used for special lines of insurance or for lines of insurance not requiring rates to be approved by the state. But in certain cases and for certain lines of insurance, the legislation may have a bearing on the underwriting decision concerning rate determination.

23.3.2 Manual Rating

Under manual rating, predetermined rates located in manuals are used to set rates for each policy. This method of rate determination is more and more commonly applied, particularly in closely regulated lines of insurance. Manual rates may be specified by the state insurance department or developed within the insurance company or by a rating agency. The manual rating method is more objective and less subjective. The uniformity in procedure for underwriting is the biggest advantage of this method. Of course, the rating manuals have to be updated regularly depending upon the results of medico-actuarial investigations. Though the method may appear to be mechanical in operation but still has a lot of scope for individual judgement and experience of the medical officer and the actuary in the interpretation of ratings in several cases.

23.3.3 Merit Rating

Under merit rating method, manual rates are used and then modified based on certain risk attributes. Rates modification may be based on the experience of the insured over a specified period. It may even be based on a schedule that quantifies applicable risk characteristics. Thus, rates are modified on the merit of the case, which may be done on any of the following basis:

Experience merit rating: Under experience merit rating method, the applicant is generally asked about pertinent behaviour or occurrences associated with the insurance coverage over a specified period and rates are determined on the basis of the experience of the insured during the specified period. For instance, a driver may be asked about traffic infringements that occurred during the last three years. Rates are partly based on the number of such infringements over that period.

Retrospective merit rating: Under this type of merit rating method the underwriter reviews the loss experience during the policy period and then sets a rate based on that loss experience. Retrospective merit rating is commonly applied in commercial lines of insurance and also in *workers compensation* insurance.

Scheduled merit rating: Scheduled merit rating is said to be a sophisticated form of manual rating as the base rates used under this method are indeed the manual rates to/from which, addition/subtraction may be made. This addition/subtraction is based on the amounts determined for various risk characteristics. For instance, the standard rate under this type of rating system may be lowered in cases where, fireproof construction materials are used.

Notwithstanding the type of method used to assign rates, rates are ultimately determined by evaluating the proportional incidence and gravity of a risk. Gravity, in this context, refers to the amount of financial loss that is likely to occur due to the risk. Incidence refers to the number of times or the frequency with which the loss is likely to occur. The rate for a small, occasional loss would obviously be low in comparison to an occasional but large loss while the rate for a loss that is both recurrent and large would be rather high.

23.4 TYPES OF UNDERWRITERS

Most insurance companies, nowadays deal in different types of insurance and issue a variety of policies for each type of insurance. On the other hand, most underwriters perform their responsibilities as experts, specializing in one or few types of insurance, that is, property or personal or professional, and so on. Thus, the different types of underwriters are:

23.4.1 Property and Casualty Underwriters

Property and casualty underwriters normally specialize in a particular type of property or casualty coverage rather than the complete domain concerned with property and casualty. Within this domain there may be fire underwriters, homeowners underwriters, automobile insurance underwriters, marine underwriters, commercial property underwriters, personal property underwriters, commercial general liability underwriters, professional liability underwriters, etc. A good understanding of the risks involved with each line of insurance underwritten by an underwriter is essential for the efficient discharge of his responsibilities. They must also be aware of the practical methods that are available for dealing with these risks and have a thorough knowledge of the resources used to evaluate each application and ascertain whether the applicant match company underwriting standards. The resources generally used for this purpose include site inspection reports, business or personal financial statements and reports, and where a business is insured, statistical reports prepared by the industry that the business belongs to, in addition to the statistical reports from the property and casualty insurance industry as applicable to the risk.

23.4.2 Personal Line and Commercial Lines

Property and casualty underwriters may further be classified depending on whether they underwrite personal lines or commercial lines. Different risks affect individuals and businesses differently. Accordingly, the insurance needs of an individual are very different from the needs of a business. Of course, both need protection in the form of property and liability insurance. Moreover, there are several types of businesses, each involving different types of risks associated with the business. Hence, there may be many specialized underwriting functions even within the domain of commercial lines and accordingly a commercial property and casualty underwriter may even specialize in underwriting specific types of businesses. For instance, if an insurer deals with clients needing boilers and machinery insurance along with clients needing cover for extensive data processing facilities, one group of underwriters may work with the boilers and machinery applicants and another group with those requiring data processing protection. Similarly, where a property and casualty underwriter works with personal lines applicants, the underwriter will have an intense insight of the specific risks facing individuals, who may, for instance be homeowners or drivers, etc. An underwriter working with exceedingly precious personal property of an individual will be aware of the assessment reports and suitable security measures that should be taken to protect the property.

23.4.3 Life and Health Underwriters

Life and health insurance is yet another domain in which the underwriters may specialize. A life and health insurance underwriter is acquainted with the effect of medical history, personal habits, lifestyle and other health related issues on insurability. The health or life underwriter is capable of analyzing and comprehends medical reports and information collected from the Medical Information Bureau. Health insurance being closely regulated, health insurance underwriters are also well conversant in regulations governing health coverage.

23.4.4 Liability Underwriters

Liability insurance underwriters must understand the liability risks affecting commercial businesses, professionals or individuals. They should be capable of evaluating past losses, judgments and settlements in terms of the probability of re-emergence in order to ascertain relative future risk. They must also have knowledge of the latest trends in court judgments and with liability laws in order to accurately appraise high-risk applicants.

23.4.5 Group Underwriters

Many types of insurance, including health insurance, are underwritten on group basis. Underwriting of group insurance is different from underwriting of individual policies. In such cases, a common rate, established after due analysis of the characteristics of the whole group, as well as individuals within the group, is applied to the entire group to be insured. The rate is normally reviewed and revised on an annual basis. In certain cases, individual rates may be allocated to individuals within the group. However, the allocated rate is generally a discounted rate for the reason that the individual is only a part of the group; accordingly the insurer's marketing costs are reduced on a per coverage basis. Various types of group insurance, particularly the ones that are offered as part of an employer's benefit package, are governed by state regulations. Thus, specialized underwriters for group insurance are required because group underwriting differs from individual underwriting both in terms of operations as well as regulations.

23.5 ROLE OF AGENTS IN UNDERWRITING

The agent plays a significant role in the selection of risks. The agent establishes the bond between the insurer and the insured. He is an agent of the insurer, and hence, he has to first and foremost look to the interests of the insurer. On the other hand, he is the guide of the insured who has no or very little knowledge of insurance. From the insurer's viewpoint, the agent's contribution in appraising the risk is so crucial that he is also called the **first line or primary underwriter**. The complete knowledge of the insured that is the prerequisite to deciding the degree of the risk is made available to the insurer through the field force, in particular, the agent. The agent manages to get all the information about the insured as required by the underwriter either through his personal knowledge or through careful enquiries and investigations.

KEY TERMS

Acceptance letter Letter issued by the insurance company to the proposer, formally communicating its acceptance of the proposal.

First premium receipt Receipt issued by the insurance company as an acknowledgement of payment of first instalment of premium. It is an evidence of insurance contract.

Moral hazard report Report on hazards or conditions that increase the chances of loss arising from individual moral weaknesses or general, social and economic conditions.

Primary underwriter The term used for insurance agents as they are the primary source of information about the insured.

Risk A potential source of loss, injury or damage, which is the subject matter of insurance itself.

Underwriting policy Basic philosophy or fundamental principles of underwriting followed by an insurance company.

REVIEW QUESTIONS

23.1 Explain the concept of underwriting. What are the purposes of underwriting?

23.2 Explain the fundamental principles of underwriting.

23.3 Describe the important methods of rate determination in underwriting.

23.4 Discuss the role of different types of underwriters in the business of insurance.

23.5 'The agents are also called as the **first line** or primary underwriters'. Comment.

24

Policy Servicing and Claims Settlement

Learning Objectives

After going through this chapter we will be able to:

- Describe various insurance documents.
- Explain the procedure involved in policy servicing.
- Describe the procedure towards alterations; revival.
- Distinguish between nomination and assignment.
- Elucidate the concept of surrender value; paid-up value.
- Comprehend the rules governing policy loans and lost policies.
- Understand the procedure for settlement of death claims in life insurance.
- Describe the procedure for settlement of maturity claims in life insurance.
- Discuss some recent improvements in policy servicing.

Insurance is a contract between the insurer and the insured. Although verbal agreements are as much valid as written agreements, a contract of insurance has to be in the document form. Thus, the first step in the process of insurance involves the written proposal made by the potential insured (also known as the **proposer**) in a prescribed application form issued by insurance companies. After selecting a policy, the proposer is required to provide information about income, age and health. Where the terms of the policy so require, the agent also sends the insured's medical examination report in confidence, to the insurance company. Normally, the agent or the development officer does preliminary underwriting. The agent or the development officer, as the case may be, sends a report to the company, giving details about the financial position of the proposer besides defining the need and adequacy of insurance for the proposer. The information gathered by the agent/development officer from his personal sources or inquiries is also included in the report along with the information supplied by the proposer. The insurance company then conducts a detailed scrutiny of the documents that are submitted to it.

24.1 INSURANCE DOCUMENTS

Policy servicing involves the following documents:

24.1.1 Proposal Forms

Proposal form issued by the company is used for making an application for the requisite insurance policy. The proposal form contains queries intended to extract all material information concerning the particular risk that the insurance policy proposes to cover. The number and nature of queries would depend on the particular class of insurance covered.

In marine cargo insurance, proposal forms are not generally required. Instead, a questionnaire or a declaration form, duly completed may be asked for. Proposal forms are used for hull insurance.

In fire insurance, the procedure varies among the companies. Generally, proposal forms are used only in cases involving simple risks and are not required in cases of large industrial risks. For such cases, inspection of the risk is essentially undertaken before acceptance of the proposal.

In miscellaneous insurance, proposal forms are essentially required and they include a declaration, in accordance with the general principles of good faith.

Proposal forms generally contain the following items:

(i) Name of the proposer (in full)
(ii) Address of the proposer
(iii) Profession, occupation or business of the proposer
(iv) Particulars of previous and present insurance
(v) Loss experience
(vi) Sum insured
(vii) Other sections—signature, date, place, etc.

The proposal form must be accompanied with—(i) a valid proof of age, and (ii) medical report. The significance of these documents is discussed hereinafter.

Proof of age: Age is the main basis of calculation of premium on life insurance policies. Since, old age people have high probability of dying than the younger ones, premium is calculated on the basis of age groups. In other words, the rate of premium varies with the age of the life assured at the time of taking out a policy. Age is also significant from the point of view of underwriting decision, as the physical health of a person is generally consistent with his age. It is, therefore, essential that the correct age should be stated in the proposal papers. Currently all policies are issued with the age being duly admitted. Where the age has not been admitted, the policyholders may be advised to furnish the age proof without any delay.

Documents that are considered valid *proofs of age* are:

- Certified extract from municipal or other records made at the time of birth
- Baptism certificate or certified copy from family Bible, if it contains age or date of birth
- Certified copy of school or college-certificate, if age or date of birth is stated therein
- Certified extract from service register in case of govt. employees and employees of quasi govt; institutions including public limited companies
- Passport issued by the passport authorities in India

Besides this, some other documents like identity cards issued by the election commission, electoral roll record, etc. may also be accepted as proofs of age.

Medical report: Where the age of the insured is high or the first level examination carries some adverse remarks, the insurer may refer the proposal for a thorough medical examination, particularly when the amount of insurance is also very high. However, the medical examination may be waived, like in rural areas, with no or little medical facilities. The medical report, where required, along with other documents is delivered to the underwriter who has the power to accept or reject the proposal or accept the proposal with such conditions, exclusions or omissions as he may deem fit. He may even recommend a change in the sum assured or the amount of premium to be charged and manner in which the premium is to be paid.

According to section 45 of the Insurance Act, 1938, the policy shall be declared void and all claims in respect of it shall cease in case of any untrue or incorrect statement contained in the proposal, personal statement, declaration and other documents or in the case of concealment of any material information.

24.1.2 First Premium Receipt

The insurance company issues the first premium receipt after the insured has paid the first instalment of premium. This receipt is an acknowledgement of the proposal and contains all the particulars of the policy.

24.1.3 Policy Bond/Form

A policy bond/form is an evidence of the contract of insurance. Different policy forms are used for different classes of insurance. A policy bond must be duly executed and stamped in compliance with provisions of the Indian Stamp Act, 1899. If the insurance policy belongs to the class of insurance that is governed by a tariff or a market agreement, it would be mandatory for the insurers to apply the policy wording prescribed therein.

The following are the common constituents of policy forms:

Recital clause: The opening section of the policy is termed as *recital clause* as it recites the parties to the contract.

Operative clause: The operative clause defines the conditions under which the insurer agrees to make payment to the insured. In other words, it spells out the mutual responsibilities and obligations of both parties to the contract of insurance.

Attestation clause: This clause sets out the rules for the signing of the policy, which depend upon the practice of the insurers responsible for the execution of documents.

Conditions: All policies of insurance contain conditions, necessary to legalize the contract. The conditions that are printed on the policy form are called **express conditions**. Certain other conditions like good faith, insurable interest, etc. are implied.

Schedule: The schedule, commonly include details of the policy number, first and annual premiums, renewal date, name and address of the parties and the period of insurance, with the date of maturity of the policy.

Endorsement: If it is proposed at the time of issue of the policy to alter the terms and conditions of the policy, it is done by setting out the alteration in a memorandum, which is attached to the policy and forms part of it. The memorandum is called an **endorsement**.

In fire insurance, the operative clause of a fire cover note is issued in consideration of the proposer named in the schedule having proposed the outcome of an insurance against fire for the period mentioned, on the usual terms and conditions of the company's policy.

In motor vehicle insurance, motor cover notes are required to be issued in the form prescribed by the motor tariff.

24.1.4 Certificate of Insurance

In motor insurance, in addition to the policy, a certificate of insurance is required by the Motor Vehicle Act, 1988. This certificate provides evidence of insurance to the police and registration authorities. It contains the essential features of the cover including the terms and conditions.

In marine insurance, certificate of insurance is issued to provide evidence of cover on shipments insured under cargo open cover or floating policies.

24.1.5 Cover Note

Issue of a document called **cover note** precedes the policy. It is issued when the policy cannot for some reason or the other, be issued at once. Cover notes are issued when the negotiations for insurance are underway, and it is necessary to provide cover on a provisional basis. The cover note is issued for a temporary period of time during which the policy is prepared and is an evidence of protection to prove that cover is in force. It contains a brief detail of a cover. In marine insurance, marine cover notes are usually issued when all the details required for the issue of policy such as name of the steamer, number of packages or exact value, etc. are not known.

24.2 NOMINATION AND ASSIGNMENT: A COMPARISON

There are two ways by which a policyholder can ensure that on the claim arising by death, the policy moneys could be paid without requiring production of a succession certificate or letters of administration. The two methods are to make either an assignment or a nomination. These methods are discussed here.

24.2.1 Nomination

Nomination is the process whereby a person so named in the policy becomes entitled to receive the policy amount in the event of the death of the policyholder. Section 39 of the Insurance Act, 1938 governs nomination of an insurance policy. Accordingly, nomination may be done at the time of commencement of the policy by giving particulars of the nominee in the proposal form. It may even be done later by giving notice in a prescribed form to the insurer and endorsing it on the policy bond. The policyholder can similarly change nomination any number of times during the term of the policy. The right to nominate, vests only with a policyholder; that too on a policy covering his own life. However, nomination under joint life policy in order to be valid, can only be a joint nomination by the joint holders. Nomination so notified to the insurance company should be registered by it in its records. Nomination does not confer any right on the nominee if the policyholder is alive but if he dies before the policy expires, the nominee would be legally recognised as the person entitled to the payment of the policy amount. Death of the nominee would lead to automatic revocation of the nomination. Nomination, however, is not allowed in the case of children's policies, until the child attains majority. In case of other policies where the nominee is a minor, an appointee has to be appointed to receive the policy amount in the event of the policyholder's death. No nomination is allowed under a policy financed from HUF funds.

24.2.2 Assignment

An assignment of a policy may be defined as an instrument whereby the beneficial interest, title and the right under a policy is transferred either absolutely or conditionally by one person to another person. Thus, it is a method by which one living person who is entitled to transferable interest in a policy conveys it to another living person or to himself and another living person/s. The assignor forgoes all his rights, title and interest in the policy to the assignee immediately on execution of assignment in favour of the assignee. The premium/loan interest notices, etc. in such cases will also be sent by the insurer to the assignee and not to the policyholder that is, the assignor.

Section 38 of the Insurance Act, 1938 governs assignment of a life insurance policy. The assignor, being a major, either by endorsement on the policy or by a separate duly stamped Deed, can make assignment. This may be done out of feelings or emotions or even for financial consideration. Assignment must be made in writing under the signature of the assignor, which should be witnessed by a person. Notice of assignment is required to be submitted to the insurance company. Assignments are of two kinds:

Conditional assignment: Under this kind of assignment, the assignor and the assignee may agree to suspend or revoke the assignment, either wholly or partially, on the happening of a specified event provided the event does not depend on the will of the assignor. Conditional assignment is typically effected out of feelings of natural love and affection and not for monetary consideration.

Absolute assignment: This kind of assignment is irreversible. The assignor's rights, title and beneficial interest that he has in the policy gets transferred to the assignee without any possibility of reversion thereof, to the assignor or his estate in any event. Absolute assignment is usually done for valuable consideration.

Generally, an assignment once legally made cannot be cancelled. If necessary, it can be done only by another legally valid assignment. The assignee however, has the right to reassign the policy. He also has a right to sue under the policy. Assignment of the policy results in automatic cancellation of a prior nomination unless of course, the policy is assigned to the insurer for loan, etc. Under conditional assignment, if the assignee dies, the benefit under the policy goes back to the policyholder or to his nominee, if the policyholder has died. On the other hand, the policy benefits get passed on to the legal representatives of the deceased assignee in case of absolute assignment.

24.2.3 Nomination vs. Assignment

For a clear understanding of the effects of nomination and assignment, it is important to distinguish between the two. The distinction between nomination and assignment is given hereinafter.

(i) Nomination can be made only by the life assured. While assignment can be made by the absolute owner of the policy, (either proposer or the life assignee) or the person having requisite authority from such owners.

(ii) Nomination is effected where Insurance Act, 1938 applies, i.e., in India or where similar enactment apply viz., in Pakistan and Ceylon. Assignment can be executed anywhere in the world according to the law of that country.

(iii) Notice of nomination is required to safeguard the nominee's interest notice of assignment is required to enable the assignee to acquire priority over earlier assignee.

(iv) Appointment can be incorporated in the wording of the nomination but not in the wording of the assignment as in this case, appointment of a guardian would be necessary.

(v) Nomination can be made before issue of the policy but a policy cannot be assigned until it is issued as the life assured acquires the property under the policy only after it has been issued to him.

(vi) Nomination made after the issue of the policy requires an endorsement on the policy document. It cannot be done by a deed whereas policy may be assigned after the policy has been issued, either by an endorsement on the policy or by a stamped deed.

(vii) Nomination does not transfer the rights of the assured in respect of the policy and he can deal with the policy in any manner without requiring the consent of the nominee. Assignment creates vested interest in favour of the assignee whose consent is necessary in all businesses relating to the policy. The assured, thus, loses control over the policy.

(viii) Nomination need not be made for a monetary consideration whereas assignment unless done among blood relations, is always against some pecuniary consideration.

(ix) Nomination would be valid even if it is not witnessed but a valid assignment must be witnessed.

(x) Nomination is normally in favour of relatives. Assignment can be in favour of anybody.

(xi) The right to sue under the policy is possessed by the assignee and not by the nominee, so long as the assured is alive.

(xii) Cancellation of the nomination is possible by a change of nomination, or by an assignment but there is no way by which an assignment may be cancelled. In fact, reassignment of the policy can be done only by the assignee.

(xiii) Nomination of a minor requires only the appointment of an appointee by the policyholder. Appointment of a minor as an assignee, requires appointment of a guardian the assignee's father or any other authorised person.

(xiv) In case of nomination, the creditors of the life assured can attach the policy moneys whereas the creditors cannot attach the policy moneys in case of assignment unless the assignment was made to defraud the creditors.

(xv) Nominee's right is only to collect policy moneys on the death of the assured and when paid by the insurer. On receipt of the notice the insurer has to recognize the assignee as the person legally entitled to receive the policy benefits.

(xvi) If nominee dies, the nomination becomes ineffective. If a conditional assignee dies, the right under the policy reverts to the life assured, depending upon the terms of assignment. If an absolute assignee dies the right devolves upon his/her heirs.

(xvii) If the nominee dies after the life assured and before settlement of the claim, the policy moneys would be payable to the heirs of the life assured. If the assignee (absolute or conditional) dies after the life assured and before settlement, the policy moneys would be payable to the heirs of the assignee.

24.3 ALTERATIONS

If the policyholder so intends he/she may get the terms of the policy altered after it is issued provided the policy is operational and has not become fully paid up. However, the prospectus issued by the insurer must clearly provide that no alteration from one class of assurance to another, subject to a lower scale of premium is allowed. An alteration from the 'with-profits limited payment plan' to the 'with-profits endowment assurance plan' may be allowed as an exception.

Some of the commonly sought alterations include:

(a) Alteration in name
(b) Reduction in the sum assured
(c) Adding double accident benefit and extended disability benefit
(d) Alteration in class or term
(e) Removal of an extra premium
(f) Alteration in the mode of payment of premiums
(g) Alteration form without profits plan to with-profits plan
(h) Correction in policies

However, no alterations except for the following are generally allowed within one year of the policy's commencement:

1. Required alterations such as alteration in name, corrections in policies, alteration involving currency of payment of policy moneys and alteration regarding age proving higher or lower than what was stated at the time of proposal.
2. Requests for addition of double accident benefit, extended disability benefit.
3. Mode of payment of premium to *monthly* so as to bring the policy under salary saving scheme or to finance the same from provident fund account.
4. Conversion of ordinary policies to those issued under Married Women's Property Act, as provided in the manual on the subject of *Married Women's Property Act*.

24.3.1 Alteration Fee

Alteration fee is charged in the following cases:

(i) Alteration in the mode of payment resulting in increase in the frequency of payment of premium instalments, e.g., alteration from yearly to half-yearly, quarterly or monthly, etc.
(ii) Alteration involving addition of double accident benefit or extended disability benefit after the issue of the policy and such benefit is not granted from the commencement.
(iii) Alteration involving reduction in the sum assured.
(iv) Alteration requesting for addition of premium waiver benefit under a child deferred annuity policy after its issue and such benefit is not granted from the commencement.

The following alterations do not require any payment of alteration fee:

(i) Alteration essentially required to be made when the policyholder's age is stated incorrectly in the policy.

(ii) The age declared in the policy may be understated or overstated.

(iii) Alteration to reduce the frequency of payment of premium instalments in a year.

(iv) Alteration required in the name of the assured, nominee, assignee, etc. in the policy.

24.4 REVIVAL

If the policyholder commits a default in making payment of the premium within the grace period, the policy would lapse. However, in such a case, the policy can be revived through a fresh contract within a period of 5 years from the date when the default in premium payment is first made, that is, the date of first unpaid premium. Thus, revival of the policy grants the insurer the right to impose fresh terms and conditions. There are various ways to get the policy revived. Where the policy is revived within 6 months from the date when the first unpaid premium became actually due, the policy is revived as ordinary revival on payment of delayed premiums along with interest. The rate of interest would depend on the date of commencement of the policy. The policyholder is not required to submit a personal statement regarding health in this case. Where the revival of the policy is done on non-medical basis, the amount to be revived cannot exceed the prescribed limit for non-medical assurance and where it is done on medical basis the required medical requirements, varying with the amount to be revived must be fulfilled. The insurance companies may also offer some other schemes like revival by instalments, loan-cum-revival, survival benefit-cum-revival, special revival scheme, etc.

24.5 POLICY LOANS

The insurance companies, generally offer loans on certain policies to the policyholders although subject to certain terms and conditions. For this, an application on a prescribed form, duly completed is required to be submitted by the policyholder to the insurance company along with the policy bond. The loan amount however, is calculated on the basis of the policy's surrender value (explained later in the chapter). The maximum loan amount granted by the insurance companies may vary. For instance, LIC of India grants a maximum loan amount of upto 90 per cent under a policy. However, in case of paid-up policies, it is 85 per cent of the surrender value of the policy including cash value of bonus. Similarly, the rate of interest charged on loans taken on insurance policies and the terms and conditions of repayment too vary from company to company and from time to time. For instance, LIC of India provides for a minimum repayment of ₹50 followed by multiples of ₹10. Moreover, loan is granted for a minimum period of six months from the date of its payment. If however, claim on the policy accrues due to maturity of the policy or death of the policyholder within six months from the date of loan, interest will be charged only upto the date of maturity or death, as the case may be. The amount of loan plus interest thereon, if any, is deducted from the claim amount payable by the insurance company, if the loan amount is not repaid during the term of the policy or early claim and the claimant would be paid only the balance amount. LIC of India provides for charging of interest on *compound interest* basis in case if the interest is not paid regularly, every half-year. If the premiums are not paid regularly, that is, if the policy is not kept in force, there is a possibility that the loan amount along with accrued interest would exceed the surrender value inviting action of foreclosure against the policy. Some insurance plans are not eligible for loan. For example, loans are not available against children plans, special plans like Jeevan Griha; deferred annuity/pension plans and money back plans.

24.6 SURRENDER VALUE AND PAID-UP VALUE

The life insurance is essentially a cooperative enterprise. The premiums paid by the policyholders are pooled together and the balance of amount after paying the claims of those policyholders who have unfortunately died and meeting the expenses of management, etc. is formed into a fund, which mounts up at interest. Accordingly, when any one of the policyholders desires to opt out of the cooperative enterprise, he is not entitled for refund of the entire amount paid by him. Hence, the amount paid as cash value on surrender of a policy contract is lower than the premiums paid, which is also called **surrender value** of the policy. Thus, surrender value is the cash value of the policy that is payable by the insurance company if the policy contract is voluntarily terminated before the expiry of the term of the policy by the insured. LIC of India allows surrender of the policy only after premiums have been paid for at least three years. Although the method of calculating surrender value varies from company to company but generally, it is restricted to the amount of premiums paid up to the time of surrender, along with attached bonuses, if any. Surrender value would also depend upon the remaining duration of the policy and duration of the policy that has already elapsed on the date of surrender. Duration elapsed under the policy is the time gap between date of surrender and date of commencement of the policy as rounded off to the nearest 'half-year'. The final calculation of the surrender value is based on the appropriate surrender value factor per ₹100 paid-up value, in relation to the plan, duration elapsed and original term of the policy. The paid-up value too is proportional to the number of years the premium has been paid but the *paid-up value* is much more than the *surrender value*. If the policy is turned into *paid-up*, the amount receivable would be much more than the surrender value. Moreover, no further premiums would be payable by the insured. However, the amount would not be payable by the insurer immediately. Rather payment would become due only on the maturity of the policy or on the death of the insured during the term of the policy.

Thus,

Surrender value (SV) =

$$\frac{\text{Paid-up value (inclusive of vested bonus, if any)} \times \text{SV factor}}{100}$$

where,

$$\text{Paid-up value} = \frac{\text{Number of years' premium paid} \times \text{Sum assured}}{\text{Number of years' premium payable}}$$

For example, if the sum assured for a policy is ₹5,00,000, plan and term of the policy is endowment policy (with profits), for 20 years; mode of payment of premium is half-yearly; the date of commencement of the policy is January 1, 1994; due date of last premium paid is March 1, 2006; the date of calculation of surrender value is March 1, 2006 and accumulated vested bonus is ₹3,85,000, then the surrender value and the paid-up value in respect of the policy would be calculated as follows:

Number of years' premium paid = (01.01.2006 – 01.01.1994)
= 12 years

Term of the policy = 20 years

Paid-up value = $\frac{12}{20} \times 5,00,000$ = ₹3,00,000

Vested bonus = ₹3,85,000

Then

Paid-up value (including vested bonus)

= Paid-up value + Vested bonus

= ₹3,00,000 + ₹3,85,000 = ₹6,85,000

and,

$$\text{Surrender value} = \frac{\text{Paid-up value} \times \text{Surrender value factor}}{100}$$

24.7 ISSUE OF DUPLICATE POLICY

The insurer may issue a duplicate policy in certain cases, as for instance when the original policy is lost. However, the issue of the duplicate policy does not mean change in the rights and obligations in respect of the original policy. They remain unaffected. The following are the requirements for issuing a duplicate policy:

1. Where the policy is reported to have been lost, an advertisement at the cost of policyholder in any English daily newspaper having wide circulation in the state in which the policy is said to be lost is a prerequisite. A copy of the newspaper in which the advertisement appeared should be sent to the servicing office within one month of its appearance. If no objection has been lodged with the insurance company regarding the policy, a duplicate policy will be issued after complying with the requirements of *indemnity bond* and payment of charges for preparing duplicate policy and stamp fee.
2. The requirement of advertisement and indemnity bond may be dispensed with or modified in certain circumstances like loss of policy by theft, destruction of policy by fire, mutilated, dog-eared or damaged policy.

24.8 LOST POLICIES

The life insurance policy is an instrument substantiating a contract and defining in it the obligations of the insurer on the one hand, and the insured on the other. Since this document provides a security transferable by the owner, it should be taken proper care of. The importance of the policy document is particularly felt in the following cases:

1. On a claim arising from the policy when the policy document is required to be delivered to the insurer for settlement of claim.
2. When the policyholder desires to raise a loan on the security of the policy, the document is required to be lodged with the insurer or a bank from which the loan is to be raised.
3. If the policyholder proposes to take the surrender value of the policy in cancellation of the policy document, the policy is required to be submitted to the insurer before the payment is made.

However, sometimes, the policy gets lost and the policyholder is anxious to have a duplicate policy issued in the place of the lost one. The loss or destruction of a policy document does not, in any way, absolve the insurance company of the liability of payment of policy moneys when the claim arises. If the policy is lost or destroyed, claim will be paid to the claimant who furnishes an indemnity bond jointly with one surety.

24.9 CLAIMS SETTLEMENT IN LIFE INSURANCE

Every agent has certain responsibilities towards his clients who have taken insurance policies through his agency. The duty begins as soon as a policy is issued and ends when the claim is settled. During this period the agent is expected to meet his policyholders and help them to get whatever service desired from the insurer promptly in respect of the policies sold. However, the best opportunity, which an agent gets to serve his policyholders, arises when the policy results into claim by death or maturity of the policy. The agent has to help the policyholders in complying with the requirements swiftly, so that no delay is caused in settlement of claims. If the agent gives *after sales service* to his clients satisfactorily, he will create goodwill for himself in the minds of his clients and also improve his chances of getting additional business. This would also help in building a positive image about the insurer in the society. An agent should know among other things the various requirements for settlement of claims by death and claims on maturity in order to serve his policyholders in a better way.

The life insurance claims can be classified into two categories: (i) Death claims, and (ii) Maturity claims. The procedure involved in settlement of claims in these cases is as follows:

24.9.1 Death Claims

Death claim arises in cases where the insured dies before the expiry of the term of the policy. The insurer has to be informed about the death of the life assured in writing. The insurer may be intimated by the nominee or his representative; the assignee or his representative; a nearest relative of the life assured; the employer and the agent of the deceased insured or development officer. Particulars like policy number, name of the life assured, the date of death, the cause of death and the relationship of the informant to the deceased are to be mentioned. The intimation must be made by a concerned person who shall also be required to confirm the identity of the deceased person as the life assured under the policy.

The insurer may even get the necessary information from other sources like obituary columns, or newspaper reports in case of accidents or air crashes. The action towards settlement of the claim can be initiated as soon as the information reaches the insurance office without waiting for the intimation of the claim to be received. However, identity of the deceased assured must of course be established.

The following information is required to be submitted by the claimant:

(i) Date of death
(ii) Reason and place of death
(iii) Complete details of the policies held by the life assured

Death claims are further categorized into following two types:

Non-early death claims: It arises in cases where the death of the life assured occurs after 3 years from the date of commencement of policy or the date of last revival/reinstatement of the policy. If the policy is operative till the date of death of the life assured by regular payment of premiums, full sum assured becomes payable along with bonus (in case of with profits policy). The following documents are required to be submitted for the settlement of the death claim:

- Policy document (policy bond)
- Death certificate from the appropriate authority
- A legal evidence of title where the claimant is neither an assignee nor a nominee
- Abridged claim form
- Discharge form duly signed
- Assignment/reassignment deed, if any
- Age proof only where age is not already admitted

Once the above documents are received and if they are found in order, claim is settled by making the payment to the person entitled thereto.

Early death claims: It arises in cases where the death of life assured occurs within 3 years from commencement of the policy. The following documents, duly completed are required to be submitted for the settlement of the death claim:

- Statement from the medical attendants who last treated the deceased life assured
- Certificate of the treatment issued by the hospital authorities where the deceased was last treated
- Certificate issued by the employer where the deceased was an employee
- Certificate of the burial/cremation signed by a responsible person who attended the funeral of the deceased

The documents that must be tendered for settlement of death claims would depend upon the cause of the death, and thus vary with each case as discussed hereinafter.

- Cases of accidental death must first be reported to the police and an FIR (first information report), police inquest report (PIR), and post-mortem report (PMR) if conducted, are required to be submitted.
- Where death takes place within 2 years from date of commencement of the policy, an investigation is conducted to establish the authenticity of the claim and accordingly the accidental benefits are settled.
- In case of murder of the life assured, FIR and the report that a legal case was initiated against the accused are necessary. In such cases the settlement of the claim will be withheld until the decision of the case.

- In case of death due to an air crash, a certificate issued by airline authorities certifying that the assured was a passenger on the plane would be needed.
- In case of death caused by a ship-accident, a certified extract from the logbook of the ship would be required.
- In case of sudden heart failures, the doctor's certificate must be attached.
- In case of defence personnel, a certificate from the commanding officer of the unit is obligatory.
- Where a court enquiry is ordered, the report of the enquiry should be obtained.

The death claim amount is payable to the nominee or the assignee as the case may be. In the absence of assignment or nomination of the policy, a legal evidence of title such as *succession certificate* or *letters of administration* or *probate of will* would be mandatory to be entitled to the claim. In case of policies involving very small amounts the proof of title may, however be waived by the insurer. This is usually allowed in those cases where, the deceased has left no other estate and there is no dispute among the survivors about the policy claims.

The assignee is entitled to the payment in the case of absolute assignment. But if the absolute assignee dies, then the benefit goes to the estate of the assignee and in case if the conditional assignee dies, the right of claim gets passed back to the assured.

In case of loss of policy document, an advertisement regarding the loss of the policy is necessary as a preventative measure. Payment can be made by the insurer on being satisfied about the bona fides of the case and on the execution of an indemnity bond by the claimant.

The intimation claim must be made within a maximum of 3 years from the death. Otherwise, the same becomes time barred and the claimant must accordingly be informed. In case if the death occurred within 3 years from the date of commencement or revival of the policy, the insurance company is required to conduct investigations without knowledge of the claimant, on receiving the claim forms. If no fraud or concealment of material facts is exposed in the investigation the insurance company issues the required discharge forms for completion.

Sometimes, insurers may grant concessions while settling the claims. That is, under certain plans payment of full sum assured is made by the insurer after deduction of unpaid premiums with interest till the date of death and in the event of the death of the life assured within a period of six months or one year from the date of the first unpaid premium. Payment of full sum assured is made after unpaid premiums falling due before the next anniversary of the policy are deducted provided premiums have been paid for at least three years and five years, respectively. However, the insurance companies may decline death claims in cases where the material information is fraudulently concealed, but only after an opportunity is given to the claimant to make a representation for consideration, and by the review committees of the zonal office and the central office. The final decision is based on the merits of each case.

24.9.2 Maturity Claims

Payment of maturity claims is made in accordance with the terms and conditions of the policy. Life insurance policies are generally endowment policies including money back policies. These policies have predetermined date of maturity, which is shown in the policy bond. The amount payable at the time of maturity includes sum assured and bonuses payable on the policy. The branch office of the insurance company that services the policy generally send intimations regarding the maturity claims in advance through *claim intimation letter* along with the required *discharge voucher* to be executed by the assured. If no intimation is received from the concerned branch office, the policyholder may contact the office, mentioning the policy number. Where the policy document is either not available or is lost, the settlement of claim can be on the basis of an indemnity bond from the policyholder. For large amounts a reliable surety of sound financial means may also be asked for.

The following documents are needed in the case of maturity claims:

(i) Original policy bond
(ii) Age proof, if the age was not admitted earlier
(iii) Assignment deed, if any
(iv) Discharge form duly completed and executed

Procedure for settlement of maturity claims: After the duly completed, stamped discharge form is received along with the policy documents, the insurance company settles the claim by issuing an account payee/ crossed/order cheque. In the case of *money back plans* where periodical survival benefits are paid in instalments, the policy document will be returned to the policyholder after due endorsements are made on the policy document and in policy records. If the discharge form is lost, say, in transit, the insurance company can issue a duplicate discharge form. Policy bond and discharge form are not required for survival benefit payment of upto ₹60,000.

However, if the assured or the person authorized to sign the discharge form becomes mentally unstable, a court certificate issued under the Indian Lunacy Act, appointing a person to act as his/her guardian would be required to be presented. In case if the assured has been adjudged insolvent by a court of law after the issue of the policy but before the maturity of the policy, the official assignee appointed by the court will have to be informed by the insurance company about the date of maturity and other details of the policy. But, in this case, the official assignee will be required to send a notice along with a certified copy of the court's order declaring the assured as insolvent and appointing him as the assignee. The insurer would be legally bound to comply with any prohibitory order of court or a notice from income tax department under section 226(3) of the Income Tax Act, unless the assured has obtained a proper withdrawal order.

Where the life assured is reported to have died before the date of maturity, the claim is settled as death claim but if he is reported to have died after the date of maturity the claim is settled by the insurance company as a maturity claim and paid to the legal heirs.

The Indian Evidence Act provides that death may be presumed, if a person is not heard of for a continuous period of seven years by those who would have heard of him if he were alive. In this case the premiums are paid until presumption of death on receiving a decree of presumption of death from a court of law or else the payment would be made after obtaining the court decree as per the status of the policy as on the date when the premiums stopped.

As per the law relating of HUF, all income earned in respect of the property of HUF, shall belong to HUF. As such where policies are taken on the lives of members of HUF and premiums there-under are paid out of HUF funds, insurance amount when due would belong to HUF and it becomes a part of assets of HUF. However, under policies effected by the family members on their own lives and where premiums are paid out of their own separate income, policy moneys when due become the part of the estate of the lives assured. It is also important to note that neither the Karta of HUF nor any member thereon can take out policies on their own lives for their own benefits or for the benefit of their dependents and finance them to the detriment of joint family funds. If, therefore, policy is financed through HUF funds irrespective of contractual positions enumerated in the policy document, with regard to the title thereto, the policy would belong to HUF entirely and as such the policy moneys would be payable only to the Karta of HUF who represents HUF as Manager. However, a member of HUF can take a policy on his own life for the benefit of his immediate family, provided the premiums there are not paid from HUF funds.

Payments of claims to non-resident claimants are governed by the foreign exchange control regulations.

Section 6 of the Married Women's Property Act, 1874, (MWP ACT) provides that a policy of insurance effected by any married man on his own life, and expressed on the face of it to be for the benefit of his wife, or of his wife and children, or any of them, shall ensure and be deemed to be a trust for the benefit of his wife, or of his wife and children, or any of them according to the interest so expressed, and shall not, so long as any object of the trust remains, be subject to the control of the husband, or to his creditors, or form part of his estate. Section 6 thus not only provides for a simple method by which a married man can make a settlement for the benefit of his dependents without the formality of a deed of settlement but operates to give the beneficiaries under such a policy certain statutory privileges by virtue of which they secure decidedly better protection than they would get under a voluntary settlement outside the Act.

No claim is legally acceptable in respect of a lapsed policy or if the life assured dies within 3 years from the date of commencement of the policy except where premiums are paid for at least 3 years before the payment of premiums stopped. Here, the nominee is paid a proportionate paid-up value on the policy. But if a minimum of 2 years' premiums are paid and life assured dies within 3 months from the date of first unpaid premium, then full sum assured is payable along with payment of bonus, subject to reclamation of the premium already fallen due in addition to the premium that falls during the policy anniversary. If the life assured dies any time between 3 and 6 months from first unpaid premium, only an amount equal to 59 per cent of the basic sum assured is payable. However, in this case neither any bonus is paid and nor are any arrears of premium allowed to be received. And if the life assured dies any time between 6 months and 1 year from first unpaid premium, only notional paid-up value is paid.

Additional benefits offered in settlement of claims include

Double accident benefit: A life insurance policy may offer an additional benefit in cases where the cause of the death is an accident, in addition to and proportionate to the basic sum assured in accordance with the policy contract. The claimant has to provide required evidence as per the policy conditions regarding the accident being the cause of death in order to claim the benefit. For this, documents like FIR, post-mortem report, etc. are required to be submitted.

Disability benefit claims: Some policies provide for waiver of all future premiums under the policy along with an extended disability benefit of a regular monthly payment in accordance with the policy conditions provided that the disability is total and permanent making the person incapable of earning any wage/compensation/salary or profit as a result of the accident

24.10 IMPROVEMENTS IN POLICY SERVICING

With the increasing competition levels in the insurance industry, all the major insurance players are making a conscious effort at serving their clients to the best of their capabilities within the constraint of their resources. Life Insurance Corporation of India endeavours to take the lead in providing efficient service to its clients. All 2048 branches of LIC of India are fully computerized covering all policy servicing aspects to give timely and efficient computerized services from new policy introduction, acceptance of renewal premium, revivals, loans, etc. to final claims settlement. Green channel facility introduced by the corporation ensures speedy completion of proposals. Provision of premium payment through internet and through service providers, viz. HDFC bank, ICICI bank, UTI bank, etc. is of great convenience to the customers. Policy records are transferred from one branch office to another for servicing on the request of the policyholder. However, the policyholder must, without delay, inform the branch office, responsible for servicing the policy, about the change of his/her address for better service and quicker settlement of claims.

The LIC of India has set-up claims review committees, which give opportunity to the claimant to make representation in cases of repudiation, for consideration by the review committees at the zonal office and the central office. The grievance redressal machinery has been further expanded with the appointment of insurance ombudsman at different centres. At present, there are 12 centres operating all over the country.

The following types of complaints fall under the purview of the ombudsman:

1. Any partial or total repudiation of claims by an insurer
2. Any dispute in regard to premiums paid if payable in terms of the policy
3. Any dispute on the legal construction of the policies in so far as such disputes relate to claims
4. Delay in settlement of claims
5. Non-issue of any insurance document to customers after receipt of premium

Policyholder can approach the insurance ombudsman for the redressal of their complaints free of cost.

KEY TERMS

Claim intimation letter Formal notice to the insurer about the loss and claiming payment for the loss in accordance with the terms of contract.

Endorsement A clause added to an insurance policy that changes the coverage.

Ombudsman Official or agency responsible for impartially investigating complaints from consumers against a public authority, institution or a company.

Paid-up value The reduced amount payable by the insurer in the event of discontinuation of payment of premiums after premiums are paid for the first three years.

Policy bond Policy contract, duly executed and containing the terms and conditions of the contract.

Proposal form Prescribed form issued by the insurance company duly executed for securing an insurance policy.

Redressal Compensation or reparation for a loss or wrong experienced by a party.

Surrender value The amount of money that a policyholder can withdraw on his surrendering his right under a policy before its maturity and terminating the contract of insurance.

REVIEW QUESTIONS

24.1 Write a note on the important documents used in a contract of insurance.

24.2 Elucidate the procedure involved in servicing of insurance policies.

24.3 What are the particulars required for evaluating an insurance proposal?

24.4 Distinguish between nomination and assignment.

24.5 Can a life insurance policy once issued be altered? If yes, how and on what basis? How is the 'surrender value' of a life insurance policy determined? How does it differ from 'paid-up value' of a policy?

24.6 Explain the requirements for settlement of death claims.

24.7 Discuss the rules governing policy loans and lost policies.

24.8 Describe the procedure for settlement of maturity claims.

24.9 Discuss some recent improvements in policy servicing.

24.10 Distinguish between death claims and maturity claims.

24.11 How can a policy be assigned? What are the effects of assignment of a policy?

24.12 Write short notes on

(i) Proposal form
(ii) Policy bond
(iii) Policy revival
(iv) Cover note
(v) Lost policies
(vi) Issue of duplicate policy
(vii) Alteration fee
(viii) Surrender value vs. Paid-up value

25

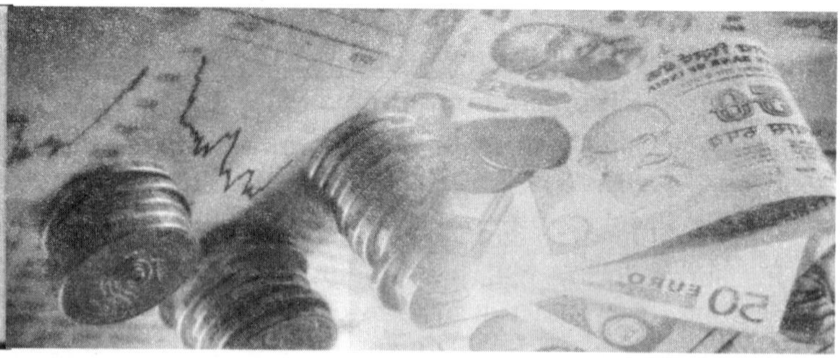

Channels of Distribution

Learning Objectives

After going through this chapter we will be able to:

- Understand the role of various insurance intermediaries.
- Describe the regulations governing insurance intermediaries.
- Understand the concept of bancassurance.
- Discuss the advantages of bancassurance.
- Discuss the significance of bancassurance for Indian insurance sector.
- Describe the different bancassurance models.

Recently the insurance industry has been under tremendous focus throughout the world due to a number of events. Frequent unforeseen claims have beleaguered the insurance industry resulting adversely. Persistent anxiety for improved services has blocked the insurance organizations to revamp the way the services are being provided. Such and other factors have indeed made the insurance business a complex one. Looking at the complexity of the industry it is becoming increasingly necessary for the insurance companies to work closely with clients using the domain experts and incisive technological understanding to create customized solutions that bring expected business returns.

25.1 INSURANCE INTERMEDIARIES AND THEIR FUNCTIONING

In today's scenario, businesses face increasingly complex risks and challenges. All the divisions of an organization—sales, customer services, human resources, technology, legal and finance—are intricately linked and dependent upon one another for smooth, profitable operations. Today insurers are chiefly relying on external service providers to build up and manage applications that will provide a rapid return on investment (ROI). In insurance and risk management, the expert external service providers assist in identifying, evaluating, reducing and managing risks. The service delivery network provides the benefit of ensuring that the insurance strategy and programmes are implemented consistently throughout the organization, and that no local gaps remain unattended. There have been significant changes in the insurance industry even in India, particularly as a consequence of the liberalization policy. As a result, a number of private companies have entered the insurance sector in India. Both, products as well as service front have witnessed a lot of innovations like provision of call centre facilities, e-servicing of products, etc.

From the point of view of consumers and marketers the role of various insurance intermediaries is discussed as follows:

25.1.1 Insurance Agents

Insurance agent has been defined under section 2(10) of the Insurance Act, 1938, as *an agent, licensed under the Act, who receives or agrees to receive payment by way of commission or other remuneration in consideration of his soliciting or procuring insurance business including business relating to continuance, renewal or revival of policies of insurance*. Insurance agents working solely for a particular insurance company are called **captive agents**. Independent insurance agents, also called **brokers** work for several companies. The Insurance Act, 1938, lays down the conditions governing the appointment and licensing of insurance agents, but the manner and the procedural details of the process of licensing as also other matters concerning agents are governed by insurance regulatory and development authority which has notified the rules under the IRDA (licensing of insurance agents) regulations, 2000. These rules provide that an insurance agent can be an individual, a firm, or a company formed under the Companies Act, 1956, including a banking company. Further, in order to be eligible, an individual besides being a major, must have passed the senior school level board examination, i.e., must have passed 12th standard examination. An insurance agent is required to obtain a licence from IRDA before conducting insurance business and to follow a code of conduct prescribed thereunder. Separate licences are required by agents to sell life and general insurance. Licences are issued only to applicants who manage to complete specified pre-licensing courses and also pass IRDA examinations. After the licence has been issued, the agent procures a letter of appointment from the insurance company for which he would be working. The letter formalizes the appointment and serves as the basis of his duties, responsibilities, authorities and obligations.

Life insurance products have customarily been marketed through insurance agents and these insurance agents have proved to be highly successful as means of distribution of insurance products. Insurance companies insist on forming an efficient, well trained team of agents who would be able to draw the attention of their prospective clients towards their own and their family's financial security and propose suitable policies for their requirements. The intensified use of the electronic media has altered the manner in which the agents interact with their clients. These days, insurance quotes are also obtained from a company's website. This development has helped in reducing the time the agents aggressively spend on the lookout for prospective clients. Insurance agents may also be able to get many new customers through referrals. The insurance companies obviously rely on their agents for the growth of their business. Insurance sales agents held approximately 11,00,000 jobs in 2005 out of which LIC of India alone accounted for over 6,51,000 agents. This speaks volumes about their contributions as insurance intermediaries. In case of non-life also the agents or development officers do much of the distribution work.

A life insurance agent is not authorized to conclude the contract with the buyer but simply forward the proposal form and other documents to the insurance company. He is responsible for preparing reports, maintaining records, find new clients, and assist both the insurer as well as the insured in settlement of claims on the occurrence of the loss. Since an effective sales force is a prerequisite for the success of the insurance business, agents are made to undergo rigorous, professional training programmes, which are both generic and particular. IRDA rules also require the agents to take a formal training programme. The 100-hour training programme conducted by the insurance companies takes care of the statutory requirement by the IRDA apart from providing training with regard to the insurance product offered by the company. Ultimately, of course, the success of the insurance agent would depend on the personal qualities of the agent like confidence, discipline, willingness to work hard, problem-solving ability, communicative skills, leadership qualities, etc. In India, a large number of people today, consider insurance sales agency as a good career option. This is because there are several benefits of becoming an insurance agent. The agents are constantly recognized and rewarded for their performance. They enjoy the most luring remuneration package.

25.1.2 Insurance Brokers

The Indian insurance market is in transitory phase, the sector has been opened up to compete with the entry of private insurance companies in late 1999. The global practice of using brokers to act as the principal distribution arm of the insurance companies, however, is growing in fits and starts. The primary role of the broker is to inspire in underwriters, on a case-by-case basis, the confidence to accept the risk presented. There can be no universal solution that will transform every risk into an attractive proposition for insurers, and for some employers this may well be impossible. Each case must be considered on its merits and individual problems addressed. Insurance broker is an individual or body corporate who canvasses insurance and places the same with insurance companies. An insurance broker is an agent of the insured. A broker is an independent professional and an expert in insurance matters, who assesses the specific insurance requirements of his clients, appraises the risk and recommends a suitable insurance cover for the clients. According to the IRDA annual report (2001–02), brokers are *professionals, who make provision for particular insurance needs of the client by evaluating the risk on behalf of the client, recommending ways to reduce the particular risk, finding out the most favourable insurance policy structure, bringing the insured and insurers together, carrying out preliminary task necessary for insurance contracts and providing assistance in the administration and performance of such contracts, if needed, particularly when claims arise.* Thus, while insurance agents are the agents of insurance companies, brokers are the agents of the insured and therefore their principal accountability is towards the insured.

The guidelines for issue of licence and regulation of affairs governing insurance brokers and insurance consultants have been issued by IRDA in 2002. The guidelines have categorized the brokers into the following categories:

Category I Direct general insurance broker

Category II Direct life insurance broker

Category III Reinsurance broker

Category IV Composite broker

Category V Insurance consultant

Some important provisions under the IRDA guidelines are discussed here[1]:

(i) The guidelines expressly provide for the qualification criteria and the functions that are expected to be performed by various classes of brokers. No person can function as a broker or an insurance intermediary unless a licence under regulations of the authority has been granted to him.

(ii) The net worth requirement fixed for composite insurance brokers is ₹2.50 crore with a cap of 26 per cent on non-Indian interest (foreign equity participation). For the purposes of these regulations, the calculations of non-Indian interest shall be made in the same manner as specified in insurance regulatory and development authority (registration of Indian insurance companies) regulations, 2000. The net worth requirement fixed for direct brokers and reinsurance brokers is ₹50 lakh and ₹2.00 crore, respectively. In addition, insurance consultants are required

[1] *Source:* www.irdaindia.org.

to furnish a bank guarantee of ₹5.00 lakh to IRDA. The capital in the case of a company limited by shares and a cooperative society shall be in the form of equity shares while in the case of other applicants shall be brought in cash. The applicant shall exclusively carry on the business of an insurance broker as licensed under these regulations.

(iii) IRDA determines the brokerage in compliance with market practices.

(iv) A solvency margin equal to ₹25 lakh or 10 per cent of the gross brokerage and fees received in the previous year, whichever is higher, is required to be maintained by every broker, who shall also furnish a statement of solvency margin from the auditors to the IRDA.

(v) The guidelines also require brokers to maintain the books of accounts as specified and in the manner as prescribed. Brokers are also required to submit the audited financial statements and report thereon to IRDA within 60 days from the end of the accounting year. Every insurance broker shall, within ninety days from the date of the auditor's report take steps to rectify any deficiencies, made out in the auditor's report and inform the authority accordingly.

(vi) The brokers shall have to furnish information on various matters as and when the authority requires it and also facilitate inspection whenever ordered by the authority. All the books of account, statements, documents, etc. shall be maintained at the head office of the insurance broker or such other branch office as may be designated by him and notified to the authority, and shall be available on all working days to such officers of the authority, authorized in this behalf by it for an inspection. All the books and documents, statements, contracts, notes etc. referred to in this regulation and maintained by the insurance broker shall be retained for a period of at least ten years from the end of the year to which they relate.

(vii) The remuneration (including royalty or licence fees or administration charges or such other compensation), payable to an insurance broker cannot be allowed to exceed the following limits:

In the case of direct general insurance business:

- On tariff products—10 per cent of the premium on that part of the business which is compulsory under any statute or any law in force and 12½ per cent of the premium on others.
- On non-tariff products—17½ per cent of the premium on direct business.

In the case of direct life insurance business:

- On individual insurance—30 per cent of first year's premium and 5 per cent of each renewal premium.
- On immediate annuity or a deferred annuity in consideration of a single premium, or where only one premium is payable on the policy—2 per cent of premium and on deferred annuity in consideration of more than one premium—7½ per cent of first year's premium and 2 per cent of each renewal premium.
- On group insurance and pension schemes
  - One year renewable group term insurance, gratuity, superannuation, group savings linked insurance—7½ per cent of risk premium
  - Single premium—2 per cent of risk premium
  - Annual contributions, at new business procurement stage—5 per cent of non-risk premium with a ceiling of ₹3 lakh per scheme.
  - Single premium new business procurement stage—0.5 per cent with a ceiling of ₹5 lakh per scheme
  - Remuneration for subsequent servicing—on one year renewable group term assurance—2 per cent of risk premium with a ceiling of ₹50,000 per scheme

On reinsurance business: As per market practices prevalent from time to time, that is, the settlement of accounts by insurers in respect of remuneration of brokers shall be done on a monthly basis and it must be ensured that there is no cross settlement of outstanding balances. Moreover, for purposes of the procurement of business, an insurer shall not pay any agency commission or allow a special discount and pay remuneration to brokers for the same insurance contract.

(viii) The business of the insurance broker shall be carried in such a manner that, not more than 50 per cent of the premium (quantum, receipts, etc. as the case may be) in the first year of business, 40 per cent of the premium in the second year of business, and 30 per cent of the premium from the third year of business onwards shall emanate from any one client. For the purposes of this regulation, the term *client* shall include, in the case of a firm or a company, an associate or a subsidiary or a group concern under the same management. The decision of the authority as to whether a company, a business or an organization is under the same management shall be final.

(ix) Every insurance broker shall before the commencement of his business, deposit and keep deposited with any scheduled bank a sum equivalent to 20 per cent of the initial capital in fixed deposit, which shall not be released to him unless prior permission of the authority is obtained provided that the authority may impose a separate limit of deposit, in any case not exceeding ₹1 crore for a person covered by regulation 2(1)(j)(v) of the IRDA (Insurance Brokers) Regulations 2002. Every insurance broker shall furnish to the authority as and when called upon to do so a statement certified by the bank in which such fixed deposit is kept.

(x) Any dispute arising between an insurance broker and an insurer or any other person either in the course of his engagement as an insurance broker or otherwise may be referred to the authority by the person so affected, and on receipt of the complaint or representation, the authority may examine the complaint and if found necessary proceed to conduct an enquiry or an inspection or an investigation in terms of these regulations.

Brokers have provided valuable services and benefited the Indian insurance industry in various ways, some are discussed as follows:

(i) Insurance brokers have helped in the introduction of new and innovative products and services in the Indian insurance industry as a result of which corporates and consumers are able to secure suitable and yet, more economical insurance cover.

(ii) Insurance brokers apply international standards, in technical skills, products, training programmes, systems, technology and managerial techniques. The broker's skill in designing and obtaining market support for more sophisticated programmes are essential in achieving and maintaining the optimum balance between retained and transferred risk for each individual client.

(iii) Most of the global insurance players feel very comfortable to work with brokers. They find it simpler and speedier to interact with them because they need to discuss only the tricky aspects or special requirements in detail and leave the rest to the broker.

(iv) Brokers provide great service in creating insurance awareness, increasing market penetration, promoting competition and improving customer service.

(v) The retention capacities of Indian insurers tend to increase as the brokers apply international reinsurance skills that help in making reinsurance programmes more effective and result in further savings in foreign exchange outflows.

(vi) The insurance brokers virtually eliminate the need for the customers to keep track of their insurance programme they offer complete solution, right from risk profiling to claims administration, which makes it easier for clients to concentrate on their core business.

25.1.3 Surveyors and Loss Assessors

When a claim is reported under a policy issued by an insurance company it is required to evaluate the loss or damage suffered. For this purpose, it appoints surveyors and loss assessors, who are independent professionals, duly licensed by the insurance regulatory and development authority. In order to obtain the licences, they have to be qualified in insurance business and should be fellows or associates of the insurance institutes of India or chartered insurance institute of London or any other technically qualified like engineering graduates or diploma holders in any discipline, chartered accountants, graduates in medical sciences. A licensed surveyor may be included on the panel of one or more insurance companies in India.

Surveyors and loss assessors are responsible for the following duties:

(i) Look into, and verify the causes of loss or damage

(ii) Recommend ways to save the damaged property or goods from further destruction and make sure that the insured takes all necessary steps to alleviate or reduce the loss

(iii) Determine the extent of the loss and ascertain the liability of the insurers in accordance with the terms and conditions attached to the policy

(iv) Step into the shoes of the insurance company in disposing of damaged property or goods in order to realize maximum worth

Moreover, surveyors are expected to observe a high degree of professionalism in the discharge of their duties. This is particularly necessary in view of the fact that the insurance companies appoint surveyors. But this relationship should not be allowed to come in the way of an objective and fair assessment of the loss.

25.1.4 Third Party Administrators

Third party administrators are intermediaries operating in the health insurance sector. They make it possible for all categories of policyholders to avail the services of a number of hospitals and nursing homes. Full-time medical practitioners working under the employment of third party administrators (TPAs) who freely take decisions regarding the claim settlements as for instance, whether the ailment is covered under the policy.

TPAs extend valuable service to both, the insurer and the insured. The insured gets improved services and the insurers benefit by considerable reduction in the administrative costs. With the introduction of TPAs the insured can avail of the hospitalization services without having to pay for the same, as was the practice earlier when the insured was compensated later for all the hospitalization expenses. TPA licence is granted, usually for a period of 3 years, to companies registered under the Companies Act 1956, having a minimum paid-up capital of ₹1 crore with foreign participation not exceeding 26 per cent. Insurers pay commission to TPAs on mutually agreeable terms but the IRDA guidelines do not permit it to exceed 15 per cent of the premium amount. TPAs can be associated with any number of hospitals offering hospitalization services and work for any number of insurance companies. Similarly, insurance companies are also free to include any number of TPAs on their panel.

Settlement of claims in this case involves the following procedure:

(i) Insurer transfers the records pertaining to medical insurance policies to the TPA. The appointed TPA issues identity cards to all the policyholders. These identity cards have to be shown to the hospital authorities before taking advantage of any hospitalization services. For the purposes of settlement of a claim, the policyholder is required to inform TPA on its 24-hour toll free line.

(ii) Policyholder is then directed to a hospital with which the TPA has a tied-up agreement. The policyholder may choose to join any other hospital, but in such a case payment is made on reimbursement basis.

(iii) An authorization letter for the treatment is issued to the hospital by the TPA whereby it is agreed to pay for the treatment. TPA pursues the insured's case at the hospital. All the bills are sent to TPA for payment on discharge of the insured from the hospital.

(iv) After settling the payment with the hospital, TPA forwards all the necessary documents, along with bills to the insurance company for consideration of claims.

(v) Finally, the insurance company compensates the TPA.

25.1.5 Corporate Agents

As the name itself suggests, corporate agents, is a corporate body set up with the explicit objective of selling insurance products. The concept of corporate agents was introduced in India by IRDA in order to facilitate *bancassurance,* a new *distribution channel* corporate agents are bound by the Companies Act, 1956, and IRDA (insurance regulatory and development authority) regulations. IRDA has issued guidelines in respect of minimum educational qualifications, practical training requirements and code of conduct for the purpose of licensing of corporate agents. Although basically they are agents, yet their role is slightly different. For instance, unlike individual agents, corporate agents must necessarily have three directors all of whom have to be certified by the IRDA for selling insurance. Simply stated, corporate agents are more professional in their approach and a lot more systematic in comparison to individual agents. A lot of individual agents go in for the profession on a part-time basis to enhance their current professional or business aims. These part-time agents are not always available. On the other hand, corporate agents work in a team of at least 3 agents. This provides a certain degree of stability and convenience to the business. Moreover, an individual agent is the sole proprietor of his business. In case if he shifts his business or if he passes away, his clients would be left in the lurch. Insurance is a long-term contract ranging from 10–30 years. An agent must be able to provide the needed service to his clients for that long a period. To that extent a corporate agency is more capable of servicing clients than an individual agent. Corporate agents are also more professional as they have a brand name to protect and cannot afford to waver on professional principles. They are expected to be more methodical in their approach. They are careful not to do anything that might damage their reputation and restrict their business prospects. As corporate agents work in a team, their knowledge base is extensive. Corporate agents are more updated with respect to developments in the insurance sector and also products offered by other insurers. They are able to give a broader perspective to their clients to help them make suitable decisions.

25.2 BANCASSURANCE

The concept of *bancassurance* originated in France before it became popular in other European countries as well. Bancassurance is the distribution of insurance products through the bank's distribution channel whereby, along with a complete range of banking and investment products and services, insurance products are also offered through the vast network of banking services. Thus, it is in the nature of a partnership between an insurance company and a banking institution through which an attempt is made to exploit synergies between both the insurance companies and banks. Bancassurance if taken in right spirit and implemented properly can be win-win situation for all the participants viz. banks, insurers and the customers.

25.2.1 Advantages of Bancassurance

(i) The traditional channels of insurance in India are not only outdated but also they cost more. For instance, insurance companies pay commission to their agents throughout the length of the issued policy at a rate that varies between 5–10 per cent of annual premium. On the other hand, the cost is much lesser for the insurance company using the banking channel because it will have to pay just around 20 per cent, that too only for one time.

(ii) With the increasing competition as result of the liberalization of the Indian economy it is becoming difficult for the insurers to sustain their market share. More and more insurers are turning to bancassurance in order to take advantage of the gigantic customer database available with the banks. Customer database like customers' financial standing, spending habits, investment and purchase capability can be used to customize products and sell accordingly. Since banks have already established relationship with customers, the conversion ratio of leads-to-sales is likely to be high. Further service aspect can also be tackled easily.

(iii) The banking sector also benefits through bancassurance. Besides other ways, banks also increase return on assets (ROA), through fee income, assuming a constant asset base, which enables them to cover more of their operating expenses. The sale of insurance products is one of the best ways to build fee income and thus to increase ROA.

(iv) Bank is an effective channel for the sale of insurance, particularly personal insurance. This is not only because of the face-to-face contact with the customers but also due to their vast distribution and processing capabilities. Most retail banks generate a lot of confidence amongst large section of consumers, which helps the banks in selling them personal line insurance products. Thus, by utilizing their strengths and overcoming their weaknesses, banks can make significant contribution as insurance distributors.

(v) Due to additional advantages in terms of huge customer base and brand awareness within their geographic regions, banks have lower cost per sales lead and lower per lead cost of advertising through various mediums in comparison to traditional insurance distributors helping them to expand their customer base and increase their market share.

(vi) Marketing and processing capabilities are valuable assets of a bank. Banks have wide experience in marketing their products to existing customers as well as outsiders. Existing customers forms a ready market for retention and cross selling and outside customers are relied on for acquisition and awareness Their access to multiple communication channels, as for instance, direct mail, ATMs, telemarketing, etc. has further resulted in improvements in transaction processing and customer service.

25.2.2 Bancassurance in India

Government of India, through its notification dated August 3, 2000, has recognized *insurance* as a permissible form of banking business under the provisions of the Banking Regulation Act, 1949. The RBI too has recognized *bancassurance,* allowing banks with prior permission to offer physical infrastructure to insurance companies within the premises of some selected branches authorizing them to sell their insurance products to the banks' customers and in exchange earn referral fees based on the premium collected. Banks too stand to gain in the process, as bancassurance is an important source of revenue for them. A number of insurers have already engaged banks for the purpose and the future of bancassurance in India is extremely bright. Indian banks with huge branch network, enormous customer base, customer confidence and experience, have all the essential constituents for the growth of bancassurance. The potential for banks as a significant distribution option in India can be gauged by the fact that there are 27 public sector banks and 196 regional rural banks with over 60,000 branches of commercial banks and an average population of 15,000 being served by each branch. The network includes 33,000 rural branches and 14,000 semi-urban branches. If properly implemented, India could lead the world in bancassurance. However, insurer-banks should be careful in their strategies because selling risk products in an upcoming competitive market is not easy. The banking and insurance sectors in India are regulated by two different authorities (banking by the RBI and insurance by the IRDA). Being a combination of these two sectors, bancassurance is governed by both the regulators.

The Reserve Bank of India has provided the following guidelines for banks entering into the insurance sector:

(i) Joint ventures will be allowed for financially strong banks interested in undertaking insurance business with risk participation
(ii) Those banks, which are not eligible for this joint venture option can avail of the investment option of up to 10 per cent of the net worth of the bank or ₹50 crore, whichever is lower
(iii) All commercial banks are allowed to undertake insurance business as agents of insurance companies. This will be on a fee basis with no-risk participation

The guidelines for bancassurance provided by the insurance regulatory and development authority (IRDA) include the following:

(i) Each bank dealing in insurance must have a chief insurance executive to manage various insurance activities
(ii) All the persons involved in selling should undergo compulsory training at an institute accredited by IRDA. They must also pass the examination conducted by the authority
(iii) Commercial banks, including cooperative banks and regional rural banks, are allowed to become corporate agents for one insurance company
(iv) Banks are not authorized to become insurance brokers.

Some of the bancassurance alliances in India are given in Table 25.1.

Table 25.1 Bancassurance Alliances in India

Insurance company	*Bank*
Birla Sun Life Insurance Co. Ltd.	Bank of Rajasthan, Andhra Bank, Bank of Muscat, Development Credit Bank, Deutsche Bank and Catholic Syrian Bank.
Dabur CGU Life Insurance Company Pvt. Ltd.	Canara Bank, Lakshmi Vilas Bank, American Express Bank and ABN Amro Bank.
HDFC Standard Life Insurance Co. Ltd.	Union Bank of India.
ICICI Prudential Life Insurance Co. Ltd.	Lord Krishna Bank, ICICI Bank, Bank of India, Citibank, Allahabad Bank, Federal Bank, South Indian Bank, and Punjab and Maharashtra Cooperative Bank.
Life Insurance Corporation of India	Corporation Bank, Indian Overseas Bank, Centurion Bank (Centurion Bank of Punjab), Satara District Central Cooperative Bank, Janata Urban Cooperative Bank, Yeotmal Mahila Sahkari Bank, Vijaya Bank, Oriental Bank of Commerce.
MetLife India Insurance Co. Ltd.	Karnataka Bank, Dhanalakshmi Bank and J&K Bank.
SBI Life Insurance Company Ltd.	State Bank of India.
Bajaj Allianz General Insurance Co. Ltd.	Karur Vysya Bank and Lord Krishna Bank.
National Insurance Co. Ltd.	City Union Bank.
Royal Sundaram General Insurance Company	Standard Chartered Bank, ABN Amro Bank, Citibank, Amex and Repco Bank.
United India Insurance Co. Ltd.	South Indian Bank.

25.2.3 Bancassurance: Some Emerging Issues

Since, the banks and insurers in a bancassurance tie-up play different roles involving varied skills, it is likely that the road to a successful tie-up would be a demanding task. Some of the issues that need to be addressed are

(i) In order to ensure the success of bancassurance, it is essential to develop innovative products and services rather than depend on the traditional methods of banking and insurance. The kinds of products the banks would be allowed to sell is another crucial issue. For instance, an intricate unit-linked life insurance product should rather be sold through brokers or agents, whereas a standard term product or simple products like auto insurance, home loan and accident insurance cover can be allowed to be handled by banks.

(ii) There should be absolute clarity regarding the operational activities of the bancassurance, i.e., will the insurance company prefer to place its own person at the bank branch, or will the bank branch train and place one of its own people.

(iii) Although the banks enjoy a clear edge due to the face-to- face contact that they have with their clients, a high degree of pro-active marketing and skill is required to sell the insurance products. This necessitates proper training of the persons on the job.

(iv) There are risks of direct competition to traditional banking products. Bank personnel may resist selling insurance products out of the fear of becoming redundant if savings were diverted from banks to their insurance subsidiaries.

The following factors are essential for the successful execution of bancassurance:

(i) Strategies coherent with the bank's goals, knowledge of the needs of target customers, distinct sales process for introducing insurance services, simple yet complete product offers, effective service delivery procedure, efficient management, harmonized planning across all business lines and subsidiaries, complete assimilation of insurance with other bank products and services, effective, extensive training, pertinent and pliable database systems.

(ii) Another essential requisite of successful bancassurance is the efficient handling of customers. With the increase in the levels of awareness amongst the customers, their demand for greater convenience in financial services is also increasing.

(iii) The emergence of remote distribution channels, such as PC-banking and Internet-banking, as also newer distribution channels looking for a market share in the network may encumber the distribution of insurance products through banks. The banks have to be better prepared to face this challenge.

25.2.4 Bancassurance Models

Distribution alliance: Under the distribution alliance model, the insurance company ties up with the bank for distribution of insurance product.

Joint venture: Joint venture as distribution model refers to partnership between insurer and bank wherein the bank provides the head start and its reputation and brand name, while the insurer brings products and underwriting and servicing proficiency. The partners combine their individual strengths to create an ideal bancassurance process.

Leveraged life distribution: Under this model, the life insurance company takes the lead in partnership, while several banks act as corporate agents to provide access to middle-market leads.

Leveraged bank distribution: Under leveraged bank distribution, it is the bank that takes the lead as in the joint-venture model, while the life insurance companies supply products for its bancassurance efforts. This model requires a large bank with a number of efficient distribution channels. For instance, branches, ATMs, mail, phones, etc.

KEY TERMS

Bancassurance Insurance coverage that is manufactured and underwritten by a commercial bank's own insurance company and distributed through the bank's distribution channels.

Joint venture A jointly undertaken business enterprise.

Leverage A position of extended gains or losses created by putting up partly fixed costs against a variable return, thereby, leaving a residual return which is left with far higher impact of variability. The residual class has, therefore, leveraged risk and reward position.

Reinsurance broker A third party that acts as a go-between for a ceding company and a reinsurer in effecting a reinsurance transaction.

REVIEW QUESTIONS

25.1 What do you understand by the term insurance agent? Discuss the role of insurance agent in the Indian insurance sector.

25.2 Define the term bancassurance. Explain the various bancassurance models.

25.3 What are prerequisites for the successful execution of bancassurance?

25.4 What is the contribution of agents and brokers as means of distribution of insurance products?

25.5 In what ways have insurance brokers benefited the Indian insurance industry?

25.6 What are the duties of surveyors and assessors?

25.7 Describe the contribution of third party administrators in the Indian health insurance sector.

25.8 Write short notes on

(i) Insurance agents

(ii) Corporate agents

(iii) Brokers

(iv) Third party administrators

(v) Surveyors and assessors

26

Legal Framework

Learning Objectives

After going through this chapter we will be able to:

- Understand the essential features of valid contract.
- Classify different types of contracts.
- Decipher the relevance of the Consumer Protection Act (CPA).
- Elucidate important definitions under the CPA.
- Describe complaint procedure prescribed under the CPA.
- Discuss redressal of consumer's grievances.
- Explicate the functions of the general insurance corporation of India (GIC).
- Discuss powers of the Central Government under the General Insurance Business (Nationalization) Act, 1972.
- Shed light on the constitution, functions and powers of the corporation under the Life Insurance Corporation Act, 1956.
- Interpret duties, powers, functions and composition of authority under the Insurance Regulatory and Development Authority Act, 1999.
- Decode the stipulations in the Insurance Act, 1938.
- Comprehend the powers of the authority to make rules in respect of advisory committee, etc. under the Insurance Act, 1938.

The insurance sector in India has gone through a full circle of phases from being unregulated to completely regulated and then currently being partly deregulated. It is governed by a number of acts, namely, the Insurance Act,

1938, the IRDA Act, 1999, the General Insurance Business (Nationalization) Act, 1972, the LIC Act, 1956 and the Consumer Protection Act, 1986, The Indian Contract Act, 1872 does not directly govern the business of insurance, however, the provisions of the Act are significant since the insurance transactions are based on a contractual relationship between the insured and the insurance company. Similarly, the provisions of *the Consumer Protection Act* have bearing on the insurance business because in every contract of insurance, the insured is the buyer (consumer) and the insurance company is the seller (supplier) of the insurance product (policy).

26.1 THE INDIAN CONTRACT ACT, 1872

The Indian Contract Act, 1872 deals with

1. The general principles of the law of contract, and
2. Some special contracts only.

The Act does not directly deal with the contracts related to partnership, sale of goods, negotiable instruments, bill of lading, insurance, etc. There are separate Acts that deal with these contracts. Thus, although the Act does not directly govern insurance business, every contract of insurance must satisfy the basic requisites of a valid contract.

Law of contract is neither the whole law of agreements nor the whole law of obligations. That is, to say all agreements do not lead to legal obligations and are, thus, not contracts in quite the same way as many obligations do not necessarily originate from an agreement, e.g., torts or civil wrongs, quasi-contracts, etc. and so are not contractual but still enforceable.

Section 2(h) of the Act defines a contract is an agreement made between two or more parties which is enforceable by the law.

26.1.1 Nature of an Agreement

All contracts comprise two elements, namely, agreement, and enforceability of an agreement by law.

Section 2(e) of the Act defines *agreement* as *every promise and every set of promises, forming consideration for each other.* A promise, in turn, is defined as a proposal (offer), which has been accepted, Sec. 2(b). Hence, an agreement is an accepted proposal. In order, therefore, to form an agreement, there must be a proposal or offer by one party and its acceptance by the other. It can be concluded as

Agreement = Offer + Acceptance

However, an agreement, to become a contract, must give rise to a legal obligation or duty. The term obligation denotes legal binding (and not a social compulsion), upon a person to do something or not.

Examples, (a) *A* agrees to sell his house to B for ₹50 lakh. The agreement gives rise to an obligation on the part of A to transfer the house to B and on the part of B to pay the amount to *A*. This agreement is a contract. Thus, all contracts are agreements but all agreements are not necessarily contracts.

Contract = Agreement + Enforceability at law

26.1.2 Requisites of a Valid Contract

Section 10 of the Act provides that all agreements made by the free consent of parties competent to contract, for a lawful consideration and with a lawful object and are not expressly declared to be void are valid contracts. In order to become a valid contract, an agreement must have the following essential elements:

Offer and acceptance: There must be two parties to an agreement, one making the offer and the other accepting it. Offer must be capable of being accepted and giving rise to legal relationship between the parties to the agreement. It must also be definite, unambiguous and not loose or vague. In order to be accepted, it must also be communicated with the intention of obtaining the assent. Acceptance, on the other hand, must be absolute and unconditional or unqualified. It must be communicated to the offerer within a reasonable time.

Intention to create legal relationship: There can be no contract unless both the parties to the agreement intend to establish a legal relationship between them.

Lawful consideration: *Consideration* means *something in return,* which may be an advantage/benefit passed from one to the other and need not necessarily be in cash or kind but must be valid and lawful. It can even be an act or promise to do or not to do something. However, it must move at the desire of the promisor though it may also move from the promisee or any other person. Consideration may be past, present or future.

Capacity to enter into the contract: The parties to the agreement must possess the legal competence to contract. A person loses the capacity to contract if he has not attained the age of majority, is of unsound mind and is disqualified from contracting by any law to which he is subjected (Sec. 11 and 12). Agreements contracted by such a person are not enforceable.

Free and genuine consent: The consent of the parties to the agreement is said to be free when they are at agreement with each other on all the material terms of the contract (Sec. 13) and when the consent is not brought about by coercion, undue influence, fraud, misrepresentation, mistake, etc. (Sec. 14). When there is no consent, there is no contract.

Lawful object: The purpose/object of the agreement must also be lawful in order for it to be enforceable. That is, the object must not be illegal, immoral, or opposed to public policy (Sec. 23) or else, it would not be enforceable by law.

Agreement not declared void: The agreement must not have been expressly declared void by any law in force in the country (Sec. 24–30 and Sec. 56).

Certainty and possibility of performance: The agreement must be certain, distinct and definite rather being vague (Sec. 29).

Legal formalities: It is immaterial whether the contract is verbal or written in order to enforce it though it is otherwise in the interest of the parties to the contract that it should be in writing. (Sec. 10, para 2).

26.1.3 Classification of Contracts

Contracts may be classified on the following basis:

Classification according to validity:

Valid contract: An agreement that fulfils all the essential requisites as per the requirements of law is a valid contract.

Voidable contract: An agreement which is enforceable by law at the option of one or more of the parties thereto, but not at the option of the other or others, is a voidable contract. This happens when one of the requisites of validity, viz. free consent, is absent in a contract. In such a case the party whose consent is not free may either rescind the contract or accept it. However, the contract continues to be regarded as valid till it is avoided by the party entitled to do so.

For example, A promises to sell his shop to B for ₹90,000. His consent, however, is obtained forcibly. The contract is voidable at the option of A. He may avoid the contract or elect to be bound by it.

Void agreement and void contract. According to Sec. 2(g) of the Act, agreements not enforceable by law are said to be void agreements, which create no legal rights or obligations, are a nullity and completely destitute of legal effects. They are void ab initio, i.e., from the very beginning as, for example, an agreement with a minor or an agreement lacking consideration.

A void contract, on the other hand, is a contract which subsequently ceases to be enforceable by law. Such a contract becomes void when it so ceases to be enforceable. That is, a contract may be valid and binding when originally entered into but may later become void, e.g., a contract to export goods to a foreign country is a perfectly valid contract till a war breaks out between the importer's and exporter's country, in which case the contract will become void. Thus, a void contract is never originally entered into but is a valid contract that subsequently becomes void due to certain circumstances.

Illegal agreement. An agreement, which violates some rule of basic public policy or is criminal or immoral in nature is called an **illegal agreement**. Such an agreement is a nullity. All illegal agreements are void but all void agreements or contracts are not necessarily illegal.

Unenforceable contract. Contracts, which cannot be enforced in a court of law because of some technical defect such as absence of writing or because the remedy has become time-barred are called **unenforceable contracts**. These contracts may still be carried out by the parties concerned, but in the event of breach or denial, the aggrieved party will not be entitled to the legal remedies.

Classification according to formation:

Express contract. In an express contract, the terms and conditions of a contract are expressly agreed upon (in spoken or written words) at the time of formation of the contract. An express promise results in an express contract.

Implied contract. A contract, which is inferred from the acts or behaviour of the parties or course of dealings between them is an implied contract. It is not the result of any express promise or promises by the parties but may result from a particular act or acts. An implied promise results in an implied contract. For instance, there is an implied contract when A gets into a public transport or eats at a restaurant.

Quasi-contract. A quasi-contract is not really a contract since it is not entered into by the parties but is created by law. It bears resemblance to a contract as a legal obligation is imposed on the party, which is required to perform it. It is based on the principle of justice that "a person shall not be allowed to enrich himself unjustly at the expense of another". For instance, if A a salesman, leaves goods at B's house by mistake and B treats the goods as his own then he is bound to pay for the goods.

E-commerce contract. An e-commerce contract is one which is entered into between two parties through internet.

Classification according to performance:

Executed contract. An executed contract is one in which both the parties have executed/discharged their respective obligations.

For example, A agrees to sell his car to B for ₹1,00,000 and accordingly transfers the car to B on getting the agreed amount from B. The contract is a duly executed contract.

Executory (bilateral) contract. Executory or bilateral contract is a contract in which both the parties are yet to execute their respective obligations. Such contracts are also known as 'contracts with executory consideration'. In the above example, if B had paid but A was still to transfer the car to B, it would have been an executory contract.

Unilateral (one-sided) contract. Where only one party has to discharge his obligation while the other party has already complied with his obligation, the contract is a unilateral or one-sided contract, also known as 'contract with executed consideration'.

26.1.4 Agency Law

Chapter X (Sec. 182–238) of the Indian Contact Act, 1872, contains Law of Agency.

An *agent* has been defined as a person employed to do any act for another, or to represent another in dealings with third persons. The person for whom such an act is done, or who is so represented in the Act, is called the **principal** (Sec. 182). It has further been provided that any person who is of the age of majority and who is of sound mind may, according to the law to which he is subjected, employ an agent. Any person who is of the age of majority and of sound mind, may be employed by the principal to act as his agent in a particular transaction or for a particular deal, so as to be responsible to the principal. Where the person employed as agent does not have the legal capacity to contract, he would not be responsible towards the principal for acts done in his capacity of being the agent. However, payment of consideration is not a prerequisite for creation of a principal–agent relationship because *agency* is based on agreement and not necessarily on contract.

Accordingly, agency may arise either by express or by an implied agreement. An express authority is derived by the agent when it is given by words spoken or written by the principal. On the other hand, an agent's authority is said to be implied when it is to be inferred from the circumstances of the case, and things either spoken or written. In addition, the ordinary manner of dealing, may also be considered as *circumstances of the case*. Moreover, an agent, employed by the principal to do an act, shall have the authority to do every lawful thing that may be necessary for doing such act. An agent employed to carry on a business has implied authority to do every lawful thing required for the purpose of that business and in accordance with usual custom of that business. In a crisis situation too, an agent has authority, to do all such acts for the purpose of safeguarding the interest of his principal as would normally be done by a person of ordinary prudence, in his own case, under parallel circumstances.

26.1.5 Termination of Agency

An agency can be terminated by the principal by revoking his authority and by the agent in any of the following cases:

(i) When he renounces the business for which he was employed

(ii) When the business is complete

(iii) Either the principal or agent has died, has become of unsound mind or the principal has been adjudicated an insolvent

Where the agent has himself an interest in the property forming subject-matter of the agency, the agency cannot, without an express contract, be terminated to the prejudice of such interest For instance, if Ram gives authority to Sham to sell Ram's house and to pay himself, out of the proceeds, the debts due to him from Ram. This authority cannot be revoked by Ram, nor can it be terminated by his insanity or death.

The principal may revoke the authority given to his agent at any time before the authority has been exercised. But, where the authority has been partly exercised, the principal cannot revoke the authority given to his agent, with regard to such acts and obligations that arise from the acts already done in the agency. In any case, reasonable notice of revocation or renunciation must be given, otherwise the damage thereby resulting to the principal or the agent, as the case may be, must be made good to the one by the other.

In the case of an express or implied contract to carry on the agency for a specified period of time, the principal must make compensations to the agent, or the agent to the principal, as the case may be, if the agency is revoked or contract renounced without sufficient cause, before the expiry of that period. Revocation or renunciation can either be expressed or implied in the conduct of the principal or of the agent. For example, Ram authorizes Sham to let Ram's house. Later, Ram lets it himself. This is an implied revocation of Sham's agency.

From the point of view of an agent, termination of an agency does not become effective unless and until, it is communicated to him and, as far as the third parties are concerned, before it is communicated to them. However, if an agency is terminated as a result of death of the principal or his becoming of unsound mind, the agent is bound to take all reasonable steps for safeguarding the interests entrusted to him by the deceased principal, for the benefit of his representative.

26.1.6 Agent's Duty to Principal

An agent has to discharge the following duties towards the principal:

(i) An agent is bound to conduct the business of his principal in accordance with the directions given by the principal, and where no directions are given, in accordance with the general business customs, of which his business is a part. Otherwise, the agent would be liable to compensate the principal for any loss suffered by him. Contrarily, if any profit accrues, he must account for it.

(ii) An agent is bound to exercise such skill, diligence and prudence in the discharge of his duties as would generally be expected of any person engaged in similar business. An agent is liable compensate his principal in respect of the direct consequences of his own neglect, want of skill, or misconduct. He is, of course, not responsible for any loss or damage caused indirectly or remotely due to such neglect, want of skill, or misconduct.

(iii) The agent maintain and hand over, on demand, proper accounts to his principal. The agent must, in case of any difficulty, communicate with his principal and obtain his instructions. If he chooses to deal on his own account, in the conduct of the business of agency without seeking the principal's consent and acquainting him with all material facts, which have come to his knowledge on the issue, the principal may repudiate the deal.

(iv) If an agent, without the knowledge of his principal, deals in the business of the agency on his own account instead of on account to his principal, the principal is entitled to claim from the agent any benefit which may have resulted to him from the transaction.

(v) If any amount is received by the agent on account of the principal, he may retain out of that amount all moneys due to him from the principal, towards advances made or expenses incurred in the conduct of such business, and also such remuneration as may be payable to him for acting as the agent. Except for such deductions the agent is bound to transfer to his principal, all sums received on his account.

26.1.7 Principal's Duty to Agent

The principal has to discharge the following duties towards the agent:

(i) The principal must indemnify the agent against the consequences of all lawful acts done by him in carrying out the authority conferred upon him.

(ii) Where the agent has acted in good faith, the principal is liable to compensate him against the consequences of his action, though it may have caused an injury to the rights of third persons.

(iii) Where the principal has appointed an agent to do an act which is criminal, the employer is not liable to the agent, either upon an express or an implied promise to indemnify him against the consequences of that act.

(iv) The principal must make compensation to his agent for any injury caused to such agent by the principal's neglect or lack of skill.

26.1.8 Effect of Agency on Contracts with Third Persons

The effects of agency on the contracts with the third parties may be discussed as follows:

(i) Contracts entered into through an agent, and the consequent obligations arising therefrom are enforceable in the same manner, and with the same legal consequences as if the contracts had been entered into by the principal himself. However, where an agent partly exceeds his authority such that the part of what he does, being within his authority, can be separated from the part, which is in excess of his authority, then only that part, which is within his authority would be binding on the principal.

(ii) Where an agent has partly exceeded his authority in such a way that the part of his action which is beyond the scope of his authority cannot be separated from what was within the authority limits, the principal is not bound by the transaction.

(iii) Any notice given to or information obtained by the agent that is supposed to be given or obtained in the course of the business transacted by him on behalf of the principal, shall, as between the principal and third parties, have the same legal consequences as if it had been given to or obtained by the principal.

(iv) Unless otherwise provided in the contract, an agent cannot personally enforce contracts entered into by him on behalf of his principal. On the same grounds, he is not personally bound by these contracts. However, such a contract shall be presumed to exist

- Where the contract is made by an agent for the sale or purchase of goods for a merchant resident abroad
- Where the name of the principal is not disclosed by the agent, or
- Where the principal, though disclosed, cannot otherwise be sued

(v) If a contract is made by the agent with a person who neither knows nor has reason to suspect, that he is an agent, his principal may still want the performance of the contract, but the other contracting party shall, as against the principal, have the same right as he would have had against the agent, had he been the principal. But, if the principal discloses himself before the completion of the contract, the other contracting party may refuse to fulfil the contract, provided he can show that, if he had known who the principal in the contract was, or had known that the agent was not the principal, he would not have entered into the contract.

(vi) Where a person makes a contract with another, neither knowing nor having reasonable ground to suspect that the other is an agent, the principal can, if he requires, obtain performance of the contract subject to the right and obligations as between the agent and the other party to the contract.

(vii) When an agent has, in the absence of an authority, done acts or incurred obligations to a third person on behalf of his principal, the principal is bound by such acts or obligations, provided he has, by his word or conduct induced such a third person to believe that such acts and obligations were within the scope of the agent's authority.

(viii) Where an agent commits any fraud or misrepresentation in the course of the business conducted on behalf of his principal, in respect of matters affecting his authority, the legal effect of such misrepresentations or frauds on agreement made by the agent would be the same as if it had been committed by the principal himself; but misrepresentations made, or frauds committed, by agents, in matters which do not affect their authority, do not affect their principals.

26.2 THE CONSUMER PROTECTION ACT, 1986

An important landmark in the history of socio-economic legislation in the country is the enactment of the Consumer Protection Act, 1986, a comprehensive Act designed to protect the interests of consumers by providing easy, prompt and economical redressal to the consumers' grievances and related matters through the establishment of consumer councils and other authorities, namely, District Forum, the State Commission and the National Commission, besides Central Consumer Protection Council and State Consumer Protection Councils. The provisions of this Act are compensatory and not punitive in nature. The Act has been amended from time to time in order to extend its coverage and scope and to expand the powers of the redressal machinery.

The salient provisions of the Consumer Protection Act, 1986, are as follows:

26.2.1 Important Definitions Under the Act

Goods: As in the Sale of Goods Act, 1930, means every kind of movable property, including stock and shares, growing crops, grass, and things attached to or forming part of the land that are agreed to be cut off before sale or under the contract of sale and excluding actionable claims and money.

Service: Includes any kind of service including facilities in connection with banking, financing, insurance, transport, processing, supply of electrical or other energy, boarding/lodging/both, house construction, entertainment, news or other information passed on to the potential users but excluding the rendering of any service free of charge or under a contract of personal service.

Restrictive trade practice: Means a trade practice requiring a consumer to buy, hire or avail of some goods or services as a pre-condition to buying, hiring or availing of other goods or services.

Defect: Implies any flaw, defect or deficiency in the quality, quantity, effectiveness, purity or standard which is required to be maintained by or under any law for the time being in force or under any contract express or implied or as is claimed by the trader in any manner whatsoever in relation to any goods.

Deficiency: Denotes any fault, imperfection, shortcoming or inadequacy in the quality, nature and manner of performance which is required to be maintained by or under any law for the time being in force or has been undertaken to be performed by a person in pursuance of a contract or otherwise in relation to any service.

Unfair trade practice: As amended by the Consumer Protection (amendment) Act, 1993 means a trade practice, which for the purpose of promoting the sale, use or for the supply of any goods or for the provision of any service adopts such unfair trade practices as untrue or misleading statement (misrepresentation), bargain price, offering of gifts, prizes, contests, etc. Non-compliance of product safety standards, hoarding or destruction of goods, and so on.

Consumer: Consumer Protection Act defines the term *consumer* separately for *goods* and *services* as explained as follows:

From the point of view of ***goods***. Consumer means a person who buys or agrees to buy any goods for some consideration, which has been paid or promised or is partly paid and partly promised or under any system of deferred payment, including any user of such goods other than the person who actualy buys goods, and such use is made with the approval of the purchaser but, excluding a person who purchases goods for commercial or resale purposes unless the goods were bought and used by him exclusively for the purpose of earning his living, by way of self-employment.

From the point of view of ***services***. *Consumer* means a person who hires or avails of any service or services for a consideration which has been paid or promised or partly paid and partly promised or under any system of deferred payment, including any beneficiary of such service excluding one who actually hires or avails of the service for consideration and such services are availed with the approval of such person.

Complaint: The term *complaint* as defined under the Act, stands for an allegation made in writing by a person, called a complainant, with reference to

- Any unfair trade practice as defined in the Act or any restrictive trade practice
- One or more defects or deficiencies in services in goods
- Hazardous goods being offered for sale to public in violation of the provisions of any law for the time being in force
- A trader charging excess of price displayed on goods or on the package containing such goods or that fixed by or under any law for the time being in force

Complainant: Refers to a person/party entitled to file a complaint. Under the provisions of the Act, the term includes a consumer, a voluntary consumer organization, registered under any relevant law for the time being in force, the Central or the State Government, Union Territory administrations. It also includes one or more consumers complaining on behalf of numerous other consumers having the same interest.

26.2.2 Extent and Coverage of the Act

The Act pertains to all goods and services unless expressly exempted by the Central Government and covers all the sectors whether private, public or cooperative. Its provisions are compensatory and not corrective in nature. Moreover, the provisions of the Act are in addition to and not in derogation of the provisions of any other law for the time being in force.

26.2.3 The Objects of the Act

The main object of the Act is to safeguard the basic consumers' rights. These include the following:

Right to protection: The Act provides protection to the consumer against the marketing of goods and services that could prove hazardous to the consumer's life and property.

Right to information: Consumers have the right to information regarding the quantity, potency, purity standard and price of goods or services and protection against unfair trade practices.

Right to use (i.e., choice): Consumers must be provided access to a variety of goods and services at competitive prices.

Right to be heard (i.e., right to representation): Consumers must have the assurance that their interests will receive due consideration at appropriate forums.

Right to seek redressal: Consumers have the right to seek redressal against unfair trade practices leading to unscrupulous exploitation of consumers.

Right to consumer education: The consumers' right to acquire knowledge about the products being bought by them and to seek awareness about their rights and the remedies available to them, is well accepted by the provisions of the Act. In order to achieve this purpose, Consumer Protection Councils at the central and state levels are established under the Act.

However, consumers are also expected to discharge certain **duties and responsibilities**, which may be described as follows:

To provide appropriate information to the seller: The consumer must provide adequate information about his needs and expectation to the seller.

To exercise caution in buying: The consumer must make reasonable efforts to get complete information on quality, quantity, price, etc., of the product before buying it.

To press for receipt or cash memo: In order to make a complaint to the seller regarding any defect in the goods bought, a proof of purchase in the form of cash memo or receipt becomes necessary.

Not to compromise on quality: The consumer must look for standard quality marks such as Agmark, Woolmark, ISI, FPO, etc., and should not compromise on the quality of goods.

To file complaint against genuine grievances: It is not only the right of a consumer but also his duty to file a complaint with the seller or manufacturer about any defect or shortcoming in the product or service.

26.2.4 Protection of Consumers' Interests

The Act proposes to protect the interests of consumers with the setting up of different authorities, viz. the Central Consumer Protection Council, the State Consumer Protection Council and the District Consumer Protection Council.

Central consumer protection council: Central Consumer Protection Council has been set up by the Central Government with the Minister in charge of consumer affairs in the Central Government as its Chairman, and other official and non-official members representing varied interests. The central council comprises 150 members appointed for a term of 3 years. The council meets as and when required but at least one council meeting is held in a year.

State consumer protection council: The Minister in charge of consumer affairs in the State Government is the Chairman of the state council. Other official and non-official members of the council represent varied interests. The state council meets as and when required but not less than two meetings must be held every year.

District consumer protection council: In order to promote and protect the rights of the Consumers, the District Consumer Protection Councils are established by every State Government with respect to each district in the State. The Collector of the district is the Chairman of the council. Other offical and non-offical members of the council represent interests prescribed by the State Government. The council is required to meet at least twice a year at such time and place within the district as the Chairman may think fit. However, the manner in which the business is to be conducted at the council meetings is prescribed by the State Government.

25.2.5 Composition of Redressal Agencies

With the aim to provide uncomplicated, prompt and economical redressal of consumer grievances, the Act provides for a three-tier, quasi-judicial machinery at the National, State and District levels. That is,

National commission: The Act provides that anyone who is or has been a judge of the Supreme Court can be appointed by the Central Government (in consultation with the Chief Justice of India) to be the President of the National Consumer Disputes Redressal Commission (the National Commission). The appoint-ments of other four members (one of whom must a woman) shall be made by the Central Government on the recommendation of a selection committee, which shall consist of a Judge of the Supreme Court to be nominated by the Chief Justice of India, the Secretary in the department of legal affairs and the Secretary in charge of consumer affairs in the Government of India. The members of the National Commission shall hold office for a term of five years or upto the age of seventy years, whichever is earlier. The members cannot be reappointed. A member may resign by giving written notice to the Central Government.

State commission: The State Government (in consultation with the Chief Justice of the High Court) is empowered to appoint any person who is or has been a judge of a High Court to be the President of The Consumer Disputes Redressal Commissions (the state commission). Other two members (one of whom must be a woman) shall be appointed by the State Government on the recommendation of a selection committee consisting of the President of the State Commission, Secretary law department of the state and secretary in charge of consumer affairs in the state. Every member of the District Forum holds office for five years or upto the age of sixty five years, whichever is earlier. The members are not eligible for reappointment. A member may resign by giving written notice to the State Government and the vacancy thus created shall also be filled up by the State Government.

District forums (consumer disputes redressal forums): Each district forum shall consist of a person who is, or who has been, or is qualified to be a District Judge, who shall be its President and two other members, one of whom shall be a woman. Appointments to the forum shall be made by the State Government on the recommendation of a selection committee consisting of the President of the state committee, the Secretary—Law Department of the State and the secretary in charge of the department dealing with consumer affairs. Every member of the district forum holds office for 5 years or upto the age of 65 years, whichever is earlier. The members are not eligible for re-appointment. A member may resign by giving written notice to the State Government and the vacancy thus created shall also be filled up by the State Government but a member cannot be re-appointment.

26.2.6 Procedure for Filing the Complaint

Subject to the other provisions of the Act, the District Forum shall have jurisdiction to entertain complaints where the value of the goods or services and the compensation, if any, claimed does not exceed ₹20 lakh, while the State Commission shall have jurisdiction to entertain complaints where the value of the goods or services and the compensation, if any, claimed does not exceed ₹1 crore. Where the value of goods or services and the compensation, if any, exceeds ₹1 crore, the complaint can be filed before the National Commission at New Delhi.

The complaint procedure is very simple. No fee is charged for filing a complaint. All that is required of the complainant is to file three to five copies of the complaint on plain paper, giving requisite information. The following information is required to be included in the complaint:

(i) The name, description and the address of both the complainant as well as the opposite party or parties, to the extent they can be ascertained
(ii) The facts relating to the complaint, giving details as to when and where it took place
(iii) Documents supporting the allegations, if any, contained in the complaint; and
(iv) The relief sought by the complainant

The complaint, duly signed by the complainant or his authorized agent may be presented by the complainant or his authorized agent, in person or sent by post to the appropriate forum/commission. The complaint must be filed within two years from the date on which cause of action surfaced.

26.2.7 Relief Available to the Consumers

Based on the facts of the case and the type of relief sought by the consumer, the forums/commission may direct

(i) Elimination of the defects from the goods, or
(ii) Substitution of the goods, or
(iii) Repayment of the price paid, or
(iv) Reimbursement for the loss or damage suffered by the consumer, or
(v) Elimination of defects or deficiencies in the services, or
(vi) Cessation of unfair trade practices/restrictive trade practices, or
(vii) Withdrawal of the hazardous goods from being offered for sale.

26.2.8 Procedure for Filing the Appeal

An appeal to the State Commission in the prescribed form and manner may be filed by the complainant feeling distressed or perturbed with any directive given by the forum. Likewise, appeal against orders of a State Commission may be filed before the National Commission and that against any directive/order of the National Commission, before the Supreme Court. All appeals must be filed within thirty days of receiving such order/directive. No fee is charged for filing an appeal before the State Commission or the National Commission. The procedure laid down under the Act, for filing the appeal is the same as that of a complaint with a difference that the appeal should accompany the orders of the District Forum/State Commission, as the case may be. As provided by the Act, it is mandatory for the forum/commission to decide complaints, to the extent feasible, within a period of three months from the date of notice received by the opposite party where complaint does not require analysis or testing of the commodities and within five months if it requires analysis or testing of commodities; and for the commission to decide the appeal within a maximum period of 90 days from the first date of hearing.

It is compulsory for the complainant/appellant as well as the opposite parties to appear before the forum/commission on the date of hearing/ adjourned hearing. Failure or omission by a trader or other person against whom a complaint is made or the complainant to comply with any order of the State Commission or the National Commission shall be punishable with imprisonment or fine or both.

26.2.9 Consumer Protection Act, 2019—Key Highlights

The Consumer Protection Act, 2019 was enacted on 9 August 2019. The new Act seeks to replace the more than 3 (three) decades old Consumer Protection Act, 1986.

Some of the Key Highlights of the new Act are discussed below:

1. The new Act has widened the definition of 'consumer'. The term 'consumer' now includes any person who buys goods, whether through offline or online transactions, electronic means, teleshopping, direct selling or multi-level marketing. E-Commerce transactions were not explicitly included in the previous Act of 1986.
2. Revised monetary limits have been fixed under the new Consumer Protection Act. Consequently, the district forum can now entertain consumer complaints where the value of goods or services paid does not exceed ₹1 crore. The State Commission can entertain disputes where such value exceeds ₹1 crore but does not exceed ₹10 crore, and the National Commission can exercise its jurisdiction in cases where such value exceeds ₹10 crore.
3. The new Act contains provision whereby the consumer enjoys flexibility of filing complaints with the jurisdictional consumer forum located at the workplace or the place of residence of the consumer. This is in dissimilar to the existing provision of filing it at the place of purchase or where the seller has its registered office address. Provisions are also made under the new Consumer Protection Act for consumers to file complaints electronically and for hearing and/or examining parties through video-conferencing. The objective is to provide procedural facility and diminish inconvenience and harassment for the consumers.
4. The new Act recommends the establishment of a regulatory authority known as the Central Consumer Protection Authority (CCPA), with extensive powers of enforcement. The Act will have an investigation wing, headed by a Director-General for conducting inquiry or investigation into consumer law violations. The Central Consumer Protection Authority has been granted wide powers to take suo-moto actions, recall products, order reimbursement of the price of goods or services, cancel licenses and file class action suits, wherever a consumer complaint affects more than one individual.
5. The CCPA may impose a penalty of up to ₹10 lakhs on a manufacturer or an endorser, for a false or misleading advertisement. The accused may also be sentenced to imprisonment for up to two years for the same. In case of a supervening offence, the fine may extend to ₹50 lakhs and imprisonment of up to five years. The CCPA can also prohibit the endorser of a misleading advertisement from endorsing that particular product or service for a period of up to one year. The period of prohibition may extend to three years for every successive offence.

6. The new Act has also introduced the concept of 'product liability' and includes within its scope, the product manufacturer, product service provider and product seller, for any claim for compensation. The term 'product seller' is defined to include a person involved in placing the product for a commercial purpose and would also include e-commerce platforms as well. Under the new Act, there are added liability risks for manufacturers in comparison to product service providers and product sellers. In other words, a manufacturer shall be liable in product liability action even where it is proved that he was not negligent or fraudulent in making the express warranty of a product. On the other hand, certain exceptions from liability claims have been provided under the new Consumer Protection Act. For example, the product seller will not be liable if the product has been misused, altered or modified.
7. The new Act enlarges the definition of Unfair Trade Practices, which also includes sharing of personal information given by the consumer in confidence, save when such disclosure is made in accordance with the provisions of any other law.
8. The new Act provides for arbitration as an 'Alternate Dispute Resolution' mechanism, making the process of dispute adjudication trouble-free and prompter for speedy resolution of disputes and reduce burden on consumer courts.

26.3 THE GENERAL INSURANCE BUSINESS (NATIONALIZATION) ACT, 1972

The General Insurance Business (Nationalization) Act, 1972, provides for the acquisition and transfer of shares of Indian insurance companies and undertakings of other existing insurers. It is designed to bring about improvement in the economy through the development, regulation and control of general insurance business, in the best interests of the community. The main purpose of the Act was to nationalize the 100 odd general insurance companies and subsequently merging them into four companies. All the companies were amalgamated into National Insurance, New India Assurance, Oriental Insurance, United India Insurance which were headquartered in each of the four metropolitan cities.

The most significant provisions of the Act are summarized here:

26.3.1 Important Definitions (Sec. 3 of the GIB Act, 1972)

Acquiring company: Means any Indian insurance company where a scheme has been framed involving the merger of one Indian insurance company in another or the amalgamation of two or more such companies, means the Indian insurance company in which any other company has been merged or the company which has been formed as a result of the amalgamation.

Appointed day: Means such day, not being a day later than the 2nd day of January, 1973, as the Central Government may, by notification, appoint.

Companies Act: Means the Companies Act, 1956.

Corporation: Refers to the General Insurance Corporation of India formed under Sec. 9.

Existing insurer: Means every insurer, the management of whose undertaking has vested in the Central Government under Sec. 3 of the General Insurance (emergency provisions) Act, 1971, and includes the undertaking of the Life Insurance Corporation insofar as it relates to the general insurance business carried on by it.

Foreign insurer: Means an existing insurer incorporated under the law of any country outside India.

General insurance business: Means fire, marine or miscellaneous insurance business, whether carried on singly or in combination with one or more of them, but does not include capital redemption business and annuity certain business.

Government company: Means a Government company as defined in Sec. 617 of the Companies Act.

Indian insurance company: Means an existing insurer having a share capital who is a company within the meaning of the Companies Act.

Insurance Act: Means the Insurance Act, 1938.

Life Insurance Corporation: Means the Life Insurance Corporation of India established under the Life Insurance Corporation Act, 1956.

Notification: Means a notification published in the official gazette.

Prescribed: Means prescribed by rules made under this Act.

Schedule: Means the Schedule to this Act.

Scheme: Means the scheme framed under Sec. 16 and Sec. 17A of the Act.

Further, it has been clarified that (a) Words and expressions used in this Act but not defined herein and defined in the Insurance Act, shall have the meanings respectively assigned to them in that Act, and (b) Words and expressions used in this Act but not defined herein or in the Insurance Act and defined in the Companies Act, shall have the meanings respectively assigned to them in the Companies Act.

26.3.2 Transfer to Public Ownership of General Insurance Business

By virtue of this Act, all the shares in the capital of every Indian insurance company shall, on the appointed day, stand transferred to and vested in the Central Government free of all trusts, liabilities and encumbrances affecting them.

26.3.3 Transfer of Undertakings of Other Existing Insurers

The Act further provides that on the appointed day, the undertaking of every existing insurer who is not an Indian insurance company shall stand transferred to and vested in the Central Government.

26.3.4 Formation of General Insurance Corporation of India

Section 9 of the Act lays down that the Central Government shall, soon after commencement of this Act, form a Government company in accordance with the provisions of the Companies Act, to be known as the General Insurance Corporation of India for the purpose of superintending, controlling and carrying on the business of general insurance and with the authorized capital of ₹250 crore.

According to the provisions carried under Sec. 10 all the shares in the capital of every Indian insurance company which stand transferred to and vested in the Central Government by virtue of provisions of this Act shall, immediately after such vesting, stand transferred to and vested in the corporation and every Indian insurance company shall forthwith give effect to such transfer of shares and rectify its register of members by including therein the Corporation as the holder of such shares.

26.3.5 Functions of the Corporation

Section 18 of the GIB Act defines the functions of the corporation to include the following:

(i) The carrying on of any part of the general insurance business, if it thinks it is desirable to do so

(ii) Aiding, assisting and advising the acquiring companies in the matter of setting up of standards of conduct and sound practice in general insurance business and in the matter of rendering efficient service to holders of policies of general insurance

(iii) Advising the acquiring companies in the matter of controlling their expenses including the payment of commission and other expenses

(iv) Advising the acquiring companies in the matter of the investment of their funds

(v) Issuing directions to acquiring companies in relation to the conduct of general insurance business

26.3.6 Functions of Acquiring Companies

The functions of the acquiring companies are laid u/s 19 of the Act

(i) That subject to the rules, if any, made by the Central Government in this behalf and to its memorandum and articles of association, it shall be the duty of every acquiring company to carry on general insurance business.

(ii) Each acquiring company shall so function under this Act as to secure that general insurance business is developed to the best advantage of the community.

(iii) For the removal of doubts it is hereby declared that the corporation and any acquiring company may, subject to the rules, if any, made by the Central Government in this behalf, enter into such contracts of reinsurance or reinsurance treaties as it may think fit for the protection of its interests.

26.3.7 Acquiring Companies to have the Exclusive Privilege of Carrying on General Insurance Business (Sec. 24)

Except to the extent expressly provided in this Act, on and from the appointed day, the corporation and the acquiring companies shall have the exclusive privilege of carrying on general insurance business in India.

26.3.8 The Manner in which Acquiring Companies shall Utilize Balance of Profits

Section 20 prescribes the rules for utilization of balance of profit by an acquiring company, requiring that after making provision for bad and doubtful debts, depreciation in assets, provident, superannuation, welfare and other funds, debts due to government and all other matters for which provision is necessary under any law or which are usually provided for by insurance companies, every acquiring company shall distribute the balance of profit as dividends. Any profit made by the corporation and any sums received by the corporation by way of dividends or otherwise shall be dealt with by it in such manner as may be prescribed.

26.3.9 Indemnity (Sec. 32)

Every officer of the Central Government and every officer or other employee of the corporation and of any acquiring company shall be indemnified by the Central Government or the corporation or the acquiring company, as the case may be, against all losses and expenses incurred by him in, or in relation to, the discharge of his duties under this Act except such as have been caused by his own wilful act or default.

26.3.10 Dissolution of Corporation and Acquiring Companies

According to Sec. 33 of the Act, no provision of law relating to the winding up of companies shall apply to the corporation or to an acquiring company, and neither the corporation nor any such company shall be placed in liquidation save by order of the Central Government and in such manner as it may direct.

26.3.11 Powers of the Central Government Under the Act

Power to transfer employees: Under the provisions of Sec. 22 of the Act, the corporation may at any time transfer any officer or employee from an acquiring company or the corporation to any other acquiring company or the corporation, as the case may be, and the officer or employee so transferred, shall continue to have the same terms and conditions of service as were applicable to him immediately before such transfer.

Power to issue directions: According to Sec. 23, the corporation and every acquiring company shall, in the discharge of its functions, be guided by such directions in regard to matters of policy involving public interest as the Central Government may give.

Power to make rules: Section 39 provides as follows:

- The Central Government may, by notification, make rules to carry out the provisions of this Act.
- In particular, and without prejudice to the generality of the foregoing power, rules made under this section may provide for
  - (a) The manner in which the profits, if any, and other moneys received by the corporation may be dealt with
  - (b) The conditions, if any, subject to which the corporation and the acquiring companies shall carry on general insurance business
  - (c) The terms and conditions subject to which any reinsurance contracts or treaties may be entered into
  - (d) The form and manner in which any notice or application may be given or made to the Central Government
  - (e) The reports which may be called for by the Central Government from the corporation and the acquiring companies
  - (f) Any other matter which is required to be, or may be, prescribed

Note: Every rule made under this section and every notification issued under Sec. 35 (application of Insurance Act) shall be laid, as soon as may be after it is made, before each House of Parliament, while it is in session, for a total period of thirty days which may be comprised in one session or in two or more successive sessions, and if, before the expiry of the session immediately following the session or the successive sessions aforesaid, both Houses agree in making any modification in the rule or notification or both Houses agree that the rule or notification should not be made, the rule or notification shall thereafter have effect only in such modified form or be of no effect, as the case may be; so, however, that any such modification or annulment shall be without prejudice to the validity of anything previously done under that rule or notification.

Power to frame/amend a scheme (Sec. 17): If the Central Government is of opinion that for the more efficient carrying on of general insurance business it is necessary so to do, it may, by notification, frame one or more schemes. The Central Government may, by notification, add to, amend or vary any scheme framed under this section. A copy of every scheme, and every amendment thereto, framed under this section shall be laid, as soon as may be after it is made, before each House of Parliament.

Power to regulate the terms and conditions of service of officers and other employees (Sec. 17A): The Central Government may, by notification in the official gazette, frame one or more schemes for regulating the pay scales and other terms and conditions of service of officers and other employees of the corporation or of any acquiring company.

26.3.12 Properties in India Not to be Insured with Foreign Insurers Except with Permission of Central Government

Section 25(1) states that no person shall take out or renew any policy of insurance in respect of any property in India or any ship or other vessel or aircraft registered in India with an insurer whose principal place of business is outside India save with the prior permission of the Central Government. If any person contravenes any provision of subsection (1), he shall be punishable with imprisonment for a term which may extend to one year, or with fine which may extend to one thousand rupees, or with both.

26.3.13 Application of Insurance Act

Section 35 provides that subject to such exceptions, restrictions and limitations, if any, as the Central Government may, by notification, specify in this behalf, the Insurance Act shall apply to or in relation to the corporation and every acquiring company as if the corporation or the acquiring company, as the case may be, were an insurer carrying on general insurance business within the meaning of that Act.

26.4 LIFE INSURANCE CORPORATION ACT, 1956

Although the first legislation in India came into force in 1938, when the Insurance Act was enacted, but the life insurance business in India could be completely nationalized only in 1956, with the enforcement of the Life Insurance Corporation Act, 1956, and the government's action of taking over the management of the insurance companies, which were operating in India during that time. The Life Insurance Corporation of India was formed in accordance with the provisions of the LIC of India Act, and has since then grown up to be the largest insurance company in India.

The major provisions of the Life Insurance Corporation Act, 1956, are discussed here.

26.4.1 Important Definitions

Section 2 of the Act contains the definitions adopted under the Act. Some of the important definitions in this Act, unless the context otherwise requires are:

Appointed day: Means the date on which the corporation is established under Sec. 3.

Composite insurer: Means an insurer carrying on in addition to controlled business any other kind of insurance business.

Controlled business: Means

- in the case of any insurer specified in sub-clause (a) or sub-clause (b) of clause (9) of Sec. 2 of the Insurance Act, and carrying on life insurance business
    - (a) all his business, if he carries on no other class of insurance business
    - (b) all the business appertaining to his life insurance business, if he carries on any other class of insurance business also
    - (c) all his business, if his certificate of registration under the Insurance Act in respect of general insurance business stands wholly cancelled for a period of more than six months on the 19th day of January, 1956
- in the case of any other insurer specified in clause (9) of Sec. 2 of the Insurance Act and carrying on life insurance business
    - (a) all his business in India, if he carries on no other class of insurance business in India
    - (b) all the business appertaining to his life insurance business in India, if he carries on any other class of insurance business also in India
    - (c) all his business in India, if his certificate of registration under the Insurance Act in respect of general insurance business in India stands wholly cancelled for a period of more than six months on the 19th day of January, 1956

Corporation: Means the Life Insurance Corporation of India established under Sec. 3

Insurance Act: Means the Insurance Act, 1938 (4 of 1938)

Insurer: Means an insurer as defined in the Insurance Act who carries on life insurance business in India and includes the government and a provident society as defined in section 65 of the Insurance Act

Member: Means a member of the corporation

Prescribed: Means prescribed by rules made under this Act

Tribunal: Means a tribunal constituted under Sec. 17 and having jurisdiction in respect of any matter under the rules made under this Act

All other words and expressions used herein but not defined and defined in the Insurance Act shall have the meanings respectively assigned to them in that Act.

26.4.2 Establishment and Incorporation of Life Insurance Corporation of India

Section 3 of the Act provides that

(i) With effect from such date as the Central Government may, by notification in the official gazette, appoint, there shall be established a corporation called the **Life Insurance Corporation of India**.

(ii) The corporation shall be a body corporate having perpetual succession and a common seal with power, subject to the provisions of this Act, to acquire, hold and dispose of property, and may by its name sue and be sued.

The Life Insurance Corporation of India (Nationalised Public Sector Undertaking) came into being on September 1, 1956 for the achievement of the following objectives:

- Spread life insurance generally and in particular to the rural areas and to the socially and economically backward classes in order to reach all insurable persons in the country and provide them adequate financial cover against death at an affordable cost.
- Making insurance-linked savings adequately attractive for maximizing mobilization of people's savings.
- To deploy the funds raised from the policyholders to the best advantage of the investors as well as the community as a whole, keeping in view national priorities and obligations of attractive return.

- Conduct business with utmost economy and with the full realization that the moneys belong to the policyholders.
- To act as trustees of the insured public in their individual and collective capacities.
- To fulfil the various life insurance needs of the community that would arise in the changing social and economic environment.
- To involve all people working in the Corporation to the best of their capability in promoting the interests of the insured public by providing efficient service with courtesy.
- Stimulate a sense of participation, pride and job satisfaction amongst all agents and employees of the Corporation through discharge of their duties with dedication towards achievement of the corporate goals.

26.4.3 Constitution of the Corporation

According to Sec. 4 of the Act

1. The corporation shall consist of such number of persons not exceeding 2 as the Central Government may think fit to appoint thereto and one of them shall be appointed by the Central Government to be the Chairman thereof.
2. Before appointing a person to be a member, the Central Government shall satisfy itself that that person will have no such financial or other interest as is likely to affect prejudicially the exercise or performance by him of his functions as a member, and the Central Government shall also satisfy itself from time to time with respect to every member that he has no such interest, and any person who is, or whom the Central Government proposes to appoint and who has consented to be, a member shall, whenever required by the Central Government so to do, furnish to it such information as the Central Government considers necessary for the performance of its duties under this subsection.
3. A member who is in any way directly or indirectly interested in a contract made or proposed to be made by the corporation shall, as soon as possible after the relevant circumstances have come to his knowledge, disclose the nature of his interest to the corporation, and the member shall not take part in any deliberation or discussion of the corporation with respect to that contract.

26.4.4 Capital of the Corporation

The corporation shall have the capital in accordance with the provisions in Sec. 5 of the Act, that is

(i) The original capital of the corporation shall be five crores of rupees provided by the Central Government after due appropriation made by Parliament by law for the purpose, and the terms and conditions relating to the provision of such capital shall be such as may be determined by the Central Government.

(ii) The Central Government may, on the recommendation of the corporation, reduce the capital of the corporation to such extent and in such manner as the Central Government may determine.

26.4.5 Functions of the Corporation (Sec. 6)

The Act depicts the functions of the corporation as follows:

(i) Subject to the rules, if any, made by the Central Government in this behalf, it shall be the general duty of the corporation to carry on life insurance business, whether in or outside India, and the corporation shall so exercise its powers under this Act as to secure that life insurance business is developed to the best advantage of the community.

(ii) Without prejudice to the generality of the provisions contained in subsection (1) but subject to the other provisions contained in this Act, the corporation shall have power

(a) To carry on capital redemption business, annuity certain business or reinsurance business in so far as such reinsurance business appertains to life insurance business.

(b) Subject to the rules, if any, made by the Central Government in this behalf, to invest the funds of the corporation in such manner as the corporation may think fit and to take all such steps as may be necessary or expedient for the protection or realization of any investment, including the taking over of and administering any property offered as security for the investment until a suitable opportunity arises for its disposal.

(c) To acquire, hold and dispose of any property for the purpose of its business.

(d) To transfer the whole or any part of the life insurance business carried on outside India to any other person or persons, if in the interests of the corporation it is expedient so to do.

(e) To advance or lend money upon the security of any movable or immovable property or otherwise.

(f) To borrow or raise any money in such manner and upon such security as the corporation may think fit.

(g) To carry on either by itself or through any subsidiary any other business in any case where such other business was being carried on by a subsidiary of an insurer whose controlled business has been transferred to and vested in the corporation under this Act.

(h) To carry on any other business which may seem to the corporation to be capable of being conveniently carried on in connection with its business and calculated directly or indirectly to render profitable the business of the corporation.

(i) To do all such things as may be incidental or conducive to the proper exercise of any of the powers of the corporation.

It is further provided that the corporation must, in the discharge of any of its functions, act so far as may be, on business principles. Furthermore, in the discharge of its functions under this Act, the corporation shall be guided by such directions in matters of policy involving public interest as the Central Government may give to it in writing, and if any question arises whether a direction relates to a matter of policy involving public interest the decision of the Central Government thereon shall be final.

26.4.6 Constitution of Tribunals

(i) The Central Government may, for the purposes of and in accordance with the provisions in Sec. 17 of this Act, constitute one or more tribunals. Each tribunal shall consist of three members appointed by the Central Government one of whom shall be a person (i.e., the Chairman thereof) who is, or has been, a Judge of a High Court or that of the Supreme Court.

(ii) Tribunal may choose one or more persons possessing special knowledge of any matter relating to any case under inquiry to assist the tribunal in determining any question which has to be decided by it under this Act.

(iii) Every tribunal shall have the powers of a civil court in respect of matters relating to

(a) Summoning and enforcing the attendance of any person and examining him on oath

(b) Requiring the discovery and production of documents

(c) Receiving evidence on affidavits

(d) Issuing commissions for the examination of witnesses or documents

26.4.7 Management of the Corporation

The central office of the corporation shall be at such place as the Central Government may, by notification in the official gazette, specify. The corporation shall establish a zonal office at each of the following places, namely, Mumbai, Kolkata, Delhi, Kanpur and Chennai, and, subject to the previous approval of the Central Government, may establish such other zonal offices as it thinks fit. The territorial limits of each zone shall be such as may be specified by the corporation. There may be established as many divisional offices and branches in each zone as the zonal manager thinks fit.

The corporation may entrust the general superintendence and direction of its affairs and business to an Executive Committee consisting of not more than five of its members and the Executive Committee may exercise all powers and do all such acts and things as may be delegated to it by the corporation. Besides, an Investment Committee may also be constituted for the purpose of advising the corporation in matters relating to the investment of its funds., and the Investment Committee shall consist of not more than eight members of whom not less than four shall be members of the corporation and the remaining members shall be persons (whether members of the corporation or not) who have special knowledge and experience in financial matters, particularly, matters relating to investment of funds.

The corporation may constitute such other committees as it may think fit for the purpose of discharging such of its functions as may be delegated to them. It may appoint one or more persons to be the Managing Director or directors of the corporation, and every managing director shall be a whole-time officer of the corporation, and shall exercise such powers and perform such duties as may be entrusted or delegated to him by the Executive Committee or the corporation. The superintendence and direction of the affairs and business of a zonal office may be entrusted to a person, whether a member or not, who shall be known as the **zonal manager** and the zonal Manager shall perform all such functions of the corporation as may be delegated to him with respect to the area within the jurisdiction of the zonal office. For the purpose of advising the zonal Manager in respect of such matters as are referred to it under the regulations made by the corporation, a board consisting of such number of persons as it thinks fit to appoint thereto, may be constituted by the corporation for each zone.

The corporation shall also constitute in the prescribed manner for each zonal office an Employees and Agents Relations Committee consisting of such number of persons as it thinks fit and every such committee shall consist of representatives of the corporation and its employees and agents, so however, that the number of representatives of the employees and agents on the committee shall not be less than the number of representatives of the corporation and it shall be the duty of the committee to advise the zonal manager on matters which relate to the welfare of the employees and agents of the corporation or which are likely to promote and secure amity and good relations between them and the corporation.

26.4.8 Funds of the Corporation (Sec. 24)

The corporation shall have its own fund and all receipts of the corporation shall be credited thereto and all payments of the corporation shall be made therefrom.

26.4.9 Audit of Accounts of the Corporation (Sec. 25)

The accounts of the corporation shall be audited by auditors duly qualified to act as auditors of companies under the law for the time being in force relating to companies, and the auditors shall be appointed by the corporation with the previous approval of the Central Government and shall receive such remuneration from the corporation as the Central Government may fix. The auditors shall submit their report to the corporation and shall also forward a copy of their report to the Central Government.

26.4.10 Actuarial Valuations (Sec. 26)

The corporation shall, once at least in every two years, cause an investigation to be made by actuaries into the financial condition of the life insurance business of the corporation, including a valuation of the liabilities of the corporation in respect thereto, and submit the report of the actuaries to the Central Government.

26.4.11 Annual Report of Activities of Corporation (Sec. 27)

The corporation shall, as soon as may be, after the end of each financial year, prepare and submit to the Central Government in such form as may be prescribed a report giving an account of its activities during the previous financial year, and the report shall also give an account of the activities, if any, which are likely to be undertaken by the corporation in the next financial year.

26.4.12 Policies to be Guaranteed by Central Government (Sec. 37)

The sums assured by all policies issued by the corporation including any bonuses declared in respect thereof and, subject to the provisions contained in Sec. 14 the amounts assured by all policies issued by any insurer the liabilities under which have vested in the corporation under this Act, and all bonuses declared in respect thereof, whether before or after the appointed day, shall be guaranteed as to payment in cash by the Central Government.

26.4.13 Liquidation of the Corporation (Sec. 38)

No provision of law, as provided in the Companies Act, relating to the winding up of companies or corporations shall apply to the corporation established under this Act, and the corporation shall not be placed in liquidation save by order of the Central Government and in such manner as the Government may direct.

26.4.14 Application of the Insurance Act (Sec. 43)

(i) The following sections of the Insurance Act shall, so far as may be, apply to the corporation as they apply to any other insurer, namely—Sections 2, 2B, 3, 18, 26, 33, 38, 39, 41, 45, 46, 47A, 50, 51, 52, 110A, 110B, 110C, 119, 121, 122 and 123.

(ii) The Central Government shall as soon as may be after the commencement of this Act, by notification in the official gazette, direct that the following sections of the Insurance Act shall apply to the corporation subject to such conditions and modification as may be specified in the notification, namely—Sections 2D, 10, 11, 13, 14, 15, 20, 21, 22, 23, 25, 27A, 28A, 35, 36, 37, 40A, 40B, 43, 44, 102 to 106, 107 to 110, 111, 113, 114 and 116A.

(iii) The Central Government may, by notification in the official gazette, direct that all or any of the provisions of the Insurance Act other than those specified in subsection (1) or subsection (2), shall apply to the corporation subject to such conditions and modifications as may be specified in the notification.

(iv) Every notification issued under subsection (2) or subsection (3) shall be laid for not less than thirty days before both Houses of Parliament as soon as possible after it is issued, and shall be subject to such modifications as Parliament may make during the session in which it is so laid or the session immediately following.

(v) Save as provided in this section, nothing contained in the Insurance Act shall apply to the corporation.

26.4.15 Power of the Central Government to make rules (Sec. 48)

The Central Government may, by notification in the Official Gazette, make rules to carry out the objectives of this Act. In particular, and without prejudice to the generality of the foregoing power, such rules may provide for all or any of the following matters, namely:

(i) The term of office and the conditions of service of members

(ii) The manner in which the moneys and other assets belonging to any such fund as is referred to in Sec. 8 shall be apportioned between the trustees of the fund and the corporation

(iii) The services which the chief agent should have rendered for the purpose of the proviso to Sec. 12; and, the terms and conditions of service of the employees and agents of the corporation, including those who became employees and agents of the corporation on the appointed day under this Act

(iv) The jurisdiction of the tribunals constituted under Sec. 17

(v) The manner in which, and the persons to whom, any compensation under this Act may be paid

(vi) The time within which any matter which may be referred to a tribunal for decision under this Act may be so referred

(vii) The manner in which and the conditions subject to which investments may be made by the corporation

(viii) The manner in which an Employees and Agents Relations Committee may be constituted for each zonal office

(ix) The form in which the report giving an account of the activities of the corporation shall be prepared

(x) The conditions subject to which the corporation may appoint employees

(xi) The fees payable under this Act and the manner in which they are to be collected

(xii) Any other matter which has to be or may be prescribed

Every rule made by the Central Government under this Act shall be laid, as soon as may be after it is made, before each House of Parliament while it is in session, for a total period of thirty days which may be comprised in one session or in two or more successive sessions, and if, before the expiry of the session immediately following the session or the successive sessions aforesaid, both Houses agree in making any modification in the rule or both Houses agree that the rule should not be made, the rule shall thereafter have effect only in such modified form or be of no effect, as the case may be; so, however, that any such modification or annulment shall be without prejudice to the validity of anything previously done under that rule.

26.5 THE INSURANCE REGULATORY AND DEVELOPMENT AUTHORITY ACT, 1999

Owing to the nationalization of the insurance sector there were no private insurance companies operating in India till 1999, when the Government of India introduced the Insurance Regulatory and Development Authority Act, thereby deregulating the insurance sector and allowing private companies into the insurance. Further, foreign investment was also allowed and capped at 26 per cent holding in the Indian insurance companies. Thus, the objective of the IRDA Act, 1999, was to provide for the establishment of an authority to protect the interests of holders of insurance policies, to regulate, promote and ensure orderly growth of the insurance industry and for matters connected therewith or incidental thereto and further to amend the Insurance Act, 1938, the Life Insurance Corporation Act, 1956 and the General Insurance Business (Nationalization) Act, 1972.

The most significant provisions of IRDA Act, 1999, are briefly explained hereinafter.

26.5.1 Extent and Coverage

The Act shall come into force on such date as the Central Government may, by notification in the official gazette, appoint and its provisions shall extend to the whole of India. The provisions of this Act shall be in addition to, and not in derogation of, the provisions of any other law for the time being in force.

26.5.2 Important Definitions (Sec. 2)

In this Act, unless the context otherwise requires,

Appointed day: Means the date on which the authority is established under subsection (1) of Sec. 3.

Authority: Means the Insurance Regulatory and Development Authority established under subsection (1) of Sec. 3.

Chairperson: Means the Chairperson of the authority.

Fund: Means the Insurance Regulatory and Development Authority fund constituted under subsection (1) of Sec. 16.

Interim Insurance Regulatory Authority: Means the Insurance Regulatory Authority set up by the Central Government through Resolution No. 17(2)/94-Ins.-V, dated the 23rd January, 1996.

Intermediary or insurance intermediary: Includes insurance brokers, reinsurance brokers, insurance consultants, surveyors and loss assessors.

Member: Means a whole-time or a part-time member of the authority and includes the Chairperson.

Notification: Means a notification published in the official gazette.

Regulations: Means the regulations made by the authority.

Words and expressions used and not defined in this Act but defined in the Insurance Act, 1938 (4 of 1938), or the Life Insurance Corporation Act, 1956 (31 of 1956), or the General Insurance Business (Nationalization) Act, 1972 (57 of 1972), shall have the meanings assigned to them in those Acts, respectively.

26.5.3 Establishment and Incorporation of Authority (Sec. 3)

With effect from such date as the Central Government may, by notification, appoint, there shall be established, for the purposes of this Act, an authority to be called the **Insurance Regulatory and Development Authority**. The authority shall be a body corporate by the name aforesaid having perpetual succession and a common seal with power, subject to the provisions of this Act, to acquire, hold and dispose of property, both movable and immovable, and to contract and shall, by the said name, sue or be sued. The head office of the authority shall be at such place as the Central Government may decide from time to time. The authority may establish offices at other places in India.

26.5.4 Composition of Authority (Sec. 4)

The authority shall consist of a Chairperson, along with not more than five whole-time members and not more than four part-time members, who shall be appointed by the Central Government.

The Chairperson and every other whole-time/part-time member, as per Sec. 5 of the Act, shall hold office for a term of five years from the date of his appoinment and shall be eligible for reappointment. The Chairperson shall have the powers of general superintendence and direction in respect of all administrative matters of the authority. Further, no person shall hold office as a Chairperson after he has attained the age of sixty-five years and no person shall hold office as a whole-time member after he has attained the age of sixty-two years. Members may resign by giving a written notice of not less than three months to the Central Government. Section 8 of the Act provides that the Chairperson and the whole-time members shall not, for a period of two years from the date on which they cease to hold office as such, except with the previous approval of the Central Government, accept any employment either under the Central Government or under any State Government or any appointment in any company in the insurance sector.

Besides, the authority may, as provided for u/s 12, appoint officers and such other employees as it considers necessary for the efficient discharge of its functions under this Act. The terms and other conditions of service of officers and other employees of the authority appointed under subsection (1) shall be governed by the regulations made under this Act.

26.5.5 Removal from Office (Sec. 6)

The Central Government may remove from office any member who

(i) Is, or at any time has been, adjudged as an insolvent

(ii) Has become physically or mentally incapable of acting as a member

(iii) Has been convicted of any offence which, in the opinion of the Central Government, involves moral turpitude
(iv) Has acquired such financial or other interest as is likely to affect prejudicially his functions as a member
(v) Has so abused his position as to render his continuation in office detrimental to the public interest

26.5.6 Salary and Allowances of Chairperson and Members

The Act u/s 7 prescribes the salary and allowances payable to, and other terms and conditions of service of, the members other than part-time members.

26.5.7 Meetings of Authority (Sec. 10)

The Authority shall meet at such time and places and shall observe such rules and procedures in regard to transaction of business at its meetings (including quorum at such meetings) as may be determined by the regulations. The Chairperson, or if for any reason he is unable to attend a meeting of the authority, any other member chosen by the members present from amongst themselves at the meeting shall preside at the meeting. All questions which come up before any meeting of the authority shall be decided by a majority of votes by the members present and voting, and in the event of an equality of votes, the Chairperson, or in his absence, the person presiding shall have a second or casting vote. The authority may make regulations for the transaction of business at its meetings.

26.5.8 Duties, Powers and Functions of Authority (Sec. 14)

Subject to the provisions of this Act and any other law for the time being in force, the authority shall have the duty to regulate, promote and ensure orderly growth of the insurance business and re-insurance business.

The **powers and functions** of the authority shall include

(i) Issue to the applicant a certificate of registration, renew, modify, withdraw, suspend or cancel such registration
(ii) Protection of the interests of the policyholders in matters concerning assigning of policy, nomination by policyholders, insurable interest, settlement of insurance claim, surrender value of policy and other terms and conditions of contracts of insurance
(iii) Specifying requisite qualifications, code of conduct and practical training for intermediary or insurance intermediaries and agents
(iv) Specifying the code of conduct for surveyors and loss assessors
(v) Promoting efficiency in the conduct of insurance business

(vi) Promoting and regulating professional organizations connected with the insurance and reinsurance business

(vii) Levying fees and other charges for carrying out the purposes of this Act

(viii) Calling for information from, undertaking inspection of, conducting enquiries and investigations including audit of the insurers, intermediaries, insurance intermediaries and other organizations connected with the insurance business

(ix) Control and regulation of the rates, advantages, terms and conditions that may be offered by insurers in respect of general insurance business not so controlled and regulated by the Tariff Advisory Committee under Sec. 64U of the Insurance Act 1938

(x) Specifying the form and manner in which books of account shall be maintained and statement of accounts shall be rendered by insurers and other insurance intermediaries

(xi) Regulating investment of funds by insurance companies

(xii) Regulating maintenance of margin of solvency

(xiii) Adjudication of disputes between insurers and intermediaries or insurance intermediaries

(xiv) Supervising the functioning of the Tariff Advisory Committee

(xv) Specifying the percentage of premium income of the insurer to finance schemes for promoting and regulating professional organizations referred to in clause (f)

(xvi) Specifying the percentage of life insurance business and general insurance business to be undertaken by the insurer in the rural or social sector

(xvii) Exercising such other powers as may be prescribed

26.5.9 Constitution of Fund (Sec. 16)

There shall be constituted a fund to be called the **Insurance Regulatory and Development Authority Fund** and there shall be credited thereto all Government grants, fees and charges received by the authority, all sums received by the authority from such other source as may be decided upon by the Central Government and a percentage of the prescribed premium income received from the insurer.

The fund shall be applied for meeting the salaries, allowances and other remuneration of the members, officers and other employees of the authority as well as other expenses of the authority in connection with the discharge of its functions and for the purposes of this Act.

26.5.10 Accounts and Audit (Sec. 17)

The authority shall maintain proper accounts and other relevant records and prepare an annual statement of accounts in such form as may be prescribed by the Central Government in consultation with the Comptroller and Auditor-General of India.

The accounts of the authority shall be audited by the Comptroller and Auditor-General of India at such intervals as may be specified by him and any expenditure incurred in connection with such audit shall be payable by the authority to the Comptroller and Auditor-General.

The Comptroller and Auditor-General of India and any other person appointed by him in connection with the audit of the accounts of the authority shall have the same rights, privileges and authority in connection with such audit as the Comptroller and Auditor-General generally has in connection with the audit of the Government accounts and, in particular, shall have the right to demand the production of books of account, connected vouchers and other documents and papers and to inspect any of the offices of the authority.

The accounts of the authority as certified by the Comptroller and Auditor-General of India or any other person appointed by him in this behalf together with the audit report thereon shall be forwarded annually to the Central Government and that Government shall cause the same to be laid before each House of Parliament.

26.5.11 Powers of Central Government Under the Act

Power to issue directions (Sec. 18): Without prejudice to the foregoing provisions of this Act, the authority shall, in exercise of its powers or the performance of its functions under this Act, be bound by such directions on question of policy, other than those relating to technical and administrative matters, as the Central Government may give in writing to it from time to time.

Power to supercede authority (Sec. 19): If, at any time the Central Government is of the opinion that, on account of circumstances beyond the control of the authority, it is unable to discharge the functions or perform the duties imposed on it by or under the provisions of this Act; or that the Authority has persistently defaulted in complying with any direction given by the Central Government under this Act and as a result of such default the financial position of the authority or the administration of the Authority has suffered; or that circumstances exist, which render it necessary in the public interest so to do, the Central Government may, by notification and for reasons to be specified therein, supercede the authority for such period, not exceeding six months, as may be specified in the notification and appoint a person to be the Controller of Insurance under Section 2B of the Insurance Act, 1938.

The Central Government shall cause a copy of the notification issued under subsection (1) and a full report of any action taken under this section and the circumstances leading to such action to be laid before each House of Parliament at the earliest.

Power to make rules (Sec. 24): The Central Government may, by notification, make rules, in respect of the following matters:

- The salary and allowances payable to, and other terms and conditions of service of, the members other than part-time members under Sec. 7(1)
- The allowances to be paid to the part-time members under Sec. 7(2)
- Such other powers that may be exercised by the authority under clause (q) of Sec. 14(2)
- The form of annual statement of accounts to be maintained by the authority u/s 17(1);
- The form and manner in which and the time within which returns and statements and particulars are to be furnished to the Central Government under Sec. 20(1)
- Matters u/s 25(5) on which the Insurance Advisory Committee shall advise the authority
- Any other matter which is required to be, or may be, prescribed, or in respect of which provision is to be or may be made by rules

Power to remove difficulties (Sec. 29): If any difficulty arises in giving effect to the provisions of this Act, the Central Government may, by order published in the official gazette, make such provisions not inconsistent with the provisions of this Act as may appear to be necessary for removing the difficulty.

Grants by Central Government (Sec. 15): The Central Government may, after due appropriation made by Parliament by law in this behalf, make to the authority grants of such sums of money as the Government may think fit for being utilized for the purposes of this Act.

26.5.12 Furnishing of Returns, etc. to Central Government (Sec. 20)

The authority shall furnish to the Central Government at such time and in such form and manner as may be prescribed, or as the Central Government may direct to furnish such returns, statements and other particulars in regard to any proposed or existing programme for the promotion and development of the insurance industry as the Central Government may, from time to time, require.

Within nine months after the close of each financial year, the authority shall submit to the Central Government, a report giving a true and full account of its activities including the activities for promotion and development of the insurance business during the previous financial year. Copies of such reports shall be laid, as soon as may be after they are received, before each House of Parliament.

The Chairperson, members, officers and employees of the authority shall in this regard be deemed to be public servants.

26.5.13 Delegation of Powers (Sec. 23)

The authority may, by general or special order in writing, delegate to the Chairperson or any other member or officer of the authority subject to such conditions, if any, as may be specified in the order, such of its powers and functions under this Act as it may deem necessary or likewise, form committees of the members and delegate to them the powers and functions of the authority as may be specified by the regulations.

26.5.14 Establishment of Insurance Advisory Committee (Sec. 25)

The authority may, by notification, establish with effect from such date as it may specify in such notification, a committee to be known as the Insurance Advisory Committee. The Insurance Advisory Committee shall consist of not more than twenty-five members excluding ex officio members to represent the interests of commerce, industry, transport, agriculture, consumer forums, surveyors, agents, intermediaries, organizations engaged in safety and loss prevention, research bodies and employees' association in the insurance sector. The Chairperson and the members of the authority shall be the ex officio Chairperson and ex officio members of the Insurance Advisory Committee. The objects of the Insurance Advisory Committee shall be to advise the authority on matters relating to the making of the regulations under Sec. 26.

26.5.15 Power to Make Regulations (Sec. 26)

The authority may, in consultation with the Insurance Advisory Committee, by notification, make regulations, consistent with this Act and providing for all or any of the following matters:

(i) The time and places of meetings of the authority and the procedure to be followed at such meetings including the quorum necessary for the transaction of business.

(ii) The transaction of business at its meetings u/s 10(4)

(iii) The terms and other conditions of service of officers and other employees of the authority under subsection (2) of Sec. 12

(iv) The powers and functions which may be delegated to committees of the members under subsection (2) of Sec. 23

(v) Any other matter which is required to be, or may be, specified by regulations or in respect of which provision is to be or may be made by regulations

26.5.16 Rules and Regulations to be Laid Before Parliament (Sec. 27)

Every rule and every regulation made under this Act shall be laid, as soon as may be after it is made, before each House of Parliament, while it is in session, for a total period of thirty days, which may be comprised in one session or in two or more successive sessions, and if, before the expiry of the session immediately following the session or the successive sessions aforesaid, both Houses agree in making any modification in the rule or regulation or both Houses agree that the rule or regulation should not be made, the rule or regulation shall thereafter have effect only in such modified form or be of no effect, as the case may be.

26.5.17 Penalty for Default in Complying with, or Act in Contravention of, this Act

If any person, who is required, under this Act or rules or regulations made thereunder

(i) To furnish any document, statement, account, return or report to the authority, fails to furnish the same

(ii) To comply with the directions, fails to comply with such directions

(iii) To maintain solvency margin, fails to maintain such solvency margin

(iv) To comply with the directions on the insurance treaties, fails to comply with such directions, he shall be liable to a penalty not exceeding five lakh rupees for each such failure and punishable with fine.

If a person makes a statement, or furnishes any document, statement, account, return or report which is false and which he either knows or believes to be false or does not believe to be true, he shall be liable to a penalty not exceeding five lakh rupees and shall be punishable with imprisonment which may extend to three years or with fine for each such failure.

26.5.18 Offences by Companies (Sec. 105A)

Where any offence under this Act has been committed by a company, every person who, at the time the offence was committed, was in charge of, and was responsible to, the company for the conduct of the business of the company as well as the company shall be deemed to be guilty of the offence and shall be liable to be proceeded against and punished accordingly.

26.6 INSURANCE (AMENDMENT) ACT, 2015

The long overdue Insurance (Amendment) Act, 2015 came into force on 23 March, 2015.

The major highlights of the new Act may be summarized as below:

1. Foreign investment ceiling that applies to the "paid-up equity capital" of an insurance company has been increased from 26% to 49%.
2. A new requisite levied by the amendment is that the joint ventures must be Indian controlled. But there is no clear definition of what shall satisfy this prerequisite. In the absence of any clear definition, the determination of whether an insurer is 'Indian controlled' would have to be made on the basis of individual case.
3. Prior to the enactment of the Amendment Act, 2015, insurance companies were permitted only to issue equity shares with uniform face value. The amendment now authorises insurance companies to issue "such other form of capital as may be specified by the regulations." Permission to issue preference shares or debentures that do not carry voting rights, would enable the insurer to raise more foreign capital without having any impact on its compliance with the 49% ceiling on foreign ownership that only applies to equity capital or to the requirement for Indian control.
4. The new Amendment Act provides that even after ten years of commencement of business; a promoter can hold more than 26% (even upto 100%) of shares in the business. Previously, the Insurance Act required the Indian 'promoter' of an insurance company to divest its stake in excess of 26% within 10 years of commencing business.
5. A key highlight of the new Act is that *Health Insurance,* which was formerly regulated as a part of the general insurance business shall now be proposed to be regulated on a stand-alone basis under the provisions of the new Amendment Act, 2015. The aim of this amendment is to bestow priority on health insurance business through a more focused regulatory regime.
6. The Amendment Act allows foreign reinsurers to operate out of wholly owned branch offices. Previously, only domestic insurance companies were permitted to sell reinsurance. The government has now dispensed with the requirement for reinsurance business to be conducted only through a company incorporated in India.

7. The Insurance Regulatory and Development Authority of India (IRDAI) has been bestowed with greater flexibility under the new amendment to regulate insurance companies through its rule-making powers on matters such as management fees, commissions and composition of the insurance company's investment portfolio. Earlier, these were included within the provisions of the Insurance Act itself.
8. The penalties for violation of the provisions of the Act have considerably been increased under the new Amendment Act, 2015. For example, as per Section 102, where a company fails to comply with the directions of Insurance Regulatory and Development Authority of India, the penalty has been markedly increased from ₹5 Lakhs to ₹1 Lakh for each day or ₹1 crore, whichever is less.
9. The Insurance Laws Amendment Act, 2015 has made Securities Appellate Tribunal (SAT) as the appellate authority to the Insurance Regulatory and Development Authority.
10. Section 3A of the Insurance Act, 1938 that provides for annual renewal of registration of insurance company has been amended under the 2015 Amendment Act. The new Act mandates merely for annual fee and no annual renewal is now required. In other words, it provides for permanent registration of the companies. IRDA has the authority to suspend or cancel such registration under certain specified conditions.

26.7 THE INSURANCE (AMENDMENT) ACT, 2021

The significant objective of the Insurance (Amendment) Act, 2021 is to realise the purpose of the Government's FDI (Foreign Direct Investment) Policy by raising the threshold limit of the foreign investment in the Indian insurance companies from the prevailing 49% to 74%, and to permit the foreign ownership and control with certain precautions. The enhanced investment limit is hoped to induce competition and thus growth.

Three sections (Sections 2, 27 and 114) under The Insurance Act, 1938 have been amended by the Insurance Amendment Act, 2021. Section 2 (7A) defines "Indian insurance company" as "any insurer" which is a company and is limited by shares. It is incorporated under the Companies Act of 2013 in the nature of a public company or is transformed into the same within a duration of 1 year since the commencement of the Insurance Laws (Amendment) Act, 2015 (5 of 2015) [sub-clause *(a)*]. Sub-clause *(b)* of Sec. 2 has now been changed to define an Indian insurance company as a company in which "the aggregate holdings of equity shares by foreign investors including portfolio investors, do not exceed 74% of the paid-up equity capital of such Indian insurance company, and the foreign investment in which shall be subject to such conditions and manner, as may be prescribed." Earlier ceiling of 49% has now been enhanced to 74% and the words "Indian owned and controlled" have been substituted by "foreign investment".

Section 27 of the Insurance Act contains provisions related to the investment of assets. Section 27(7) of the Act provides that the Indian assets invested by a foreign investor "shall be held in trust for the discharge of liabilities" and "shall be vested in trustees resident in India and approved by the Authority, and the instrument of trust under this sub-section shall be executed by the insurer with the approval of the Authority and shall define the manner in which alone the subject-matter of the trust shall be dealt with."

Section 114 of the Act gives the power to Central Government to make rules for the purposes of this Act. Under Sec. 114(2) of the Act the rules so made could earlier prescribe "the manner of ownership and control of Indian insurance company under sub-clause *(b)* of clause *(7A)* of section 2" [clause *(aaa)*]. The words "manner of ownership and control of Indian insurance company" have been replaced by "the conditions and manner of foreign investment" by the 2021 amendment.

KEY TERMS

Consideration Price for which the promise of the other is bought and the promise thus obtained is legally enforceable.

Corporation The term refers to—(i) General Insurance Corporation of India u/s 9 of the GIB Act, 1972, and (ii) Life Insurance Corporation of India u/s 3 of the LIC Act, 1956.

Insurance intermediary The term includes insurance brokers, insurance agents, reinsurance brokers, insurance consultants, surveyors and loss assessors (as defined under the IRDA, Act, 1999).

Investigation The term broadly means to examine the managerial affairs of the insurance company in order to find out whether any irregularities have been committed or not.

Liquidation Process by which the business is dissolved or shut down by discharging its debts and liabilities out of the proceeds of realisation of its assets.

Misrepresentation Making, circulating, issuing or causing to be issued or circulated an estimate, an illustration, a notice or statement that does not represent the true nature of the terms and conditions of the policy.

Obligation Legal tie imposing the compulsion to do or not to do an act or acts upon particular person or persons.

Redressal machinery The mechanism of providing relief against the grievances of consumers in accordance with the provisions under the CPA, 1986.

REVIEW QUESTIONS

26.1 What is the object and nature of the law of contract? Classify and define various contracts.

26.2 "All agreements are not contracts but all contracts are agreements." Discuss the statement explaining the essential elements of a valid contract. When does an agreement become void?

26.3 Distinguish between the following classes of contracts:

(i) Express and implied contracts
(ii) Executed and executory contracts
(iii) Valid, void and voidable contracts
(iv) Void agreements and void contracts

26.4 Discuss the legal provisions governing the relationship between an agent and the principal.

26.5 What are the rights and the duties of an agent?

26.6 What is the relevance of the Consumer Protection Act in insurance business?

26.7 Discuss the redressal of consumer's grievances under the CPA.

26.8 Briefly explain the rights of consumers under the Consumer Protection Act.

26.9 What are the powers and functions of General Insurance Corporation of India? Briefly explain the important provisions of GIC Act, 1972.

26.10 What are the objectives of LIC? Describe the constitution of the LIC.

26.11 Elucidate the functions and powers of the LIC of India.

26.12 Discuss the role of IRDA in the Indian insurance service sector.

26.13 Discuss the powers and duties of IRDA.

26.14 Explain the objectives of IRDA Act, 1999. What are the powers, duties and functions of the authority under the Act?

26.15 What are the superceding powers of the Central Government under the IRDA Act, 1999?

26.16 Briefly discuss the important features of Insurance (Amendment) Act, 2015.

26.17 What role has been assigned to the advisory committee by the provisions of the Insurance Act?

26.18 Write short notes on

(i) Licensing of surveyors and loss assessors
(ii) Tariff advisory committee

(iii) Insurance business in rural or social sector
(iv) Management of the Life Insurance Corporation
(v) Controlled business
(vi) Acquiring companies
(vii) Protection of consumers' interests under CPA
(viii) 'Consumer' as defined in CPA
(ix) IRDA fund
(x) Insurance Amendment Act, 2021
(xi) Consumer Protection Act, 2019

27

Indian Insurance Industry: Transition and Prospects

Learning Objectives

After going through this chapter we will be able to:

- Trace the historical background of insurance in india.
- Describe the major reforms in the Indian insurance sector.
- Explicate the meaning and implications of liberalization.
- Envisage future trends in the Indian insurance industry.
- Elucidate the macro insurance prospects for India.
- Examine the role of major insurance players in India.
- Discuss budget 2007 proposals for the Indian insurance Industry.

The saga of insurance is presumably as old as that of mankind itself. The inclination to secure oneself against loss and adversity stimulated ancient men as much as it motivates today's ambitious folks. The beginning of insurance can thus be traced back to ancient times. In fact, it is said to have started with the code of Hammurabi in 2100 BC, which formalized the concepts of civic responsibilities, bottomry and respondentia. Bottomry and respondentia loans refer to marine contracts covering vessels and cargo.

27.1 INSURANCE IN INDIA: HISTORICAL BACKGROUND

In India, the concept of insurance was prevalent even during ancient times. In fact, there are references of insurance in the Vedas. For instance, yogakshema, the name of life insurance corporation of India's corporate headquarters, stems from the Rig Veda. Insurance in its earliest form existed in the shape of marine insurance. In the ancient land of Babylonia, nearly 4,500 years ago, the practice of traders giving loans, which were to be repaid with interest when the goods arrived safely, was a means of bearing (i.e., insuring) risk of the trade-convoy. Thus, a system was devised whereby the financial loss unbearable to an individual could be spread over the group of traders. However, the concept of insurance as understood today came to exist in England in the 17th century at the Lloyd's coffee house in London, a meeting place for merchants, shipowners and underwriters where they discussed and transacted business. Later by the 18th century, the business of Lloyd's flourished to such an extent that it turned to be one of the first modern insurance companies.

The onset of life insurance was seen in England in the 16th century. In 1693, astronomer Edmond Halley worked out the first mortality table on the basis of statistical laws of mortality and compound interest, which helped in establishing a correlation between the life insurance premium and the average life spans. Joseph Dodson modified the table in 1756, to bring out the linkage of premium rate with age. The earliest stock companies indulging into the business of insurance were chartered in England in 1720. However, it was only after 1840, that life insurance really bloomed in a big way. In India, the first life insurance company named The Oriental Life Assurance Co. Ltd., was set up mainly by Europeans in Bengal in 1818, followed by the establishment of Bombay Mutual Life Assurance Society in 1871. Indian policyholders were charged 15 per cent higher premium than their European counterparts.

The 19th century witnessed rapid changes in the field of insurance, with newer products being conceived to cope up with the emergent requirements of the post-industrialization era. Fire insurance originated in Germany but gained momentum after the catastrophic fire in England in 1866, which drew people's attention to the need to provide insurance for unexpected, huge losses simultaneously suffered by a large section of people. Since, it was impractical to imagine a single company to provide protection against such gigantic losses, the practice of reinsurance was developed, whereby the risks are spread among a number of companies, was developed particularly for such eventualities. In India, the Triton Insurance, Calcutta, started fire insurance in 1850, but it could not make much headway. In the 19th century, many innovations in insurance took place, which benefited the society as a whole.

In India, the insurance industry started flourishing in the early 20th century with the setting up of many new companies. By the middle of the 20th century, India had approximately 170 insurance companies and nearly 80 provident fund societies providing life insurance cover. With the growth in the business conducted by these companies, the government felt the need to regulate them. Thus, the first attempt at regulation of the insurance business in India was through the passing of the Indian Life Assurance Companies Act in 1912, which was later amended and passed as the Insurance Act in 1938. Life assurance business in India was nationalized with the amalgamation of about 250 life insurance companies before being taken over and setting up of the Life Insurance Corporation of India by the government in 1956. The result was the monopolization of the insurance business by the public sector for a long period of time.

Some of the significant landmarks in the insurance sector in India may be summarized as:

1818: Oriental Life Insurance Company, the first life insurance company started functioning in India.

1850: The British established the first general insurance company named the Triton Insurance Company Ltd. in Calcutta.

1870: Bombay Mutual Life Assurance Society, the first Indian life insurance company started its business.

1907: The Indian Mercantile Insurance Ltd., the first company to transact all classes of general insurance business was set up.

1912: The Indian Life Assurance Companies Act was passed to legalize and control the life insurance business in India.

1928: The Indian Insurance Companies Act was passed to empower the government to gather statistical information concerning both life and non-life insurance businesses.

1938: The Insurance Act was passed with the objective of protecting the interests of the insuring public.

1956: 250 Indian and foreign insurers and provident fund societies were taken over by the Central Government and nationalized. LIC was formed as a statutory corporation under an Act of Parliament, namely, The LIC Act, 1956.

1957: The General Insurance Council, a wing of the Insurance Association of India, framed a code of conduct to ascertain reliable and sound business practices.

1968: The Insurance Act was amended to regulate investments and set minimum solvency margins and for setting up the Tariff Advisory Committee.

1972: The General Insurance Business (Nationalization) Act, 1972 was passed.

27.2 REFORMS IN THE INDIAN INSURANCE SECTOR

The financial reforms paving way to liberalization of the Indian economy in the early 1990s resulted in the recognition of the insurance sector as an important part of the overall financial system. Thus, it was found necessary to bring about appropriate reforms in the insurance sector as well. In 1993, Malhotra Committee, led by former finance secretary and RBI governor, R.N. Malhotra was formed to assess the state of insurance industry in India and submit its recommendations.

The Malhotra Committee was formed with the following purposes:

1. To propose the structure of the insurance industry, to evaluate its strengths and weaknesses with the intention of creating an efficient and feasible insurance industry that would offer wide-ranging insurance services, covering a variety of insurance products with a high quality of services to the public and operating as an efficient means for mobilization of financial resources for development of the economy.
2. To formulate recommendations for modifying structure of insurance industry, for amending the general policy-framework, etc.
3. To make precise proposals regarding Life Insurance Corporation of India and General Insurance Corporation of India with a view to improve their functioning.
4. To make suggestions on regulation and supervision of the insurance sector in India.
5. To give advice on role and working of surveyors, intermediaries like agents, etc. in the insurance sector.
6. To make proposals on any other matter relevant to the development of the insurance industry in India.

The Committee submitted its report in 1994, recommending the following, in respect of:

Structure:

- Government stake in the insurance companies should be brought down to 50 per cent.
- Government should take over the holdings of General Insurance Corporation of India and its subsidiaries in order that these subsidiaries can act as independent corporations
- All insurance companies to be given greater autonomy to operate.

Competition:

- Private companies with a minimum paid-up capital of ₹100 crore should be allowed to enter the industry
- No company should deal in both life and general insurance through a single entity
- Foreign companies may be allowed to enter the industry in collaboration with the domestic companies
- Postal life insurance should be allowed to operate in the rural market

- Only one state level life insurance company should be allowed to operate in each state
- The Insurance Act, should be suitably changed
- An insurance regulatory body should be set up
- Controller of insurance (currently a part of the Finance Ministry) should be made independent

Investments:

- Mandatory investments of LIC life fund in government securities to be reduced from 75 per cent to 50 per cent.
- GIC and its subsidiaries are not to hold more than 5 per cent in any company (there current holdings to be brought down to this level over a period of time).

Customer services:

- LIC should pay interest on delays in payments beyond 30 days
- Insurance companies must be encouraged to set up unit-linked pension schemes
- Computerization of operations and updating of technology to be carried out in the insurance industry

The main emphasis in the recommendations made by the Committee was on opening up of the insurance industry to competition in order to provide better services at economical rates to the customers. However, these recommendations also carried a word of caution as any fiasco on the part of new players could drastically diminish public confidence in the industry. Consequently, it was resolved to regulate competition by stipulating the minimum capital requirement of ₹100 crore. Since this sum is rather insignificant for foreign companies, the foreign equity participation was to be restricted to only 40 per cent. In 1999, Insurance Regulation and Development Act, was passed allowing the entry of new players/joint ventures into the insurance business. An independent regulatory body (the authority) was set up in order to protect the interests of policyholders and to regulate, promote and ensure orderly growth of the insurance industry and to propose suitable amendments in the existing insurance laws.

27.3 LIBERALIZATION: MEANING AND IMPLICATIONS

Privatization, globalization and liberalization are interrelated terms. Privatization is often referred to as the pillar on which the structure of new economic policy of our government has been standing since 1991. *Privatization* is used in different senses. In its narrow sense, it may mean the induction of private ownership in publicly owned enterprises, while in a broader sense, it also suggests the introduction of private management and control in the public sector enterprises with or without ownership. The rationale behind the government policy towards privatization is the growing dissatisfaction with the performance of the public sector undertakings and state owned enterprises. Liberalization is an essential prerequisite for meaningful privatization. Without liberalized rules and regulations, the private players would not feel motivated enough to undertake the risk of business.

The term *globalization* refers to the expanding interrelationships and interdependence among organizations belonging to different countries of the world. It means that the entire world is deemed as one entity, one unit and thus, one market. Under this *one market model,* the business in any part of the globe can be considered as a global business, which is always extremely competitive in a free market.

Globalization and liberalization are closely linked terms. Liberalization has got two facets, namely, domestic liberalization consisting of general curbs and guides on production, investment, prices, the role of market, resource allocation, etc. and external sector liberalization on international flow of goods and services, technology and capital. Globalization is branded with external sector liberalization. Globalization of the Indian insurance industry, therefore, means that while global companies and multinationals enter the Indian market, Indian companies too should have the chance to carry out its business in a foreign country without much limitation. The government attempts at liberalization and privatization have indeed set a trend towards a global business environment in India and this trend is expected to further progress in the future.

Liberalization of the insurance sector has contributed towards the economic development of the country in the following ways:

1. The growth scenario in the insurance sector has created numerous employment opportunities in the economy. There is an upsurge in the demand for marketing experts, finance specialists, human resource professionals, statisticians, etc. Experts in the new specialty areas like underwriting, claims managements, actuarial management, etc. are also being occupied in the industry.
2. The Indian economy has been witnessing huge inflow of funds since the deregulation of the insurance sector. There is a huge influx of foreign players in the insurance sector in India in the recent past.
3. Insurance related service-domains like training, workshops, risk assessment and rating, and risk management too have positively changed making it possible for the industry to explore new policy covers. Besides, the increase in the insurance players will significantly boost up related fields like advertising, brand building, etc., which in turn would promote the ancillary industries. Further,

the intense competition caused by the presence of innumerable insurance companies would compel these companies to follow customer-friendly pricing structure that would foster healthy competition throughout the insurance industry.

4. Before deregulation of the insurance industry, the purpose of life insurance policies in India was merely to seek tax benefits and very little attention was paid to the risk covers. But now most of the new entrants have shifted the focus from tax benefit to protection.
5. The developments in the insurance industry have created the need for widening the channels of distribution of insurance products. The new players have started an extensive variety of products that calls for need based selling technologies. Banks too have been involved in the task of distributing insurance products. The traditional sales procedures have been substituted with modern techniques like bancassurance to sell insurance products to customers. So much, so that the insurance companies are entering into tie-ups with the manufacturers of consumer goods in order to speed up the process of reaching the customers at their doorsteps.
6. The need for quicker delivery of insurance products has provoked the competing insurance players to follow more sophisticated, automated systems. This has taken IT sector to new heights.

27.4 FUTURE TRENDS IN THE INDIAN INSURANCE INDUSTRY

The crucial impetus, intensified through evolving reforms in the financial sector in India since the early 1990s, has accelerated overall economic growth. The government is making all efforts to refurbish the existing basic laws to enable the industry to perform in line with the global trends and expectations. The market is developing and is expected to improve in the days to come.

The latest form of insurance is the cyber-insurance, which is the result of increasing dependence of the modern business organizations on electronic media. Most companies these days conduct their businesses through the internet and are therefore, exposed to security risks involving cyber crime. Such crimes have become worldwide phenomena. No organization whose internal computer systems are connected to the internet is absolutely safe from the deadly curse of cyber criminals. Moreover, the probable loss from cyber crimes can be gigantic. The risk covered through cyber-insurance involves the probability of loss as a result of computer related criminal activity. The risks covered include alleged defamation, violation of privacy rights, copyrights and trademark infringement. Risks due to negligent acts, errors and omissions in the provision of internet services, loss of interruption of service as also transmission of computer viruses are all insured under cyber-insurance policies, besides errors of omission in programming, consulting, data processing, system installation and training. In India, Tata AIA is the first private insurance player to provide insurance cover against cyber threats. The company occupies nearly 70 per cent of the global e-insurance market. Cyber-insurance is offered in tailor-made packages to suit the varying needs of the customers.

The Indian insurance industry has undergone numerous changes in trends and strategies in the recent past. The US$ 41 billion industry is considered the fifth largest life insurance market, and is growing at a rapid pace of 32–34 per cent annually, according to the Life Insurance Council. There are currently 58 insurance companies in India, of which 46 are from the private sector. There are 24 life insurance and 34 non-life insurance companies in India. The market share of private sector players has increased over the years. In the non-life insurance sector, the market share of private companies rose from 15% in 2004 to 49.3% in the FY 2021. In the life insurance sector, private companies had a market share of approximately 36% in FY 2021 while The Life Insurance Corporation of India held approximately 64% of the sector's total insurance premiums in FY 2021. The life insurance industry is expected to increase at a CAGR of 5.3% between 2019 and 2023. In terms of insurance density, India's overall density stood at US$78 in FY 2021. Further, private life insurers are expected to grow their retail APE at a CAGR of over 17% between 2021–23 and new retail term premiums are expected to double in five years. The private non-life insurance sector is predicted to grow at 16% in FY 2022 and 14% in FY 2023. Gross first year premiums in India reached $ 29.54 billion in FY 2021–22, i.e., ₹2,27,188 crore (until 31st January 2022) in Life insurance. Life insurance companies collected 13% additional premium in FY 2022 compared to the year before. Life insurers collected premium of ₹3.10 lakh crore in FY 2022 as against ₹2.70 lakh crore in FY 2021 as per the latest IRDAI data. Non-life insurance companies had a gross premium business worth ₹17,251.10 crore in April 2021. And it grew nearly 24% to ₹21,326.58 crore in April 2022. The market share of private sector companies in the non-life insurance market rose from 15% in FY 2004 to 49.3% in FY 2021.

With a GDP of $3.1 trillion, India is the world's sixth largest economy. India's GDP is likely to grow by 8–8.5% in FY 2022 according to the 2021–22 Economic Survey. It is expected that India will grow by 7.1%–7.6% in FY 22–23 and 6%–6.7% in FY 23–24. This will ensure that India reigns as the world's fastest-growing economy over the next few years, driving world growth even as many developed economies brace themselves for a slowdown or possibly even a recession. In the Indian insurance sector, the life insurance industry is predicted to grow at a compound growth rate (CAGR) of 10.3% from ₹7 trillion in 2021 to ₹11.4 trillion in 2026. The general insurance industry in India, which grew by 5% in 2021 is projected to grow at a CAGR of 9.9% from ₹2172.03 billion in 2021 to ₹3484.35 billion in 2026.

The evaluation is quite encouraging; taking into view the fact that nearly 80 per cent of India, despite being second most populous country in the world, is still uninsured. Moreover, India also ranks third in the world in terms of purchasing power parity (PPP). With the average annual GDP growth rate of 7 per cent and a Gross savings (% of GDP) in India being reported at 30.23% in 2021, the Indian market surely offers rewarding prospects for the global players.

27.4.1 The Opportunities Ahead

The Indian Insurance industry has big opportunity to expand, given the large population and untapped potential. The insurance market in India has witnessed dynamic changes with the entry of a number of global insurers. Most of the private insurance companies are joint ventures with recognized foreign institutions across the globe. Saturation of markets in many developed economies has made the Indian market even more attractive for global insurance majors. The total insurance penetration, which is the ratio of insurance premium as a percentage of GDP, has increased from 2.32 in 2000–01 to 5.10 in 2010–11, according to IRDAI. India's insurance penetration was pegged at 4.2% in FY 2021 with life insurance penetration at 3.2% and non-life insurance penetration at 1%. However, despite healthy growth India's share in the global insurance market was meagre 1.72% during 2020. These figures clearly reflect the enormous untapped potential in the Indian insurance market.

The insurance market is likely to witness a sea change in the marketing mix, namely, product, price, place (distribution channel) promotion and communication mechanism. The market will get customer-centric and result in lot of flexibilities and innovations with the advanced technology playing major role. The IRDA guidelines will need to be fine-tuned to promote competition, fairness, and reliability.

The induction of modern channels of distribution, such as bancassurance, the electronic media and the internet, would require new strategies for strengthening and making the distribution channels more effective. At the same time, communication will continue to play a significant role in creating greater demand for insurance products. Stringent checks and controls, however, would be required to discourage unscrupulous or misleading advertisements.

With the factors of production and distribution undergoing a makeover in the Indian insurance market, the magnitude of competition and profitability, survival and growth will be determined by such forces as bargaining power of buyers and suppliers, risk of substitution, rivalry among current competitors, the entry norms and the rules related to conduct of insurance business. Application of IT (information technology) and BPR (business process reengineering) will also help in augmenting the scale and speed of market operations.

The last decade ended with a wielding of insurance mergers and acquisitions across the world. The Asian markets have a significant contribution in this development. The emergent Indian market provides enormous opportunities for growth, outshining the already saturated markets in the West. The number of mergers and acquisition will move up considerably in the near future. Large-scale companies, capable of influencing the market, would alone reap best benefits of globalization. On the other hand, achieving growth through internal developments will be impossible in the current competitive environment. Thus, a focused merger and acquizition strategy is the only key to success. India is already geared to face the challenges posed by the developments in the international markets. Liberalization of the insurance sector has allowed foreign insurers to enter the market. Most of the foreign insurers are endeavouring to find local partners within the local market. India offers enormous opportunities to foreign insurers since it is the world's most populous country, having over a billion people.

27.5 MACRO INSURANCE: THE INDIAN PERSPECTIVE

The significant changes in the Indian insurance industry in the last few years were caused by a number of external influences. Firstly, the changing socio-economic and political environment provided an appropriate ground for these developments to take shape. The worldwide tendency towards mergers, combinations and globalization had its influence on the insurance industry as well. Fast changing technology, new and widening patterns of distribution and the changing profile of the customer were powerful drivers of change. The policy of deregulation in many Asian countries further accelerated the pace of change. The complacent insurers, who believed that size alone was enough to dominate the market and lower costs, soon realized that in the global environment, no company could afford the kind of capital required for global domination or succeed in all business sectors.

Though international insurance players look at internet as the best distribution channel and are spending huge amounts on developing business strategies with the use of internet hoping that it will bring in huge cost savings but they cannot undermine the contribution of the traditional agent in ensuring regular business. The traditional agent will continue to dominate the insurance scene because the generally complex insurance products require personal meetings and discussions with the prospective customers. Moreover, the reason for buying insurance itself has undergone a radical change. Earlier, premature death used to be the main motivation behind life insurance. But today, the risk of 'living too long without visible means of support' is the real motivator. Consequently, people cautiously plan their retirement savings and wealth management products, for which they have to depend on the advice of insurance agents. In fact, the agent's role has widened.

The growing awareness amongst the customers of their rights has made them very demanding. As a result, the enterprising and ambitious insurers are focused on maintaining good market profile, corporate governance and market conduct. The insurers are competing hard to impart value and quality service to their customers in order to retain them. Realizing the importance of brand building, the global insurance companies are working hard in this direction. This has posed fresh challenge for the Indian brands, as they will have to build a global brand before the global players capture their market.

Transformations in the financial services market have bearing on the insurance industry in a big way. One stop financial services shops or financial services supermarkets are also providing insurance services. Bancassurance is gaining momentum in many Asian countries including India, Malaysia and Singapore.

Internet and other IT advancements have helped global insurance companies set up their back office operations in low-priced countries, manage capital on a global basis, make use of their special skills worldwide and use their superior managerial capabilities to secure their hold in the industry. The flourishing BPO industry in India is a case in reference wherein the growth is driven by the need to reduce costs, differentiate products in an increasingly competitive environment, and ensure regulatory compliance.

Thus, in the emergent conditions, the aggressive strategies alone cannot ensure success; quick adaptation and more importantly, efficient execution of the strategies would be necessary. Keeping pace with international changes would need to be the guiding force.

27.6 MAJOR PLAYERS IN INDIAN INSURANCE INDUSTRY

Earlier the insurance industry in India consisted of only two state-owned insurers, namely, Life Insurance Corporation of India (LIC) and General Insurance Corporation of India (GIC), including its four subsidiary companies. With effect from December 2000, these subsidiaries have been delinked from parent company and converted into independent insurance companies—Oriental Insurance Company Limited, New India Assurance Company Limited, National Insurance Company Limited and United India Insurance Company Limited.

The insurance regulatory and development authority (IRDA) issued the initial batch of licences in 2001. Categorized as life insurers and non-life insurers, following are the major insurance players in the Indian insurance market:

27.6.1 Non-life Insurers

Bajaj Allianz General Insurance Company Limited: Incorporated on 19th September 2000, Bajaj Allianz General Insurance Company Limited is a joint venture between Bajaj Auto Limited and Allianz AG of Germany. The company has an authorized and paid up capital of ₹110 crore. Bajaj Auto holds 74 per cent and the remaining 26 per cent is held by Allianz, AG. The company's headquarter is in Pune. The company offers both tariff and non-tariff products. Its tariff products include consequential loss (fire) insurance; industrial all-risk insurance; motor insurance; workmen's compensation and engineering insurance and the non-tariff products include critical illness; health guard; personal accident; burglary and public liability (Act).

ICICI Lombard General Insurance Company Limited: The ICICI Lombard General Insurance Company Limited (ICICI Lombard) is a joint venture between ICICI Bank Limited, which is India's second largest bank and Lombard Canada Limited, one of the oldest property and casualty insurance companies in Canada.

- The major product offerings of the company are in the following categories:
- Personal needs like home insurance
- Personal care business needs like Project Insurance, Fire and Special Perils Policy, Burglary Insurance, All-risks Insurance, Money Insurance, Contractor's All-risk Policy, Marine (Export-Import) Insurance Policy.
- Liability products like Public Liability Insurance Act Policy, Workmen's Compensation Insurance.

IFFCO-TOKIO General Insurance Company Limited: IFFCO-TOKIO General Insurance (ITGI) is a joint venture between the Indian Farmers Fertilizer Cooperative (IFFCO) and its associates and Tokio Marine and Nichido Fire Group, the largest listed insurance group in Japan. IFFCO owns 74 per cent of ITGI together with its associate companies. ITGI was incorporated on December 4th, 2000 with a capital worth of ₹100 crore. Its head office is situated in Gurgaon, Haryana. It has been providing tailor-made products to its customers and quality services.

Some of the major products offered by the company are—Contractor's Plant and Machinery, Machinery Breakdown, Electronic Equipment Insurances, Machinery Loss of Profit, Public Liability (Industrial/Non-industrial), Marine (cargo), Motor (Private/Personal Car/Commercial Vehicles), Group Medshield; Overseas Travel Insurance and Sankath Haran Policy, which is innovative insurance cover for farmers.

National Insurance Company Limited: National Insurance Company incorporated in 1906, and has been carrying out general insurance business as a private concern till its nationalization in 1972. 22 foreign companies along with 11 Indian insurance companies were amalgamated with National Insurance Company Limited, as a subsidiary company of

General Insurance Corporation of India that year. Since 2002, with the passage of Insurance Amendment Bill (2002), National Insurance Company has been delinked from GIC and has been functioning as an independent company. Besides general insurance products, the company has also been providing customized and innovative insurance products to its customers. The company is also carrying out reinsurance and foreign operations.

New India Assurance Company Limited: The New India Assurance Company was incorporated in 1919. In 1972, the company was nationalized along with all other non-life insurers in the country. After the passing of Insurance Amendment Bill (2002), it was also delinked from GIC and has since been functioning as an independent company.

Oriental Insurance Company Limited: The Oriental Insurance Company Ltd. is a public sector company and is one of the four subsidiaries of the General Insurance Corporation of India. The Oriental Fire and General Insurance Co. Ltd., incorporated in the year 1947, as a subsidiary of Oriental Government Security Life Assurance Co. Ltd., became a subsidiary of the Life Insurance Corporation of India in 1956. The government took over the management of the company in 1971 along with other general insurance companies in India. With the nationalization of general insurance business in 1973, Oriental Fire and General Insurance Company became a subsidiary of the General Insurance Corporation of India and commenced operations in 1975.

Later, as a result of the Insurance Amendment Bill (2002), the company was delinked from GIC in 2002, and has since been independently functioning as the Oriental Insurance Company Ltd. with its head office in New Delhi. The company has 21 regional offices, 311 divisional offices and 635 branch offices in various cities of the country. The company has overseas operations in Nepal, Kuwait and Dubai.

United India Insurance Company Limited: United India Insurance is another subsidiary of the General Insurance Corporation of India, which was delinked from GIC in 2002. It has been functioning as an independent company with its head office at Chennai and a network of 1123 offices and manpower of over 21,000 employees. The organizational structure comprises 22 regional offices, 313 divisional offices, and 789 branch offices.

Besides the common insurance covers, the company also offers protection in the form of

Sports Insurance, Suhana Safar Policy, Baggage Insurance, Bhagyashree Insurance, Rajrajeshwari Mahila Sampoorna Suraksha Bima, Gun Insurance, Mediclaim Policy, Traffic Accident Insurance, Erection All-risks Insurance, Aquaculture Insurance, Plantation/Horticultural Poultry Insurance, T.V. Policy, Advance Loss of Profits Insurance, Jeweller's Block Policy, LPG Dealers Policy, Office Umbrella Policy, Product Liability Insurance, Lift Irrigation/Sprinkler Insurance, Floriculture Insurance, Farmer's Package Policy, Agriculture Insurance, Cattle Insurance, Failed Well Insurance.

Tata AIG General Insurance Company Limited: Tata AIG General Insurance Company Ltd., and Tata AIG Life Insurance Company Ltd., are a joint venture between the Tata group, India's most trusted industrial house contributing 74 per cent to the company's capital worth of ₹125 crore and American International Group (AIG), Inc., the leading US-based international insurance and financial services organization, making the balance 26 per cent capital contribution. Tatas were the pioneers in the private insurance sector in India before nationalization of insurance business. The New India Assurance Co. was set up by the Tata group in 1919. By 1973, the Tata Company had registered a global presence for itself with 56 overseas offices. The AIG companies, on the other hand, entered India in 1945, and established offices in several Indian cities.

Tata AIG General Insurance Company Ltd. is the first Indian insurance company to offer a comprehensive policy cover against various risks in the IT sector. Its chief products on offer are property, casualty, marine, directors and officers liability, accident and health, homeowners and automobile insurance.

Royal Sundaram General Insurance Company Limited: Royal Sundaram General Insurance Company Limited, a joint venture between Royal and Sun Alliance Insurance and Sundaram Finance Limited, started its operations in 2001. The share of Sundaram Finance Limited and Associates is 74 per cent in the total capital of the company while that of Royal and Sun Alliance is to the tune of 26 per cent. It gains distinction as the first foreign joint venture to obtain a licence for conducting insurance business in the non-life segment. It has its headquarters at Chennai. The company offers insurance in the form of Travel Shield, Accident Shield, Health Shield and Home Shield.

Cholamandalam General Insurance Company Limited: Cholamandalam General Insurance Company Limited is promoted by Chennai based Murugappa group. The company has a capital worth of ₹105 crore with 75 per cent being held by tube investment, a Murugappa group company. While Cholamandalam Investment and Finance Company Ltd. holds 15 per cent equity and the balance by other privately held Murugappa companies having 5 per cent share each. A variety of insurance products are offered by the general insurer—Motor Insurance, Electronic Equipment, Neon Sign Insurance, Machinery Breakdown Insurance, Marine Insurance, Casualty and Financial Lines Insurance, Plate Glass Insurance, Property and Crime Insurance, Pet Insurance, to name a few.

Reliance General Insurance Company Limited: Reliance General Insurance Company Limited (RGICL), a subsidiary of Reliance Capital, is one of the first private sector non-life insurance companies to be granted licence by the IRDA. Reliance General Insurance is the fastest growing general insurance company in India with innovative product offerings and customer service standards comparable with the best insurance practices in the world. It offers a comprehensive range of insurance products that covers most, if not all risks including property, marine, casualty and liability.

Export Credit Guarantee Corporation of India Limited: Export Credit Guarantee Corporation of India Limited, was incorporated in 1957, by the Government of India with the objective of strengthening the export promotion campaign by insuring the risk associated with exporting on credit. Since, it is basically an export promotion organization, it functions under the administrative control of the Ministry of Commerce, Government of India. Its board of directors is comprised of representatives of the government, Reserve Bank of India, banking, insurance and exporting community. ECGC is the fifth largest credit insurer of the world in terms of national coverage.

HDFC Chubb General Insurance Limited: HDFC Chubb General Insurance Ltd., a joint venture between HDFC, India's premier financial services company and Chubb Corporation, the leading global non-life insurer, came to be established in 2002. The initial capital worth of the joint venture stood at ₹100 crore with HDFC share being 74 per cent and the Chubb having a stake of 26 per cent.

The company has earned distinction for introducing leading edge insurance products and services to meet the changing needs of consumers in diverse markets.

Star Health and Allied Insurance Co. Ltd.: Founded in 2006, Star Health and Allied Insurance is a stand alone health insurer headquartered in Chennai. Star Health and Allied Insurance is a joint venture between Indian venture capitalist firms—Star Health Investments, ICICI Venture, Sequoia Capital and foreign investors which include Oman Insurance Company—Middle East insurance solution provider and ETA Ascon Group—UAE contracting firm.

Apollo Munich Health Insurance Co. Ltd.: Previously known as Apollo DKV Insurance Co. Ltd., it is a joint venture company promoted by the Apollo Hospitals Group and Munich Health, Munich Re's newest business segment. The products include health, personal accident and travel insurance plans for individual as well as families.

Shriram General Insurance Co. Ltd.: Headquartered in Jaipur, Shriram General Insurance is a non-life insurance company. Shriram General Insurance is joint venture between Shriram Group—US$ 8 million corporate giant and Sanlam Limited—South Africa's financial services group. Shriram Group holds 74 per cent equity and Sanlam Limited has the rest 26 per cent equity in the joint venture.

SBI General Insurance Company Limited: SBI General Insurance Co. Ltd. is a joint venture between the State Bank of India and Insurance Australia Group (IAG). SBI owns 74 per cent of the total capital and IAG the remaining 26 per cent. Current policy offering of SBI General covers Motor & Home Insurance for Individuals and fire, marine, package, construction & engineering, group health & miscellaneous insurance for businesses.

Max Bupa Health Insurance Company Limited: Founded in 2008, Max Bupa is a joint venture between Max India—multibusiness conglomerate and Bupa Group—UK-based healthcare company. Max India holds 74 per cent and Bupa holds 26 per cent equity in the joint venture. The company is headquartered in New Delhi. Max Bupa offers health insurance for individual as well as family.

Universal Sompo General Insurance Co. Ltd.: Universal Sompo General Insurance Co. Ltd. is a collective effort of three Indian banks along with Dabur Investments and Sompo Japan Insurance, an insurance company from Japan. Universal Sompo General Insurance Co. Ltd. is a joint partnership between the Allahabad Bank, Sompo Japan Insurance Inc., Dabur Investments, Karnataka Bank and Indian Overseas Bank. In November 2007, the Insurance Regulatory and Development Authority granted a License of Registration to this company.

Bharti AXA General Insurance: The Bharti AXA General Insurance is a joint venture between Bharti—India's leading corporate group with interests in telecom, agricultural business and retail; and AXA—the world leader in financial protection and wealth management. Bharti Group holds 74 per cent of equity and AXA holds 26 per cent of the equity in this joint venture. The company was incorporated on July 13, 2007 with its headquarters at Bangalore.

Raheja QBE General Insurance Company Limited: The Raheja QBE General Insurance Company Limited is a joint venture general insurance company promoted by Prism Cements Limited, India and QBE Holdings (AAP) Pty Limited, a wholly owned subsidiary of QBE, Australia has been registered as a General Insurer by IRDA on December 12, 2008.

L&T General Insurance Company Limited: Also known as (L&T Insurance), it is a wholly owned subsidiary of Larsen & Toubro Limited.

27.6.2 Life Insurers

Bajaj Allianz Life Insurance Company Limited: Bajaj Allianz Life Insurance Co. Ltd. is a joint venture between two leading conglomerates—Allianz AG and Bajaj Auto Limited. Allianz Bajaj Life Insurance Co. Ltd. was incorporated in 2001. The various products offered by the company may be classified into:

Individuals: Consisting of Risk Care Plan, Term Care Plan, Save Care Plan, Cash Care Plan, Life Time Plan.

Groups: Consisting of Group Risk Care Plan, Employer-employee Group Risk Care Plan, Non-employer-employee Group Credit Care Plan, Employer-employee Group Risk Credit Plan, Non-employer-employee Invest Gain Plan.

Birla Sun Life Insurance Company Limited: Birla Sun Life Insurance (BSLI) is a joint venture between Birla Group and Sun Life Corporation of US. The company claims to have unique products, rendering an effective mixture of returns, liquidity, security, tax benefits, transparency and expediency. The insurance products of the company are—Flexi Save Plus Endowment Plan, Flexi Life Line Whole Life Plan, Flexi Cash Flow Money Back Plan, Single Premium Bond, Flexi Secure Life Retirement Plan (pension) and Birla Sun Life Term Plan.

HDFC Standard Life Insurance Company Limited: HDFC Standard Life Insurance Company Limited was incorporated in 2000 as a joint venture of HDFC and Standard Life. It was the first joint venture to enter life insurance business. HDFC is the substantial shareholder having a holding of 81.4 per cent in the company while Standard Life owns 18.6 per cent.

The products offered by the company include—With-profits Endowment Assurance, With-profits Money Back, Single Premium Whole of Life, Loan Cover Term Assurance, Personal Pension Plan, Children's Plan, Group Term Insurance, Development Insurance Plan.

ICICI Prudential Life Insurance Company Limited: ICICI Prudential Life Insurance Company Ltd. was incorporated in 2000, with an authorized capital of ₹230 crore. It is a joint venture of ICICI (having a share of 74 per cent) and Prudential Public Ltd. Co., UK. (having a share of 26 per cent). The company has its offices in Mumbai, New Delhi and other 8 major cities. The categories of products offered by ICICI Prudential Life Insurance Company Ltd. include Individual products; investment products and Group insurance plans.

Life Insurance Corporation of India Limited: Life Insurance Corporation of India Ltd. (LICI) was established in 1956, and is the dominant leader in life insurance business in India. It has 7 zonal offices, over 100 divisional offices and more than 204 branches in India.

Tata AIA Life Insurance Company Limited: Tata AIA Life Insurance Co. Ltd. has capital base of ₹185 crore out of which 74 per cent belongs to Tata Sons and the balance 26 per cent belongs to its American partner, the American Insurance Group. Headquartered in Mumbai, Tata AIA Life has sales offices in major cities and towns across in India. The company offers a broad array of insurance products to individuals, associations and businesses of all sizes. It is one of the major private sector insurers in India offering life, health and group insurance products covering entire life-stage needs. The products of the company include—Protection; Wealth; Savings; Child; Retirement; Health and other solutions.

SBI Life Insurance Company Limited: SBI Life Insurance Company Ltd. is a joint venture between the State Bank of India (SBI), India's largest bank and Cardiff S.A., a leading insurer in France. Cardiff S.A. the foreign partner has a contribution of 26 per cent in the company's paid capital of ₹250 crore while SBI's contribution is the balance 74 per cent. The company's products include—Sanjeevan, Sudarshan, Young Sanjeevan, SBI Scholar.

Kotak Life Insurance Company Ltd.: Kotak Life Insurance Company Ltd. is a joint venture between Kotak Mahindra Bank and Old Mutual Public Ltd. Co. (OM), headquartered in London. It was incorporated with an initial net worth of ₹150 crore, with 74:26 stake belonging to Kotak Mahindra Bank and OM, respectively. Partnership with Old Mutual Public Ltd. Co. has granted an international perspective and expertise to Kotak Mahindra group in the business of life insurance. The official name of the company is Kotak Old Mutual Life Insurance Company. The major products offered by this partnership include—Gramin Bima Yojana, Retirement Plan, Child Plans, Savings and Investment Plans.

Max New York Life Insurance Co. Ltd.: Max New York Life Insurance Co. Ltd. is a joint venture between Max India Limited, one of India's leading multi-business corporations and New York Life, a Fortune 100 company. The paid-up capital of the Joint Venture is ₹250 crores. Max India Ltd. is developing its business in the diversified, flourishing fields involving Healthcare, Financial Services and Information Technology. The company offers a wide range of insurance plans embracing Whole Life; Endowment and Term Assurance plans.

Exide Life Insurance Company Limited: Exide Life Insurance Company Limited (formerly ING Vysya Life Insurance Company Limited) commenced operations in 2001. The company is 100% owned by Exide Industries Limited and is proud to be part of a 100 year old brand heritage in India. The company's headquarter is at Bangalore while its operations extend to Mumbai and Delhi as well. The company's main products on offer are: Exide Life Wealth Maxima Child; Exide Life New Fulfilling Life; Exide Life New Creating Life Insurance Plus; Exide Life Jeevan Uday.

Aviva Life Insurance Company Limited: Aviva Life Insurance Company Ltd. is a joint venture between Dabur India and CGU, a wholly owned subsidiary of Aviva Public Limited Company (Plc). The joint venture is capitalised at ₹110 crore. Aviva Plc is the largest life and general insurance group of UK and the world's 7th largest insurer. Aviva Plc is the holding company of Aviva group of companies, which is conducting business in the areas of life assurance, general insurance and long-term savings fund management. Aviva Life has tied up with ABN AMRO, Canara Bank, Laxmi Vilas Bank and American Express for distribution of its products. The company is headquartered in Gurgaon, Haryana, with branch offices in Mumbai, Chennai, New Delhi, Hyderabad, Bangalore and Kolkata. Its major products are—Life Long, Life Saver, Life Bond, Corporate Life, Credit Plus, Secure Life, Easy Life Plus, Pension Plus.

Reliance Nippon Life Insurance Company Limited: Reliance Capital acquired AMP Sanmar Life Insurance Company in 2005. AMP Sanmar Life Insurance Company was formed in 2001 as a joint venture between AMP, holding 26% stake and the Sanmar Group, having a stake of 74%. The company's name was changed to Reliance Life Insurance Company Limited in 2006. Reliance Life Insurance Company Ltd. (RLIC), is a wholly owned Indian company and an associate of Reliance Capital Ltd., a part of Reliance—Anil Dhirubhai Ambani Group. The company thus had an advantage of a pre-established infrastructure and a product portfolio base to develop it further to attract the Indian customers. Reliance Capital Ltd. has its presence in Communications, Energy, Natural Resources, Media, Entertainment, Healthcare and Infrastructure segments in India. RLIC is amongst the leading private sector life insurance companies in terms of new business. By 2008 it became the 4th largest private insurer in the country. Nippon Life Insurance Company acquired 26% interest in equity share capital of the Company in 2011 subsequent to receipt of all regulatory approval. Nippon Life Insurance (26% share), also called Nissay, is Japan's largest private life insurer. The company life insurance products targeted at individuals and groups, catering to four distinct segments: protection, children, retirement and investment plans. Reliance Life Insurance has tied up with five insurance repositories—Database Management Limited, Central Insurance Repository Limited, SHCIL Projects Limited, CAMS Repository Services Limited and Karvy Insurance Limited—to enable and encourage policyholders to hold their insurance policies in demat form.

Met Life India Insurance Company Private Limited: Met Life India Insurance Company Private Limited was incorporated in India in 2001, as a joint venture between Met Life International Holdings Inc., The Jammu and Kashmir Bank, Punjab National Bank Limited (PNB), M. Pallonji and Co. Private Limited and other private investors. Metropolitan Life Insurance Company (Met Life), the number one insurer in the US is headquartered in New York and operates in 13 countries throughout America, Europe and Asia through its affiliates, subsidiaries and representative offices. PNB Met Life was previously known as Met Life India Insurance Company Limited (Met Life India) and has been present in India since 2001.

Bharti-AXA Life Insurance Company Limited: Bharti-AXA Life Insurance Company Limited commenced its operations in India with the inauguration of the first branch in Hyderabad in 2006. It is a joint venture between AXA, the French insurance giant and Bharti Enterprises, the private telecom major. In its endeavour to be amongst the top three life insurers in the country, the company is following a multi-product, multi-featured and multi-distribution approach. Bharti's distribution capabilities and knowledge of the domestic market (AIRTEL is market leader in cellular space) together with AXA's global experience and technical expertise, is a perfect blend to success.

Canara HSBC Oriental Bank of Commerce Insurance Company Limited: Canara HSBC Oriental Bank of Commerce Insurance Company Limited was launched in 2008 with a capital base of ₹325 crore wherein Canara Bank holds the majority 51 per cent stake in the company while HSBC and OBC hold 26 per cent and 23 per cent respectively. The company's Headquarter is located in Gurgaon. The company has launched several products with a mix of traditional and unit-linked schemes.

Future Generali India Life Insurance Co. Ltd. and Future Generali India Insurance Co. Ltd.: Future Generali is an insurance joint venture between the Italy-based Generali Group and the India-based Future Group and is headquartered in Mumbai. Future Generali operates life and non-life insurance businesses through 'Future Generali India Life Insurance Co. Ltd.' and 'Future Generali India Insurance Co. Ltd.'.

IDBI Federal Life Insurance Co Ltd.: IDBI Fortis Life Insurance Co. Ltd. is a joint venture between three leading financial corporations—India's premier development and commercial bank, IDBI, India's leading private sector bank, Federal Bank and Ageas, a multinational insurance giant based out of Europe, each of which enjoys a significant status in their respective business segments. In this venture, IDBI owns 48% equity while Federal Bank and Ageas own 26% equity each.

Sahara India Life Insurance Co. Ltd. (SILICL): SILICL is the first wholly Indian-owned private-sector life insurance company. The reinsurance of Sahara Life Insurance Co. is in the hands of Gen Re and Munich Re Insurance Companies. Some of the products being issued by the company are Sahara Utkarsh—Jeevan Bima Plan; Sahara Sugam Jeevan Bima Plan; Sahara Dhanvriddhi Jeevan Bima; Sahara Dhanversha-Jeevan Bima Plan; Sahara Shrestha Nivesh-Jeevan Bima plan; Sahara Pay Back Jeevan Bima; Sahara Dhanviddhi-Jeevan Bima.

Shriram Life Insurance Company: Shriram Life Insurance Company is a joint venture between the Shriram Group and the Sanlam Group. The Shriram Group is one of the largest financial services conglomerates in

India. Sanlam Life Insurance Limited, a part of the Sanlam Group, is one of the largest providers of life insurance in South Africa. The major products of Shriram Life Insurance company include—New Shri Life; New Shri Raksha; New Shri Vidya; New Shri Vivah; Wealth plus; Ujjwal life; Star Shri Family Care; Shri Sahay; New Akshay Nidhi.

AEGON Religare Life Insurance Company Limited: AEGON, one of the world's largest life insurance and pension groups, Religare, one of India's leading integrated financial services groups and Bennett, Coleman & Company Ltd., India's largest media house, have come together to launch AEGON Religare Life Insurance Co. Ltd. The company offers protection, savings, child, and retirement plans. The company was incorporated in 2007 and is based in Mumbai.

DHFL Pramerica Life Insurance Co. Ltd.: The company was founded in 2008 and is based in Gurgaon, India with a network of offices in India. DHFL Pramerica Life Insurance Company Ltd. was formerly known as DLF Pramerica Life Insurance Company Limited. As a result of its acquisition by Dewan Housing Finance Corporation Limited, its name was changed. DHFL Pramerica Life Insurance Company Ltd. (DPLI) is a joint venture between Dewan Housing Finance Corporation Ltd. (DHFL), India's second largest private sector housing finance company and Prudential International Insurance Holdings, Ltd. (PIIH), a fully owned subsidiary of Prudential Financial, Inc. (PFI), a financial services leader headquartered in the U.S. As DLF Pramerica Life Insurance Company Ltd. started operations in India on September 01, 2008 it has a pan India presence through multiple distribution channels which have been customized to address the specific insurance needs of diverse customer segments. DHFL, the company is one of India's leading mortgage finance institutions with presence in over 450 locations across the country, in addition to representative offices in Dubai and London. The joint venture is committed to providing protection and quality financial advice to its customers. It provides various life insurance products and services in India.

Star Union Dai-ichi Life Insurance Co. Ltd.: Star Union Dai-ichi Life Insurance Co. Ltd. is a joint venture company floated by the Bank of India and Union Bank of India, two leading public sector banks in India and the Dai-ichi Life Insurance Co. Ltd., a leading Japanese company in the life insurance market for undertaking life insurance business in India. The Company, was incorporated in September, 2007. The Company has a capital stake of 48 per cent by Bank of India, 26 per cent by Union Bank of India and 26 per cent by Dai-ichi Life Insurance Co. Ltd. The Company has authorized capital of ₹250 Crore.

India First Life Insurance Company Limited: India First Life Insurance was incorporated in November, 2009 with its headquarters located in

Mumbai, India. It is a joint venture between two of India's public sector banks – Bank of Baroda (44 per cent) and Andhra Bank (30 per cent), and UK's financial and investment company.

Edelweiss Tokio Life Insurance Co. Ltd.: Edelweiss Tokio Life Insurance Co. Ltd. is a joint venture between Edelweiss Financial Services, one of India's leading diversified financial services companies and Tokio Marine Holdings Inc. Edelweiss Tokio Life Insurance Company Limited, a joint venture life insurance company established in India by Tokio Marine Holdings, Inc., one of the oldest and the biggest insurance companies in Japan and the India-based financial services company "Edelweiss Capital Limited" "ECL" was established on May 10, 2011.

KEY TERMS

Autonomy A system of self-governance or self-determination.

Controller of insurance Officer appointed by the Central Government to perform the duties prescribed under the Insurance Act, 1938.

Credit wrap insurance Insurance against defined credit risks. It is a credit guarantee insurance plan.

Cyber-insurance Insurance cover against damages or losses resulting from cyber crimes.

Global companies Companies that serve a range of overseas markets both by exporting and direct investment.

Globalization The process by which social or business institutions become adopted on a global scale, i.e., become international or start operating at international level.

Joint venture Business enterprise jointly undertaken by two or more companies/partners who share the initial investment, risks and profits.

Liberalization Reforming and becoming less strict.

Privatization Practice of transferring a public utility (or an economic enterprise) from state ownership to private ownership.

Reforms Reorganization or improvement of an institution or system (in this case, improvements in the economic system).

Subsidiary A company controlled and owned by a larger one, known as its holding company.

REVIEW QUESTIONS

27.1 Describe some of the significant landmarks in the history of insurance sector in India.

27.2 How has the insurance industry developed in India? Describe the major reforms in the Indian insurance sector.

27.3 What were the objectives of the Malhotra Committee? Describe the recommendations of the Committee.

27.4 Comment on the present state of Indian insurance market.

27.5 What were the objectives of liberalization of the Indian insurance industry? How has it contributed towards the economic development of the country?

27.6 Explain the concept of macro-insurance. What, in your opinion are the future prospects for the Indian insurance industry?

27.7 Explain the challenges currently facing the Indian insurance market in the light of globalization.

27.8 Give a brief description of the major private players in the Indian life insurance industry.

27.9 Briefly give the company profile of

(i) Reliance General Insurance Co. Ltd.

(ii) Bajaj Allianz General Insurance Co. Ltd.

(iii) ICICI Prudential Life Insurance Co. Ltd.

(iv) Royal Sundaram General Insurance Co. Ltd.

(v) Aviva Life Insurance Company Ltd.

(vi) Reliance Life Insurance Co. Ltd.

APPENDIX A

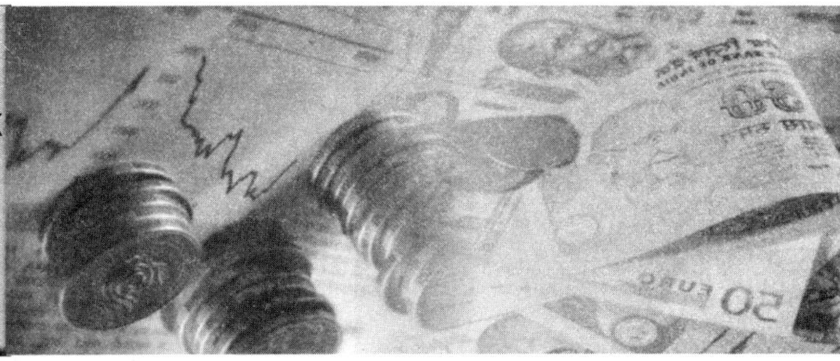

Public Sector Banks

PUBLIC SECTOR BANKS

State Bank of India

Punjab National Bank

Indian Overseas Bank

Indian Bank

Bank of Baroda

Canara Bank

Bank of India

Union Bank of India

Bank of Maharashtra

UCO Bank

Central Bank of India

Punjab and Sind Bank

APPENDIX B

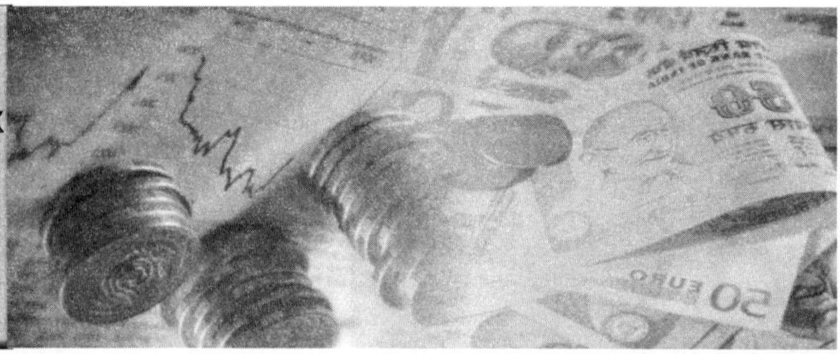

Foreign Banks in India

ABN Amro

Abu Dhabi Commercial

American Express Bank

Antwerp Diamond Bank

Arab Bangladesh Bank

Bank International Indonesia

Bank Muscat S.A.O.G.

Bank of America, N.A.

Bank of Bahrain & Kuwait, B.S.C.

Bank of Ceylon

Barclays Bank PLC

Bank of Nova Scotia

Bank of Tokyo–Mitsubishi UFJ

BNP Paribas

Calyon Bank

Chinatrust Commercial Bank

Cho Hung Bank

Citibank, N.A.

Commerzbank AG

Credit Agricole Indosuez

Credit Lyonnais

DBS Bank

Deutsche Bank

Development Bank of Singapore Ltd.

Dresdner Bank AG

HSBC Ltd.

ING Bank N.V.

JP Morgan Chase Bank (The Chase Manhattan Bank)

Krung Thai Bank

Mashreq Bank

Mizuho Corporate Bank (The Fuji Bank Ltd.)

Oman International

Oversea–Chinese Banking Corporation Ltd.

Societe Generale

Sonali Bank

Standard Chartered Bank

Standard Chartered Grindlays Bank Ltd.

Sumitomo Mitsui Banking Corporation (The Sumitomo Bank Ltd.)

The Bank of Tokyo–Mitsubishi Ltd.

The Siam Commercial Bank

The Toronto–Domonion Bank Ltd.

UFJ Bank Ltd. (The Sanwa Bank Ltd.)

APPENDIX C

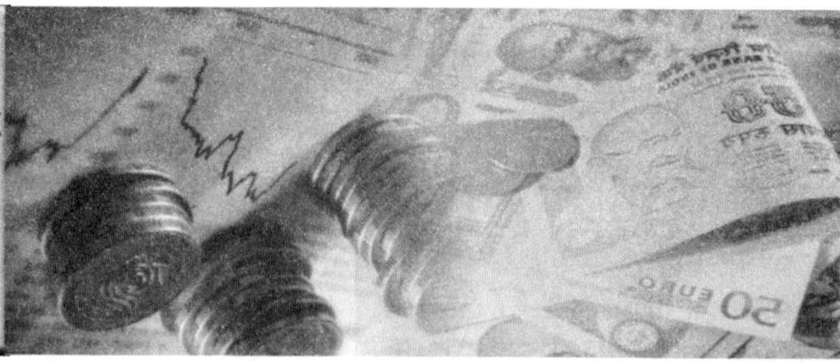

Private Sector Banks

OLD PRIVATE SECTOR BANKS

Bank of Rajasthan Ltd.

Bharat Overseas Bank Ltd.

Catholic Syrian bank Ltd.

City Union Bank Ltd.

Development Credit Bank Ltd.

Dhanalakshmi Bank Ltd.

Federal Bank Ltd.

Ganesh Bank of Kurundwad

Jammu and Kashmir Bank Ltd.

Karnataka Bank Ltd.

Karur Vysya Bank Ltd.

Lakshmi Vilas Bank Ltd.

Nainital Bank Ltd.

Ratnakar Bank Ltd.

Sangli Bank Ltd.

SBI Commercial and International Bank Ltd.

South Indian Bank Ltd.

Tamil Mercantile Bank Ltd.

United Western Bank Ltd.

NEW PRIVATE SECTOR BANKS

HDFC Bank Ltd.

ICICI Bank Ltd.

IDBI Bank Ltd.

Indus Ind Bank Ltd.

Kotak Mahindra Bank Ltd.

Bandhan Bank

CSB Bank

City Union Bank

Development Credit Bank

IDFC First Bank

YES Bank

RBL Bank

Federal Bank

APPENDIX D

Cooperative Banks

Abhyudaya Cooperative Bank
Ahmedabad Mercantile Cooperative Bank
Andhra Pradesh State Cooperative Bank Ltd.
Apana Sahakari Bank
Bhandari Cooperative Bank
Bharat Cooperative Bank
Bihar State Cooperative Bank Ltd., Patna
Bombay Mercantile Cooperative Bank Ltd., Bombay
Charminar Cooperative Urban Bank Ltd., Hyderabad (AP)
Chembur Nagarik Sahakari Bank
Citizencredit Cooperative Bank
Cooperative Bank of Ahmedabad Ltd., Ahmedabad (Gujarat)
Cosmos Cooperative Bank
Deccan Merchants Cooperative Bank
Development Cooperative Bank Ltd.
Excellent Cooperative Bank
Goa State Cooperative Bank Ltd.
Greater Bombay Cooperative Bank
Gujarat State Cooperative Bank Ltd.
Haryana State Cooperative Bank Ltd.
Jain Sahakari Bank
Jankalyan Sahakari Bank
Janseva Sahakari Bank

Kapool Cooperative Bank
Kokan Mercantile Cooperative Bank
Mahanagar Cooperative Bank
Mahesh Sahakari Bank
Mandvi Cooperative Bank
Mangal Cooperative Bank
Maratha Sahakari Bank
Model Cooperative Bank
Mumbai District Central Cooperative Bank
Municipal Cooperative Bank
New India Cooperative Bank
NKGSB Cooperative Bank
Parsik Janata Sahakari Bank
Pondicherry State Cooperative Bank
Punjab and Maharashtra Cooperative Bank
Saraswat Cooperative Bank
Shamrao Vithal Cooperative Bank
Shreeji Bhatia Cooperative Bank
Thane Janata Sahakari Bank
Vaishya Sahakari Bank
Veerashaiva Cooperative Bank
Zoroastrian Cooperative Bank

APPENDIX

E

Cases

CASE 1 BANK MERGERS

State Bank of India and merger of its subsidiaries

The State Bank of India (SBI) came into existence in July 1955 when the government of India nationalized the Imperial Bank of India to introduce public sector banking. In 1959 eight state banks of erstwhile princely states were also nationalized to form subsidiaries of the SBI. Over time the subsidiaries of SBI were merged with it—the State Bank of Saurasthra was merged with the SBI in 2008 and State Bank of Indore in 2013. The remaining five subsidiaries (State Bank of Bikaner had already been merged with State Bank of Jaipur), have since been merged with SBI and have started functioning as branches of SBI from April 1, 2017. The mergers were expected to help drive synergies, reduce duplication and save resources. Post-merger SBI ranks as the 43rd largest bank in the world and number 221 in the Fortune Global 500 companies. It is the only Indian bank to feature in this list. It is the largest Indian PSB with 23% of market share by assets and 25% share of total loan and deposit market.

Mergers of other commercial banks

It was hoped that mergers of banks will result in a number of benefits of consolidation namely: higher operational efficiency gains to reduce cost of lending, increase in income from services, higher return on equities, boost to economy by increasing liquidity. Mergers were also expected to diversify risk and tackle NPA issues. Combined synergy enhances efficiency and performance and increases value. Potential competitors are absorbed into one entity and this helps to reduce competition in the market. The risk of bankruptcy is also reduced after mergers..

In 1993 New Bank of India was merged with Punjab National Bank. It was hoped that this shall improve adequacy of capital, reduce weaknesses and provide a competitive edge but it failed to create significant energies.

The merger of Dena and Vijaya Banks with Bank of Baroda took place in 2019 but little obvious improvement was noticed.

In August 2019, ten PSBs were merged into four

1. Oriental Bank of Commerce and United Bank were merged with PNB thus making it the second largest state run bank after SBI. (total loan plus deposit business 17.95 trillion).
2. Syndicate Bank was merged with Canara Bank to make it the fourth largest PSU (total business 15.2 trillion).
3. In the third merger Union Bank of India was merged with Andhra Bank and Corporation Bank to build Indi's fifth largest PSB (total business of ₹14.59 trillion).
4. Indian Bank merger with Allahbad Bank will make it the seventh largest PSB (total business 8.08 trillion).

It was hoped that this measure will

(i) Strengthen the balance sheets of those banks which were struggling under a mountain of debt.
(ii) The merged entity will be able to increase credit offering which is crucial to increase spending and consumption.
(iii) Government will be able to rationalize demand for capital and ease future bailout packages.

After mergers of 10 PSBs into 4 and subsequent infusion of ₹2.9 lakh crore in the last five years the capital adequacy ratio of PSBs has increased from 11.8 in March 2016 to 14.3% in December 2021. As a result the PCA restrictions of some banks have been lifted. It was widely speculated that the mergers will be postponed due to impact of the Corona virus pandemic but as on April 1, 2020, the mergers have become effective.

However, some apprehensions about bank mergers still remain. The increase in market power of merged institution has concomitantly affected financial inclusion as less competition means less choices for the consumer. Another grave concern is that capital infusion does not become a substitute for improved governance and risk controls. Banks should not depend upon repeated capitalization and implicit government guarantees but maintain strict market discipline.

CASE 2 PUNJAB AND MAHARSHTRA COOPERATIVE BANK

Cooperative banks have historically been a socio-political answer to the absence of a proper banking system. The cooperative movement grew in sugarcane and sugar mills in Maharashtra and then spread to credit, whereas in Gujarat it started from milk cooperatives. The structure of cooperative banks is such that depositors are shareholders and vice-versa.

As a result, almost always the prominent depositors, shareholders and borrowers are the same group. This can have disastrous consequences. Apparently, no lessons were learnt from the Madhavpura Mercantile Co-operative Bank in Gujarat which had lent 90% of it's deposits to broker Ketan Parekh who could not repay after the market crash of 2001.

More recently the Punjab and Maharashtra Co-operative Bank has been in a similar predicament. This bank too had committed the mistake disbursing most of it's loans to a single borrower group—Housing Development and Infrastructure (HDIL). This real estate company filed for bankruptcy on 21.8.19. The PMC bank had lent ₹6,500 crore to this company out of it's 11,800 crore of deposits. However as disclosed by Mr. Joy Thomas, the erstwhile Managing Director of the bank, only ₹440 crores were disclosed in the balance sheet and the balance was hidden through multiple accounts. Approximately a month later the RBI superseded the Board, appointed an Administrator and restricted withdrawals to ₹1000 per account to prevent a run on the bank by it's depositors as that could easily end up endangering the stability of the entire financial system because of a contagion effect. But because of wide spread panic and hardship amongst the depositors withdrawals was increased to ₹50,000 per month after six months. This fraud could be easily manipulated as the PMC's Chairman Mr. Waryam Singh as he was a family friend of the Wadhawans who were the promoters of HDIL and DHFL, having served on the boards of both these companies for several years. The rate of mortality of cooperative banks is very high. On an average 16 such banks default and die annually. Such high incidents of failure and bankruptcy raise doubts about the viability and success of cooperative banks. However after the PMC bank debacle the RBI has made numerous changes to prevent such incidents in the future and to provide relief to the depositors:

(i) Prudential exposure limits for UCBs for a single borrower and a group of connected borrowers were lowered to 10% and 25% respectively (from 15% and 40% earlier), of their tier—I capital.

(ii) Priority Sector Lending targets were hiked to 75% from 40% of adjusted net bank credit in a phased manner—50% by March 2021, 60% by March 2022 and 75% by 31 March 2023.

(iii) The portfolio mix of the UCBs should have at least 50% of loans should not be more than ₹25 lakh per borrower including all types of funded and non-funded exposures in the nature of credit.

(iv) The DICGC Bill was amended to provide deposit insurance of up to ₹5 lakh form ₹1 lakh. To provide quicker relief to depositors of stressed banks this will cover lenders currently under moratorium (like PMD) and depositors will not have to wait till the bank is declared bankrupt.

CASE 3 NATIONAL ASSET RECONSTRUCTION COMPANY LIMITED (NARCL)

The tremendous accumulation of non-performing assets restricts the flow of cash due to provisioning, drains profits and has a negative effect on equity value as well as the reputation of the bank. This may either result in depositors withdrawing their money or invite PCA action by the RBI which can have grave consequences for the bank. This led to the plan to set up a bad bank. It was first announced in the Union Budget of FY 22, but initially the RBI was not happy with the proposed structure. Subsequently the lenders submitted a revised proposal and the NARCL was finally set up (Mint 1.4.22). The NARCL has been incorporated under the Company's Act and has applied to RBI for license as an Asset Reconstruction Company (ARC). It aims to ease stress on state run banks by freeing their capital and help spur lending. NARCL is basically a bad bank created by the government in the mold of an ARC. An ARC is a specialized financial institution which buys stressed assets from banks at a mutually agreed price, thereby helping banks to clean up their Balance Sheets and concentrate on delivering normal banking services. Thereafter, the recovery or realization of the asset becomes the responsibility of the ARC.

Bad loans above a certain thresh hold will be picked up by NARCL which will also be responsible for valuing them and determining the price at which they would be sold. State owned banks will have 51% stake while FIs or Debt management companies will hold 49% stake in the NARCL.

A total of 38 NPA accounts worth 82,845 crores have been identified to be transferred to NARCL. This will be done in a phased manner. 15 NPA accounts worth 50,00 crores will be transferred in the first phase. India Debt Resolution Company Limited (IDRCL) will handle the resolution process under an exclusive arrangement. IDRCL will manage these stressed assets through engaging market professionals and turnaround experts. They will acquire stressed assets through 15% cash payment to banks after valuation and rest 85% will be given as Security Receipts (SRs). The government will give sovereign guarantee for these SRs issued by NARCL.

CASE 4 BANK FRAUDS

In recent years a spate of frauds has hit the banking industry. Bank frauds have increased sevenfold in just five years from a total of ₹10,171 crores in 2013–14 to 71,543 crores in 2018–19. This has majorly stemmed from malpractices at PSBs—with the collusion of bank employees millions of rupees have been syphoned off by unethical businessmen. A whopping 90% of the fraud value and 55% of the number of frauds between April and September 2019 was made by PSBs (Mint 11.12.19)—SBI recorded the highest losses 25,417 crores, followed by PNB with 10,822 crores and Bank of Baroda, ₹8,273 crores. More recent data shows that in financial year 2021, RBI reported bank frauds amounting to ₹1.38 trillion. This was 1.85 trillion less than in 2020 (ET Feb. 21, 2022). In fact the RBI has mandated that all NPAs of more than ₹50 crores should be examined for possible fraud. The following table highlights some of the bank frauds under CBI lens:

Accused	*Figures in ₹ crores*
Nirav Modi and Mehul Choksi	13,578
Vijay Mallya (Kingfisher)	9,000
Transstory India Limited, Guntur	7,926
IVRCL&MD, Hyderabad	4,837
Rana Kapoor (Former CEO, Yes Bank)	4,300
Shakti Bhog Foods & MD	3,269
Chanda Kochhar (ex ICICI Bank CEO)	1,875

(HT 26.3.21)

In just three years from 2018 to 2020 ₹1 lakh crore bank frauds were registered with CBI. The highest figure being 70,000 crores in 2020, in just 200 bank fraud cases.

The latest case of bank fraud is that of ABG Shipyard—a repairer and builder of ships company which is based in Gujarat, has duped a consortium of 28 banks to the tune of ₹22,842 crores by opening shell companies in 26 countries. The biggest lenders are ICICI bank, IDBI bank and the SBI. The company is accused of diversion of funds, misappropriation and criminal breach of trust.

Cyber crime too is witnessing an alarming spike in the number of incidents. The following figures highlight the rate at which such incidents have grown in the last four years alone:

Year	*Number of incidents*
2018	2,08,456
2019	3,84,499
2020	11,58,208
2021	14,20,809
2022 (first two months)	2,12,485

With online shopping and payment of utility bills, salaries, etc., electronic banking transactions now run into trillions and hackers are having a field day. Phishing, account hacking, internet fraud, Ransom ware, Malware, website spoofing, identity theft, online harassment and cyber stalking incidents are proliferating. While the ease, convenience, speed and cost of electronic transfer of funds is a boon but safety of funds has become a matter of concern and greater safeguards are needed.

Bibliography

Books

Baye, M.R. and Jansen, D.W., *Money, Banking and Financial Markets: An Economic Approach*, A.I.T.B.S. Publishers & Distributors (Regd.), Delhi, 1996.

Bhole, L.M., *Financial Institutions and Markets: Structure Growth and Innovations*, Tata McGraw-Hill, New Delhi, 2004.

Chatterjee, Arun, *Bank Lending: Law, Practice and Recovery*, Skylark Publications, New Delhi, 2003.

Dorfman, M.S., *Introduction to Risk Management and Insurance*, Seventh Edition, Prentice Hall Upper Saddle River, New Jersey, 2001.

Fredricke G. Crane, *Insurance Principles and Practice*, John Wiley & Sons, England, 1980.

Gupta, C.B., *Business Organization and Management*, Mayur Paperbacks, Noida, 2005.

Gupta, P.K., *Fundamentals of Insurance*, Himalaya Publishing House, Mumbai, reprinted, 2006.

Gupta, P.K., *Insurance and Risk Management*, Himalaya Publishing House, Mumbai, 2004.

Guruswamy, S., *Financial Services and Systems*, Thompson, Vijay Nicole Imprints, Chennai, 2004.

Harrington and Niehaus, *Insurance and Risk Management*, Tata McGraw-Hill Pub. Co. Ltd., New Delhi, 2004.

Heffernan, Shelagh, *Modern Banking*, John Wiley & Sons, West Sussex, England, 2005.

Indian Institute of Banking and Finance, *Workbook on Principles of Banking, Accounting and Finance for Bankers, Legal Aspects of Banking,* Taxmann, New Delhi, 2006.

James Lam, *Enterprise Risk Management: From Incentives To Controls,* John Wiley & Sons, England, 2003.

Jindal, K.K., *Banking and Financial Institutions,* Skylark Publications, New Delhi, 2000.

Kapoor, N.D., *Business Law,* Sultan Chand & Sons, New Delhi, 2005

Kripa, S.S., *Development of Commercial Banks in India,* Sunrise Publications, New Delhi, 2007.

Kuchhal, M.C., *Mercantile Law,* Vikas Publishing House, New Delhi, 2005.

Mishra, M.N., *Insurance Principles and Practice,* S. Chand & Co., New Delhi, 2006.

Nigam, B.M. Lal, *Banking Law and Practice,* Konark Publishing, New Delhi, 1988.

Periasamy, P., *Principles and Practice of Insurance,* Himalaya Publishing House, Mumbai, 2005.

Rejda, G.E., *Insurance and Risk Management,* Pearson Education, London, 2002.

Risk Management, ICAI, New Delhi.

Seth, Rajeev K., *Marketing of Banking Services,* Macmillan India, New Delhi, 1997.

Shekhar, K.C. and Shekhar Lekshmy, *Banking Theory and Practice,* Vikas Publishing House, New Delhi, 2005.

Sobti Renu, *Banking and Financial Services in India, Market Redefined,* New Century Publication, New Delhi, 2003.

Study material-post qualification programme on Insurance and Risk Management, ICAI, New Delhi, 2006.

Thomas, Lloyd B., *Money, Banking and Financial Markets,* McGraw-Hill Companies, Inc., United States of America, 1997.

Toor, N.S., *Bank Finance for Industry & Trade,* Skylark Publications, New Delhi, 1999.

Toor, N.S., *Handbook of Banking Information,* Skylark Publications, New Delhi, 2006.

Uppal, R.K. and Rimpi, Kaur, *Banking Sector Reforms in India: A Review of Post–1991 Developments,* New Century Publications, New Delhi, 2006.

Varshney, P.N., *Banking Law and Practice,* Sultan Chand & Sons, Delhi, 2004.

Reports, Journals, Newspapers, Magazines

The Professional Banker, The ICFAI University Press, Hyderabad

RBI Annual Report 2005–06

The Economic Times

The Hindustan Times

Business Standard (Banking Annual, Nov. 2006)

Acts

Reserve Bank of India Act, 1934

Banking Regulation Act, 1949

Websites

Export Credit Guarantee Corporation of India Website

HDFC Standard Life Insurance Company Website

http://finmin.nic.in/law/index.htm

ICICI Lombard General Insurance Company Website

IFFCO-Tokio General Insurance Company Website

Insurance Regulatory and Development Authority India Website-Acts passed in Indian Parliament

Life Insurance Corporation of India Website

Max Life Insurance Company Website

New India Assurance Website

Reliance Life Insurance Company Website

Star Health & Allied Insurance Company Website

www.bimaonline.com

www.fiuindia.gov.in

www.getmeinsure.com

www.hdfcbank.com

www.hsbc.co.in

www.icicibank.com

www.indiacode.nic.in

www.indiacore.com

www.licindia.com

www.irdaindia.org

www.mib.com.
www.rbi.org.in
www.royalsundaram.com
www.statebankofIndia.com
www.taxmann.net/insurancelaws
www.utibank.com

Index